INBOARD ENGINES & DRIVES SERVICE MANUAL
(2nd Edition — Volume 1)

CONTENTS

ENGINES

BMW
- B190, B220 3
- D12 9
- D35, D50 19
- D150, D190 26

CHRYSLER
- 40 Hp 37
- M225D, MH225D 39
- 273, 318, 360 42
- 383, 413, 440 47
- MN4-33, MN6-33 53
- CM6-55 59

CRUSADER
- 185 67
- 220, 270, 350 69

FORD
- YSD-424, YSD-635 73
- SSD-437, SSD-655, SSD-681 ... 82
- 254, 362, 363, 380 93
- CSG-850M, WSG-858M, LSG-875M 101
- 302, 351, 460 101

MERCRUISER
- 233, 255, 350 111

DRIVES

BERKELEY
- 12JB, 12JC & 12JE 118

CHRYSLER 120

HURTH 122

JACUZZI
- 12YJ 125

O.M.C. 128

PANTHER 450E 131

PARAGON
- SA0 133
- SA1 136
- P200, P300 & P400 138
- PV300 & PV400 141
- SSR 142

TWIN DISC
- MG-502 IN-LINE & V-DRIVE 143
- MG-506L & MG-506R 146

VELVET DRIVE
- 70, 71 & 72 149

Cover photo credit: Peugeot Engines

PUBLISHED BY

ABOS MARINE PUBLICATIONS DIVISION

INTERTEC PUBLISHING CORP.
P.O. Box 12901, Overland Park, Kansas 66212

©Copyright 1984 by Intertec Publishing Corp. Printed in the United States of America.

All rights reserved. Reproduction or use, without express permission, of editorial or pictorial content, in any manner, is prohibited. No patent liability is assumed with respect to the use of the information contained herein. While every precaution has been taken in the preparation of this book, the publisher assumes no responsibility for errors or omissions. Neither is any liability assumed for damages resulting from use of the information contained herein. Publication of the servicing information in this manual does not imply approval of the manufacturers of the products covered.

All instructions and diagrams have been checked for accuracy and ease of application; however, success and safety in working with tools depend in a great extent upon individual accuracy, skill and caution. For this reason the publishers are not able to guarantee the result of any procedure contained herein. Nor can they assume responsibility for any damage to property or injury to persons occasioned from the procedures. Persons engaging in the procedures do so entirely at their own risk.

ABOS Publications is grateful to the manufacturers whose trade names appear below for their cooperation in supplying photos, drawings, technical information and dimensional data for this manual. Also to National Marine Manufacturers Association and to the many individuals who have supplied technical assistance and encouragement.

BMW

Chrysler

Ford

Mercury

Thermo Electron

INBOARD ENGINES BMW

BMW

BMW OF NORTH AMERICA
1 BMW Plaza
Montvale, New Jersey 07645

ENGINE SERVICE DATA

NOTE: Metric fasteners are used throughout engine.

ENGINE MODEL	B190	B220
General		
Cylinder	6	6
Bore	86 mm	89 mm
Stroke	80 mm	86 mm
Displacement	2788 cc	3205 cc
Compression Ratio	8.2:1	8.4:1
Compression Pressure at Cranking Speed	950 kPa	
Main Bearings, Number Of	7	
Firing Order	1-5-3-6-2-4	
Numbering System (Front to Rear)	1-2-3-4-5-6	
Tune-Up		
Valve lash (cold)	0.25-0.30 mm	
Valve Seat Angle	45°	
Valve Face Angle	45°30'	
Valve Seat Width:		
Intake	1.6-2.0 mm	
Exhaust	2.0-2.4 mm	
Valve Spring Pressure:		
Installed	273-279 N @ 37.6 mm	
Loaded	659-715 N @ 28.5 mm	
Valve Stem Clearance:		
Intake	0.025-0.055 mm	
Exhaust	0.040-0.070 mm	
Timing Mark Location	Flywheel	
Ignition Timing	22° BTDC @ 2300 rpm	
Cam Angle (Dwell)	35°-41°	
Breaker Point Gap	0.35 mm	
Spark Plug Type	Bosch W 125 T30	
Spark Plug Gap	0.6 mm	
Carburetor Type	Solex 4A1	
Float Level	5.5-8.5 mm	
Engine Idle Speed	700-800 rpm	
Sizes — Capacities — Clearances		
Crankshaft Journal Diameter:		
Color Code Red	59.980-59.990 mm	
Color Code Blue	59.971-59.980 mm	
Main Bearing Clearance	0.030-0.070 mm	
Rod Journal Diameter	47.975-47.991 mm	
Rod Bearing Clearance	0.023-0.069 mm	
Crankshaft End Play	0.085-0.174 mm	
Pin Bore In Piston	22.000-22.004 mm	
Pin Clearance In Piston	0.001-0.006 mm	

Illustration courtesy BMW

BMW INBOARD ENGINES

ENGINE SERVICE DATA (CONT.)

ENGINE MODEL	B190	B220
Sizes — Capacities — Clearances (Cont.)		
Pin Bore In Rod	22.005-22.010 mm	
Piston Clearance	0.045 mm	
Piston Rings—		
Top Compression Ring:		
End Gap	0.3-0.5 mm	
Side Clearance	0.060-0.092 mm	
2nd Compression Ring:		
End Gap	0.3-0.5 mm	0.2-0.4 mm
Side Clearance—		
Mahle Pistons	0.030-0.062 mm	0.050-0.082 mm
KS Pistons	0.040-0.072 mm	
Alcan/Nural Pistons	0.030-0.062 mm	
Oil Control Ring:		
End Gap	0.25-0.50 mm	0.25-0.40 mm
Side Clearance—		
Mahle Pistons	0.020-0.052 mm	
KS Pistons	0.030-0.062 mm	
Alcan Nural Pistons	0.020-0.052 mm	
Camshaft Journal Diameters:		
Front Journal	45.959-45.975 mm	
2nd Journal	44.959-44.975 mm	
3rd Journal	43.959-43.975 mm	
4th Journal	33.959-33.975 mm	
Camshaft Bearing Clearance	0.034-0.075 mm	
Camshaft End Play	0.03-0.18 mm	
Valve Guide Bore	8.0-8.015 mm	
Valve Stem Diameter:		
Intake	7.960-7.975 mm	
Exhaust	7.945-7.960 mm	
Maximum Total Stem/Guide Wear	0.15 mm	
Cyl. Head Rocker Arm Shaft Bore	15.50-15.543 mm	
Rocker Arm Shaft Clearance In Cyl. Head	0.016-0.077 mm	
Rocker Arm Bushing Diameter	15.500-15.518 mm	
Rocker Arm Bushing Clearance	0.016-0.052 mm	
Rocker Arm Shaft Diameter	15.466-15.484 mm	
Cylinder Bore:		
Standard	86.010-86.020 mm	89.010-89.020 mm
Maximum Out-Of-Round	0.01 mm	
Maximum Taper	0.01 mm	
Maximum Total Piston/Cylinder Wear	0.10-0.15 mm	
Crankcase Capacity W/Filter	5¾ liter	
Oil Pressure at 4000 rpm	400-500 kPa	
Fuel Pump Pressure at 4000 rpm	30 kPa	
Tightening Torques		
(All values are in newton meters.)		
Carburetor Mounting Nuts	9.8-11.7	
Connecting Rod Cap	52-57	
Cylinder Head	77-81	
Exhaust Manifold	30-33	
Flywheel	98-113	
Fuel Pump	9.8-13.7	
Intake Manifold	25	
Main Bearing Cap	56.8-61.7	
Oil Distributor Cap		
Hollow Screw	11-13	
Spark Plugs	24-29	
Starter	43-48	
Timing Chain Tensioner Plug	29.4-39.2	
Timing Gear Upper Cover	8.8-10.7	
Valve Adjuster Locknut	9-11	

Illustration courtesy BMW

INBOARD ENGINES
BMW

MAINTENANCE

LUBRICATION

Use of a high quality API specification SE grade 20W-50 oil is recommended. Oil and filter should be changed after each 50 hours of operation or seasonally, whichever is more frequent.

OIL COOLER

Oil cooler/filter assembly must be removed from engine as a unit when servicing cooler insert. This is necessary to prevent water, which is trapped in cooler unit, from leaking into oil pan. See Fig. B1-1.

DISTRIBUTOR

Ignition system incorporates a centrifugal cut-off switch, which is located just below distributor rotor. The cut-off switch shuts off electrical current to ignition system when engine speed exceeds 5900 rpm.

FUEL SYSTEM

FUEL BY-PASS VALVE. B190 and B220 engines are equipped with a fuel by-pass valve which is located on top of the intake manifold towards front of engine. This valve reduces fuel pressure to 0.25-0.30 bar at the carburetor. Fuel by-pass valve is available only as a unit assembly.

CARBURETOR. All models are equipped with Solex 4A1 carburetor. Carburetor adjustments should only be made after engine is at normal operating temperature and valve clearance has been set to specification. Dwell angle, ignition timing and plug gap should also be checked and brought to specification before carburetor adjustments are made.

IDLE ADJUSTMENTS. Always perform idle mixture and idle speed adjustments with flame arrestor installed.

Fig. B1-1 – Remove oil cooler/filter housing (H) from engine before removing cooler (C) to prevent raw water from leaking into crankcase and contaminating engine oil. Oil filter (F) may be removed at any time for service.

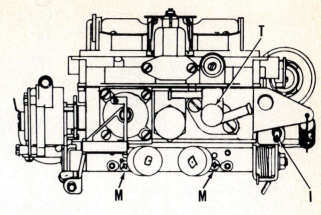

Fig. B1-2 – Illustration shows location of some Solex 4A1 carburetor components.

I. Idle speed adjustment screw
M. Idle mixture adjustment screws
T. TN-Starter

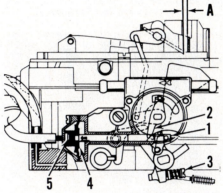

Fig. B1-3 – Illustration shows adjustment points for vacuum break. See text for adjustment procedure.

1. Vacuum break rod
2. Choke lever
3. High idle speed adjustment screw
4. Vacuum break diaphragm
5. Vacuum break housing screw
A. Distance between lower edge of choke plate and air horn wall should be 3.1-3.3 mm.

Adjust idle mixture screws (M – Fig. B1-2) alternately until a smooth and even idle has been achieved. Set idle speed at 700-800 rpm using screw (I).

VACUUM BREAK ADJUSTMENT. Adjustment of vacuum break must be performed with engine cold and not running. Open throttle slightly, close choke plate completely and release throttle lever. Using a thin drift or similar tool, push vacuum break rod (1 – Fig. B1-3) towards vacuum diaphragm until stop pin of rod touches choke lever (2). While holding vacuum break rod in this position, turn screw (3) until distance (A) between lower edge of choke plate and air horn wall is 3.1-3.3 mm.

Open choke plate until choke lever (2) is released, then push vacuum break rod (1) in until it bottoms on vacuum break diaphragm (4). While holding vacuum break rod in this position, turn vacuum break housing screw (5) until distance (A) between lower edge of choke butterfly and air horn wall is 4.1-4.3 mm.

FLOAT ADJUSTMENT. Remove air horn assembly and gasket, then siphon

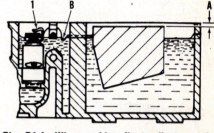

Fig. B1-4 – When making float adjustment be sure float tang (1) is properly seated on needle valve. Bend float arm at point (B) to obtain proper float depth (A) as specified in ENGINE SERVICE DATA section.

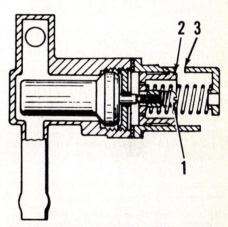

Fig. B1-5 – See text for adjustment procedure for TN-Starter.

1. Adjustment screw
2. Plunger
3. Housing window

excess fuel from fuel bowl assembly. While gently holding needle in its seated position using float arm (1 – Fig. B1-4), measure distance (A) from top of float toe to fuel bowl gasket surface. Bend float arm at point (B) to achieve a measurement of 3.0 to 4.0 mm.

TN-STARTER ADJUSTMENT. Remove TN-Starter (T – Fig. B1-2) from carburetor and place it in a 20°C water bath for 30 minutes. After heat-soak period, turn screw (1 – Fig. B1-5) to establish a gap of 2.2-2.4 mm between edge of plunger (2) and opposite edge of housing window (3). After adjustment reheat TN-Starter for a few minutes and

Illustration courtesy BMW

BMW — INBOARD ENGINES

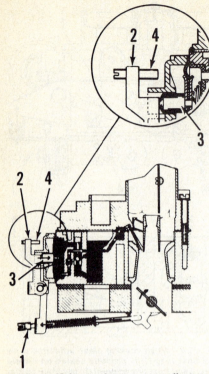

Fig. B1-6 — Make accelerator pump adjustments as outlined in text refering to illustration shown for adjustment point locations.

1. Adjustment screw
2. Pump lever
3. Pump rod
4. Set screw

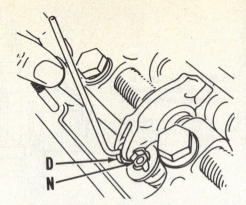

Fig. B1-7 — To adjust valve clearance, loosen locknut (N) and using a suitable Allen wrench turn adjustment disc (D) until specified valve clearance has been obtained.

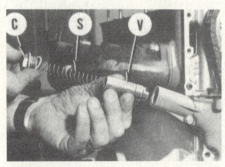

Fig. B1-7A — To relieve pressure on timing chain tensioner shoe remove plug (P), spring (S) and valve (V) from front timing case cover as shown.

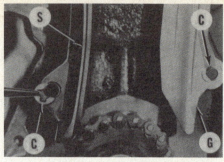

Fig. B1-7B — Remove circlip (C) from tensioner shoe (S) and chain guide (G) then slip shoe and guide off their support pins.

```
3  5 11 13  9  7  1
2  8 10 14 12  6  4
```

Fig. B1-8 — When removing cylinder head loosen cylinder head bolts in sequence shown.

Fig. B1-9 — Overhaul of cylinder head requires use of BMW special tool number 111060.

recheck adjustment before installation on carburetor.

ACCELERATOR PUMP ADJUSTMENT. To adjust accelerator pump remove carburetor from engine and place on a flat surface. Install a 2.5 mm feeler gage between idle adjustment screw (I – Fig. B1-2) and throttle lever stop. Turn screw (1 – Fig. B1-6) in until all play has been removed between pump lever (2) and pump rod (3). Remove feeler gage and supply carburetor with fuel under a pressure of 20 kPa. Operate accelerator pump through 10 full strokes in 30 seconds and collect discharged fuel from each bore in a separate graduated container. Divide total quantity of fuel collected from each bore by 10 to establish average fuel delivery per stroke. Correct amount is 0.5-0.7 cubic centimeters per stroke for each bore. Adjust amount of fuel delivery using set screw (4). Turn screw in for less fuel and out for more fuel.

VALVE ADJUSTMENT

To adjust valve lash, loosen locknut (N – Fig. B1-7) and rotate eccentric disc (D) using a suitable tool until a clearance of 0.25-0.30 mm is achieved. Valve adjustment should be performed on a cold engine in firing order sequence.

REPAIR

TIMING CHAIN AND GEARS

To gain access to the timing chain and timing gears the front crankshaft pulley and vibration damper must first be removed. Next remove the rocker arm cover and both upper and lower front cover halves. Note that rocker arm cover and front cover halves are sealed to their respective mating surfaces using an RTV type sealant. Therefore it will be necessary to tap them loose using a soft mallet. To relieve tension on timing chain remove tensioner plug, spring and piston as shown in Fig. B1-7A. Remove bolts retaining camshaft timing gear to camshaft and lift off gear and timing chain. Using a suitable puller withdraw crankshaft timing gear from crankshaft. If desired chain tensioner shoe (S – Fig. B1-7B) and chain guide (G) may now be removed for inspection or renewal by removing circlip (C) and sliding shoe and/or guide off their shafts. Inspect all parts for wear or damage and renew as necessary.

Install parts in opposite order of removal making sure the camshaft and crankshaft timing gears are properly timed as follows: Position number 1 piston at TDC on compression stroke. Rotate camshaft until both valves of number 1 cylinder are closed and dowel hole of camshaft timing gear is in the 7 o'clock position as shown in Fig. B1-13. Without moving either the camshaft or crankshaft install the timing chain onto the timing gears. Install the tensioner piston, spring and plug to hold the timing chain in position.

CYLINDER HEAD

Before attempting cylinder head service note that BMW special tool number 111060 is required for disassembly and overhaul of cylinder head. To remove cylinder head position number 1 piston at TDC on compression and remove timing chain tensioner plug, spring and piston as shown in Fig. B1-7A. Mark position of chain on camshaft timing gear and detach camshaft timing gear. Cylinder head bolts should be loosened evenly, but not removed, in the sequence shown in Fig. B1-8.

INBOARD ENGINES

BMW

Fig. B1-10 — Install upper half of BMW special tool 111060 on cylinder head as shown to compress valve springs as described in text.

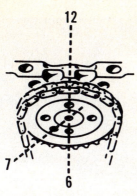

Fig. B1-13 — When installing camshaft timing gear be sure dowel hole in gear is in the 7 o'clock position as shown.

Remove the oil distributor pipe and four adjacent head bolts. Insert knurled pins contained in special tool kit 111060 into empty head bolt holes to secure rocker shafts in position. Note that pins the same diameter as the cylinder head bolts may be used if special knurled pins are not available. Remove cylinder head and place on special tool stand shown in Fig. B1-9.

To disassemble cylinder head, loosen rocker arm locknuts and turn eccentric adjusting discs (Fig. B1-7) so that all intake valves have maximum clearance and all exhaust valves have zero clearance, then retighten locknuts. Install special tool valve spring compressor as shown in Fig. B1-10 making sure that each compressor tab is on top of its corresponding adjustment disc. Tighten the four valve spring compressor nuts evenly starting on exhaust valve side while checking the valve heads frequently with a feeler gage (Fig. B1-11) to insure they do not touch as tool is tightened down on cylinder head. Camshaft retainer and camshaft can now be removed. Remove valve spring compressor and knurled pins. Remove C-clips which hold rocker arms in position and pull out rocker arm shafts while noting position of components so they can be installed in their original positions.

NOTE: All four shafts are different.

Place the wooden support supplied with the special tool under the holding fixture and remove valve springs and valves as shown in Fig. B1-12.

Valve seats and guides are renewable with 0.10, 0.20 and 0.30 inch oversizes available. Valve seats and guides are a shrink fit in the cylinder head, and if renewal is required, it should be performed by a professional machine shop where the cylinder head can be oven heated to 250°C and the valve seat or guide cooled to −70°C.

Refer to ENGINE SERVICE DATA table for cylinder head component specifications.

```
12 10 4  2  6  8 14
13  7 5  1  3  9 11
```

Fig. B1-14 — When installing cylinder head tighten cylinder head bolts in three steps in sequence shown as outlined in text.

Reassemble the head and install valves, valve springs, rocker arms, rocker shafts and springs in their original positions. After installing rocker shafts, insert knurled alignment pins of special tool in their head bolt holes to align and retain rocker shafts. Install camshaft so that with both valves on number 1 cylinder closed, the dowel in the camshaft is in 7 o'clock position. See Fig. B1-13. Make sure that number 1 piston is on TDC. Install cylinder head and hand tighten all head bolts with the last four being those that replace rocker shaft alignment pins. Tighten head bolts in sequence shown in Fig. B1-14 using the following steps: 1st 34-44 N·m, 2nd 67-71 N·m, 3rd 77-81 N·m, 4th 77-81 N·m. Install camshaft gear and chain using previously made marks on gear and chain to check for proper camshaft timing. Install timing chain tensioner with red spring end next to plug. Fill chain tensioner with oil before installing plug. Adjust valve clearance as previously outlined.

OIL PUMP

Oil pump can be removed from engine after removal of timing chain as previously outlined. Oil pump is chain driven off of the crankshaft timing gear. Remove oil pump drive gear retaining screws then remove gear and drive chain as a unit. Remove pump and pickup tube assembly from crankcase. After removing oil pump assembly from engine disconnect pickup tube from pump and remove pump cover. See Fig.

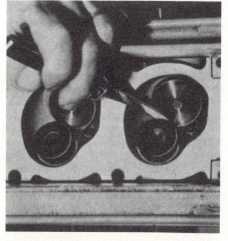

Fig. B1-11 — Use a feeler gage to check that intake and exhaust valves do not come into contact with each other when compressing valve springs for camshaft removal.

Fig. B1-12 — After rocker arms and shafts have been removed use BMW special tool to remove valve springs from valves.

Illustration courtesy BMW

BMW   INBOARD ENGINES

Fig. B1-15 – Using a feeler gage and straightedge measure oil pump rotor wear at the positions shown.

1. Outer rotor axial wear
2. Outer rotor-to-housing clearance
3. Inner-to-outer rotor clearance

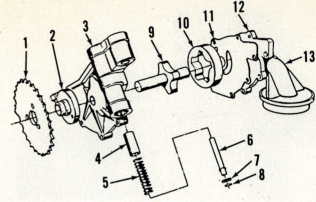

Fig. B1-16 – Exploded view of oil pump assembly.

1. Pump drive gear
2. Gear flange
3. Pump housing
4. Pressure relief valve
5. Pressure relief spring
6. Support pin
7. Washer
8. Circlip
9. Inner rotor
10. Outer rotor
11. Spacer plate
12. Pump cover
13. Pickup tube

B1-16 for an exploded view of oil pump assembly. Use a straightedge and feeler gage (1–Fig. B1-15) to check inner and outer rotor end play, which should be 0.035-0.095 mm. Use a feeler gage to check outer rotor to pump housing clearance (2), which should be 0.10-0.15 mm. Inner rotor-to-outer rotor clearance is checked with rotors positioned as shown (3–Fig. B1-15); this clearance should be 0.12-0.20 mm. If any of the above clearances are found to be excessive oil pump should be renewed as a unit assembly. Pressure relief valve spring (5–Fig. B1-16) should have a free length of 68.0 mm, and may be renewed separately if necessary. Pressure relief valve (4) is not available separately, therefore, renewal of pump assembly is required if valve is found to be damaged or its freedom of movement in any way impaired. If desired, gear flange (2) may be removed from inner rotor shaft (9) using a suitable press. When installing flange on shaft distance from face of flange to parting line of pump housing should be 42.6-42.8 mm.

PISTON AND ROD UNITS

Pistons are stamped + or – and must be replaced with a piston bearing the same mark. Piston and pin must be renewed as a unit. Pistons and rings are available in standard size, 0.25 and 0.50 mm oversize. Piston rings should be installed with their manufacturers mark facing up in order shown in Fig. B1-17. Space ring end gaps 180 degrees apart. Connecting rods are grouped in weight categories by color. If a connecting rod requires renewal it should be replaced by a rod having same color marking as the original. Total weight variation of all rods should not exceed 4 grams, excluding bearing shells. Connecting rod bearings are available in standard size, 0.025, 0.25, 0.50 and 0.75 mm oversize. When assembling connecting rod to piston be sure piston pin oil supply hole and arrow on piston crown face the same direction and are installed in engine with piston arrow facing front (timing gear) end of engine.

CRANKSHAFT

Preparation for crankshaft removal requires the removal of cylinder head, timing chain and gears, oil pump, flywheel, and piston and rod units. Using a suitable puller remove crankshaft timing gear. Remove crankshaft rear main seal housing. Before removing main bearing caps mark each one as to its position and front of engine. Remove main bearing caps then lift crankshaft out of crankcase. Two different crankshafts are used interchangeably and are color coded either red or blue. All specifications as shown in ENGINE SERVICE DATA section are the same for either crankshaft, except for main bearing journal sizes as noted in the data table. Main bearing inserts are available in standard size, 0.20, 0.50 and 0.75 mm oversize.

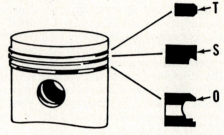

Fig. B1-17 – Install piston rings as outlined in text in sequence shown.

S. Second compression ring
T. Top compression ring
O. Oil control ring

Illustration courtesy BMW

INBOARD ENGINES — BMW

BMW

ENGINE SERVICE DATA

NOTE: Metric fasteners are used throughout engine.

MODEL

	D12
General	
Cylinders	1
Bore	82 mm
Stroke	100 mm
Displacement	528 cc
Compression Ratio	22:1
Dry Weight with Gearbox	108 kg
Gearbox	Hurth HBW5/ZF Bw3
Gearbox Reduction	
Forward	2.7:1
Reverse	1.9:1
Maximum Installation Angle	15°
Tune-Up	
Engine Oil Capacity	2.0 liter
Transmission Oil Capacity	0.4 liter
Injection Pressure	11.2-12.0 MPa
Injection Pump	PFR 1 K 70A 343/II
Valve Clearance (cold)	0.35 mm
Fuel Injection Ends	9.5°-10.5° BTDC
Sizes — Clearances	
Rocker Arm Shaft Diameter	11.96-11.97 mm
Rocker Arm Bore ID	11.998-12.006 mm
Rocker Arm Radius	8 mm
Valve Stem Diameter	6.96-7.03 mm
Valve Head Diameter	31.0 mm
Valve Head Protrusion	0.25-0.55 mm
Valve Guide ID	7.0-7.009 mm
Valve Guide OD	12.028-12.036 mm
Valve Guide Bore in Cylinder Head	12.0-12.011 mm
Valve Face Angle	45°
Valve Seat Angle	45°
Valve Spring Free Length	39.3 mm
Piston Diameter	81.97 mm
Piston Ring End Gap	0.3-0.5 mm
Piston to Cylinder Head Clearance	0.8-0.9 mm
Connecting Rod Piston Pin Bushing ID	28.040-28.073 mm
Connecting Rod Small End ID	32.0-32.16 mm
Connecting Rod Big End ID	54.0-54.01 mm
Connecting Rod Bearing ID	....
Connecting Rod Bearing Clearance	0.04-0.08 mm
Connecting Rod Bearing Journal Diameter	47.93-47.94 mm
Crankshaft Rod Bearing Journal Width	40.0-40.06 mm
Main Bearing Journal Diameter	35.0 mm
Crankshaft Fuel Control Ball-Hub Diameter	29.028-29.41 mm
Crankshaft Fuel Control Ball-Sleeve Diameter	27.959-27.97 mm
Crankshaft Timing Gear Sleeve Diameter	22.035-22.048 mm
Tightening Torques	
(All values are in newton meters.)	
Camshaft Follower Retainer Screw	60
Connecting Rod	60
Counterweight	65
Cylinder Head	50

Illustration courtesy BMW

BMW

MODEL
D12

Tightening Torques (Cont.)
Flywheel	250-300
Injector Mounting Nut	15
Injector Nozzle Nut	85
Injection Pump Delivery Valve	40
Rear Main Bearing Housing	30

MAINTENANCE

LUBRICATION

Model D12 incorporates a splash lubrication system. On a new or overhauled engine, oil and filter should be changed after first 10 hours of operation. Thereafter, oil and filter should be changed after each 50 hours of operation or seasonally, whichever is more frequent. Always use a high quality API specification CC/CD SAE 30 oil.

Transmission oil should be changed after each 150 hours of operation or seasonally, whichever is more frequent. Always use a high quality Dexron ATF.

FUEL SYSTEM

BLEED FUEL SYSTEM. All Model D12 engines incorporate a fully automatic air-bleed system. Prior to starting engine after lay-up or when fuel system has been worked on, operate priming pump 30-50 strokes. Place throttle in full speed position and start engine. Model D7 priming pump is integral with fuel supply pump while Model D12 priming pump is located on the fuel inlet side of the primary fuel filter.

FUEL SUPPLY PUMP. After each 100 hours of operation or seasonally, filter screen located in fuel supply pump must be removed and cleaned in fresh diesel fuel. Remove cover screw (1–Fig. B2-1), cover (2), gasket (3), and screen (4). When installing screen always install a new gasket. Apart from cleaning filter screen no other maintenance or repair of pump is possible. Fuel supply pump must be renewed as a unit assembly.

FUEL INJECTION TIMING. Fuel injection pump timing is adjusted by varying thickness of shims (2–Fig. B2-2) between injection pump and mounting surface. Proceed as follows to set or check fuel injection timing.

Remove fuel supply and return lines. Cap fuel return line nipple so fuel cannot leak off during timing procedure. Remove delivery valve (1–Fig. B2-2) and install a spill tube with dial indicator as shown in Fig. B2-3. Note that spill tube and dial indicator pin are offered by BMW as special tool number 74 64 1 333 535. Connect a gravity-fed fuel supply to injection pump inlet; do not use a pressurized fuel supply. Turn crankshaft counterclockwise by hand (viewed at flywheel; clockwise if hand starter crank is used) until air-free fuel flows from spill tube. Continue to turn crankshaft until fuel stops flowing from spill tube and preload dial indicator 1 mm. Slowly continue to rotate crankshaft until fuel again flows from spill tube, this is the end of fuel injection. Check timing marks of flywheel and see ENGINE SERVICE DATA section for specifications.

If end of fuel injection timing is not to specification correct timing by adding or removing timing shims (2–Fig. B2-2). Adding shims retards injection timing; fuel delivery ends later (lower number of degrees). Deleting shims advances injection timing; fuel delivery ends earlier (higher number of degrees).

To determine correct thickness of timing shims, set dial indicator to "O" at end of injection then turn flywheel to cor-

Fig. B2-3 – Connect a gravity-fed fuel supply (1) to fuel injection pump and block off fuel return line (2). Install spill tube and dial indicator (3) as shown to check fuel injection timing as outlined in text.

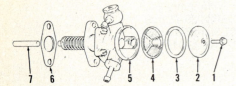

Fig. B2-1 – Exploded view of fuel pump used on D12 engines.

1. Cover screw
2. Cover
3. Cover gasket
4. Filter screen
5. Pump body
6. Pump gasket
7. Pump push rod

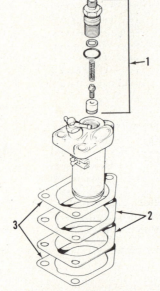

Fig. B2-2 – Partially exploded view of Bosch injection pump used on D12 engines.

1. Delivery valve assy.
2. Timing shims
3. Pump gaskets

Fig. B2-4 – Loosen screws (1) and turn starter body (2) using BMW special tool number 74 64 1 333 528 (3) to properly set injection stroke as outlined in text.

INBOARD ENGINES

BMW

Fig. B2-5 — To set high idle speed loosen locknut (1) and turn screw (2). To set low idle speed loosen locknut (3) and turn screw (4).

Fig. B2-6 — To adjust valve gap loosen locknut (1) and turn adjusting screw (2). Insert correct thickness feeler gage (3) between valve stem and rocker arm.

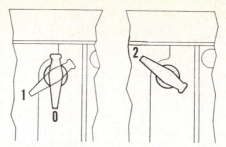

Fig. B2-7 — Illustration of the three positions used when adjusting decompression device clearance as outlined in text.

Fig. B2-8 — Following procedure given in text, loosen locknut (1) and turn adjusting screw ½ turn beyond point of first contact when adjusting decompression device.

rect timing mark. Dial indicator will indicate thickness of shims to be added or removed.

After establishing and installing correct timing shims, injection stroke must be measured and adjusted. Set dial indicator to "0" and turn crankshaft by hand in counterclockwise direction (as viewed at flywheel) until a lift of 1.54 mm is indicated. At this point fuel should just start flowing from spill tube. If necessary loosen set screws (1 – Fig. B2-4) and then turn starter body (2) using BMW special tool number 74 64 1 333 528 (3) as necessary to provide minimum fuel flow at this point. Tighten set screws and secure with lock wire. Remove dial indicator and spill tube. Reinstall delivery valve and fuel lines. Bleed air from fuel system as previously outlined. Start engine and check for fuel leaks.

ENGINE SPEED ADJUSTMENTS

Engine speed is measured at the camshaft using a hand held mechanical tachometer. Camshaft has a 4 to 1 reduction, therefore indicated speed should be multiplied by 4.

To enable engine to reach correct operating speed under full load, it is necessary to set unloaded speed to 3160 rpm. To set high idle speed loosen locknut (1 – Fig. B2-5) and turn adjusting screw (2). Idle speed is adjusted by loosening locknut (3) and turning screw (4) until an engine speed of 780-800 rpm has been achieved.

VALVE ADJUSTMENT

Valve clearance should be checked and adjusted after each 100 hours of operation. Remove rocker arm cover and bring piston to TDC on compression. Loosen locknut on rocker arm to be adjusted and backout adjusting screw. Insert correct thickness feeler gage between rocker arm and valve stem as shown in Fig. B2-6. Slowly tighten adjusting screw until a slight drag is felt on feeler gage. While holding adjusting screw in place tighten locknut. Repeat above procedures for remaining rocker arm.

DECOMPRESSION DEVICE

Decompression device should be adjusted after each 100 hours of operation or whenever valve clearance is adjusted.

Check and adjust valve clearance as previously outlined. Turn decompression lever to the "1" position shown in Fig. B2-7. Loosen decompression device adjusting screw locknut (1 – Fig. B2-8). Backout adjusting screw (2) until there is noticeable clearance between adjusting screw and decompression device cross shaft. Bring piston to TDC on compression and place decompression lever in the "2" position shown in Fig. B2-7. Slowly tighten adjusting screw until exhaust valve rocker arm just touches exhaust valve stem, then turn adjusting screw ½ turn tighter and hold screw in that position while locknut is being tightened.

Install rocker arm cover and place decompression lever in the "0" position. This adjustment must be made carefully to insure piston does not contact exhaust valve head when decompression device is in use.

REPAIR

WATER PUMP

Model D7 and D12 engines are direct, raw-water cooled with raw water fed by an impeller type pump located on front of engine and driven by crankshaft. Water is circulated through cylinder block and cylinder head jackets and finally discharged through a thermostat controlled outlet into the exhaust manifold.

R&R AND OVERHAUL. Remove water pump suction and discharge hoses. Loosen both mounting nuts evenly and remove water pump assembly. Remove cover plate (2 – Fig. B2-9), and

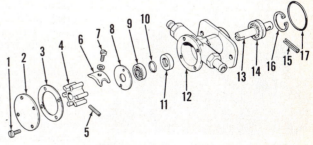

Fig. B2-9 — Exploded view of raw-water pump used on D12 engines.

1. Cover screw
2. Cover
3. Gasket
4. Impeller
5. Impeller drive pin
6. Shoe
7. Shoe retaining screw
8. Seal plate
9. Seal
10. "O" ring
11. Seal
12. Pump body
13. Shaft
14. Bearing
15. Pump drive pin
16. Snap ring
17. "O" ring

Illustration courtesy BMW

BMW

INBOARD ENGINES

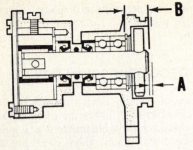

Fig. B2-10—Install shaft in housing so end of shaft is 2 mm (A) below mounting flange. Install bearings on shaft so distance (B) is 12 mm.

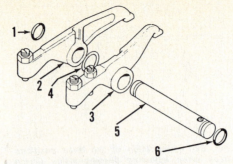

Fig. B2-12—Exploded view of rocker arm and shaft assembly.

1. "O" ring
2. Intake rocker arm
3. Exhaust rocker arm
4. Spacer
5. Shaft
6. "O" ring

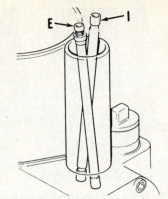

Fig. B2-13—View showing correct installation of intake (I) and exhaust (E) push rods. Exhaust (E) push rod decompression valve cup must be up.

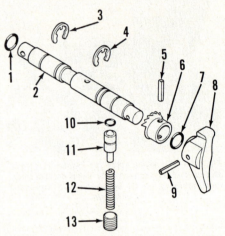

Fig. B2-14—Exploded view of decompression device.

1. "O" ring
2. Shaft
3. "E" ring
4. "E" ring
5. Roll pin
6. Gear
7. "O" ring
8. Handle
9. Roll pin
10. "O" ring
11. Detent pin
12. Spring
13. Set screw

gasket (3). Remove shoe mounting screw (7), withdraw impeller (4) and shoe (6). Remove drive pin (5) from impeller. Lift out seal plate (8) and remove circlip (16) from pump body (12). From impeller side of pump body, tap out shaft (13) and bearing (14) as an assembly. Remove drive pin (15) from shaft (13). Push out seals (9 and 11) and "O" ring (10).

Carefully inspect all parts for wear and renew as necessary. Upon assembly pack all bearings and seals with grease. Assemble water pump in opposite order of teardown. Install bearing (14) on shaft (13) so rear surface of bearing is 12 mm from rear end of shaft. Install shaft and bearing assembly in pump body (12) so crankshaft end of shaft (13) is 2 mm below rear surface of pump body as shown in Fig. B2-10. Coat "O" ring (17—Fig. B2-9) with petroleum jelly prior to pump installation. Before installing impeller into pump body, coat vanes of impeller and shoe (6) with petroleum jelly and then rotate impeller in direction of operation during installation. Install pump on engine being sure to properly engage pump drive pin in slot in end of crankshaft. Tighten retaining nuts, install suction and discharge hoses, open raw water inlet valve, start engine and carefully check cooling system for leaks.

CYLINDER HEAD

Cylinder head should be renewed if valve seats are cracked or worn beyond

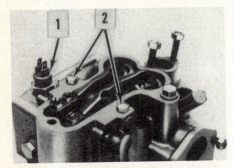

Fig. B2-11—To remove rocker arm shaft, temperature sensor (1) and shaft retaining screws (2) must first be removed.

repair, or cylinder head gasket surface is warped more than 0.5 mm. Valve guides are renewable and should be reamed to specification after installation. Valve guides are removed from combustion chamber side of cylinder head. Install new valve guide from rocker arm side of cylinder head using a minimum press force of 889.6 newtons. After installation of new valve guide, valve and seat should be ground to a true 45-degree angle. After surface grinding of cylinder head or valve renewal, check that valve head protrusion is within specifications given in ENGINE SERVICE DATA section. Install assembled cylinder head on engine using new gaskets and torque fasteners to specification. Insert a piece of soft solder through injector hole and position it between valve head and top of piston. By hand, slowly rotate crankshaft through TDC, remove solder and measure piston to valve clearance. See ENGINE SERVICE DATA section for specification. Repeat procedure for remaining valve. If clearance is correct, complete installation of cylinder head. If clearance is too small, valve and/or seat must be reground or cylinder head renewed.

ROCKER ARMS AND PUSH RODS

To remove rocker arm and shaft assembly first remove rocker arm cover, temperature sensor (1—Fig. B2-11) and both retaining bolts (2) with tab washers. Loosen valve adjustment screw locknuts and back out both adjusting screws until rocker arms are completely free. Using a suitable drift, tap rocker arm shaft (5—Fig. B2-12) out of cylinder head being careful not to lose shim (4). Lift out intake (3) and exhaust (2) rocker arms. If desired push rods may also be removed at this time. Inspect all parts for wear or damage and renew as necessary.

Install exhaust push rod (E—Fig. B2-13) in front valve lifter with cup towards top. Install intake push rod (I) in rear (flywheel side) valve lifter, then position both push rods as shown in Fig. B2-13. Lightly oil rocker arm shaft (5—Fig. B2-12) and insert it through cylinder head bore, from either direction, installing rocker arms (2 and 3) along with shim (4) as shaft is pushed through cylinder head. Be sure to install the intake and exhaust rocker arms in the correct sequence. As rear of shaft approaches cylinder head install a new "O" ring (1) and continue to push shaft into cylinder head until opposite end protrudes far enough to install second "O" ring (6). After installation of second shaft "O" ring carefully center shaft in cylinder head and install retaining bolts (2—Fig. B2-11) with tab washers and temperature sensor (1). Note that when installing temperature sensor a new copper sealing washer between cylinder head and sensor should be used. Adjust valve clearance and decompression

INBOARD ENGINES

BMW

Fig. B2-15 — Exploded view of injector used on D12 engines.

1. Injector body
2. Adjusting shim
3. Spring
4. Pin
5. Valve
6. Seat
7. Nozzle
8. Nozzle nut
9. Seal
10. Sealing ring

cylinder head and install "O" ring (1) and "E" ring (3). Turn cylinder head over and install "O" ring (10) onto pin (11) then push pin into place followed by spring (12) and set screw (13). From top of cylinder head, place lever (8) in position "1" (Fig. B2-7). Make sure gear teeth face away from push rods, then insert roll pin (5) to secure gear (6) to shaft.

INJECTOR

Injector can be tested on engine using BMW special tool 74 64 1 333 545, and injection pump.

Before removing injection nozzle, clean injector and surrounding cylinder head area. Remove and cap fuel supply and return lines. Loosen injector retaining nuts evenly and pull injector from cylinder head. Remove seal (9–Fig. B2-15) and sealing ring (10) from injector bore and renew upon installation of injector.

Unscrew nozzle nut (8–Fig. B2-15) and remove nozzle (7), seat (6), needle (5), pin (4), spring (3) and shim (2). Injector should be renewed as a unit if needle (5) is damaged or corroded, needle or nozzle (7) are blued from overheating or needle does not properly seal in seat (6).

Clean all dirt and carbon from injector parts using clean diesel fuel and a brass brush. Reassemble injector in opposite order of disassembly and tighten nozzle nut (8) to 85 N·m.

Install BMW special tool number 74 64 1 333 545 as shown in Fig. B2-16, turn crankshaft counterclockwise by hand and note injector spray pressure.

WARNING: Fuel leaves injection nozzle with sufficient force to penetrate skin. When testing nozzle keep yourself clear of nozzle spray.

Spray pressure should be 11.2-12.0 MPa and is adjusted by adding or removing shims (2–Fig. B2-15). Spray from injector should be conical in shape and well atomized. At end of injection, spray should stop abruptly and fuel should not drip from nozzle.

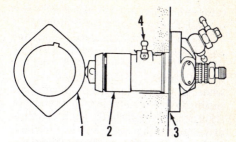

Fig. B2-18 — Install injection pump (2) on base circle of cam (1). Be sure control rack (4) lines up with throttle linkage. Use shims (3) to adjust injection timing.

After injector passes above tests it can be returned to service. Install new seal (9) and sealing ring (10) in cylinder head. Firmly seat injector by hand in cylinder head and tighten retaining nuts evenly to 15 N·m.

INJECTION PUMP

Injection pump leakage can be tested on engine using BMW special tool number 74 64 1 333 545.

Remove injection pump discharge line and install BMW special tool number 74 64 1 333 545 as shown in Fig. B2-17. Plug all unused fittings. Place throttle control lever in "Start" position. Turn crankshaft by hand in direction of normal rotation until gage pressure of 30-40 MPa has been reached and observe gage for any signs of pressure loss. If pressure drops below 25 MPa pump is faulty and should be repaired or renewed.

Injection pump should be tested and repaired by a shop qualified in diesel injection pump repair.

To remove injection pump, place throttle lever in "Start" position, remove retaining nuts and pull injection pump straight out of cylinder block. Do not lose injection pump timing shims (3–Fig. B2-18).

To install injection pump, place throttle lever in "Start" position. Rotate crankshaft by hand in direction of normal rotation until base of cam (1–Fig. B2-18) can be seen through injector pump opening. Install gaskets and timing shims (3) over injector pump mounting studs. Push injection pump gently down over studs making sure that fuel rack (4) is properly engaged by fuel control linkage. Install retaining nuts and torque to specification given in ENGINE SERVICE DATA section. See FUEL INJECTION TIMING section.

CAMSHAFT/COUNTERWEIGHT

Camshaft/counterweight assembly removal is accomplished after cylinder head and timing gear cover have been

device as previously outlined. Install rocker arm cover.

DECOMPRESSION DEVICE

To disassemble decompression device, cylinder head must first be removed. Remove rocker arm assemblies. Tap out roll pin (5–Fig. B2-14). Turn cylinder head over and remove set screw (13), spring (12), detent pin (11) and "O" ring (10). From top of cylinder head remove "E" rings (3 and 4) then, using a suitable drift, tap shaft (2) from head.

Inspect parts for wear and renew as necessary. Install lever (8) on shaft (2) and secure with roll pin (9). Lightly grease and install "O" ring (7) on lever end of shaft and push shaft halfway into place. Install "E" ring (4) and gear (6) then push shaft (2) rest of the way into

Fig. B2-16 — Install BMW special tool number 74 64 1 333 545 (1) between injection pump and injector (2) as shown. Attach pressure gage (3) and cap off unused fitting (4).

Fig. B2-17 — Install BMW special tool number 74 64 1 333 545 (1) between injection pump and pressure gage (2) then block off all unused fittings to test injection pump as outlined in text.

BMW

INBOARD ENGINES

removed. Refer to CRANKSHAFT section for timing gear cover removal.

Loosen intermediate gear casing and withdraw locating dowel (1 – Fig. B2-19). Turn camshaft until counterweight is next to crankshaft and lock flywheel in place. Maneuver intermediate casing so that a suitable puller can be installed on crankshaft counterweight drive gear (Fig. B2-19), then remove gear. Stand engine on flywheel end and position intermediate casing in its installed position. Secure camshaft followers away from camshaft cams, and using BMW special tool number 74 64 1 333 556, or other suitable puller, remove camshaft/counterweight assembly as shown in Fig. B2-20. If necessary, remove camshaft bearing in cylinder block by heating area around bearing to 80°C then using a suitable puller to extract bearing.

To disassemble camshaft/counterweight assembly, first detach snap ring (8 – Fig. B2-21). Using a suitable puller remove cams and large gear from camshaft, one piece at a time, as shown in Fig. B2-22. Lift off spacer (1 – Fig. B2-21), counterweight (2). Remove bearing (3) from counterweight (2) using a press. Remove key (7) from camshaft (6), then heat inner bearing race (4) to 80°C and remove it from camshaft. Lift off thrust washer (5).

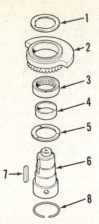

Fig. B2-21 – *Exploded view of camshaft/counterweight assembly.*

1. Spacer
2. Small gear and counterweight
3. Bearing
4. Bearing inner race
5. Thrust washer
6. Camshaft
7. Key
8. Snap ring

Inspect all parts for wear and cams for blueing, renew as necessary. Assemble camshaft/counterweight assembly in opposite order of disassembly. Install large gear with "O" timing mark facing counterweight. When installing cams, wide (exhaust) cam is installed with chamfer next to large gear and narrow (intake) cam is installed with step next to exhaust cam.

With engine standing on flywheel end, intermediate case dowel installed and intermediate case properly positioned, lower camshaft/counterweight assembly into crankcase. Align timing marks on camshaft gear and crankshaft gear as shown in Fig. B2-23. Install crankshaft counterweight drive gear on crankshaft by heating gear to 80°C and tapping it into place. Align counterweight gear and crankshaft counterweight drive gear timing marks (T – Fig. B2-24) while tapping crankshaft gear onto crankshaft. Check valve adjustment and fuel injection timing as previously outlined.

GOVERNOR

Camshaft/counterweight assembly must be removed, as previously outlined, prior to disassembly of governor mechanism. Place throttle lever (22 – Fig. B2-25) in "stop" position. Remove snap ring (1) from shaft (3) and extract shaft using a suitable puller. Unhook spring (16) from yoke (2) and lift out yoke. Using a suitable puller remove crankshaft gear. Remove nylon washer (6), ball sleeve (7) and steel balls (9). Using BMW special tool number 74 64 1 333 557 remove ball hub (8) and nylon washer (11). Remove pin (13) and washer (17) from shaft (12) and lift off spring (16). Remove locknuts (24), pull lever (22) with washers (21 and 23) from shaft (12) then remove key (14). Pull

Fig. B2-19 – *To remove crankshaft counterweight drive gear (2), first remove dowel (1) from crankcase, then maneuver intermediate gearcase so a suitable puller can be installed on crankshaft gear.*

Fig. B2-20 – *Using BMW special tool number 74 64 1 333 556, or other suitable puller, remove camshaft/counterweight as shown.*

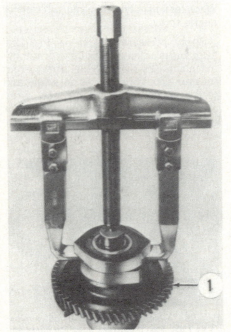

Fig. B2-22 – *Remove cams and large gear (1) individually from camshaft.*

Fig. B2-23 – *Align timing marks (M) on camshaft large gear and crankshaft small gear.*

Fig. B2-24 – *Align timing marks (T) on camshaft counterweight gear and crankshaft counterweight drive gear.*

INBOARD ENGINES
BMW

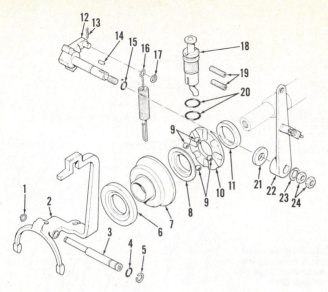

Fig. B2-25 — Exploded view of governor assembly.

1. Snap ring
2. Yoke
3. Shaft
4. "O" ring
5. Snap ring
6. Nylon washer
7. Ball sleeve
8. Ball hub
9. Steel balls
10. Ball plate
11. Nylon washer
12. Shaft
13. Pin
14. Key
15. "O" ring
16. Spring
17. Washer
18. Starter body
19. Set screws
20. "O" rings
21. Washer
22. Lever
23. Washer
24. Locknuts

Lightly clamp cylinder to crankcase and bring piston to TDC. Measure piston standout as shown in Fig. B2-26. Next measure thickness of new head gasket to be installed. Subtract piston standout measurement from head gasket thickness as shown in the following example:

Head Gasket Thickness	0.70 mm
Piston Standout	0.15 mm
Difference	0.55 mm

The example calculation results in a piston-to-cylinder head clearance of 0.55 mm. Model D12 engine piston-to-cylinder head clearance should be 0.8-0.9 mm.

Adjust piston-to-cylinder head clearance by adding or removing copper base shims which are available in 0.1 and 0.2 mm thicknesses. If piston-to-cylinder head clearance is too small, piston and valves may be damaged. If piston-to-cylinder head clearance is too great, engine will be hard to start and will not perform properly.

shaft (12) from crankcase. Remove set screws (19) and using BMW special tool number 74 64 1 333 528 remove starter body (18).

Inspect all parts for wear and renew as necessary. Assemble governor components in opposite order of removal. Heat crankshaft gear to 80°C to aid in installation. Heat ball hub (8) to 70°C and tap into place using a suitable driver. Hold steel balls (9) in place during assembly using grease. Ball sleeve (7) must be free to slide on crankshaft. Check engine speed as outlined in ENGINE SPEED ADJUSTMENT section.

CYLINDER

After removal of cylinder head, rotate crankshaft until piston is at BDC, lift cylinder straight up and off of crankcase being careful not to lose copper shims located at bottom of cylinder bore. If necessary cylinder can be bored and fitted with oversize rings and piston.

To install cylinder, first attach original copper base shims to bottom of cylinder with grease. Space piston ring gaps around piston so that no two gaps are aligned and clamp them into place using a band type ring compressor. Place piston at BDC and gently lower cylinder into place over piston. Remove ring compressor being careful not to dislodge base shims. Slide cylinder by hand completely into position.

Fig. B2-27 — With piston at BDC use BMW special tool number 74 64 1 333 552 (1) to remove piston pin.

PISTON AND ROD

After cylinder has been removed as previously outlined, remove snap ring at each end of piston pin and, using BMW special tool number 74 64 1 333 552, press pin from piston as shown in Fig. B2-27. If necessary heat piston to 50°C to aid in pin removal.

If desired, piston and connecting rod may be removed as a unit. Place crankcase on its side, remove bottom cover, then remove crankshaft counterweights. See Fig. B2-28. After counterweights have been removed connecting rod bolts will be easily accessible for removal. Mark connecting rod and cap as an aid in

Fig. B2-26 — Using a suitable clamp (1), lightly clamp cylinder to crankcase. Bring piston to TDC and using a vernier depth gage (2) measure piston protrusion above cylinder at point (3).

Fig. B2-28 — To remove connecting rod from crankshaft first remove counterweight bolts (1) which will allow access to connecting rod bolts (2).

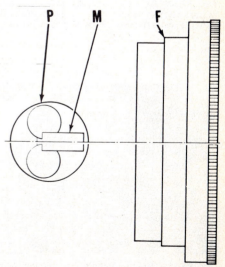

Fig. B2-29 — Install piston (P) on connecting rod so pocket (M) in piston crown is pointing towards flywheel (F).

Illustration courtesy BMW

BMW INBOARD ENGINES

proper assembly. Detach connecting rod bolts and lift rod out from top of crankcase while removing rod cap through bottom hole.

Inspect all parts for wear. Refer to ENGINE SERVICE DATA section for specifications and renew parts as necessary. Install components in opposite order of removal. Be sure connecting rod and cap are properly assembled and that pocket (M–Fig. B2-29) in piston crown points towards flywheel. Tighten connecting rod bolts to 60 N·m and crankshaft counterweight retaining bolts to 65 N·m.

CRANKSHAFT

Remove piston and connecting rod as previously outlined. Remove gearbox/clutch cover assembly, clutch and flywheel.

Remove timing cover by first removing starting-handle guide plate then removing remaining perimeter retaining screws. Attach a suitable puller to timing cover, as shown in Fig. B2-30, and pull cover from front of engine. If bearings are to be removed from timing cover, heat cover to 80°C and tap bearings out using a suitable driver.

Detach rear main bearing housing by first removing retaining nuts (1–Fig. B2-31). Heat crankcase in an oven or on

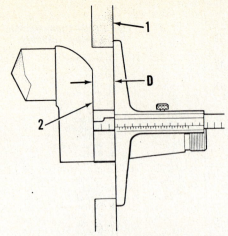

Fig. B2-32 – After installing crankshaft in crankcase use a vernier depth gage to measure distance (D) between housing mounting flange (1) and face of crankshaft web (2).

a hot plate to 80°C. Install four M8 jackscrews in holes (2), then turn jackscrews to force rear main bearing housing from crankcase. To remove bearing roller from housing, heat housing to 150°C and tap roller out using a suitable bearing driver.

Rotate crankshaft so connecting rod bearing journal lines up with cutout in crankcase, then tap crankshaft from front main bearing using a soft mallet.

If necessary to remove main bearing inner races from crankshaft, carefully heat races to 100°C at which time they should fall free of their own weight. Care should be used so bearing races are heated evenly, but quickly to prevent heat transfer to crankshaft and blueing of bearing metal. Under no circumstances should a bearing race be reused which has been blued by heat.

Inspect and measure crankshaft and compare with specifications given in ENGINE SERVICE DATA section.

To remove crankshaft front roller bearing from crankcase, remove snap ring then heat crankcase to 80°C and using a suitable driver tap bearing out from inside crankcase.

Before installing crankshaft bearing into crankcase, coat crankcase bore with grease and heat crankcase to 80°C. Tap bearing into place using a suitable driver and install snap ring. Using the same procedure, install main bearing in rear housing.

Install front main bearing inner race on crankshaft, heat crankcase to 80°C and tap crankshaft into place using a soft mallet to insure front bearing is seated against snap ring. Using a vernier depth gage, measure distance between rear main bearing housing mounting surface and face of crankshaft web as shown in Fig. B2-32. Measurement should be 15.1-15.2 mm for a warm

Fig. B2-30 – To remove timing cover (3) first remove starting handle guide plate and attach a suitable puller (1) using two timing cover screws (2).

Fig. B2-31 – Detach rear main bearing housing by unscrewing retaining nuts (1) then installing four M8 jackscrews in holes (2) and forcing housing from crankcase.

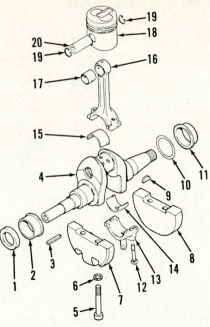

Fig. B2-33 – Exploded view of crankshaft, piston and connecting rod assembly.

1. Spacer
2. Front main bearing inner race
3. Key
4. Crankshaft
5. Counterweight bolt
6. Lockwasher
7. Counterweight (thin)
8. Counterweight (thick)
9. Key
10. Shim
11. Rear main bearing inner race
12. Connecting rod bolt
13. Connecting rod cap
14. Connecting rod bearing lower half
15. Connecting rod bearing upper half
16. Connecting rod
17. Piston pin bushing
18. Piston
19. Snap ring
20. Piston pin

crankcase or 15.3-15.5 mm for a cold crankcase. Adjust thickness of shim (10–Fig. B2-33) to achieve correct measurement. After selecting proper shim thickness, install shim and rear main bearing inner race on crankshaft using a suitable bearing driver.

Coat rear bearing housing crankcase bore with grease, heat crankcase to 90°C and pull rear housing into place using mounting nuts. Torque nuts to 30 N·m. Check for proper crankshaft end play of 0.3-0.4 mm. If end play adjustment is required, vary thickness of shim (10–Fig. B2-33).

ELECTRICAL SYSTEM

The generator produces current without mechanical contacts and has no bearings. Faults, therefore, most commonly arise from shorts and loose or corroded connections. When a fault is suspected, first check ground connections and wiring connections, then check generator operation.

IMPULSE TRANSMITTER. If warning lamp stays on after starting engine and boat wiring harness has been checked and found to be correct, check

Illustration courtesy BMW

INBOARD ENGINES   BMW

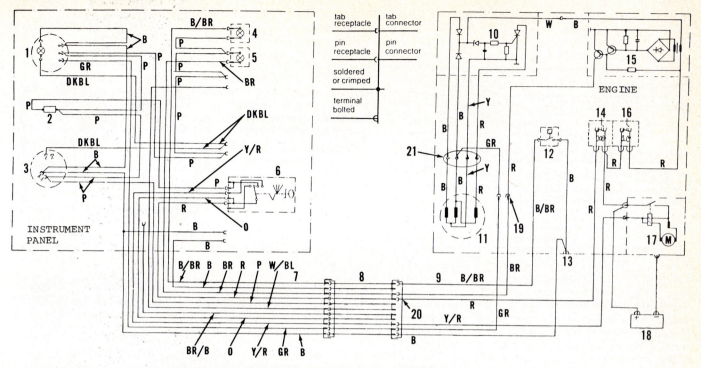

Fig. B2-34 – Diagram of wiring system used on D12 engines.

- B. Black
- BL. Blue
- BR. Brown
- DKBL. Dark blue
- GR. Gray
- O. Orange
- P. Purple
- R. Red
- W. White
- Y. Yellow
- 1. Tachometer/hourmeter
- 2. Fuse
- 3. Voltmeter
- 4. Water temperature warning light
- 5. Generator warning light
- 6. Key switch
- 7. Instrument panel wiring harness
- 8. Boat hull wiring harness
- 9. Engine wiring harness
- 10. Control unit
- 11. Generator
- 12. Water temperature switch
- 13. Engine ground
- 14. 25-amp circuit breaker
- 15. Impulse transmitter
- 16. 25-amp circuit breaker
- 17. Starter motor
- 18. 12-volt battery
- 19. Diagnostic point for impulse transmitter
- 20. Diagnostic point for control unit
- 21. Diagnostic point for generator

impulse transmitter (15 – Fig. B2-34) in the following manner. Disconnect red wire to brown wire connector at point (19) and connect to the red wire end a 12-volt test lamp, the other end of which has been connected to battery positive. With engine not running test lamp should be on. Start engine and slowly increase speed; test lamp should go out at 1150 rpm. If lamp does not light with engine off or go out at or above 1150 rpm, renew impulse transmitter and repeat test.

CONTROL UNIT. With engine shut off, disconnect 10 gage red engine wire from boat hull wiring at point (20 – Fig. B2-34) and connect a 0-40 amp ammeter in series between the disconnected wires. Start engine and turn some electrical equipment to place a load on electrical system. Refer to Fig. B2-35 for AMP/RPM chart. If no charge or an insufficient charge is shown, proceed to generator checking procedure. If correct charge rate is shown, check boat wiring for loose or corroded connections.

GENERATOR TEST. This test enables generator to be checked in- dependently of control unit and battery. With engine shut off disconnect the control unit to generator four-wire connector at point (21 – Fig. B2-34). Connect either black wire or red wire from generator to a 250 VAC voltmeter. Be sure other black wire cannot touch a ground. Start engine and run at full speed. Compare meter reading to chart in Fig. B2-36. Repeat test with remaining black generator wire. If meter reading for both black wires is correct, charging problem lies with a faulty control unit. If meter readings are not correct there are two fault possibilities. When meter reading for both black

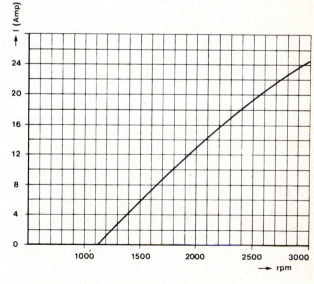

Fig. B2-35 – When testing control unit, generator output should match performance curve shown.

Illustration courtesy BMW

BMW — INBOARD ENGINES

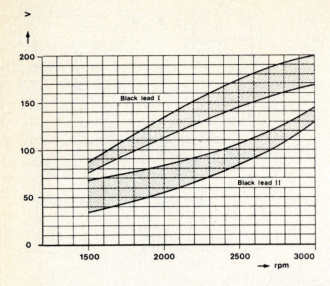

Fig. B2-36 — When performing generator test, individual black wire tests should produce voltages that fall in gray areas of adjacent chart.

Fig. B2-37 — Remove spring clip (1) using needle nose pliers to release magnetic rotor from flywheel.

Fig. B2-38 — Before removing stator retaining screws (2), remove cable clamp (1) from rear main bearing housing. Be sure cable and clamp will clear flywheel upon assembly.

wires lies below correct value, rotor magnetism is inadequate and rotor should be renewed. When only one black wire shows a low reading, a fault in stator windings is indicated and stator should be renewed.

ROTOR. REMOVE AND REINSTALL. Remove flywheel and lay flat with ring gear towards bottom. Remove spring clip (1 – Fig. B2-37) using needle nose pliers inserted in cut-out provided in rotor. Evenly and smoothly lift rotor straight out of flywheel. When inserting rotor in flywheel, it may be necessary to gently tap rotor with a soft mallet. Do not hit rotor with a metal tool or heat flywheel as loss of magnetism will result.

STATOR. REMOVE AND REINSTALL. Remove flywheel. Flatten lockwasher/cable clip (1 – Fig. B2-38) securing stator cable to rear main bearing housing. Remove retaining screws (2) and lift stator assembly off of rear main bearing housing. Assemble stator to engine in opposite order of removal; be sure cable clip is positioned so stator cable will not contact flywheel when installed.

BMW

ENGINE SERVICE DATA

NOTE: Metric fasteners are used throughout engines.

ENGINE MODEL	D35	D50
General		
Cylinders	2	3
Bore	95 mm	
Stroke	100 mm	
Displacement	1416 cc	2124 cc
Compression Ratio	19:1	
Main Bearings, Number of	3	4
Firing Order	1-2	1-2-3
Numbering System*		
(Front to Rear)	1-2	1-2-3

*Timing gear end is considered front of engine.

Tune-up		
Valve Lifter Type	Mechanical	
Valve Clearance (Cold):		
Inlet	0.45 mm	
Exhaust	0.45 mm	
Valve Seat Type	Cast in Head	
Valve Seat Angle:		
Inlet	45	
Exhaust	45	
Injection Pump	Bosch	
Injection Pressure	25.0-25.8 MPa	
Injection Timing	17-18° BTDC	
Idle Speed:		
Low	900-950 rpm	
High	3160 rpm	
Injector Nozzle	Bosch DLLA 160S760	
Engine Oil Capacity-liters	6	10
Oil Pressure:		
700 rpm	90 kPa	
3000 rpm	400 kPa	

Sizes — Capacities — Clearances		
Rocker Arm Shaft Diameter	18.967-18.980 mm	
Rocker Arm Bushing ID	18.988-19.046 mm	
Valve Stem Diameter:		
Intake	8.94-8.96 mm	
Exhaust	8.95-8.97 mm	
Wear Limit (Both)	8.90 mm	
Valve Guide ID	9.000-9.009 mm	
Wear Limit	9.050 mm	
Cylinder Bore	95.01-95.15 mm	
Connecting Rod Small End		
ID (without bushing)	35.000-35.016 mm	
Connecting Rod Big End		
ID (without bearing)	63.000-63.019 mm	
Connecting Rod Small		
Bushing OD	35.045-35.085 mm	
Connecting Rod Small End		
ID (with bushing)	32.025-32.041 mm	
Piston Diameter:		
Standard	94.94 mm	
Oversize	95.95 mm	
Piston Clearance	0.06-0.07 mm	

ENGINE SERVICE DATA (CONT.)

ENGINE MODEL	D35	D50

Sizes — Capacities — Clearances (Cont.)

	D35	D50
Piston Ring End Gap:		
1st Compression Ring	0.40-0.65 mm	
2nd Compression Ring	0.40-0.65 mm	
Oil Control Ring	0.30-0.60 mm	
Wear Limit 1st & 2nd Rings	1.0 mm	
Connecting Rod Bearing Diameter:		
Standard	60.040-60.083 mm	
Undersize	59.540-59.583 mm	
Connecting Rod Bearing Thickness:		
Standard	1.468-1.480 mm	
Undersize	1.718-1.730 mm	
Connecting Rod Bearing:		
Clearance	0.040-0.102 mm	
Wear Limit	0.2 mm	
Crankshaft Journal Diameter:		
Standard	71.981-72.000 mm	
Undersize	71.481-71.500 mm	
Connecting Rod Journal Diameter:		
Standard	59.981-60.000 mm	
Undersize	59.481-59.500 mm	
Main Bearing Clearance	0.056-0.118 mm	
Crankshaft End Play	0.16-0.44 mm	
Main Bearing Clearance (Maximum Allowed)	0.2 mm	
Main Bearing ID:		
Standard	72.056-72.099 mm	
Undersize	71.566-71.599 mm	
Main Bearing Shell Thickness:		
Standard	2.960-2.972 mm	
Undersize	3.210-3.222 mm	
Balancer Shaft:		
Diameter	27.991-28.000 mm	
Wear Limit	27.970 mm	
End Play	0.15-0.60 mm	0.15-0.70 mm
Camshaft Journal Diameter:		
Front Bearing	53.921-53.940 mm	
Intermediate Bearing	53.921-53.940 mm	
Rear Bearing (Ball Bearing Seat)	20.008-20.021 mm	
Camshaft End Play	0.1 mm	
Crankcase Bearing Bore:		
Front Bearing	54.000-54.030 mm	
Intermediate Bearing	54.000-54.030 mm	
Rear Bearing	46.982-46.993 mm	

Tightening Torques

(All values are in newton meters.)

	D35	D50
Bell Housing	140	
Connecting Rod	60	
Crankcase Halves	90	
Crankshaft Counterweights	65	
Crankshaft Gear	35	
Cylinder Head	55	
Flywheel	135	
Governor Spring Retainer	25	
Governor Weight Support	25	
Injection Advance Cams	10	
Injection Pump Pressure Valve	40	
Injector	1.5	
Injector Nozzle Nut	85	
Rear Seal Retainer	6.7	

INBOARD ENGINES — BMW

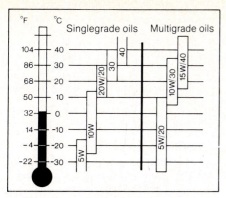

Fig. B3-1 — Correct oil viscosity as related to ambient air temperature can be found in chart shown.

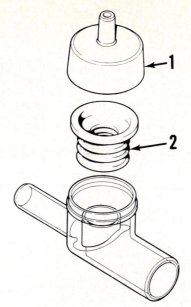

Fig. B3-2 — Crankcase ventilation valve should be serviced periodically by removing cap (1) and cleaning bellows (2).

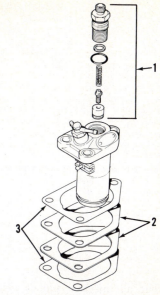

Fig. B3-3 — Exploded view of Bosch injection pump.
1. Delivery valve assy.
2. Shims
3. Gasket

Fig. B3-4 — When making injection pump control rod adjustment, as outlined in text, push control rod (1) forward then loosen lock screws (2). Adjustable forks (3) then can be moved forward to injection pump stops.

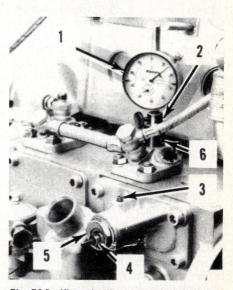

Fig. B3-5 — View showing proper installation of spill tube, dial indicator and maximum fuel setting pin.

1. Dial indicator
2. Spill tube
3. Locking screw
4. Setting pin, BMW special tool number 00 06 1 984 500
5. Cylinder
6. Fuel drip hole

MAINTENANCE

LUBRICATION

OIL. Use of a high quality API CC or CD oil is recommended. If CC oil has been extensively used in the past a change to CD oil is not recommended. See Fig. B3-1 for viscosity recommendations.

CRANKCASE VENTILATION VALVE. Pry cap (1–Fig. B3-2) off to gain access to rubber bellows (2) which should be periodically cleaned and inspected for cracks and holes. Renew bellows as necessary.

FUEL SYSTEM

FUEL PUMP. The fuel pump is actuated by a lobe on the engine's camshaft. The fuel pump incorporates a removable filter screen which should be cleaned periodically. Fuel pump is not repairable and must be renewed as a unit assembly.

INJECTION PUMP TIMING. Injection pump timing is accomplished through use of a fuel spill tube which will accomodate a dial indicator. If necessary these tools are available from BMW. Spill tube and dial indicator extension pin come as a set under BMW special tool number 00 06 0 483700.

To check injection timing first set throttle lever to full open position. Start with injection pump on number 1 cylinder. Remove pump delivery valve (1–Fig. B3-3) and install spill tube with dial indicator and extension pin installed as shown in Fig. B3-5. Connect an external fuel supply to injection pump inlet and suspend it at least 8 inches above pump. Rotate crankshaft so number 1 piston is at 20° BTDC on compression stroke using flywheel timing marks. Open spill tube cock and fuel should run out. Slowly turn flywheel counterclockwise until fuel flows at a rate of 1 drop in 5 seconds. This is the point at which fuel injection starts. Injection timing should be 17-18° BTDC. Check timing marks on flywheel to determine present injection timing. If timing is not within specifications, set dial indicator to "O". Turn flywheel in either direction so correct timing marks are aligned. Read dial indicator to obtain shim thickness adjustment necessary to correct timing. If injection pump timing is advanced, remove injection pump from crankcase and add a shim (2–Fig. B3-3) the thickness shown on dial indicator. If injection timing is retarded reduce total shim thickness by the indicated amount. After timing shim correction recheck pump timing as previously outlined. This procedure must be followed to check or adjust injection pump timing on remaining cylinders (be sure to use correct timing marks for cylinder being timed).

INJECTION PUMP CONTROL ROD. Injection pump control rod must be adjusted to synchronize injection pumps thereby providing uniform fuel delivery to all cylinders. To adjust injection pump fuel delivery control rod, remove inspection covers and cold start assembly from right side of engine. Lock throttle lever in stop position. Push control rod (1–Fig. B3-4) forward (timing gear end) to stop position. Loosen lock screws (2) of movable forks (3), and push forks forward to stop position of injection pumps and retighten screws. Procedure should be done carefully to in-

BMW INBOARD ENGINES

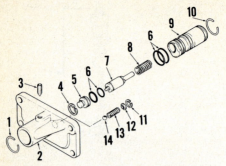

Fig. B3-6 – Exploded view of cold start assembly.

1. Circlip
2. Housing
3. Locking screw
4. Snap ring
5. Cap
6. "O" ring
7. Piston
8. Spring
9. Cylinder
10. Circlip
11. Snap ring
12. Spring retainer
13. Spring
14. Check ball

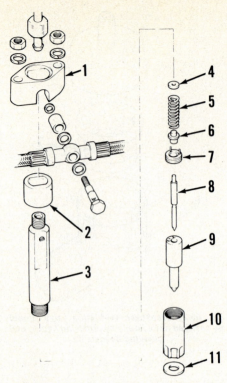

Fig. B3-7 – Exploded view of Bosch fuel injection nozzle.

1. Clamp
2. Spacer
3. Body
4. Shim
5. Spring
6. Push pin
7. Spacer
8. Valve
9. Nozzle
10. Nozzle nut
11. Washer

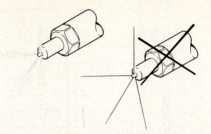

Fig. B3-8 – Fuel spray from injection nozzle should be conical in shape and well atomized as shown by left nozzle.

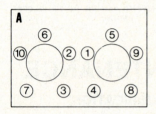

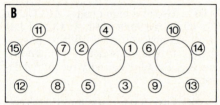

Fig. B3-9 – When installing cylinder head bolts they should be tightened using sequence (A) for D35 models or sequence (B) for D50 models.

sure that all injection pumps achieve their stop positions.

MAXIMUM FUEL SETTING. Note that BMW special tool number 00 06 1 984 500 is required to perform this procedure. Before adjusting maximum fuel setting, insure that injection pump control rod has been properly adjusted. Set throttle control lever to full speed position. Install spill point tool and dial indicator in number 1 injection pump as previously outlined in INJECTION PUMP TIMING section. Remove snap ring (4 – Fig. B3-6) and plug (5) from automatic cold start and install BMW special tool 00 06 1 984500 as shown in Fig. B3-5. Turn flywheel so fuel injection begins (1 drop every 5 seconds) which should be at 17° BTDC. Set dial indicator to "0". Turn flywheel counterclockwise until dial indicator reads 1.14 mm. Loosen set screw (3 – Fig. B3-5) and turn cylinder (5), using flats provided, until fuel spill rate is again 1 drop every 5 seconds then retighten set screw.

REPAIR

INJECTORS

After removal, clean injector of all carbon and dirt deposits using a brass brush and clean fuel. Disassemble injector after unscrewing nozzle nut (10 – Fig. B3-7). Closely inspect all parts for wear and deterioration paying particular attention to valve (8) tip for erosion or blueing from overheating, nozzle (9) for blocked spray holes or spray hole deterioration, and push pin (6) for wear. Renew parts as necessary. Note that nozzle (9) and valve (8) can only be renewed as a set. Caution must be used to insure that these parts do not become mixed with similar parts from other injectors. Lubricate all parts in clean fuel. Hold nozzle (9) vertically and insert valve (8). Valve should slide slowly down under its own weight. Complete remainder of assembly in opposite order of disassembly. Tighten nozzle nut (10) to 85 N·m.

Test injector using a suitable test stand being careful to keep injector tip pointed in a safe direction away from hands and eyes. Press handle down slowly and check for opening pressure of 2.5-2.58 MPa. Adjust pressure by adding or removing shims (4 – Fig. B3-7). Observe pattern (Fig. B3-8) by operating pump handle slowly 4-6 strokes, also listen for a light hissing sound. Finally check nozzle tip for leakage by setting injector pressure at 2.3 MPa for 10 seconds. Nozzle tip must remain dry.

AUTOMATIC COLD START

To disassemble automatic cold start device, detach unit from engine. Remove circlip (1 – Fig. B3-6) and set screw (3) then push out complete cylinder (9). Remove snap ring (4) and plug (5) to release piston (7) and spring (8). Remove snap ring (11) and shake out spring collar (12), spring (13) and check ball (14). Inspect all parts for wear, do not overlook ball seat in housing (2), and renew as necessary. Renew "O" rings and gasket. Reassemble in reverse order after oiling piston (7) and cylinder (9). Apply Loctite to four mounting screws. Do not tighten set screw (3) until adjusting MAXIMUM FUEL setting as previously outlined.

CYLINDER HEAD

Rocker arms and shafts should be removed prior to cylinder head removal.

Fig. B3-10 – After removal invert cylinder head to locate stamped shim thickness numbers (N).

Illustration courtesy BMW

INBOARD ENGINES

BMW

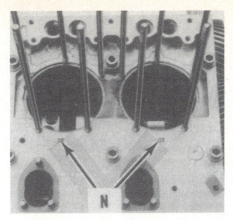

Fig. B3-11 – Location of cylinder block shim thickness number is shown by (N).

Fig. B3-13 – When installing timing gears align marks (M) as shown.

C. Crankshaft gear
F. Injection pump camshaft
I. Idler gear
M. Timing gear alignment marks
O. Oil pump drive gear
V. Camshaft

Valve face and valve seat angles are 45 degrees for both intake and exhaust valves. Depth of valve in head should be 0.85-1.25 mm as measured from valve face to cylinder head surface. If this measurement is exceeded either valve and/or cylinder head must be renewed. If measurement is less than minimum, valve seat should be cut deeper to achieve minimum clearance. Valve guides are renewable and should require a minimum press force of 1000 newtons. If valve guide can be installed using less than 1000 newtons force, cylinder head should be renewed. Valve guide should extend 23 mm above head surface on rocker arm side. See ENGINE SERVICE DATA for all other specifications. Follow tightening sequence shown in Fig. B3-9 and tighten all nuts to 55 N·m.

CYLINDER

Because the cylinder is a separate unit from the crankcase it is very important that you properly shim the cylinder to the crankcase upon assembly. Each cylinder is stamped at the top (Fig. B3-10) and the crankcase is stamped on the injection pump side of the cylinder bore (Fig. B3-11). Add these two numbers together to obtain correct shim thickness between cylinder and crankcase.

PISTONS

Pistons are accessible after removal of cylinder block. Care must be used not to damage pistons when crankshaft is rotated with cylinder block removed. Pistons may be removed after detaching snap rings which retain piston pin, and then pushing out piston pin.

Install piston so combustion chamber in piston crown is towards injection pump.

CONNECTING ROD

Connecting rods may be removed after pistons are removed. Remove one rod screw and replace it with an 8 mm headless stud that is long enough to reach bottom of crankcase. Unscrew remaining rod screw while holding rod cap with stud, then remove rod cap. Be careful not to drop bearing halves (3 – Fig. B3-12) or alignment pins (4) into crankcase.

Install connecting rods so numbers (N) on rod and cap are towards injection pump. Tighten connecting rod screws to 60 N·m.

TIMING GEARS AND FRONT COVER

Before front cover can be removed the raw-water pump, raw-water pump drive, crankcase ventilation tube and front pulley must first be removed. Remove Allen screws securing front cover to crankcase and remove cover. Front cover is sealed to crankcase with a gasket which should be renewed upon installation of cover.

To remove idler gear (I – Fig. B3-13), first remove oil slinger (1 – Fig. B3-14). Remove snap ring (3) from support shaft (8) then using a suitable puller withdraw idler gear and support bearings. After idler gear has been removed, outer bearing (4) and inner bearing (7) may be removed from gear (2). Be careful not to lose bearing spacer (6). Inspect all parts for wear or damage and renew as necessary. Removal of other gears in timing gear train is outlined in appropriate shaft assembly section, i.e., CAMSHAFT, INJECTION PUMP CAMSHAFT or CRANKSHAFT.

After installation of all other gears install idler gear assembly (I – Fig. B3-13) in opposite order of removal. Align timing marks (M) as idler gear is gently tapped onto support shaft using a suitable driver and light hammer. Be sure to tap idler gear assembly straight onto support shaft. Install snap ring (3 – Fig. B3-14) and oil slinger (1). Install front cover in opposite order of removal.

OIL PUMP

Oil pump is located behind timing gear cover on front of engine. Oil pump drive gear is supported by a needle bearing located in crankcase. If bearing is

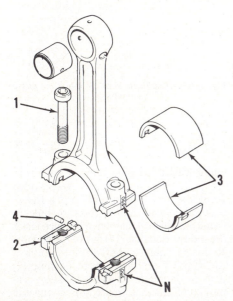

Fig. B3-12 – Exploded view of connecting rod assembly.

1. Rod screw
2. Rod cap
3. Bearing
4. Rod cap alignment pins
N. Rod and cap assembly numbers

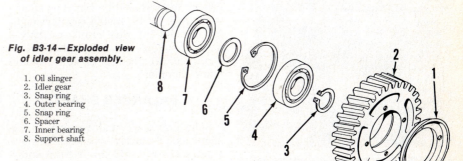

Fig. B3-14 – Exploded view of idler gear assembly.

1. Oil slinger
2. Idler gear
3. Snap ring
4. Outer bearing
5. Snap ring
6. Spacer
7. Inner bearing
8. Support shaft

Illustration courtesy BMW

BMW — INBOARD ENGINES

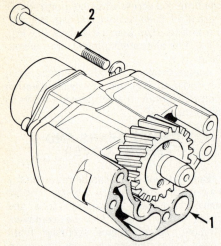

Fig. B3-15 — When installing oil pump onto engine coat mating surface (1) and bolt head (2) with sealant to prevent oil leaks.

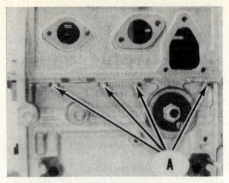

Fig. B3-17 — When separating crankcase halves remove Allen head screws (A) after those shown in Fig. B3-16.

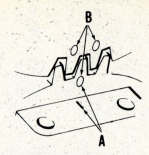

Fig. B3-19 — When installing balancer shaft drive gear onto crankshaft, be sure marks (A) are aligned as shown. Balancer shaft drive and driven gears should be aligned as illustrated by (B).

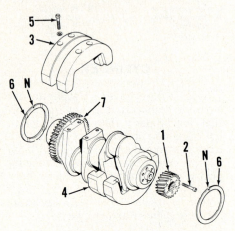

Fig. B3-18 — Exploded view of crankshaft assembly.

1. Crankshaft gear
2. Retaining screw
3. Removable counterweight
4. Removable counterweight
5. Retaining screw
6. Thrust shim
N. Alignment notch

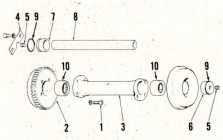

Fig. B3-20 — Exploded view of balancer shaft assembly.

1. Counterweight retaining screw
2. Gear
3. Connector shaft
4. Strap
5. Set screw
6. Front bushing
7. Rear bushing
8. Balance shaft
9. "O" rings
10. Bearings

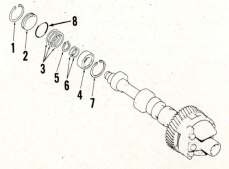

Fig. B3-21 — Exploded view of injection pump camshaft.

1. Snap ring
2. Cap
3. Shims
4. Bearing
5. Snap ring
6. Shims
7. Snap ring
8. "O" ring
9. Injection pump camshaft

removed it should be reinstalled flush with crankcase. Apply Loctite 571 or its equivalent to pump mating surface to seal oil channels (1 – Fig. B3-15) between pump and crankcase upon installation. Screw (2) threads must be sealed with Loctite 220 or similar product to ensure oil sealing.

CRANKSHAFT AND CRANKCASE

It is necessary to separate crankcase halves to remove crankshaft. Remove pistons, connecting rods, front cover, rear main oil seal and oil pump. Remove Allen screws (A – Fig. B3-16) and then Allen screws (A – Fig. B3-17). Carefully separate crankcase upper half from lower half using a plastic hammer. Crankshaft may now be lifted out of lower crankcase half.

Crankcase gear (1 – Fig. B3-18) is removed using a plastic hammer after unscrewing Allen screws (2). If necessary to remove balance shaft drive gear (7) it should be heated with a torch and driven off with a brass hammer. Counterweights (3 and 4) can also be removed by unscrewing Allen screws (5). Counterweights must be marked to insure reinstallation in original location.

To install balance shaft drive gear (7), heat gear to 150°C and install it with "0" marked tooth aligned with crankshaft index mark. See A-Fig. B3-19.

Reinstall crankshaft by first removing counterweight (3 – Fig. B3-18). Install thrust washers (6) with bronze side against crankshaft and notches (N) pointing up. Balance shaft drive and driven gears should be timed as shown in B – Fig. B3-19. Install counterweight (3 – Fig. B3-18). Seal crankcase halves using a suitable sealant. Install crankshaft gear (2). See Fig. B3-13 for timing mark alignment.

BALANCER SHAFT

Split crankcase and remove crankshaft as previously outlined. Remove screws (1 – Fig. B3-20) from counterweights (2). Note that Model D50 has a two-piece connector shaft (3) and screws connecting two halves must be removed. Remove strap (4) and set screws (5) from front and rear bushings (6 and 7). Insert a suitable drift punch through hole in front bushing (6) and drive balance shaft (8) and rear bushing (7) out of crankcase. Re-insert balance shaft (8) into connector shaft (3) and drive front bushing (6) just far enough forward to allow removal of balance shaft (8), connector shaft (3) and balance weights (2). Balancer shaft diameter should be 27.991-28.000 mm; wear limit is 27.970 mm.

To assemble, insert connector shaft (3 – Fig. B3-20) and balance weights (2)

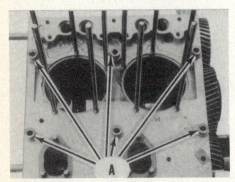

Fig. B3-16 — When separating crankcase halves remove Allen head screws (A) prior to those shown in Fig. B3-17.

INBOARD ENGINES — BMW

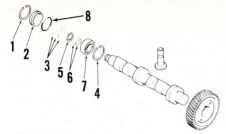

Fig. B3-22 — Exploded view of camshaft.

1. Snap ring
2. Cap
3. Shims
4. Snap ring
5. Snap ring
6. Shims
7. Bearing
8. "O" ring
9. Camshaft
10. Valve lifter

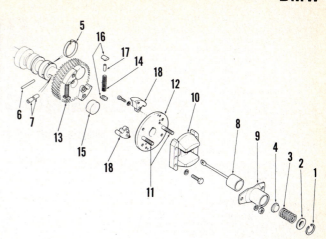

Fig. B3-23 — Exploded view of governor and injection pump advance assemblies.

1. Snap ring
2. Spring retainer
3. Spring
4. Spring seat
5. Spring clip
6. Pin
7. Thimbles
8. Spring housing and rod
9. Support bracket
10. Governor weight assy.
11. Studs
12. Driving plate
13. Gear
14. Springs
15. Weights
16. Retaining pins
17. Pins
18. Cams

into crankcase and hand-tighten Allen head screws (1). Push balance shaft (8) through connector shaft (3) and completely into front bushing (6). Drive front bushing (6) back flush with crankcase surface. This should be done with care to ensure a flush fit to prevent future oil leaks. Install rear bushing (7) and tighten connector shaft screws (1). Adjust countershaft end play by driving rear bushing (7) in until shaft end play is 0.15-0.60 mm for D35 or 0.15-0.70 mm for D50. Install set screws (5) and strap (4) using Loctite 220 or its equivalent. See Fig. B3-13 for timing mark alignment.

INJECTION PUMP CAMSHAFT

To remove injection pump camshaft, crankcase must be split and injection pumps removed. Remove snap ring (1 – Fig. B3-21), cap (2) and shims (3). Detach snap ring (7) from inside of case. Gently drive camshaft forward using a piece of 47 mm pipe and hammer. To remove injection pump camshaft bearing (4), first remove snap ring (5) and shims (6) then remove bearing (4) using a suitable puller.

Reassemble injection pump camshaft in reverse order. Bearing (4 – Fig. B3-21) end play should be zero and is adjusted using shims (6). Injection pump camshaft end play should be 0.10 mm and is adjusted with shims (3). See Fig. B3-13 for timing mark alignment.

CAMSHAFT

To remove camshaft and lifters, crankcase must be first split and some arrangement made to hold all lifters in their fully raised position. This is most easily accomplished by inverting upper crankcase half after removal of push rods and other related valve train parts.

Remove snap ring (1 – Fig. B3-22), cap (2) and shims (3) from outside of crankcase then detach snap ring (4) from inside of crankcase. Hold all valve lifters in their uppermost positions while using a piece of 47 mm pipe and hammer to gently drive camshaft forward and out. To remove camshaft roller bearing (7) first detach snap ring (5) and shims (6), then use a suitable puller to remove bearing (7).

Camshaft assembly is reverse of disassembly. Use shims (6 – Fig. B3-22) to establish zero end play for bearing (7) and shims (3) to obtain 0.1 mm camshaft end play. Install camshaft while observing timing mark alignment shown in Fig. B3-13.

GOVERNOR/INJECTION PUMP ADVANCE MECHANISM

The governor and injection pump advance are both located on the driven end of the injection pump camshaft. Injection pump camshaft must be removed in order to disassemble either unit.

To disassemble governor, remove snap ring (1 – Fig. B3-23), spring retainer (2), spring (3) and spring seat (4). Next remove spring clip (5), push out pin (6) and thimbles (7). This will allow removal of spring housing and rod (8). Lift off support bracket (9) and governor weight assembly (10). This completes the disassembly of the governor. Assembly is reverse of disassembly order while checking that governor weights are free to move and spring clip (5) is properly installed.

If available, BMW recommends the use of special tool 00 06 1 974600 to aid in disassembly of advancing mechanism. When using this tool first remove studs (11 – Fig. B3-23) from driving plate (12). Clamp BMW special tool 00 06 1 974600 in a vise, push driving plate (12) down over shaft of special tool (be careful pin in tool does not come all the way through driving plate flange) then turn gear (13) clockwise by hand against springs (14) and lift gear off. Remove weights (15), springs (14), spring retaining pins (16) and pins (17). Finally remove cams (18).

If BMW special tool is not available removal of driving plate (12) can also be achieved by carefully clamping studs (11) in a vise then pushing down and turning gear (13) clockwise as previously described. Precautions must be taken to protect the studs (11) and prevent any warping of driving plate (12).

Assembly is basically accomplished in reverse of disassembly order. Hook springs (14 – Fig. B3-23), pins (17) and pivots (16) into cams (18) of gear (13). Preload springs by turning gear (13) clockwise while pushing it down on driving plate (12). Be sure that keyways in gear (13) and driving plate (12) are aligned and that gear moves freely on plate. Install governor as previously outlined. Install injection pump camshaft as previously outlined observing timing mark alignment as shown in Fig. B3-13.

BMW

ENGINE SERVICE DATA

NOTE: Metric fasteners are used throughout engine.

MODEL	D150	D190

General
Cylinders	6	
Bore	90 mm	
Stroke	92 mm	
Displacement	3590 cc	
Compression Ratio	21:1	
Main Bearings, Number of	7	
Firing order	1-5-3-6-2-4	
Cylinder Numbering System Front to Rear	1-2-3-4-5-6	
Maximum Installation Angle	15°	
Direction of Rotation	Counterclockwise – viewed from flywheel end	
Turbocharger	KKK type 26	
Injection Pump	Bosch VE611F	
Injectors	Bosch/DNOSD 1510	
Gearbox	HBW 360	HBW 450

Tune-Up
Low Idle Speed	850 rpm	
Maximum Engine Speed	4350 rpm	
Injection Pressure	15.5 MPa	
Charge Air Pressure	85-95 kPa	
Injection Timing	4° BTDC	
Valve Clearance: Intake	0.3 mm	
Exhaust	0.45 mm	
Compression Pressure	2.4-2.6 MPa	
Thermostat Opening Temperature	77°-81°C	
Engine Oil Capacity	10 liter	
Oil Pressure at Idle	150-250 kPa	
Oil Pressure at Maximum Speed	350-650 kPa	
Oil Temperature	100°-110°C	
Gearbox Oil Capacity	1.4 liter	1.8 liter
Gearbox Ratio	1.6:1	
Fresh Water Cooling System Capacity	12 liter	

Sizes — Clearances
Rocker Arm Shaft Diameter	21.979-22.000 mm	
Rocker Arm Bushing ID	22.020-22.041 mm	
Rocker Arm to Shaft Clearance	0.020-0.062 mm	
Cylinder Head Gasket Thickness: Standard	1.70 mm	
Oversize	1.85 mm	
Valve Spring: Free Length	43.20 mm	
Installed Length	37.0 mm	
Valve Guide Protrusion	13.5-14.0 mm	
Valve Head Depth: Intake	0.8-1.1 mm	
Exhaust	0.79-1.09 mm	
Valve Lifter Diameter	14.965-14.985 mm	
Valve Lifter Bore Diameter	15.010-15.035 mm	
Valve Lifter to Bore Clearance	0.035-0.077 mm	

INBOARD ENGINES   **BMW**

ENGINE SERVICE DATA (CONT.)

MODEL	D150	D190

Sizes — Clearances (Cont.)

	D150	D190
Camshaft Lobe Height:		
Intake	←—— 45.14 mm ——→	
Exhaust	←—— 44.76 mm ——→	
Camshaft Lobe Width:		
Intake	←—— 37.88 ——→	
Exhaust	←—— 37.12 mm ——→	
Camshaft Journal Diameter:		
Standard	←—— 53.48-53.50 mm ——→	
Undersize	←—— 53.20-53.25 mm ——→	
Camshaft Bearing ID:		
Standard	←—— 53.54-53.59 mm ——→	
Undersize	←—— 53.29-53.34 mm ——→	
Camshaft Bearing OD	←—— 57.111-57.161 mm ——→	
Camshaft Bearing Bore ID	←—— 57.005-57.030 mm ——→	
Camshaft Radial Runout	←—— 0.04-0.11 mm ——→	
Camshaft End Play	←—— 0.05 mm ——→	
Camshaft Thrust Bearing Thickness	←—— 3.95-4.05 mm ——→	
Valve Stem Diameter:		
Intake	←—— 7.942-7.960 mm ——→	
Exhaust	←—— 7.922-7.940 mm ——→	
Valve Stem to Guide Clearance:		
Intake	←—— 0.040-0.073 mm ——→	
Exhaust	←—— 0.060-0.093 mm ——→	
Valve Seat Angle:		
Intake	←—— 55° 30' ——→	
Exhaust	←—— 45° 30' ——→	
Valve Seat Insert Bore ID:		
Intake	←—— 41.962-41.985 mm ——→	
Exhaust	←—— 35.964-35.988 mm ——→	
Valve Seat Insert Height	←—— 7.00-7.05 mm ——→	
Valve Seat Insert OD:		
Intake	←—— 42.076-42.086 mm ——→	
Exhaust	←—— 36.068-36.084 mm ——→	
Valve Seat Insert Depth:		
Intake	←—— 3.11 mm ——→	
Exhaust	←—— 3.00 mm ——→	
Piston Diameter:		
Piston A		
Standard	←—— 91.90-91.91 mm ——→	
Oversize	←—— 92.53-92.54 mm ——→	
Piston B		
Standard	←—— 91.91-91.92 mm ——→	
Oversize	←—— 92.54-92.55 mm ——→	
Piston Clearance	←—— 0.5 mm ——→	
Maximum Piston Weight Variation	←—— 5 grams ——→	
Piston Protrusion	←—— 1.25-1.39 mm ——→	
Piston Ring Width:		
Top Ring	←—— 2.075-2.095 mm ——→	
Second Ring	←—— 1.978-1.990 mm ——→	
Oil Control Ring	←—— 3.978-3.990 mm ——→	
Piston Ring Groove Width:		
Top Ring	←—— 2.106 mm ——→	
Second Ring	←—— 2.06-2.08 mm ——→	
Oil Control Ring	←—— 4.02-4.04 mm ——→	
Piston Ring End Gap:		
Top Ring	←—— 0.40-0.65 mm ——→	
Second Ring	←—— 0.40-0.65 mm ——→	
Oil Control Ring	←—— 0.25-0.58 mm ——→	
Piston Pin Diameter	←—— 29.990-29.996 mm ——→	
Piston Pin Bushing ID	←—— 30.030-30.045 mm ——→	
Piston Pin to Bushing Clearance	←—— 0.024-0.045 mm ——→	
Maximum Connecting Rod Weight Difference	←—— 10 grams ——→	

Illustration courtesy BMW

BMW INBOARD ENGINES

ENGINE SERVICE DATA (CONT.)

MODEL	D150	D190

Sizes — Clearances (Cont.)

Connecting Rod Weight:
- Sky Blue .... 1120-1130 grams
- White .... 1130-1140 grams
- Yellow .... 1140-1150 grams
- Red .... 1150-1160 grams
- Green .... 1160-1170 grams
- Blue .... 1170-1180 grams

Front Main Bearing Journal Diameter:
- Standard .... 62.98-63.00 mm
- 0.25 mm Undersize .... 62.73-62.75 mm
- 0.50 mm Undersize .... 62.48-62.50 mm

Bearing ID:
- Standard .... 63.06-63.11 mm
- 0.25 mm Undersize .... 62.81-62.86 mm
- 0.50 mm Undersize .... 62.56-62.61 mm

Bearing Width .... 31.75-32.25 mm
Bearing Clearance .... 0.06-0.13 mm

Intermediate Main Bearings

Journal Diameter:
- Standard .... 62.98-63.00 mm
- 0.25 mm Undersize .... 62.98-63.00 mm
- 0.50 mm Undersize .... 62.73-62.75 mm

Bearing ID:
- Standard .... 63.050-63.093 mm
- 0.25 mm Undersize .... 62.800-62.843 mm
- 0.50 mm Undersize .... 62.550-62.593 mm

Bearing Width .... 29.75-30.00 mm
Bearing Clearance .... 0.050-0.113 mm

Rear Main Bearing Journal Diameter:
- Standard .... 69.98-70.00 mm
- 0.25 mm Undersize .... 69.73-69.75 mm
- 0.50 mm Undersize .... 69.48-69.50 mm

Bearing ID:
- Standard .... 70.06-70.11 mm
- 0.25 mm Undersize .... 69.81-69.86 mm
- 0.50 mm Undersize .... 69.56-69.61 mm

Bearing Width .... 31.75-32.25 mm
Bearing Clearance .... 0.06-0.13 mm

Connecting Rod Journal Diameter:
- Standard .... 53.92-53.94 mm
- 0.25 mm Undersize .... 53.67-53.69 mm
- 0.50 mm Undersize .... 53.42-53.44 mm

Bearing ID:
- Standard .... 53.975-54.014 mm
- 0.25 mm Undersize .... 53.725-53.764 mm
- 0.50 mm Undersize .... 53.475-53.514 mm

Bearing Width .... 22.75-23.25 mm
Bearing Clearance .... 0.035-0.094 mm
Crankshaft End Play .... 0.121-0.323 mm

Oil Pump:
- Outer Rotor Width .... 32.487-32.500 mm
- Inner to Outer Rotor Clearance .... 0.152 mm
- Clearance Between Rotors and Housing Cover .... 0.081-0.097 mm
- Clearance Between Outer Rotor and Housing .... 0.050-0.070 mm

Tightening Torques

(All values are in newton meters.)

- Alternator Armature 45-50
- Alternator Bolt, lower 50-55
- Alternator Bolt, upper 100-110
- Alternator Pulley Mounting Nut 55-60
- Connecting Rod 80-85

Illustration courtesy BMW

INBOARD ENGINES — BMW

ENGINE SERVICE DATA (CONT.)

MODEL	D150	D190
Tightening Torques (Cont.)		
Cylinder Head		160
Engine Suspension		50
Exhaust Clamp		25-30
Exhaust Manifold		30-35
Flywheel		110
Flywheel Housing		50
Fuel Injector Retaining Nut		25-30
Injection Line Couplings		15-20
Injection Pump Gear		90
Injection Pump Mounting Nuts		30-32
Intake Manifold		30-35
Main Bearing Flanges		40-45
Oil Drain Plug		80
Oil Pan		10-12
Oil Pump		25-30
Oil Supply Lines Between Cooler and Crankcase		45-50
Oil Thermostat		7-8
Pulley Nut, Crankshaft		150-160
Rear Main Bearing Housing		25-30
Rocker Arm Brackets		110
Side Bolts		80
Turbocharger		23-25
Valve Covers		10
Water Collection Plate		8-10

The BMW D150 and D190 engines are fresh water-cooled, four-stroke, six-cylinder, turbocharged diesel engines with indirect fuel injection. They incorporate a dual circuit cooling system, in which the radiator, oil cooler, thermostats and expansion tank are integrated into one unit. The fresh-water circulating pump is driven by the alternator belt, while the raw-water pump is driven directly off the camshaft. The D190 engine also incorporates a charge air cooler.

Engine front is considered to be pulley end of engine.

MAINTENANCE

DRIVE BELT

Renewal of alternator-water pump drive belt requires removal of both raw water pump hoses. Before removing hoses be sure to close raw-water inlet valve. After belt renewal belt tension is adjusted by rotating alternator away from engine on adjustable mounting brackets. Belt tension is correct when thumb pressure applied halfway between alternator pulley and fresh water circulation pump pulley causes belt to deflect about 5 mm.

LUBRICATION

ENGINE OIL AND FILTER. On new or rebuilt engine, oil and filter should be changed after first 50 hours of operation. Under normal operating conditions engine oil and filter should be changed after each 100 hours of operation or seasonally, whichever is more frequent. Use of a high quality API specification CC or CD oil is recommended. Recommended oil is SAE 20W oil for ambient temperatures of −10°C to +5°C, SAE 30W for temperatures of 5°C to 30°C and SAE 40W for temperatures of 30°C or above.

When changing engine oil be sure to drain oil cooler by removing red hex head plug (1 – Fig. B4-1). After oil cooler has been drained replace hex head plug (1) and fill oil cooler with 1 liter of fresh oil after removing red hex head plug (2), this will prevent an air lock from forming in the lubrication system and ensure that all old oil has been drained from the engine.

GEARBOX OIL. Reversing gearbox oil should be changed after every 200 hours of operation or seasonally, whichever is more frequent. Use of a high quality Dexron ATF is recommended.

COOLING SYSTEM

When adding coolant to the fresh-water cooling system be sure coolant is a 50/50 mixture of antifreeze and water. This is required to ensure proper operation of the coolant temperature sensor and thermostat. With engine stopped, pour fresh antifreeze/water mixture into expansion tank until liquid level reaches bottom of filler cap neck. Start engine and allow it to reach operating temperature, if necessary, add coolant mixture until liquid level is about 11 mm below bottom of filler cap neck.

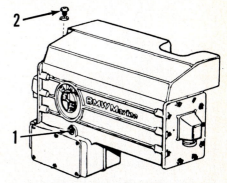

Fig. B4-1 — View showing location of oil cooler drain plug (1) and fill plug (2).

BMW INBOARD ENGINES

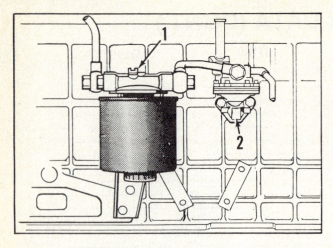

Fig. B4-2—When bleeding fuel system unscrew fuel filter bleed screw (1) and operate fuel pump manual lever (2).

FUEL SYSTEM

FUEL FILTER. Fuel filter is a cartridge type and should be drained of water and contaminants every 14 days, or less, depending on quality of fuel and condition of fuel tank. Filter cartridge should be renewed after each 100 hours of use or seasonally, whichever is more frequent.

FUEL PUMP. Fuel pump is diaphragm type and incorporates an external pump lever which is used to bleed fuel system. If necessary, pump diaphragm may be renewed after first removing fuel pump from engine. Mark pump cover and body so they may be assembled in the same position. Remove six screws that hold cover and body together and lift off pump cover. Press diaphragm down and turn counterclockwise 90 degrees. Lift diaphragm and spring out of pump body. Reassemble pump with new diaphragm in opposite order making sure pump body and cover are properly aligned before tightening cover screws. Always use a new "O" ring seal between pump and engine block.

BLEED FUEL SYSTEM. To bleed fuel system set throttle lever in full speed position. Open fuel filter bleed screw (1–Fig. B4-2) and operate fuel pump manual lever (2) until air-free fuel flows from filter bleed screw. Tighten filter bleed screw and open fuel injection pump bleed screw (1–Fig. B4-3) and again operate fuel pump manual lever until air-free fuel flows from bleed screw. Tighten injection pump bleed screw. Place throttle lever in start position and crank engine for short (not more than 15 seconds) periods of time. If after four or five attempts, engine does not start, carefully check all fuel line connections for leaks and repeat bleeding procedure. After engine starts, allow it to run until a smooth idle has been achieved.

INJECTION PUMP TIMING. To properly time fuel injection pump the use of two BMW special tools is required:
1. Adjusting disc (degree wheel), BMW special tool number 7464 1 333500.
2. Dial indicator adapter, BMW special tool number 7465 1 333510.

After removing three socket head bolts, attach the BMW degree wheel (tool number 7464 1 333500) to crankshaft vibration damper using three hex head bolts as shown in Fig. B4-4. Using a piece of wire make a pointer and install it on the engine in a convenient location. Remove number 6 cylinder rocker arm cover and bring number 1 piston to TDC on compression (valves of number six cylinder will be in an overlap condition). Mark TDC position on degree wheel and turn crankshaft counterclockwise 25°-30° (viewed at gear end).

Remove injection pump injector lines and bleed screw (1–Fig. B4-3). Install BMW dial indicator adapter (tool number 7465 1 333510) in bleed screw hole and attach a dial indicator as shown in

Fig. B4-5—After removing injection pump bleed screw install dial indicator adapter (1), BMW special tool number 7465 1 333510, and mount dial indicator (2). See text for outline of fuel injection pump timing procedure.

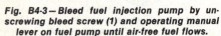

Fig. B4-3—Bleed fuel injection pump by unscrewing bleed screw (1) and operating manual lever on fuel pump until air-free fuel flows.

Fig. B4-4—View of BMW degree wheel (1) number 7464 1 333500 and gear puller (3) number 7464 1 333505 installation. Refer to text for injection pump timing and service.

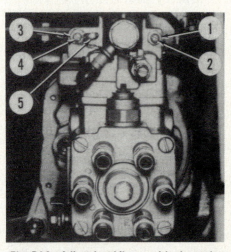

Fig. B4-6—Adjust low idle speed by loosening locknut (1) and turning idle speed screw (2). To adjust high idle speed, remove lock wire (5), loosen locknut (3) and turn high idle speed adjustment screw (4). Be sure to properly rewire and seal lock wire (5).

INBOARD ENGINES

BMW

Fig. B4-5. Preload dial indicator and set to zero. Turn crankshaft in direction of normal rotation until gage reads 0.50 mm. At this point degree wheel on crankshaft should show 4° BTDC. If not turn crankshaft in direction of rotation to 4° BTDC for number 1 piston. Loosen injection pump mounting nuts and turn pump, in adjusting slots, until dial indicator shows a reading of 0.50 mm. Without moving pump tighten mounting nuts to 30-32 N·m. Rotate crankshaft through two complete revolutions and again check dial indicator reading at 4° BTDC to verify adjustment.

Remove dial indicator, adapter, wire pointer and degree wheel. Reinstall crankshaft socket head bolts, fuel injector lines and injection pump bleed screw. Bleed fuel system as previously outlined.

IDLE SPEED ADJUSTMENT

Low idle speed is adjusted with engine running and transmission in neutral. Loosen locknut (1 – Fig. B4-6) and turn adjustment screw (2) until an idle speed of 850 rpm has been achieved. Tighten locknut (1).

Engine maximum speed adjustment is factory sealed. If adjustment becomes necessary, adjustment screw should be carefully lockwired and resealed. With engine running and transmission in neutral slowly bring engine speed up to 4350 rpm or maximum speed, whichever is slower. Loosen locknut (3) and turn adjustment screw (4) to adjust engine speed and ensure that engine speed cannot exceed 4350 rpm. Tighten locknut (3).

VALVE ADJUSTMENT

Valves should be adjusted after first 10 hours of operation on a new or rebuilt engine and every 100 hours or seasonally, whichever is more frequent, thereafter. Adjustment must be performed on a cold engine.

Fig. B4-7 – To adjust valves, bring piston of cylinder to be adjusted to TDC and loosen locknut (1). Insert proper thickness feeler gage (3) between rocker arm and valve stem then turn adjusting screw (2) until correct gap is established.

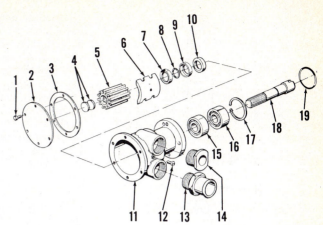

Fig. B4-8 – Exploded view of raw-water pump.

1. Cover screw (6)
2. Cover plate
3. Gasket
4. Felt shaft washers
5. Impeller
6. Shoe
7. Seal
8. "O" ring
9. Thrust ring
10. Seal
11. Pump housing
12. Shoe retaining screw
13. Metal hose adapter
14. Plastic hose adapter
15. Inner shaft bearing
16. Outer shaft bearing
17. Snap ring
18. Shaft
19. "O" ring

Remove rocker arm cover of cylinder to be adjusted and bring piston to TDC on compression. Loosen locknut (1 – Fig. B4-7) and back out adjusting screw (2) of valve to be adjusted. Insert feeler gage of correct thickness between valve stem and rocker arm. Slowly tighten adjustment screw until feeler gage can be pulled out with slight resistance. Carefully tighten locknut (1) so adjustment screw is not moved. Repeat procedure for other valve then install rocker arm cover using a new gasket. See ENGINE SERVICE DATA section for specifications.

REPAIR

COOLING SYSTEM

FRESH-WATER PUMP. Fresh-water pump is a sealed unit and must be renewed as a unit assembly. To remove pump drain cooling system, detach hoses and remove drive belt. Remove four mounting bolts and pull pump from engine. Install new pump in opposite order of removal. Coat mounting flange gasket with a non-hardening gasket sealer and fill cooling system with a 50/50 solution of anti-freeze and water.

RAW-WATER PUMP. To remove raw-water pump from engine close raw-water inlet valve and remove intake and discharge hoses. Remove four mounting nuts and pull pump from engine.

Clamp pump in a vise and remove six cover screws (1 – Fig. B4-8) and cover (2). Using two screwdrivers pry impeller (5) off shaft (18). Remove screw (12) and lift shoe (6) out of housing (11). Remove "O" ring (19) and snap ring (17) from housing (11). Using a soft mallet tap shaft (18) and bearings (15 and 16) from housing. Press shaft (18) out of bearings. Using a suitable drift carefully tap seals (7 and 10) along with thrust ring (9) and "O" ring (8) out of housing (11). If removal of hose adapters (13 and 14) is necessary, heat housing (11) to aid in adapter removal.

To assemble raw-water pump press seal (10) into pump housing (11) from drive end with lip towards outside of pump. Insert thrust ring (9) into housing from impeller end and place it against seal (10). Install "O" ring (8) and push seal (7) in from impeller end until it bottoms on housing stop with lip towards outside of pump. Press bearings (15 and 16) onto shaft (18). Install shaft and bearing assembly into housing (11) from drive end. Make sure "O" ring (8) is not damaged by shaft. Install snap ring (17) and "O" ring (19). If removed, coat threads of hose adapters (13 and 14) with Loctite and install adapters in housing (11). Install shoe (6) and secure it into place using screw (12). Coat vanes of impeller (5) with petroleum jelly and install impeller on shaft (18) using a twisting motion in direction of normal rotation. Install gasket (3), cover (2) and mounting screws (1).

Align pump shaft slot with camshaft drive key and slide pump onto mounting studs. Install and tighten mounting nuts. Install intake and discharge hoses.

Fig. B4-9 – Align injection pump shaft key way (K) with number 1 delivery valve (1) and check that key slot in injection pump drive gear is positioned as shown to ensure correct injection pump timing as outlined in text.

Illustration courtesy BMW

BMW — INBOARD ENGINES

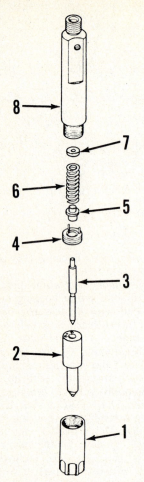

Fig. B4-10 – Exploded view of fuel injector used on BMW D150 and D190 engines.

1. Nut
2. Nozzle
3. Valve
4. Collar
5. Pin
6. Spring
7. Shim
8. Holder

Open raw-water inlet valve, start engine and check cooling system for leaks.

FUEL INJECTION PUMP

To remove fuel injection pump disconnect all fuel supply, return and injector lines. Also disconnect charge air pressure line to intake manifold and fuel shut-off solenoid wire. Close raw-water inlet valve and remove raw-water pump and hoses. Remove injection pump gear inspection cover from front of timing gear case along with gear retaining nut and washer.

Install injection pump gear puller, BMW special tool number 7464 1 333505, on injection pump drive gear and lock into place using two collar nuts as shown in Fig. B4-4. Remove injection pump mounting nuts and washers. Using center bolt of gear puller press injection pump out of drive gear and remove pump from engine. Be careful not to drop pump shaft Woodruff key into gear case.

Injection pump overhaul and repair should be performed by a shop which specializes in diesel injection pump service and repair.

To install injection pump tap Woodruff key into pump shaft. Turn pump shaft until key is lined up with number 1 pump discharge port and key slot in drive gear as shown in Fig. B4-9. Carefully slide injection pump onto mounting studs and into drive gear. Install mounting nuts and washers finger tight. Remove injection pump gear puller and collar nuts from front of gear case. Install washer then install pump gear retaining nut and tighten finger tight. Do not turn pump shaft.

Refer to INJECTION PUMP TIMING section and follow timing procedure. After timing of fuel injection pump is complete, tighten pump gear retaining nut to 90 N·m and install inspection cover. Install raw-water pump and hoses then open raw-water inlet valve. Connect fuel supply, fuel return and injector lines. Reconnect intake manifold charge air line to injection pump diaphragm. Bleed fuel system as previously outlined.

FUEL INJECTOR

REMOVE AND REINSTALL. Before removing injector clean fuel line fittings and surrounding cylinder head area with clean fuel and compressed air. If injectors are to be removed individually it is necessary to remove rocker arm cover of cylinder involved to gain access to fuel return line banjo bolt. However, if all injectors are to be removed at one time, fuel return lines can be left attached to injectors until after they have been removed as a set. Disconnect fuel supply line and hold down clamp of injectors to be removed. Pull injector straight out of cylinder head and remove seal from injector bore. Be careful that dirt and carbon are not allowed to fall into combustion chamber through open injector bore. After removal clean injector of all carbon and dirt using a brass brush and clean diesel fuel.

Before installing injector, be sure injector bore and sealing surface are clean and free from all dirt and carbon. Place a new seal on nozzle of injector and install injector in bore tightening hold down clamp nut to 25-30 N·m. Reconnect injector fuel supply and return lines.

TESTING. A complete job of testing and adjusting injectors requires use of special test equipment. Only clean, approved testing oil should be used to test injectors. Injector nozzle should be tested for opening pressure, seat leakage and spray pattern.

When operating properly during test, injector will emit a buzzing sound and cut off quickly with no fluid leakage at seat.

WARNING: Fuel emerges from injector with sufficient force to penetrate the skin. When testing the injector, keep injector tip pointed in a safe direction away from hands and eyes.

Before conducting test, operate tester lever until test oil flows, then attach injector. Close valve to tester gage and pump tester a few quick strokes to be sure nozzle valve is not stuck, which would indicate that injector may be serviceable without disassembly.

OPENING PRESSURE. Open valve to tester gage and operate tester lever slowly while observing gage reading. Opening pressure should be 15.5-16.0 MPa.

Opening pressure is adjusted by varying thickness of shim (7 – Fig. B4-10).

SEAT LEAKAGE. Injector nozzle tip should not leak at a pressure less than 14.5 MPa. To check for leakage, actuate tester lever slowly and as gage needle approaches suggested pressure, observe nozzle tip. Hold pressure for 10 seconds; if drops appear or nozzle tip becomes wet, valve is not seating and injector must be disassembled and overhauled as outlined later.

NOTE: Leakage of tester check valve or connections will cause a false reading, showing up in this test as fast leakback. If a series of injectors fail to pass this test, the tester rather than the injector units should be suspected.

SPRAY PATTERN. Spray pattern should be well atomized and slightly conical in shape, emerging in a straight axis from nozzle tip. If pattern is wet, ragged or intermittent, nozzle must be overhauled or renewed.

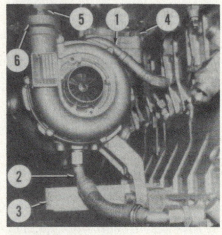

Fig. B4-11 – Grind an open-end wrench to remove turbocharger right rear mounting nut (4).

INBOARD ENGINES

BMW

OVERHAUL. Disassemble injector by removing nozzle nut (1–Fig. B4-10) from body (8). Withdraw nozzle (2), valve (3), seat (4), pin (5), spring (6) and shim (7) from body. Caution must be used to ensure that these parts do not become mixed with similar parts from other injectors. Closely inspect all parts for wear and deterioration paying particular attention to valve tip (3) for errosion or blueing from overheating, nozzle (2) for blocked spray holes or spray hole deterioration, and pin (5) for wear. Renew parts as necessary. Nozzle (2) and valve (3) can only be renewed as a set. Lubricate all parts in clean fuel. Hold nozzle (2) vertically and insert valve (3). Valve should slide slowly down under its own weight. If valve falls freely or sticks renew nozzle and valve assembly. Assemble injector in opposite order of disassembly and tighten nozzle nut (1) to 85 N·m.

TURBOCHARGER

REMOVE AND REINSTALL. Before removing turbocharger, provision to support turbocharger side of engine must be made as engine mount adjacent to turbocharger must be removed when removing turbocharger unit.

Disconnect oil supply line (1–Fig. B4-11) and return line (2). Remove exhaust pipe from turbocharger and engine. Support engine from below and remove adjacent engine mount and bracket (3) from engine block. Support turbocharger from below and remove four hex nuts holding turbocharger to exhaust manifold. It will be necessary to grind off an open-end wrench to remove rear mounting nut (4). Relieve turbocharger support pressure, remove turbocharger and gaskets from engine.

To install turbocharger, place new gasket and seal on turbocharger mounting flange. Install hose (5) and clamps (6) on compressor outlet, push turbocharger up onto exhaust manifold mounting flange and push hose onto intake manifold elbow. Start rear mounting nut (4) and use ground off open-end wrench to draw turbocharger into place. Install remaining mounting nuts and torque all four to 25-28 N·m. Install new gasket on exhaust pipe and insert pipe into turbine outlet to stop. Line up exhaust pipe mounting bracket and support and install mounting bolts. Install exhaust pipe-to-turbocharger clamp and tighten bolts evenly to 30-35 N·m. Connect oil supply and return lines (1 and 2) to turbocharger, tighten intake manifold hose clamps (6). Install engine mount and bracket (3), tighten mount bolts to 50 N·m. Lower engine into place and complete engine mount installation.

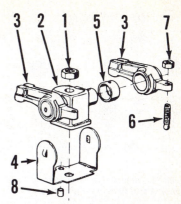

Fig. B4-15 – Exploded view of rocker arm and shaft assembly.

1. Mounting nut
2. Mounting bracket
3. Rocker arm
4. Rocker arm retainer spring
5. Rocker arm shaft bushing
6. Adjusting screw
7. Locknut
8. Guide pin

OVERHAUL. Using support bracket, clamp turbocharger in a vise as shown in Fig. B4-12. Remove oil supply line (1) and gasket from bearing housing (2). Using a scribe or similar tool mark position of bearing housing (2) and turbine housing (3) as an assembly aid. Unscrew clamping ring mounting nuts (4) and pull turbine housing off of bearing housing. Using a dial indicator as shown in Fig. B4-13 check axial play of turbine shaft. Maximum allowable end play for turbine shaft is 0.15 mm. If this measurement is exceeded renew turbocharger as a unit.

Measure radial play of turbine shaft in two locations 90 degrees apart as shown in Fig. B4-14. Maximum allowable turbine shaft radial play is 0.55 mm. If this measurement is exceeded turbocharger must be renewed as a unit.

To assemble turbocharger first install oil supply line and a new gasket on bearing housing. Install turbine housing on bearing housing then install clamping rings and retaining nuts finger tight. Rotate turbine housing until scribe marks are aligned and tighten clamping ring nuts to 30 N·m.

CYLINDER HEADS

REMOVE AND REINSTALL. To avoid distortion of cylinder head gasket surface never remove cylinder heads from a hot engine.

Remove turbocharger, intake and exhaust manifolds, water collection plate, injectors, glow plug ground straps and valve covers. Remove rocker arm assemblies from each cylinder head by unscrewing retaining nut (1–Fig. B4-15) and lifting rocker arm bracket (2) complete with rocker arms and spring plate off of mounting stud. Disconnect oil

Fig. B4-12 – Scribe marks on bearing housing (2) and turbine housing (3) before disassembly.

Fig. B4-13 – To check compressor shaft axial play, lay turbocharger flat and install a dial indicator as shown.

Fig. B4-14 – To check compressor shaft radial play install a dial indicator as shown and check shaft in at least two places 90° apart.

BMW INBOARD ENGINES

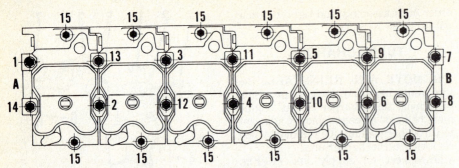

Fig. B4-16—Illustration of proper cylinder head bolt tightening sequence. Be sure to install end spacers (A and B) before tightening bolts. When loosening head bolts use reverse order of tightening sequence.

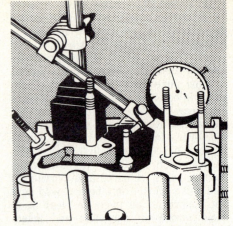

Fig. B4-19—Use a dial indicator as shown to check valve guide and stem wear from top of removed cylinder head.

pressure line, remove push rods and stamp each cylinder head with its position number. Remove cylinder head bolts in opposite order of tightening sequence shown in Fig. B4-16. If necessary, do not surface grind cylinder head more than 0.20 mm.

Prior to cylinder head installation correct cylinder head gasket thickness must be determined by measuring piston protrusion. Using BMW special tool number 7464 1 333509 compress cylinder liner by tightening special tool bolts to 30 N·m. As shown in Fig. B4-17, install dial indicator on special tool, preload gage on edge of cylinder liner and set dial to zero. Bring piston to be measured to TDC and move tip of dial indicator to top of piston and record measured distance. Two different head gaskets are available in thicknesses of 1.70 mm and 1.85 mm. If dial indicator reading is 0.065-0.20 mm use 1.70 mm thick head gasket. If dial indicator reading is 0.21-0.335 mm use 1.85 mm thick head gasket. Repeat this procedure for each piston. See Fig. B4-18 for illustration of head gaskets. Gasket (2) with extra hold is 1.85 mm thick.

Place assembled cylinder heads on cylinder block in sequential order and install head bolts with clamps finger tight. Install spacers (A and B – Fig. B4-16). Install exhaust manifold on cylinder heads and tighten mounting nuts to 30-35 N·m. Tighten cylinder head bolts in three steps in sequence shown in Fig. B4-16. First tighten all bolts to 40 N·m, then tighten all center bolts to 100 N·m and all side bolts to 80 N·m, and finally tighten all center bolts to 160 N·m and check torque of 80 N·m on all side bolts.

Complete assembly of engine in opposite order of removal. Note: After first 10 hours of operation retorque all cylinder head center bolts to 160 N·m and all side bolts to 80 N·m.

OVERHAUL. Remove rocker arm assembly from cylinder head by unscrewing retaining nut (1 – Fig. B4-15) and lifting bracket (2), complete with rocker arms (3) and spring clip (4) off mounting stud. Remove spring clip (4) and slide rocker arms off bracket (2). See ENGINE SERVICE DATA section for specifications. Coat all parts with engine oil and assemble in opposite order of removal. Torque retaining nut (1) to 110 N·m.

Check for valve guide wear using a dial indicator as shown in Fig. B4-19. Maximum allowable valve stem to guide clearance is 0.073 mm for intake valves and 0.093 mm for exhaust valves. Renew valves and guides as necessary.

To renew valve guides heat cylinder head in an oven or hot water bath to 90°C and drive old guide out of cylinder head from combustion chamber side. Using a suitable drift, install new guide from top of heated cylinder head so the distance from top of valve guide to spring seat is 13.5-14.0 mm.

Valve seat grinding and valve face refinishing should be closely coordinated and must be performed after valve guide renewal. Grind intake valve seats at a 55° angle and exhaust valve seats at a 45° angle. Face angle of intake valves should be refinished to 55°30′, while exhaust valve face angle should be refinished to 45°30′. Remove only enough stock to eliminate all scratches and pitting. Valve head thickness after refinish-

Fig. B4-17—When measuring cylinder sleeve protrusion or checking head gasket thickness use BMW special tool number 7464 1 333509 as shown to compress sleeve into bore and as a mount for a dial indicator. Point (A) shows dial indicator tip correctly placed on edge of cylinder sleeve.

Fig. B4-18—Cylinder head gasket (1), without extra hole, is 1.70 mm thick. Cylinder head gasket (2), with extra hole, is 1.85 mm thick. Be sure to use correct thickness gasket as outlined in text.

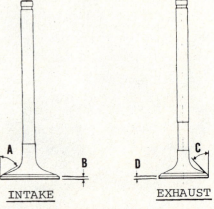

Fig. B4-20—After refacing valve be sure to check for proper face angle and rim thickness.

A. Intake valve face angle 55°30′
B. Intake valve margin thickness 1.78 mm
C. Exhaust valve face angle 45°30′
D. Exhaust valve margin thickness 1.90 mm

Illustration courtesy BMW

INBOARD ENGINES

BMW

ing should not be less than 1.78 mm for intake valves or less than 1.90 mm for exhaust valves. See Fig. B4-20. After installation of valves in cylinder head measure amount of valve head recess below cylinder head surface. Valve recess should be 0.8-1.1 mm for intake valve and 0.79-1.09 mm for exhaust valve.

TIMING GEARS

Crankshaft, idler and camshaft gears installed at time of manufacturer are marked for proper alignment as shown in Fig. B4-21. Replacement gears are not marked and timing mark from original gear should be transferred to new gear, otherwise, follow the following procedure to correctly time gears. The fuel injection pump drive gear is never marked and must be correctly timed whenever it is removed.

If removed, install crankshaft and camshaft. Remove idler gear and support so camshaft and crankshaft are allowed to rotate independently. Install BMW special tool number 7464 1 333509 on number 1 piston so dial gage will indicate piston travel as outlined in CYLINDER HEAD section. Install degree wheel, BMW special tool number 7464 1 333500, on crankshaft and using dial indicator as a gage bring number 1 piston to TDC. Place a steel rule between number 6 cylinder push rods so travel of both can be gauged simultaneously. Slowly rotate camshaft until push rods of number 6 cylinder are in exact overlap. Without moving either crankshaft or camshaft install idler gear and support bracket. Tighten three socket head bolts to 25 N·m.

NOTE: Lowermost of the three idler gear bracket mounting bolts must not be more than 16 mm long. If a longer bolt is installed oil flow to the front main bearing will be blocked off.

Camshaft and crankshaft are now properly timed to TDC for number 1 piston. Remove steel rule and dial indicator.

Using a piece of wire make a pointer for degree wheel and attach it to crankcase in a convenient location. Bring number 1 piston to TDC on compression and mark pointer position on degree wheel. Install injection pump on mounting studs and tighten retaining nuts finger tight. Rotate injection pump shaft by hand until shaft key slot lines up with number 1 delivery valve port as shown in Fig. B4-9. Install dial indicator and adapter, BMW special tool number 7465 1 333510, on injection pump using bleed screw hole as shown in Fig. B4-5. Rotate crankshaft counterclockwise (viewed at gear end) 25°-30° and install injection pump gear. Slowly turn crankshaft in normal direction until degree wheel pointer shows 4° BTDC. At this point dial indicator should show a reading of 0.50 mm. If not, rotate injection pump until a reading of 0.50 mm is obtained.

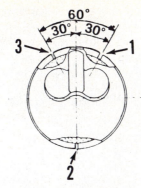

Fig. B4-22 — Position top compression ring (1), second compression ring (2) and oil control ring (3) end gaps as shown.

Tighten pump retaining nuts to 30-32 N·m.

Turn crankshaft in direction of normal rotation until number 1 piston is at TDC on compression and index mark all timing gears for future reference. Remove dial indicator and degree wheel.

PISTON AND CONNECTING ROD

Pistons should be marked prior to removal to ensure that they are reinstalled in their original positions. Upper compression ring has a straight face while second compression ring has a tapered face which should be installed with scraping edge facing piston crown. Oil control ring has a beveled edge and incorporates a rubber lined expander spring. Install rings with gaps positioned as shown in Fig. B4-22. Piston and connecting rod should be assembled so stamped numbers on connecting rod and cap face in same direction as combustion notch in piston crown. Install piston and connecting rod assembly so combustion notch and connecting rod stamped numbers face camshaft. See ENGINE SERVICE DATA section for specifications.

CRANKSHAFT

R&R AND OVERHAUL. Remove nine flywheel housing mounting bolts (1 – Fig. B4-23) and tap evenly around flywheel housing to dislodge main bearing housing from crankcase. Remove nuts (2) and use a suitable puller or BMW tool if main bearing housing does not exit easily. Before removing rear main bearing housing from flywheel housing, mark location of oil spray jet so that upon reassembly oil jet will be properly located. Remove rear main bearing housing from flywheel housing. Be sure

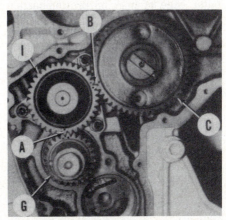

Fig. B4-21 — Factory installed timing gears are punch marked for alignment and should be installed with marks aligned as shown at (A and B). Replacement timing gears are not marked and must be timed as outlined in the text.

C. Camshaft timing gear
G. Crankshaft timing gear
I. Idler gear

Fig. B4-23 — Remove nine flywheel mounting bolts (1) before removing six rear main bearing housing retaining nuts (2) prior to removing flywheel housing from cylinder block.

Illustration courtesy BMW

35

BMW INBOARD ENGINES

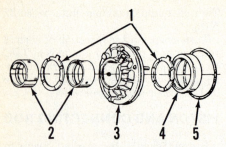

Fig. B4-24 — Exploded view of rear main bearing housing.

1. Thrust washers
2. Rear main bearings
3. Rear main bearing housing
4. Rear main bearing oil seal
5. "O" ring

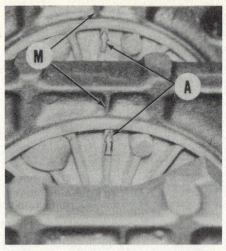

Fig. B4-26 — Install intermediate main bearing housings so arrows (A) on housings point towards casting marks (M) when installed.

Fig. B4-27 — Before installing cylinder liner in cylinder block place two red "O" rings (1) in upper grooves of liner and one black "O" ring in lower groove of liner. Groove (3) is not used. Place cylinder liner shim below upper lip of liner (4). See text for liner installation procedure.

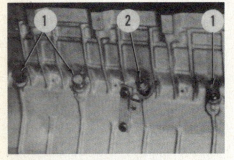

Fig. B4-25 — To remove crankshaft first remove intermediate main bearing housing locating bolts (1) and hollow locating bolt (2) from side of cylinder block. When installing locating bolts be sure that hollow bolt (2) is installed in center locating hole.

not to lose or mix up crankshaft thrust washers (1 – Fig. B4-24). Press rear main seal and bearing from housing in direction of seal. When installing rear main bearing in housing make sure oil hole in housing and bearing are properly aligned.

Using a suitable puller remove crankshaft gear from crankshaft. Remove intermediate main bearing housing locating bolts (1 and 2 – Fig. B4-25) from side of crankcase.

NOTE: Center locating bolt is hollow and must be installed in center locating hole or lubricating oil to turbocharger will be blocked.

While carefully supporting crankshaft gear end, slowly withdraw crankshaft assembly from crankcase. Before removing intermediate main bearing housings mark them as to their location and direction of installation. Unscrew two socket head bolts on each bearing housing and remove housing halves from crankshaft. Inspect all bearings and journals for wear. See ENGINE SERVICE DATA section for specifications. When checking installed ID of main bearings housing halves must be bolted together and bolts torqued to 40-45 N·m. Install new bearing shells in housing halves, making sure oil holes are properly aligned, and install housings on crankshaft in their original positions. Make sure stamped numbers on housing halves are on same side and oil spray jets face gear end of crankshaft. Tighten housing socket head bolts to 40-45 N·m. Carefully install crankshaft assembly into crankcase from rear main bearing end. Align arrows (A – Fig. B4-26) on intermediate main bearing housings with marks (M) on crankcase and install locating bolts.

NOTE: Hollow locating bolt (2 – Fig. B4-25) must be installed in center locating hole.

To install crankshaft gear, heat gear to 190°C and tap gear into place using a suitable driver. See TIMING GEAR section for outline of gear timing procedure.

Coat thrust washers (1 – Fig. B4-24) with grease and install them in rear main bearing housing with lettering facing out. Align lubrication holes in housing seat with holes in rear main bearing housing and push rear main bearing housing into place around crankshaft. Mount flywheel housing on crankcase and install nine housing bolts (1 – Fig. B4-23). Tighten flywheel housing bolts to 50 N·m. Install six rear main bearing housing retaining nuts and tighten them to 25-30 N·m. Using a dial indicator check crankshaft end play and adjust as necessary by varying thickness of thrust washers (1 – Fig. B4-24).

CYLINDER LINER

Using a suitable puller, remove cylinder liner from crankcase. Clean sealer off liners to be placed back in service. Clean sealer out of crankcase bore paying particular attention to bearing surfaces of liner flange.

Place liner, without "O" rings, in crankcase bore and install BMW special tool number 7464 1 333509, tighten tool mounting nuts to 30 N·m. See Fig. B4-17. Place tip of dial indicator on outer edge of liner on pre-combustion chamber side. Preload gage and set dial to zero. Move gage tip to cylinder block surface and record measurement. Cylinder liner protrusion must be 0.00-0.05 mm. If necessary install shims under liner to achieve correct protrusion.

Remove liner and place two red "O" rings in upper grooves (1 – Fig. B4-27) of liner, as water seals. Place one black "O" ring in bottom groove (2) of liner as an oil seal. Second groove (3) from bottom of liner is unused. Lightly coat "O" rings with engine oil. Coat bearing flange of liner with Loctite and press liner into place by hand. Be sure to install liner shim (4).

INBOARD ENGINES **Chrysler**

CHRYSLER

CHRYSLER CORPORATION
MARINE DIVISION
P.O. Box 1
Marysville, Michigan 48040

ENGINE SERVICE DATA

ENGINE MODEL	40
General	
Cylinders	4
Bore	2.960 in.
Stroke	3.267 in.
Displacement—Cu. In.	91
Main Bearing, Number of	5
Firing Order	1-3-4-2
Numbering System (Front-to-Rear)	4-3-2-1
Tune-Up	
Timing Mark Location	Centrifuge
Ignition Timing	12° BTDC
Breaker Point Gap	0.018-0.020 in.
Condenser Capacity	0.25-0.285 mfd.
Dwell Angle	55°-57°
Spark Plug Type	Champion N9Y
Spark Plug Gap	0.035 in.
Valve Lifter Type	Mechanical
Valve Lifter Gap (Hot):	
Intake	0.011 in.
Exhaust	0.015 in.
Valve Seat Angle	44°
Valve Face Angle	45°
Valve Seat Width	5/64 inch
Valve Spring Free Length:	
Inner	1.850 in.
Outer	2.286 in.
Valve Spring Pressure (Lb. at In.):	
Inner	19-23 at 1-25/64
	44-48 at 1-1/64
Outer	65-70 at 1-37/64
	108-116 at 1¼
Carburetor Type:	
Front	OM-32A
Rear	OM-31A
Carburetor Float Level	13/32 inch
Carburetor Float Drop	13/16 inch
Fuel Pump Pressure	3.5-4.2 psi

ENGINE MODEL	40
Sizes — Capacities — Clearances	
Cylinder Block Bore (See Text):	
A	2.959-2.960 in.
B	2.960-2.961 in.
C	2.961-2.962 in.
Crankshaft Journal Diameter	2.123-2.124 in.
Nominal Crankpin Diameter	1.7321 in.
Piston Pin Diameter	0.8658-0.8663 in.
Piston Ring Width:	
Compression	0.0683-0.0687 in.
Middle	0.0783-0.0787 in.
Oil	0.160-0.165 in.
Piston Ring Gap	0.019-0.025 in.
Main Bearing Clearance	0.0018-0.0026 in.
Rod Bearing Clearance	0.0018-0.0026 in.
Rod Bearing Side Clearance	0.004-0.008 in.
Piston Size At Skirt:	
A	2.957-2.958 in.
B	2.958-2.9587 in.
C	2.9587-2.959 in.
Piston Clearance:	
Top Land	0.002-0.005 in.
Skirt	0.0015-0.0025 in.
Piston Pin Clearance:	
In Piston	Press-In Piston
In Rod	No More Than 0.001
Crankshaft End Play	0.003-0.010 in.
Crankshaft Thrust Taken By	No. 3 Main Bearing
Valve Stem Diameter	0.3140-0.3145 in.
Valve Stem Clearance	0.0015-0.002 in.
Camshaft Journal Diameter:	
No. 1	1.691-1.692 in.
No. 2	1.533-1.535 in.
No. 3	0.943-0.944 in.
Camshaft Clearance	0.001-0.003 in.
Camshaft End Play	0.002-0.006 in.
Camshaft Thrust Taken By	Thrust Plate
Crankcase Capacity—Quarts	5

Tightening Torques — Ft.-Lbs.

Connecting Rod Bolt	33	Crankshaft Bolt	58
Cylinder Head Bolt	58	Centrifuge Cover	7
Main Bearing Cap Bolt	47	Timing Chain Cover	7
Spark Plug	20	Cylinder Head Cover	4
Camshaft Lockbolts	7	Heater Exchanger	4
Camshaft Thrust Plate	7	Fresh Water Tank	25
Rear Main Seal Retainer	7	Manifold	25

Illustration courtesy Chrysler

Chrysler INBOARD ENGINES

Fig. CH1-1 – Float level for OM type carburetors should be 13/32 inch. To adjust, bend tang shown in Fig. CH1-2.

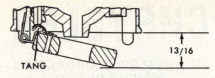

Fig. CH1-2 – Float drop for OM type carburetors should be 13/16 inch. To adjust, bend tang.

Fig. CH1-3 – With carburetors synchronized, there should be ¼-inch of over-travel with controls in neutral.

Fig. CH1-4 – Align camshaft and crankshaft sprocket timing marks as shown above.

MAINTENANCE

CARBURETOR

Model OM-31A and OM-32A

Model OM-32A is used as the front carburetor and Model OM-31A is used as the rear carburetor. Although these carburetors are similar, do not interchange parts between them. Choking is accomplished by using a solenoid actuated by the ignition key.

FLOAT ADJUSTMENT. Float level is measured between gasket surface and top edge of float. See Fig. CH1-1. Measurement should be 13/32 inch. Bend tang on float to adjust float level.

Float drop is measured between toe of float and gasket surface as illustrated to Fig. CH1-2. Float drop should be 13/16 inch. Adjust drop by bending tang on float.

IDLE MIXTURE. Turn idle mixture screw clockwise to lean mixture. Idle engine until warm and adjust idle mixture screws to obtain idle of 650 rpm.

CARBURETOR SYNCHRONIZATION. To synchronize carburetors, adjust idle stop screw (3 – Fig. CH1-3) until throttle valves just begin to open. Adjust wide open throttle stop screw (2) to fully open throttle valves, then turn screw in one turn and lock in position. Install Morse Spring Link Swivel (1) in bellcrank arm and adjust so there is ¼ inch over-travel with controls in neutral.

REPAIR

NOTE: Both metric and standard size tools are needed. Be sure correct tool size is used.

VALVE SYSTEM

Intake valve guide should protrude 0.788-0.826 inch above spring seat machined surface, and exhaust valve guide should protrude 0.689-0.727 inch. Valve seat concentricity should not exceed 0.002 inch. Align camshaft and crankshaft timing marks as shown in Fig. CH1-4.

PISTONS

Cylinder block and pistons are graded as to size. Letters are stamped on cylinder block upper face and on piston top to designate original size. Refer to ENGINE SERVICE DATA for sizes corresponding to letter. Pistons are available in oversizes of 0.008, 0.016, 0.024, 0.0315 and 0.040 inch. Install piston so notch below piston pin bore is to front of engine. Install connecting rod with number on side of big end towards camshaft. heat piston to approximately 80°C. and thumb press piston pin into piston. Piston pin is available in 0.008 inch oversize.

CYLINDER BLOCK

Main bearing caps are marked with number 1 closest to flywheel. Oversize thrust bearings are available in 0.004, 0.006, 0.008 and 0.010 inch.

INBOARD ENGINES   Chrysler

CHRYSLER

It is essential that the Chrysler serial number breakdown be used for servicing and renewing parts. Refer to Fig. CH2-1.

Propeller rotation is as viewed from drive end and engine rotation is as viewed from camshaft drive end. Engine usage code is as follows:

X – Not applicable	M – Mercruiser outdrive	N – Paragon drive (hydraulic)	K – Angle drive
Y – Service base engine	J – Turbine (jet) drive	D – Dana drive 90°	R – Paragon manual drive
P – Powernaut outdrive	W – Warner drive (hydraulic)	V – Vee drive	T – Volvo outdrive

ENGINE SERVICE DATA

ENGINE MODEL	M225D, MH225D
General	
Cylinders	6
Bore	3.41 in.
Stroke	4.12 in.
Displacement – Cu. In.	225
Compression Ratio	8.4:1
Compression Pressure at Cranking Speed	130-160 psi
Main Bearings, Number of	4
Firing Order	1-5-3-6-2-4
Numbering System (Front-to-Rear)	1-2-3-4-5-6
Tune-Up	
Valve Lifter Type	Mechanical
Valve Lifter Gap (Hot):	
Intake	0.012 in.
Exhaust	0.024 in.
Valve Face Angle:	
Intake	45°
Exhaust	47°
Valve Seat Angle	45°
Valve Seat Width Intake	5/64-3/32 inch
Exhaust	3/64-1/16 inch
Valve Spring Free Length:	
Intake	1.92 in.
Exhaust	1.92 in.
Valve Spring Pressure (Lb. at In.):	
Intake	49-57 at 1-11/16
	137-150 at 1-5/16
Exhaust	*49-57 at 1-11/16
	*137-150 at 1-5/16
Timing Mark Location	Crankshaft Pulley
Ignition Timing	See Text
Distributor Cam Angle	40°-45°
Breaker Arm Spring Tension:	
Chrysler	17-20 oz.
Mallory	26-30 oz.
Breaker Point Gap	0.020 in.
Condenser Capacity	0.25-0.285 mfd.
Engine Idle Speed	530 rpm
Spark Plug Type	Champion XN6
Spark Plug Gap	0.035 in.
Carter Carburetor Type	BBS3364S
	BBD3390S
Carburetor Float Level	BBS-7/32 inch
	BBD-¼ inch

*Valve spring with rotators should have spring pressure of: 80-90 at 1-9/16 and 178-192 at 1-5/32.

ENGINE MODEL	M225D, MH225D
Sizes – Capacities – Clearances	
Crankshaft Journal Diameter	2.7495-2.7505 in.
Crankpin Diameter	2.1865-2.1875 in.
Camshaft Journal Diameter:	
No. 1	1.998-1.999 in.
No. 2	1.982-1.983 in.
No. 3	1.967-1.968 in.
No. 4	1.951-1.952 in.
Valve Stem Diameter:	
Intake	0.372-0.373 in.
Exhaust	0.371-0.372 in.
Valve Stem Clearance:	
Intake	0.001-0.003 in.
Exhaust	0.002-0.004 in.
Piston Pin Type	Pressed-In-Rod
Piston Pin Diameter	0.9007-0.9009 in.
Piston Pin Clearance:	
In Piston	0.00045-0.00075 in.
In Rod	Pressed-In-Rod
Compression Ring Width	0.0775-0.0780 in.
Compression Ring End Gap	0.010-0.047 in.
Oil Ring End Gap	0.015-0.062 in.
Main Bearing Clearance	0.0005-0.0015 in.
Rod Bearing Clearance	0.0005-0.0015 in.
Rod Bearing Side Clearance	0.006-0.012 in.
Piston Clearance:	
At Top Land	0.025-0.030 in.
At Skirt	0.0005-0.0015 in.
Crankshaft End Play	0.002-0.007 in.
Crankshaft Thrust Taken By	No. 3 Main Bearing
Camshaft Thrust Taken By	Cylinder Block
Normal Oil Pressure	45-60 psi
Fuel Pump Pressure At Idle Speed	3½-5 psi
Tightening Torques – Ft.-Lbs.	
Connecting Rod Nut	45
Cylinder Head Bolt	65
Main Bearing Cap Bolt	85
Camshaft Lockbolt	35
Chain Case Cover Bolt	16.5
Clutch Housing Bolt: ⅜	30
5/16	15
Flywheel Bolt Nut	60
Flywheel Housing Bolt	30
Intake Manifold Bolt	10
Rocker Shaft Bolt	30
Rear Bearing Seal Retainer Bolt	30
Fuel Pump Bolt	30

Illustration courtesy Chrysler

Chrysler

INBOARD ENGINES

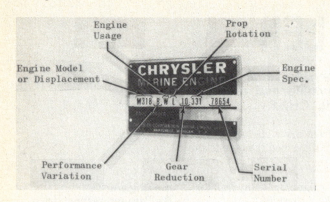

Fig. CH2-1 — Chrysler engines may be identified by identification plate attached to rear of engine. Refer to engine usage to identify drive unit originally coupled to engine.

MAINTENANCE

CARBURETOR

Model BBS

IDLE MIXTURE. Turn idle mixture adjustment screw clockwise to lean mixture.

FLOAT ADJUSTMENT. With carburetor inverted, measure float level from gasket surface of fuel bowl to crown of float. Bend float lip to adjust but do not force lip against needle when bending.

ACCELERATOR PUMP. To check accelerator pump action, back out idle speed and fast idle adjusting screws, open choke valve and close throttle valve. Be sure connector rod is in middle hole of throttle lever. Measure between end of plunger shaft and carburetor body as shown in Fig. CH2-2. Distance should be 27/32 inch. Bend connector rod to adjust.

CHOKE. To adjust choke unloader, hold choke valve closed and open throttle valve to wide open position. There should be clearance for a 3/16 inch drill between short side of choke valve and carburetor bore. Bend unloader arm on trip lever until clearance is obtained.

FAST IDLE ADJUSTMENT. To adjust fast idle speed, back out idle speed adjusting screw to close throttle valve. Hold choke valve closed with choke operating lever. There should be 0.018 inch clearance between throttle valve and carburetor bore on side opposite ports. Bend choke connecting rod to adjust.

Model BBD

IDLE MIXTURE. Turn idle mixture screws clockwise to lean mixture.

FLOAT ADJUSTMENT. With carburetor inverted, measure float level from gasket surface of fuel bowl to crown of each float. Bend float lip to adjust but do not force lip against needle when bending.

ACCELERATOR PUMP. To check accelerator pump action, back out idle speed adjusting screw, open choke valve and close throttle valve. Be sure connector rod is in middle hole of throttle lever. Measure between end of plunger shaft and carburetor body as shown in Fig. CH2-3. Distance should be 1 inch. To adjust, bend connector rod.

FAST IDLE ADJUSTMENT. To adjust fast idle speed, back out idle speed adjusting screw until throttle valves are completely closed. Invert carburetor and hold choke valves closed with choke operating lever (Fig. CH2-4). There should be 0.012 inch clearance between throttle valve and carburetor bore on side opposite ports. Bend choke connecting rod to adjust.

CHOKE ADJUSTMENT. To adjust choke unloader, hold choke valve closed and throttle valve wide open. There should be clearance for a 1/16 inch drill between short side of choke valve and carburetor bore (Fig. CH2-5). Bend unloader arm on trip lever until clearance is obtained.

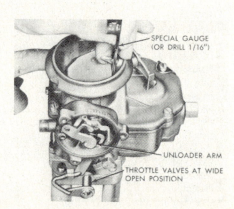

Fig. CH2-5 — View showing use of 1/16-inch drill bit for choke unloader adjustment. Refer to text.

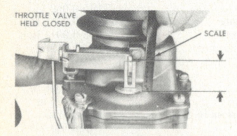

Fig. CH2-2 — Height of Model BBS accelerator pump shaft should be 27/32-inch measured as shown above.

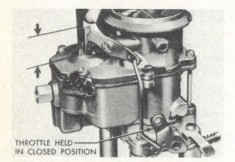

Fig. CH2-3 — Height of Model BBD accelerator pump shaft should be 1 inch measured as shown above.

Fig. CH2-4 — View showing fast idle adjustment. Refer to text.

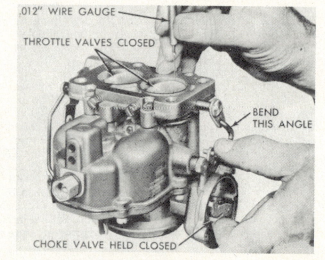

40

Illustration courtesy Chrysler

INBOARD ENGINES

REPAIR

FIRING ORDER

To determine firing order of engine refer to engine name plate (Fig. CH2-1) found at rear of engine. If engine propeller shaft rotation and gear reduction is R-10, R-13, R-15, R-25 or R-30 then engine firing order is 1-4-2-6-3-5. If engine code is L-10, L-13, L-15, L-25 or L-30 then engine firing order is 1-5-3-6-2-4.

ROCKER ARM SHAFT

Install rocker arm shaft so that flat on end of shaft is on top and to front of engine. Long rocker arm retainer should be bolted in center of rocker arm shaft.

VALVE ADJUSTMENT

To adjust valve lifter gap statically, crank engine to No. 1 TDC on compression stroke and adjust gap on Nos. 1, 2 and 4 intake valves and Nos. 1, 3 and 5 exhaust valves. Crank engine to No. 6 on compression stroke and adjust remaining valves. Gap for hot settings should be 0.012 inch for intake valves and 0.024 inch for exhaust valves. Cold settings should be 0.013 inch for intake valves and 0.027 inch for exhaust valves. It is necessary to adjust valves to above specifications when engine is cold on MH225D engines.

IGNITION TIMING

To determine correct ignition timing, on engines prior to 1969, refer to the following list of Chrysler distributor part numbers and corresponding ignition timing specifications:

2098295	2½° ATDC
2098475	2½° ATDC
2098486	2½° ATDC
2098488	2½° ATDC
2098741	TDC
2098742	TDC
2098743	TDC
2098744	TDC
2444425	15° BTDC
2444426	15° BTDC
2444415	15° BTDC
2444416	15° BTDC

PISTONS

Pistons are cam ground and must be installed so that indent in piston crown is towards front of engine and oil hole in side of connecting rod is on camshaft side of engine (Fig. CH2-6). Compression rings are marked "TOP".

MAIN BEARINGS

Number 1 upper main bearing is not interchangeable and is identified by a chamfer on tab side and a red mark on edge of bearing.

OIL PUMP

To check oil pump clearances measure inner rotor depth (Fig. CH2-7) by placing a straightedge across outer rotor face. Gap should not be greater than 0.004 inch. Inner rotor to outer rotor clearance (Fig. CH2-8) should not exceed 0.010 inch. Outer rotor to pump body clearance (Fig. CH2-9) should not exceed 0.012 inch.

Fig. CH2-6 — View of piston and connecting rod assembly. Note location of notch in piston crown and oil hole in rod.

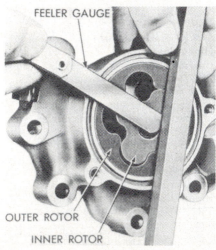

Fig. CH2-7 — Measure clearance between rotor and pump body as shown. Clearance should not exceed 0.004 inch.

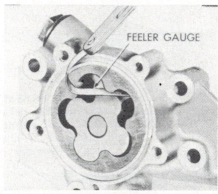

Fig. CH2-8 — Oil pump inner rotor to outer rotor clearance should not exceed 0.010 inch.

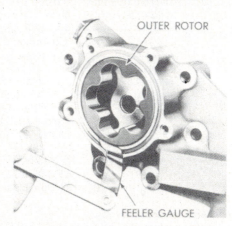

Fig. CH2-9 — Oil pump outer rotor to housing clearance should not exceed 0.012 inch.

Fig. CH2-10 — View of crankshaft and camshaft sprocket timing marks.

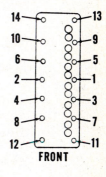

Fig. CH2-11 — Cylinder head tightening sequence.

CHRYSLER

It is essential that the Chrysler serial number breakdown be used for servicing and renewing parts. Refer to Fig. CH2-1.

ENGINE SERVICE DATA

ENGINE MODEL	M273B	LM318B	M360B
General			
Cylinders	8	8	8
Bore	3.63 in.	3.91 in.	4.00 in.
Stroke	3.31 in.	3.31 in.	3.58 in.
Displacement — Cu. In.	273	318	360
Compression Ratio	8.8:1	8.5:1	8.5:1
Compression Pressure at Cranking Speed	120-150 psi	120-150 psi	120-150 psi
Main Bearings, Number Of	5	5	5
Firing Order	See Text	See Text	See Text
Numbering System (Front-to-Rear)			
Port Bank	1-3-5-7	1-3-5-7	1-3-5-7
Starboard Bank	2-4-6-8	2-4-6-8	2-4-6-8
Tune-Up			
Valve Lifter Type	†Mechanical	Hydraulic	Hydraulic
Valve Lifter Gap (Hot):			
Intake	0.013 in.	See Text	See Text
Exhaust	0.023 in.	See Text	See Text
Valve Face Angle:			
Intake	45°	45°	45°
Exhaust	45°	45°	45°
Valve Seat Angle	45°	45°	45°
Valve Seat Width Intake	←————	0.080-0.105 in.	————→
Exhaust	←————	0.090-0.110 in.	————→
Valve Spring Free Length:			
Intake	←————	2.000 in.	————→
Exhaust	←————	1.875 in.	————→
Valve Spring Pressure (Lb. at In.):			
Intake	←————	78-88 at 1.70	————→
	←————	170-184 at 1.30	————→
Exhaust	←————	80-90 at 1.49	————→
	←————	178-192 at 1.10	————→
Timing Mark Location	←————	Harmonic Balancer	————→
Ignition Timing	2 bbl-5° BTDC #4 bbl-0° BTDC	5° BTDC	2½° BTDC
Distributor Cam Angle	←————	27°-32°##	————→
Breaker Arm Spring Tension	17-20 oz.	17-20 oz.##	##
Breaker Point Gap	0.014-0.019 in.	0.014-0.019 in. ##	##
Condenser Capacity	0.25-0.285 mfd.	0.25-0.285 mfd.##	##
Engine Idle Speed	←————	550 rpm	————→
Spark Plug Type	←————	Champion RN9Y	————→
Spark Plug Gap	←————	0.035 in.	————→
Carburetor Type	Carter BBD3979S Carter AFB3980S	Carter AFB3980S Carter AFB4329SX Carter AFB4699S Carter AFB6212S	Carter AFB6212S
Carburetor Float Level	BBD-¼ in. AFB-7/32 in.	AFB 3980S-7/32 in. AFB4329SX-5/16 in. AFB4699S-5/16 in. AFB6212S-5/16 in.	AFB 6212S-5/16 in.

†Later models have hydraulic lifters: see text.
#1972 Model M273B engine with 4bbl carburetor should have 2½° BTDC ignition timing.
##Later LM318B and all M360B models are equipped with breakerless electronic ignition. See text.

INBOARD ENGINES   **Chrysler**

ENGINE SERVICE DATA (CONT.)

ENGINE MODEL	M273B	LM318B	M360B
Sizes — Capacities — Clearances			
Crankshaft Journal Diameter	2.4995-2.5005 in.	2.4995-2.5005 in.	2.8095-2.8105 in.
Crankpin Diameter	←―――――	2.124-2.125 in.	―――――→
Camshaft Journal Diameter:			
No. 1	←―――――	1.998-1.999 in.	―――――→
No. 2	←―――――	1.982-1.983 in.	―――――→
No. 3	←―――――	1.967-1.968 in.	―――――→
No. 4	←―――――	1.951-1.952 in.	―――――→
No. 5	←―――――	1.5605-1.5615 in.	―――――→
Valve Stem Diameter:			
Intake	←―――――	0.372-0.373 in.	―――――→
Exhaust	←―――――	0.371-0.372 in.	―――――→
Valve Stem Clearance:			
Intake	←―――――	0.001-0.003 in.	―――――→
Exhaust	←―――――	0.002-0.004 in.	―――――→
Piston Pin Type	Fully Floating	Fully Floating	Pressed-in-rod
Piston Pin Diameter	0.9841-0.9843 in.	0.9841-0.9843 in.	0.9841-0.9843 in.
Piston Pin Clearance:			
In Piston	0.0000-0.0005 in.	0.0000-0.0005 in.	0.00045-0.00075 in.
In Rod	0.0000-0.0005 in.	0.0000-0.0005 in.	Pressed-in-rod
Compression Ring Width	←―――――	0.0775-0.0780 in.	―――――→
Compression Ring End Gap	←―――――	0.010-0.020 in.	―――――→
Oil Ring End Gap	←―――――	0.015-0.055 in.	―――――→
Main Bearing Clearance	←―――――	0.0005-0.0015 in.	―――――→
Rod Bearing Clearance	←―――――	0.0005-0.0015 in.	―――――→
Rod Bearing Side Clearance	←―――――	0.006-0.014 in.	―――――→
Piston Clearance:			
At Top Land	0.029-0.034 in.	0.0219-0.0340 in.	0.029-0.034 in.
At Skirt	←―――――	0.0005-0.0015 in.	―――――→
Crankshaft End Play	←―――――	0.002-0.007 in.	―――――→
Crankshaft Thrust Taken By	←―――――	No. 3 Main Bearing	―――――→
Camshaft Thrust Taken By	←―――――	Thrust Plate	―――――→
Normal Oil Pressure	←―――――	45-60 psi	―――――→
Fuel Pump Pressure At Idle Speed	←―――――	3½-5 psi	―――――→

Tightening Torques — Ft.-Lbs.			
Connecting Rod Nut	45	45	45
Cylinder Head Bolt	85	85	95
Main Bearing Cap Bolt	85	85	85
Camshaft Lockbolt	35	35	35
Camshaft Thrust Plate	17.5	....	....
Chain Case Cover Bolt:			
⅜	30	30	30
5/16	15	15	15
Clutch Housing Bolt:			
⅜	30	30	30
5/16	15	15	....
Crankshaft Bolt	135	135	135
Front Engine Mount Bolt	45	....	....
Flywheel Bolt Nut	55	55	55
Flywheel Housing Bolt	50	50	50
Intake Manifold Bolt	35	35	35
Oil Pan Drain Plug	35	35	35
Oil Pan Bolt	15	15	15
Oil Pump Attaching Bolt	35	35	35
Oil Pump Cover Bolt	10	10	10
Rocker Shaft Bolt	15	15	15
Fuel Pump Bolt	30	30	30
Vibration Damper Bolt	15	15	15
Water Pump Housing Bolt	30	30	30
Water Pump to Block Bolt	30	30	30

Illustration courtesy Chrysler

Chrysler — INBOARD ENGINES

MAINTENANCE

CARBURETOR

Carter BBD

IDLE MIXTURE ADJUSTMENT. Turn idle mixture adjusting screw clockwise to lean idle mixture.

FLOAT LEVEL ADJUSTMENT. With carburetor inverted, measure float level from gasket surface of fuel bowl to crown of each float. Measurement should be 1/4 inch. Bend float lip to adjust but do not force lip against needle when bending.

ACCELERATOR PUMP. To check accelerator pump action, back out idle speed adjusting screw, open choke valve and close throttle valve. Be sure connector rod is in middle hole of throttle lever. Measure between end of plunger shaft and carburetor body adjacent to plunger shaft. Distance should be 1 inch. To adjust, bend connector rod.

FAST IDLE ADJUSTMENT. To adjust fast idle, back out idle speed adjusting screw until throttle valves are completely closed. Invert carburetor and hold choke valve closed with choke operating lever. There should be 0.012 inch clearance between throttle valve and carburetor bore on side opposite ports. Bend choke connecting rod to adjust.

CHOKE ADJUSTMENT. To adjust choke unloader, hold choke valve closed and throttle valve wide open. There should be clearance for a 1/16 inch drill between short side of choke valve and carburetor bore. Bend unloader arm on trip lever until clearance is obtained.

Carter AFB

FLOAT LEVEL ADJUSTMENT. To check float level, invert air horn body, and with gasket in place, measure between gasket surface and outer end of float as shown in Fig. CH3-1. Carburetor float drop should be 23/32 inch on AFB3980S and 3/4 inch on all other AFB carburetors.

To measure float drop, hold air horn body in upright position and measure from outer end of float to gasket surface. In both cases, bend float arm to adjust float position.

FAST IDLE ADJUSTMENT. To check fast idle adjustment, position fast idle adjusting screw on second highest step of fast idle cam and move choke valve towards closed position. With screw on second step, there should be 1/16 inch between choke valve and wall of air horn. Bend fast idle connector rod to adjust choke valve opening. See Fig. CH3-2.

CHOKE BREAK ADJUSTMENT. Choke diaphragm adjustment may be made with carburetor on or off engine; a vacuum source is needed if carburetor is off engine. Disconnect fast idle linkage if carburetor is to be adjusted with engine running. If adjustment is made off engine, open throttle valves and move choke valve to closed position. Allow throttle valves to close, then close choke. If an external vacuum source is being used, connect vacuum hose to diaphragm as shown in Fig. CH3-3. A vacuum of at least 10 inches of mercury is required. Apply vacuum to choke diaphragm either with engine running or by external vacuum source. Carefully close choke valve until diaphragm link contacts end of choke lever slot as shown in Fig. CH3-3. Be sure diaphragm is operating correctly. Gap between air horn and choke valve should be 3/32 inch. Bend diaphragm link to obtain desired gap. Be sure bending of diaphragm link does not interfere with movement of choke valve.

CHOKE UNLOADER ADJUSTMENT. To check choke unloader adjustment, hold throttle valves in wide open position and insert a 1/4-inch drill between upper edge of choke valve and air horn as shown in Fig. CH3-4. Slight drag should be felt as drill is withdrawn while light pressure is applied against choke valve. Bend unloader tang as shown in Fig. CH3-4 to obtain desired gap between choke valve and air horn.

ACCELERATOR PUMP. Check accelerator pump adjustment by moving

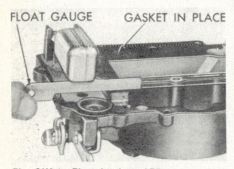

Fig. CH3-1 — Float level on AFB carburetor is measured with gasket in place.

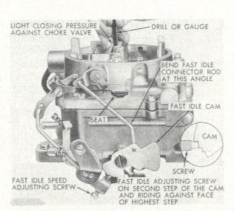

Fig. CH3-2 — View showing adjustment of fast idle. Refer to text.

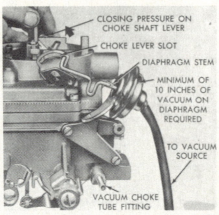

Fig. CH3-3 — Measure gap between choke valve and air horn as outlined in text for choke diaphragm adjustment.

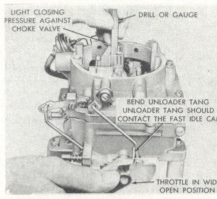

Fig. CH3-4 — Bend choke unloader tang to obtain desired gap between choke valve and horn as outlined in text.

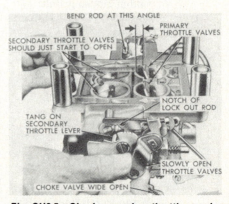

Fig. CH3-5 — Check secondary throttle opening and lock out adjustment as explained in text.

INBOARD ENGINES

Chrysler

choke valve to wide open position so fast idle cam is released. Back off idle speed adjusting screw until throttle valves are seated in their bores. Measure distance from top of air horn to accelerator pump plunger shaft. Distance should be 7/16 inch. Bend lower angle to adjust.

SECONDARY THROTTLE ADJUSTMENT. To check secondary throttle lever adjustment, block choke valve in wide open position and invert carburetor as shown in Fig. CH3-5. Slowly open primary throttle until there is 21/64 inch between lower edge of primary valve and bore. At this point, the secondary throttle valves should start to open. If adjustment is needed, bend secondary throttle operating rod. Slightly open throttle and open and close choke valve. Tang on secondary throttle lever should freely engage notch of lockout rod in Fig. CH3-5. Bend tang on secondary throttle lever to align tang and notch. With primary and secondary throttle valves completely closed, it should be possible to insert a 0.020 inch wire gage between shoes of secondary throttle levers as shown in Fig. CH3-6. Adjust by bending secondary shoe.

IGNITION SYSTEM

Model 360B and Late Model LM318B

ELECTRONIC IGNITION SYSTEM. Air gap between reluctor teeth and pole of pickup unit shown in Fig. CH3-7 should be 0.008 inch. Loosen pickup unit mounting screw and move pickup unit to adjust air gap. A non-magnetic feeler gage must be used when setting air gap to accurately determine gap. Reluctor teeth must have sharp edges. Rough or rounded edges may cause misfiring. Do not file edges of reluctor teeth.

Two types of ballast resistor are used with the Chrysler electronic ignition system. Ballast resistor designed for marine use has resistor wire totally enclosed in ceramic while automotive type ballast resistor has resistor wire exposed. Do not use automotive ballast resistor as exposed resistor wire is a fire hazard and will corrode and fail.

To troubleshoot Chrysler electronic ignition system, use Chrysler ignition tester C4166A and follow instructions on tester.

REPAIR

FIRING ORDER

Refer to engine serial number plate to determine propeller rotation and gear reduction. For R-10, R-13, R-15, R-25, R-30 and L-19 designations, the firing order is 1-2-7-5-6-3-4-8. For L-10, L-13, L-15, L-25, L-30 and R-19 designations, the engine firing order is 1-8-4-3-6-5-7-2.

VALVE SYSTEM

If mechanical lifters are used, there will be adjusting screws present on the rocker arms. Adjust mechanical lifters to the clearance specified in the ENGINE SERVICE DATA section. Hydraulic lifters are non-adjustable but may be checked for correct clearance. Rotate engine so that valve of lifter being checked is closed and lifter is on base of camshaft. Push down on push rod so that lifter is collapsed and measure clearance between end of push rod and rocker arm. Clearance should be 0.060-0.210 inch. If clearance is incorrect, inspect lifter and valve system. On 318 and 360 engines with stamped rocker arms, notch on end of rocker arm shaft must be pointing to engine centerline and to front on left bank and to rear on right bank. Do not mis-match right and left rocker arms. Install short retainers on ends and at center of rocker arm shaft. Install long retainers between first and second pairs of rocker arms. Exhaust valve rotators are used on some engines and should be inspected for proper operation.

Renew valve if valve stem wear exceeds 0.002 inch. Valve guides are non-renewable and must be reamed to next

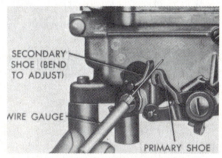

Fig. CH3-6 — Completely close primary and secondary throttle valves of AFB carburetor, and insert 0.020 inch wire gage between shoes as shown. To adjust, bend secondary shoe.

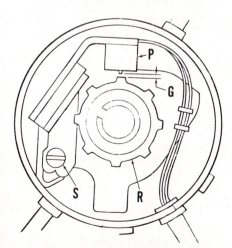

Fig. CH3-7 — Air gap (G) between pole (P) and reluctor (R) teeth should be 0.008 inch. Loosen mounting screw (S) and move pole assembly to adjust air gap.

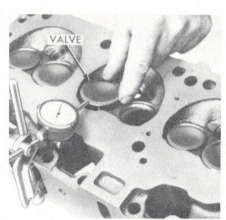

Fig. CH3-8 — Measure valve wobble as shown above.

Fig. CH3-9 — Measure clearance between rotor and pump body as shown. Clearance should not exceed 0.004 inch.

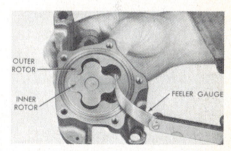

Fig. CH3-10 — Oil pump inner rotor to outer rotor clearance should not exceed 0.010 inch on 273 engines or 0.006 inch on other engines.

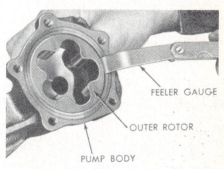

Fig. CH3-11 — Oil pump outer rotor to housing clearance should not exceed 0.012.

Chrysler

INBOARD ENGINES

oversize if valve guide wear is excessive. Valves are available in oversizes of 0.005, 0.015 and 0.030 inch. To determine if valve guide is excessively worn, install sleeve (Chrysler Tool C-3973) on valve stem and install valve in guide so sleeve supports valve. Measure valve wobble as shown in Fig. CH3-8. If wobble exceeds 0.017 inch an oversize valve must be installed.

PISTONS

Pistons are cam ground and must be installed so indent in piston crown is towards front of engine. Assemble connecting rods and pistons so large chamfer on connecting rod big end will be to front of engine on cylinders 1, 3, 5 and 7, and to rear of engine on cylinders 2, 4, 6 and 8. Compression rings are marked "TOP".

OIL PUMP

To check oil pump clearances, place a straightedge across outer rotor face and measure gap between straightedge and inner rotor face (Fig. CH3-9). Gap should not exceed 0.004 inch. Inner-to-outer rotor clearance (Fig. CH3-10) should not exceed 0.006 inch on 318 and 360 engines, or 0.010 inch on 273 engines. Outer rotor-to-pump body clearance (Fig. CH3-11) should not exceed 0.012 inch. Renew oil pump cover if it is scored or warped more than 0.0015 inch.

FLYWHEEL

Model M360B engine is externally balanced. Flywheel for Model M360B may be identified by three large holes drilled in front face of flywheel while vibration damper for Model M360B is identified by off center weight cast in hub. Do not interchange flywheel or vibration damper with other engine models.

Fig. CH3-12—Timing marks should be aligned as shown.

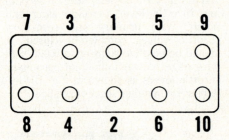

Fig. CH3-13—Use the above sequence for tightening intake manifold bolts.

Fig. CH3-14—Cylinder head bolt tightening sequence.

Illustration courtesy Chrysler

INBOARD ENGINES   Chrysler

CHRYSLER

It is essential that the Chrysler serial number breakdown be used for servicing and renewing parts. Refer to Fig. CH2-1.

ENGINE SERVICE DATA

ENGINE MODEL	M383B, M400B	M413E	M440B, M440D, M440S
General			
Cylinders	V8	V8	V8
Bore	‡4.25 in.	4.19 in.	4.32 in.
Stroke	3.375 in.	3.75 in.	3.75 in.
Displacement—Cu. In.	‡383	413	440
Fuel Required	————————*Leaded Regular————————		
Compression Pressure at Cranking Speed	————————120-150 psi————————		
Main Bearings, Number of	————————5————————		
Firing Order	————————See Text————————		
Numbering System (Front-to-Rear)			
Port Bank	————————1-3-5-7————————		
Starboard Bank	————————2-4-6-8————————		

‡M400B engine has 4.324 inch bore dimension and 400 cu. in. displacement.
*M440D and M440S require premium leaded gasoline.

Tune-Up			
Valve Lifter Type	————————See Text————————		
Valve Lifter Gap (Mechanical):			
Intake (Hot)	0.015 in.	0.015 in.	....
Exhaust (Hot)	0.026 in.	0.026 in.	....
Valve Seat Angle	————————45°————————		
Valve Face Angle	————————45°————————		
Valve Seat Width:			
Intake	————————0.060-0.085 in.————————		
Exhaust	————————0.040-0.060 in.————————		
Valve Spring Free Length:			
Intake	————————2.25 in.————————		
Exhaust	————————2.06 in.————————		
Valve Spring Pressure (LB. at In.):			
Intake	————————78-80 at 1.860————————		
	————————173-187 at 1.430————————		
Exhaust	————————76-84 at 1.73————————		
	————————163-177 at 1.37————————		
Timing Mark Location	————————Harmonic Balancer————————		
Ignition Timing	**Dist. 1889370 – 12½° BTDC Dist. 2875895 – 5° BTDC	5° BTDC	**Dist. 2098085 – 12½° BTDC Dist. 2875893 – 7½° BTDC
Distributor Cam Angle	————————28°-32°————————		
Breaker Arm Spring Tension	————————17-21.5 oz.————————		
Breaker Point Gap	————————0.014-0.019 in.————————		
Condenser Capacity	————————0.25-0.285 mfd.————————		
Engine Idle Speed	————————500-550 rpm————————		
Spark Plug Type	————————Champion RJ10Y————————		
Spark Plug Gap	————————0.035 in.————————		
Carburetor Type	————————#Carter AFB————————		
Float Level	————————7/32-in.————————		
Float Drop	————————¾-in.————————		

**Ignition timing is 5° BTDC on engines after 1970.
#Model M440S is equipped with three Holley 2 bbl. carburetors.

Illustration courtesy Chrysler

Chrysler — INBOARD ENGINES

ENGINE SERVICE DATA (CONT.)

ENGINE MODEL	M383B, M400B	M413E	M440B, M440D, M440S
Sizes — Capacities — Clearances			
Crankshaft Journal Diameter	2.6245-2.6255 in.	2.7495-2.7505 in.	2.7495-2.7505 in.
Crankpin Diameter		2.374-2.375 in.	
Camshaft Journal Diameter:			
No. 1		1.998-1.999 in.	
No. 2		1.982-1.983 in.	
No. 3		1.967-1.968 in.	
No. 4		1.951-1.952 in.	
No. 5		1.748-1.749 in.	
Piston Pin Diameter		1.0935-1.0937 in.	
Piston Pin Type		Pressed-In-Rod	
Piston Pin Clearance In Piston		0.0006-0.00075 in.	
Compression Ring Width		0.0775-0.0780 in.	
Compression Ring End Gap		0.013-0.025 in.	
Oil Ring End Gap		0.013-0.025 in.	
Main Bearing Clearance		0.0005-0.0015 in.	
Rod Bearing Clearance		0.0005-0.0015 in.	
Rod Bearing Side Clearance		0.009-0.017 in.	
Piston Clearance:			
Top Land	0.031-0.037 in.	0.031-0.037 in.	#0.032-0.040 in.
Skirt	0.0005-0.0010 in.	0.0005-0.0010 in.	0.0005-0.0015 in.
Crankshaft End Play		0.002-0.007 in.	
Crankshaft Thrust Taken By		No. 3 Bearing	
Camshaft Thrust Taken By		Cylinder Block	
Valve Stem Diameter:			
Intake		0.372-0.373 in.	
Exhaust		0.371-0.372 in.	
Valve Stem Clearance:			
Intake		0.001-0.003 in.	
Exhaust	0.002 in.	0.002 in.	0.002-0.004 in.
Normal Oil Pressure		45-65 psi	
Fuel Pump Pressure		3½-5 psi	

#Model M440S piston clearance is 0.023-0.030 inch at top land and 0.0003-0.0013 inch at skirt.

Tightening Torques — Ft.-Lbs.

Connecting Rod Nut	45
Cylinder Head Bolt	70
Camshaft Lockbolt	35
Carburetor Nut	7
Chain Case Cover Bolt:	
5/16	15
3/8	30
Clutch Housing Bolt	30
Crankshaft Rear Bearing Seal Retainer	30
Crankshaft Bolt	135
Exhaust Manifold Nut	30
Flywheel Housing Bolt	50
Fuel Pump Bolt	30
Harmonic Balancer Bolt	15
Intake Manifold Bolt	50
Main Bearing Cap Bolt	85
Oil Pan Drain Plug	35
Oil Pan Bolt	15
Oil Pump Cover Bolt	10
Oil Pump Attaching Bolt	35
Oil Filter Attaching Stud	30
Rocker Arm Cover Bolt	3.5
Rocker Shaft Bolt	30
Spark Plug	30
Starter Mounting Bolt	50
Tappet Valley Cover Bolt	9
Water Pump Housing Bolt	30
Water Pump to Block Bolt	30

Illustration courtesy Chrysler

INBOARD ENGINES

MAINTENANCE

CARBURETOR

Carter AFB

All models except M440S are equipped with a Carter AFB carburetor. Refer to ENGINE SERVICE DATA for idle speed setting.

FLOAT LEVEL ADJUSTMENT. To check float level, invert air horn body, and with gasket in place, measure between gasket surface and outer end of float as shown in Fig. CH4-1. Float level should be 7/32 inch. Bend float arm to adjust float level.

Carburetor float drop should be 3/4 inch. To measure float drop, hold air horn body in upright position and measure from outer end of float to gasket surface. Bend float arm to adjust float drop.

FAST IDLE ADJUSTMENT. To check fast idle adjustment, position fast idle adjusting screw on second highest step of fast idle cam and move choke valve towards closed position. With screw on second step, there should be 1/16 inch between choke valve and well of air horn. Bend fast idle connector rod to adjust choke valve opening. See Fig. CH4-2.

CHOKE DIAPHRAGM ADJUSTMENT. Choke diaphragm adjustment may be made with carburetor on or off engine. A vacuum source is needed if carburetor is off engine. Disconnect fast idle linkage if carburetor is to be adjusted with engine running. If adjustment is made off engine, open throttle valves and move choke valve to closed position. Allow throttle valves to close, then close choke. If an external vacuum source is being used, connect vacuum hose to diaphragm as shown in Fig. CH4-3. A vacuum of at least 10 inches is required. Apply vacuum to choke diaphragm either with engine running or with external vacuum source. Carefully close choke valve until diaphragm link contacts end of choke lever slot as shown in Fig. CH4-3. Be sure diaphragm is operating correctly. Gap between choke valve and air horn should be 3/32 inch. Bend diaphragm link to obtain desired gap. Be sure bending of diaphragm link does not interfere with movement of choke valve.

CHOKE UNLOADER ADJUSTMENT. To check choke unloader adjustment hold throttle valves in wide open position and insert a 1/4 inch drill between upper edge of choke valve and air horn as shown in Fig. CH4-4. Slight drag should be felt as drill is withdrawn while light pressure is applied to choke valve. Bend unloader tang as shown in Fig. CH4-4 to obtain desired gap between choke valve and air horn.

ACCELERATOR PUMP ADJUSTMENT. Check accelerator pump adjustment by moving choke valve to wide open position so fast idle cam is released. Back off idle speed adjusting screw until throttle valves are seated in their bores. Measure distance from top of air horn to top of accelerator pump shaft. Distance should be 7/16 inch. Bend lower angle of throttle connector rod to adjust.

SECONDARY THROTTLE ADJUSTMENT. To check secondary throttle adjustment, block choke valve in wide open position and invert carburetor as shown in Fig. CH4-5. Slowly open primary throttle valves until there is 21/64 inch between lower edge of primary valve and bore. At this point, the secondary throttle valves should start to open. If adjustment is needed, bend secondary throttle operating rod. Slightly open throttle then open and

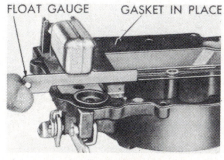

Fig. CH4-1 — Float level on AFB carburetor is measured with gasket in place.

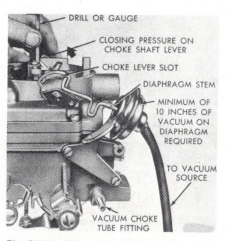

Fig. CH4-3 — Measure gap between choke valve and air horn as outlined in text for choke diaphragm adjustment.

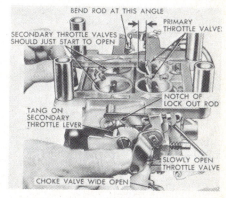

Fig. CH4-5 — Check secondary throttle opening and lock out rod adjustment as explained in text.

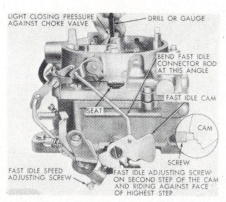

Fig. CH4-2 — View showing adjustment of fast idle. Refer to text.

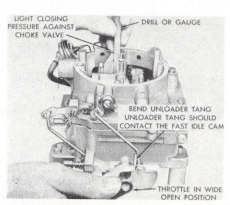

Fig. CH4-4 — Bend choke unloader tang to obtain desired gap between choke valve and air horn as outlined in text.

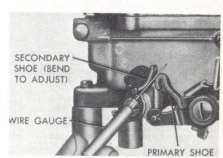

Fig. CH4-6 — Completely close primary and secondary throttle valves of AFB carburetor, and insert 0.020 inch wire gage between shoes as shown. To adjust, bend secondary shoe.

Illustration courtesy Chrysler

Chrysler — INBOARD ENGINES

close choke valve. Tang on secondary throttle lever should freely engage notch of lockout rod in Fig. CH4-5. Bend tang on secondary throttle lever to align tang and notch. With primary and secondary throttle valves completely closed, it should be possible to insert a 0.020 inch wire gage between shoes of secondary throttle levers as shown in Fig. CH4-6. Adjust by bending secondary shoe.

Holley 2300

Model M440S is equipped with two Holley Model 2300 carburetors and one Holley Model 2300C carburetor which is mounted in the center of the manifold. The front and rear carburetors are vacuum operated and do not have idle, power enrichment, accelerator pump, or choke systems. Refer to following paragraphs for adjustment of Model 2300C (center) carburetor. Due to absence of previously listed systems, only the following float and throttle synchronization adjustments are applicable to the Model 2300 (front and rear) carburetors. All adjustments can be made with carburetor in place on manifold.

ACCELERATOR PUMP LEVER CLEARANCE. Hold throttle in wide open position and use a 0.015 inch feeler gage as shown in Fig. CH4-7 to set clearance between adjusting nut and pump lever. Turn over-ride screw to adjust.

CHOKE CONTROL LEVER. Open throttle halfway and close choke valve. Measure height from top of hole in choke lever shown in Fig. CH4-8 to choke pad on manifold if carburetor is on engine or to carburetor base if carburetor is off engine. Height should be 3.750-3.781 inch to choke pad or 1.703-1.734 inch to carburetor base. Bend choke valve rod to adjust height. Be sure choke linkage moves freely.

FAST IDLE CAM. Position fast idle speed tang so it contacts second highest speed step on fast idle cam as shown in Fig. CH4-9. Gently close choke valve and insert a No. 24 drill bit between choke valve and air horn. If a slight drag is not felt when drill bit is moved, bend cam position adjusting tang until desired choke valve opening is obtained.

CHOKE UNLOADER. Hold throttle valves wide open and close choke valve while inserting a 23/64-inch drill bit between choke valve and air horn. With light finger pressure on choke lever, a slight drag should be felt as drill bit is withdrawn. To adjust, bend unloader tang shown in Fig. CH4-9.

CHOKE DIAPHRAGM. Choke diaphragm adjustment may be made with carburetor on or off engine. An external vacuum source with at least 10 inches vacuum is required if carburetor is adjusted off engine. Manipulate throttle and choke linkage so choke is in closed position with engine running or vacuum applied to diaphragm. Insert a No. 17 (0.173 in.) drill bit between choke valve and air horn while applying light pressure to choke rod to obtain minimum choke closure without moving diaphragm rod. See Fig. CH4-10. Diaphragm rod will extend as internal diaphragm spring is compressed. Spring must be fully compressed for accurate adjustment. A slight drag should be felt as drill bit is moved between choke valve and air horn. If adjustment is necessary, bend diaphragm link at U-bend (L—Fig. CH4-10) to shorten or lengthen link. Be

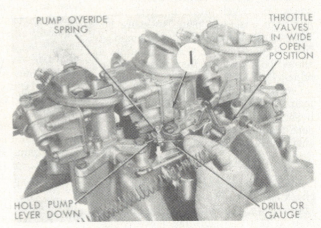

Fig. CH4-7 — View showing location of idle mixture screw on center carburetor. Use a drill bit or feeler gage as shown to set accelerator pump clearance. Refer to text.

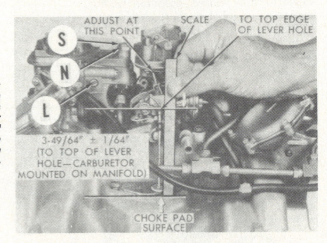

Fig. CH4-8 — Loosen lock screw (S) and turn adjusting nut (N) so fuel level reaches lower threads of hole for plug (L). Measure height of choke coil rod from choke pad to top edge of choke control lever hole. See text.

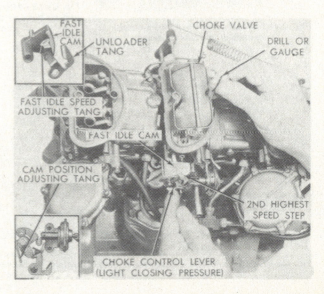

Fig. CH4-9 — View of fast idle cam and choke linkage. Refer to text for adjustment.

Illustration courtesy Chrysler

INBOARD ENGINES

Chrysler

careful not to twist diaphragm rod as diaphragm may be damaged. Be sure linkage moves without binding after adjustment.

FAST IDLE. Open throttle slightly and close choke so fast idle tang is positioned on second highest step of fast idle cam as shown in Fig. CH4-9. Run engine and note fast idle speed. Fast idle speed should be 1800 rpm and is adjusted by bending fast idle tang. Bend tang only when it is clear of fast idle cam as cam may be repositioned.

THROTTLE SYNCHRONIZATION. Back out idle speed screw on center carburetor so throttle valve will close completely. Disconnect throttle rods from center carburetor to front and rear carburetors. Note if throttle valves in front and rear carburetors are closed completely and correct if they are not. Screw throttle rods into adjuster blocks so end of each rod will fit into carburetor throttle arm without disturbing arm. Throttle linkage should now be connected to all carburetors and throttle valves on all carburetors should be closed. If not, disconnect linkage and repeat adjustment. Adjust idle speed and mixture as outlined in following paragraphs.

IDLE SPEED AND MIXTURE. Hull of boat should be as nearly level as possible during this adjustment. Preliminary setting of new or reassembled carburetor requires that idle mixture needles (I – Fig. CH4-7) be turned in, very lightly seated, then backed off one full turn. Operate engine until normal operating temperature is reached, then adjust idle speed screw until desired idle speed is obtained.

NOTE: Use of a tachometer and vacuum gage is advisable.

To adjust idle mixture, turn idle screw inward until rpm drops off (or vacuum reading falls) then back out until rpm (or vacuum) again is reduced and then adjust at a midpoint for strongest idle (or highest vacuum reading). Both idle screw adjustments should be carefully balanced for best idle mixture setting. If engine rpm increases over specifications during these adjustments, reset idle speed screw on throttle shaft. Slight readjustment of mixture needles may also be necessary.

FLOAT LEVEL SETTING—WET.

CAUTION: Take precautions to catch fuel spillage or run-over during this adjustment.

With flame arrestor removed, engine not running, remove sight plug (L – Fig. CH4-8) followed by lower fuel bowl mounting screw which is farthest from fuel inlet and allow fuel in bowl to drain into a shallow pan. Replace bowl mounting screw securely and start engine. With engine running at idle speed, fuel level should rise to just reach lower edge of sight hole. To adjust, loosen lock screw (S) and turn adjusting nut (N) clockwise to lower fuel level or counterclockwise to raise. One-sixth turn will change fuel level about 1/16-inch. Tighten lock screw after adjusting.

IGNITION SYSTEM

Models M383B, M413E, M440D, M440S and early Models M400B and M440B are equipped with a conventional breaker point ignition system. Refer to ENGINE SERVICE DATA for specifications. Later Models M400B and M440B are equipped with a breakerless electronic ignition system.

ELECTRONIC IGNITION. Air gap between reluctor teeth and pole of pick-

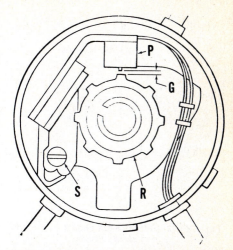

Fig. CH4-11—Air gap (G) between pole (P) and reluctor (R) teeth should be 0.008 inch. Loosen mounting screw (S) and move pole assembly to adjust air gap.

up unit shown in Fig. CH4-11 should be 0.008 inch. Loosen pickup unit mounting screw (S) and move pickup unit (P) to adjust air gap (G). A non-magnetic feeler gage must be used when setting air gap to accurately determine air gap. Reluctor teeth must have sharp edges. Rough or rounded edges may cause misfiring. Do not file edges of reluctor teeth.

Two types of ballast resistor are used with the Chrysler electronic ignition system. Ballast resistor designed for marine use has resistor wire totally enclosed in ceramic while automotive type ballast resistor has resistor wire exposed. Do not use automotive ballast resistor as exposed resistor wire is a fire hazard and will corrode and fail.

To troubleshoot Chrysler electronic ignition system, use Chrysler ignition tester C4166A and follow instructions on tester.

REPAIR

FIRING ORDER

Refer to engine serial number plate to determine propeller rotation and gear reduction. For R-10, R-13, R-15, R-25, R-30 and L-19 designations, the firing order is 1-2-7-5-6-3-4-8. For L-10, L-13, L-15, L-25, L-30 and R-19 designations, the engine firing order is 1-8-4-3-6-5-7-2.

VALVE SYSTEM

Hydraulic lifters are non-adjustable but may be checked for correct clearance. Rotate engine so valve of lifter being checked is closed and lifter is on base of camshaft. Push down on push rod so lifter is collapsed and measure clearance

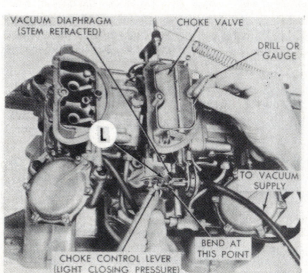

Fig. CH4-10—Adjust length of diaphragm link by bending U-bend (L). Refer to text.

Illustration courtesy Chrysler

Chrysler   INBOARD ENGINES

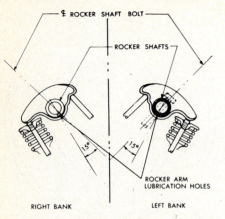

Fig. CH4-12 – Rocker arms should be installed as shown above.

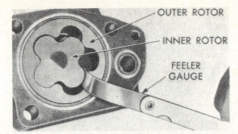

Fig. CH4-15 – Measuring oil pump inner rotor to outer rotor clearance. Clearance should not exceed 0.010 inch.

Fig. CH4-18 – View of timing marks on camshaft and crankshaft sprockets.

between end of push rod and rocker arm. Clearance should be 0.060-0.210 inch. If clearance is incorrect, inspect lifter and valve system. Install rocker shafts on 383, 400, 413 and 440 engines so oil holes point downward into rocker arms at an angle of 15 degrees toward push rod end of rocker arms. Refer to Fig. CH4-12. Stamped type rocker arms are arranged in pairs with each rocker arm having an offset push rod seat. Install rocker arms so each pair of rocker arms has push rod seats adjacent. Do not mismatch rocker arms. Install short retainers on ends and at center of rocker shaft. Install long retainers between first and second pairs and third and fourth pairs of rocker arms. Exhaust valve rotators are used on some engines and should be inspected for proper operation.

Renew valve if valve stem wear exceeds 0.002 inch. Valve guides are non-renewable and must be reamed to next oversize if valve guide wear is excessive. Valves are available in oversizes of 0.005, 0.015 and 0.030 inch. To determine if valve guide is excessively worn, install sleeve (Chrysler Tool C-3973) on valve stem and install valve in guide so sleeve supports valve. Measure valve wobble as shown in Fig. CH4-13. If wobble exceeds 0.017 inch an oversize valve must be installed.

PISTONS

Pistons are cam ground and must be installed so indent in piston crown is towards front of engine. Assemble connecting rods and pistons so large chamfer of connecting rod big end will be to front of engine on cylinders 1, 3, 5 and 7 and to rear of engine on cylinders 2, 4, 6 and 8. Compression rings are marked "TOP".

OIL PUMP

To check oil pump clearances place a straightedge across outer rotor face as shown in Fig. CH4-14 and measure gap between straightedge and inner rotor face. Gap should not exceed 0.004 inch. Inner rotor-to-outer rotor clearance (Fig. CH4-15) should not exceed 0.010 inch. Outer rotor-to-housing clearance (Fig. CH4-16) should not exceed 0.012 inch. Renew oil pump cover if it is scored or warped more than 0.0015 inch.

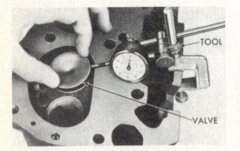

Fig. CH4-13 – Measure valve wobble as shown above.

Fig. CH4-16 – Oil pump outer rotor to housing clearance should not exceed 0.012 inch.

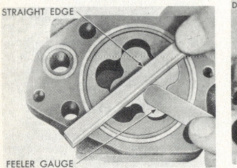

Fig. CH4-14 – Measure clearance between rotor and pump body as shown. Clearance should not exceed 0.004 inch.

Fig. CH4-17 – Slot in distributor drive gear should be parallel with crankshaft centerline when No. 1 piston is at TDC on compression.

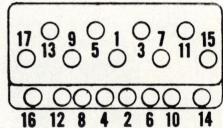

Fig. CH4-19 – Cylinder head bolt tightening sequence.

Illustration courtesy Chrysler

CHRYSLER
ENGINE SERVICE DATA
NOTE: Metric fasteners are used throughout engine.

ENGINE MODEL	MN4-33	MN6-33
General		
Cylinders	4	6
Bore	83 mm	
Stroke	100 mm	
Displacement	2164cc	3246cc
Compression Ratio	22:1	
Main Bearings, Number of	3	4
Firing Order	1-3-4-2	1-4-2-6-3-5
Numbering System (Front-to-Rear)	1-2-3-4	1-2-3-4-5-6
Compression Pressure at Cranking Speed	294 kPa	
Tune-Up		
Valve Lifter Type	Mechanical	
Valve Lifter Gap	0.35 mm	
Valve Seat Angle	45°	
Valve Face Angle	45°	
Valve Seat Type	Insert	
Valve Spring Free Length	48.7-49.3 mm	
Valve Spring Pressure	41.5 mm @ 147N	
Timing Mark Location	Crankshaft Pulley	
Injection Pump Type	Bosch Type A	
Nozzle Diameter	1 opening – 1 mm	
Injection Pressure	9.8 MPa	
Idle Speed	1000 rpm	
Injection Timing	20° BTDC	
Sizes — Capacities — Clearances		
Crankshaft Journal Diameter	70.905-70.920 mm	
Crankpin Diameter	52.910-52.925 mm	
Camshaft Journal Diameter		
Front	44.432-45.447 mm	
Center (SD22), Nos. 2 & 3 (SD33)	43.895-43.910 mm	
Rear	41.231 mm	
Piston Pin Diameter	25.983-26.000 mm	
Piston Pin Fit		
Piston	0.003 mm Loose-0.003 mm Tight	
Rod Bushing	0.025-0.047 mm	
Valve Stem Diameter		
Intake	7.970-7.985 mm	
Exhaust	7.945-7.960 mm	
Valve Spring Free Length	48.7-49.3 mm	
Valve Spring Pressure	41.5 mm @ 147N	
Main Bearing Clearance	0.035-0.095 mm	
Rod Bearing Clearance	0.035-0.090 mm	
Rod Bearing Side Clearance	0.1-0.2 mm	
Piston Clearance at Right Angle to Piston Pin Hole	0.120-0.170 mm	
Crankshaft End Play	0.06-0.24 mm	
Camshaft Bearing Clearance		
Front	0.023-0.108 mm	
Center (SD22), Nos. 2 & 3 (SD33)	0.04-0.125 mm	
Rear	0.029-0.114 mm	
Camshaft End Play	0.08-0.26 mm	
Valve Stem Clearance		
Intake	0.015-0.045 mm	
Exhaust	0.04-0.07 mm	

Illustration courtesy Chrysler

Chrysler — INBOARD ENGINES

ENGINE SERVICE DATA (CONT.)

ENGINE MODEL	MN4-33	MN6-33

Sizes — Capacities — Clearances (Cont.)

Piston Ring End Gap	0.3-0.5 mm	
Piston Ring Side Clearance		
No. 1 Compression	0.06-0.10 mm	
No. 2 & 3 Compression	0.04-0.08 mm	
Oil Rings	0.02-0.06 mm	
Connecting Rod Bushing		
Small End Fit	0.013-0.046 mm Tight	
Camshaft Lobe Height	37.3 mm	
Cylinder Bore to Liner Fit	0.01-0.03 mm Tight	
Cylinder Liner Standout	0.02-0.09 mm	
Cylinder Block Deck Height (Min.)	267.7 mm	
Flywheel Run-out (Max.)	0.1 mm	
Oil Pump Drive Shaft Diameter		
At Drive End	14.958-14.976 mm	
At Gear End	12.958-12.976 mm	
Oil Pump Idler Shaft Diameter	13.040-13.058 mm	13.033-13.044 mm
Oil Pressure, Engine Warm	345 kPa @ 2000 rpm	
Battery	12V-Neg. Grd.	

Starter Service Data

Starter Make	Hitachi S12-19K	Hitachi S13-04K
Brush Spring Tension	8.3N	17.6N
Minimum Brush Length	13 mm	
Commutator Min. Diameter	40 mm	47 mm
Max. Armature Shaft Run-out	0.1 mm	
No-Load Test:		
Volts	12	12
Amps	55	80
Rpm	6,500	4,500
Lock Test		
Volts	5	5
Amps	800	1,050
Torque	28.4 N·M	30.4 N·M

Alternator Service Data

Alternator Make	Hitachi LT123-38K or Hitachi LT123-64K
Output Current	24½ amps/14 volts @ 2500 rpm
No Load Voltage	13.8-14.8 @ 2500 rpm
Brush Spring Tension	2.94N
Min. Brush Length	7.5 mm
Min. Slip Ring Diameter	32 mm
Max. Slip Ring Run-out	0.3 mm

Tightening Torques
(All values are in newton meters.)

Camshaft Gear Mounting Bolt	44.74-48.81
Camshaft Locating Plate Bolt	4.07-5.42
Connecting Rod Cap Nut	51.52-55.59
Crank Pulley Mounting Nut	294.21-322.68
Cylinder Head Bolts:	
Small	48.81
Large	127.45
Exhaust Manifold Nut	14.91-17.63
Fan Pulley Mounting Bolt	6.78-9.49
Flywheel Housing Bolt:	
MN4-33	39.32-43.39
MN6-33	63.72-73.21
Flywheel Mounting Bolt	44.74-48.81
Front End Plate Mounting Bolt	10.17-12.20
Injection Pump Mounting Nut	19.66-24.40
Injection Pump Timer Nut	69.15-77.28
Intake Manifold Nut	14.91-17.63
Main Bearing Cap Nut:	
MN4-33	148-155
MN6-33	102
Nozzle Nut	69.15-88.13
Nozzle Overflow Nut	39.32-48.81
Oil Cooler Mounting Bolt	10.17-12.20
Oil Filter Mounting Bolt	20.34-24.40
Oil Pan Mounting Bolt	4.07-5.42
Oil Pump Mounting Bracket Bolt	10.17-12.20
Rocker Arm Shaft Mounting Bolt	19.66-24.40
Starter Motor Mounting Bolt	63.72-73.21
Timer Cover Mounting Bolt	4.07-5.42
Timing Gear Case Mounting Bolt:	
6 mm	4.07-5.42
8 mm	10.17-12.20
Water Pump Mounting Bolt:	
8 mm	10.17-12.20
10 mm	19.66-24.40

Illustration courtesy Chrysler

INBOARD ENGINES

Chrysler

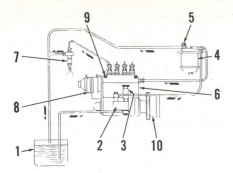

Fig. CH5-1 – Drawing of MN4-33 and MN6-33 fuel circuit.

1. Fuel tank
2. Fuel pump
3. Primer pump
4. Fuel filter
5. Overflow valve
6. Fuel injection pump
7. Injectors
8. Governor
9. Air bleed screws
10. Advance and drive assembly

MAINTENANCE
FUEL SYSTEM

Fuel is pumped from fuel tank (1 – Fig. CH5-1) by a fuel pump (2) to the fuel filter (4). An overflow valve (5) at the fuel filter directs excess fuel back to fuel tank. Fuel travels from the fuel filter (4) to injection pump (6) where it is routed to injection nozzle (7) for each cylinder. Excess fuel at each injection nozzle is returned to fuel tank.

BLEED SYSTEM. Should the fuel lines from fuel tank (1 – Fig. CH5-1) to fuel pump (2) or injection pump (6) be broken or disconnected, then fuel system must be bled. To bleed fuel system, remove air bleed screws (9) on side of injection pump (6) and actuate priming pump (3) which is integral with fuel pump (2). Operate priming pump (3) until air is no longer emitted from air bleed holes. Reinstall air bleed screws (9).

FUEL TANK. The fuel tank of any diesel engine using "cracked" fuels should be cleaned periodically to remove gum and varnish deposits. These deposits can be removed using a 50/50 mixture of uncolored denatured alcohol and benzol.

FUEL PUMP. A piston type, cam-driven fuel pump is used to pump fuel from fuel tank to fuel filter and injection pump. The fuel pump also contains a manually operated priming pump. Refer to Fig. CH5-2 for an exploded view of fuel and priming pump. Check fit of push rod (9) in bore in pump body. If excessive clearance is present, lubricating oil may be contaminated with diesel fuel. Ream hole in pump body and install an oversize push rod if necessary. Fuel pump should deliver 300 cc of fuel at 1000 rpm engine speed in 15 seconds.

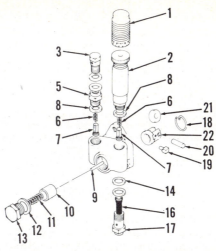

Fig. CH5-2 – Exploded view of fuel pump and primer pump.

1. Cover
2. Primer plunger
3. Banjo bolt
4. Fuel inlet
5. Nipple
6. Spring
7. Check valve
8. Washer
9. Push rod
10. Piston
11. Spring
12. Washer
13. Plug
14. Nylon washers
15. Fuel outlet
16. Filter
17. Banjo bolt
18. Snap ring
19. Retainer
20. Pin
21. Roller
22. Tappet

FUEL FILTER. A full-flow, paper type filter is used to clean fuel before entering injection pump. Fuel filter should be inspected and filter element periodically renewed if dirty or defective. Fuel filter is equipped with an overflow valve which directs excess fuel into a return line to fuel tank. Overflow valve should maintain a pressure of 147-156 kPa at discharge port of fuel filter. Renew valve if pressure is incorrect.

FUEL INJECTION PUMP. Nissan MN4-33 and MN6-33 engines are equipped with a Diesel Kiki fuel injection system. The Diesel Kiki injection pump is similar to the Bosch Type "A" pump. A mechanical flyweight governor is mounted on the injection pump. It is

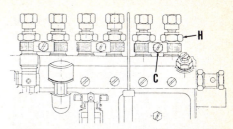

Fig. CH5-4 – View of fuel injection pump. Loosen clamp (C) before unscrewing delivery valve holder (H).

recommended that the fuel injection pump and governor assembly be taken to a qualified diesel injection service shop for overhaul and testing.

The diesel fuel system consists of three basic units; the fuel filters, injection pump and injection nozzles. When servicing any unit associated with the fuel system, absolute cleanliness must be observed. Care must also be taken not to nick or burr any of the working surfaces.

A lubrication compartment contains oil to lubricate the camshaft assembly. Fill compartment with 80cc of oil on MN4-33 engine and 180cc oil on MN6-33 engine. The governor has an oil level gage attached to the governor housing to indicate correct oil level. Fill injection pump and governor reservoirs with same oil used in engine crankcase.

FUEL INJECTION TIMING. Rotate engine so number 1 cylinder is at 20° BTDC on compression stroke by aligning timing mark on crankshaft pulley as shown in Fig. CH5-3. Disconnect number 1 cylinder fuel line from delivery valve holder (H – Fig. CH5-4) on injection pump. Loosen valve holder clamp (C) and unscrew valve holder. Remove delivery valve spring and reinstall valve

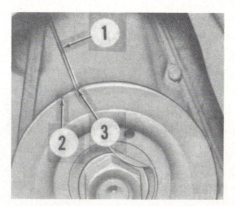

Fig. CH5-3 – Engine is at number 1 TDC when crankshaft pulley notch (2) is aligned with gear cover mark (1). Timing notch (3) indicates 20° BTDC when aligned with mark (1).

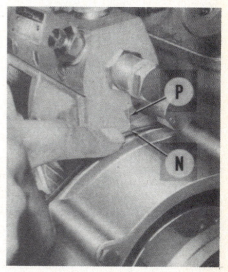

Fig. CH5-5 – Fuel injection mark (P) should align with notch (N) on end plate.

Illustration courtesy Chrysler

Chrysler   INBOARD ENGINES

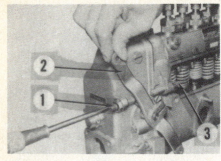

Fig. CH5-6 – Adjust idle speed by turning screw (1) and high governed speed by turning screw (3).

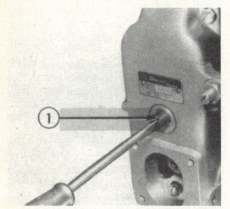

Fig. CH5-7 – Adjust idle surge by turning screw (1).

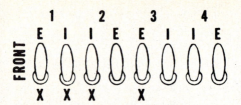

Fig. CH5-8 – Adjust valves statically on MN4-33 engine as explained in text. Valves marked "X" are adjusted when number 1 piston is at TDC on compression stroke.

VALVE ADJUSTMENT

Valve clearance is adjusted with engine shut off by rotating engine to number 1 TDC on compression stroke and adjusting valves as shown in Fig. CH5-8 or Fig. CH5-9. Adjust remaining valves by rotating engine to TDC on compression of number 4 cylinder on Model MN4-33 or number 6 cylinder on Model MN6-33. A TDC mark is located on crankshaft pulley as shown at (2 – Fig. CH5-3).

REPAIRS

INJECTION PUMP

REMOVE AND REINSTALL. Disconnect all fuel lines at fuel injection pump and control linkage to governor. Remove timing case cover and tachometer drive. Unscrew retaining nut and remove pump advance assembly and drive gear. Unscrew pump retaining nuts and remove pump from mounting plate.

To reinstall injection pump, reverse removal procedure. Before installing advance assembly and gear, rotate engine so number 1 cylinder is at TDC on compression by aligning timing marks shown in Fig. CH5-3. Install advance and drive gear assembly by aligning "Y" marks on drive gear and idler gear, as shown in Fig. CH5-10, with key and keyway in pump shaft. Reinstall remainder of assembly and follow timing procedure outlined in FUEL INJECTION TIMING section.

FUEL INJECTION NOZZLES

CAUTION: Fuel leaves the injection nozzles with sufficient force to penetrate the skin. When testing, keep exposed areas of body clear of nozzle spray.

If a single cylinder is misfiring, a faulty injector should be suspected. The faulty injector can be located by detaching the fuel line from injector and noting any change in engine operation. When faulty injector is removed from fuel circuit, its removal will have less effect on engine operation than if a good injector is disconnected.

To check spray pattern of injector, remove injector from engine then reconnect fuel line to injector. Direct injector so spray pattern can be observed and rotate engine with starter. Compare spray pattern with that shown in Fig. CH5-11. If spray pattern is incorrect injector may need cleaning or overhaul. Install a new, rebuilt or good injector

holder (H) and tighten to 30-34 N·m. Loosen four nuts which secure pump to engine. Rotate top of injection pump towards engine. Operate priming pump while rotating pump away from engine. Stop rotation when fuel ceases to flow from delivery valve holder (H). Injection to number 1 cylinder would begin at this time. Check for alignment of mark on front face of pump and notch on end plate of engine as shown in Fig. CH5-5. If marks do not align, new marks should be made. Tighten pump retaining nuts being careful not to disturb position of pump. Reinstall delivery valve spring and retighten valve holder to 30-34 N·m. Tighten valve holder clamp.

ENGINE SPEED ADJUSTMENTS

Engine idle speed may be adjusted by loosening locknut and turning adjusting screw shown in Fig. CH5-6. Maximum governed engine speed is adjusted by loosening locknut and turning adjusting screw opposite idle screw as shown in Fig. CH5-6. Engine surging at idle may be corrected by removing rear cap and turning surge screw (1 – Fig. CH5-7). Do not turn screw excessively as governor operation may be effected in other speed ranges. Other governor adjustments should be accomplished by a shop experienced in governor servicing.

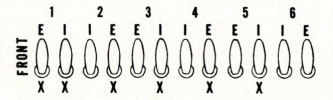

Fig. CH5-9 – Adjust valves statically on MN6-33 engine as explained in text. Valves marked "X" are adjusted when number 1 piston is at TDC on compression stroke.

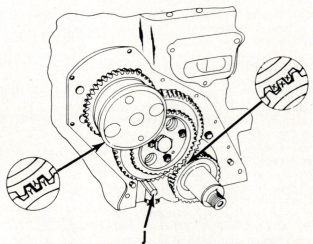

Fig. CH5-10 – View of gear train and timing marks. Oil jet (J) should point to gears referred to in text.

Illustration courtesy Chrysler

INBOARD ENGINES

Chrysler

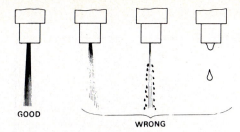

Fig. CH5-11 — View showing correct and incorrect injector spray patterns.

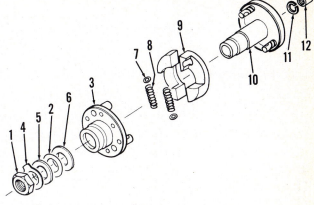

Fig. CH5-13 — Exploded view of advance mechanism mounted on injector pump.

1. Nut
2. Shim
3. Drive flange
4. Tab washer
5. Washer
6. Washer
7. Shim
8. Spring
9. Advance weights
10. Hub
11. Lockwasher
12. Nut

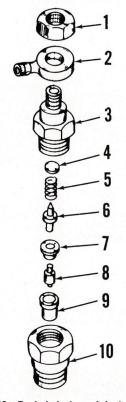

Fig. CH5-12 — Exploded view of fuel injection nozzle (injector).

1. Nut
2. Fuel return outlet
3. Holder
4. Shim
5. Spring
6. Push rod
7. Spacer
8. Nozzle valve
9. Valve seat
10. Nut

Fig. CH5-14 — Drive gear timing mark (O) and mark (M) on advance drive flange (3—Fig. 1-13) must be aligned during assembly.

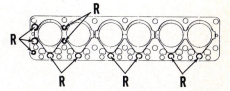

Fig. CH5-15 — Rubber rings (R) must be installed around water and oil passages between block and head. Location of rings is similar on MN4-33.

from another engine and check engine operation. If engine operation improves, then service faulty injector or install a new injector.

Before loosening any lines, wash connections and adjacent parts with fuel oil or kerosene. After disconnecting high pressure (feed) and leak-off lines, cap exposed openings in lines and fittings to prevent dirt from entering system. Unscrew injector from engine. Remove copper gasket which may have remained in cylinder head.

Hard or sharp tools, emery cloth, grinding compounds or abrasives of any kind should not be used to clean injectors. Place all parts in clean fuel oil or kerosene as they are disassembled.

Unscrew locknut (1–Fig. CH5-12) and nozzle nut (10). Disassemble injector as shown in Fig. CH5-12. Do not interchange adjusting shim(s) as injector operation will be altered if they are not returned to their original position. Nozzle valves (8) and seats (9) are a lap fit and must never be interchanged.

Soften hard carbon deposits formed on nozzle seats and valve tip by soaking in a suitable carbon solvent, then use a soft brush to remove carbon from valve and nozzle exterior. Rinse nozzle and valve immediately after cleaning to prevent the carbon solvent from corroding the highly polished surfaces.

Inspect seat (9–Fig. CH5-12) and valve (8) for wear or damage. Seat and valve should be renewed if discolored or signs of seizing are present. Check spacer (7) for proper contact between spacer and seat (9) and spacer and nozzle holder (3). Return spring (5) free length should be 22 mm. Renew components if excessively worn or damaged. Reassemble injector in opposite order of disassembly. Tighten injector nut (10) to 104.3-117 N·m.

Remove carbon from injector hole using a suitable reamer to clean hole. Install injector being careful not to strike nozzle tip against any hard surface.

ADVANCE MECHANISM

Both models are equipped with a centrifugal advance mechanism mounted on front end of injection pump shaft. Advance mechanism is accessible after removing front timing gear cover. Injection pump drive gear attaches to drive flange (3–Fig. CH5-13). Install shims (2) as needed to obtain 0.02-0.1 mm drive flange end play. Note in Fig. CH5-14 that "O" mark on injection pump drive gear must align with straight mark on drive flange. If necessary equipment is available, the following advance specifications may be checked:

RPM	Pump Degrees
500	0°
700	1°
1100	2.8°
1500	5°
1800	7.5°

CYLINDER HEAD

Valve installed height should be 39 mm. Rubber rings are used to seal oil and water passages between block and cylinder head. Refer to Fig. CH5-15 for location of rubber rings. Rocker arm and bracket assembly should be heated in 158°F. water to ease removal of brackets. Immerse brackets in 158°F. water before installing brackets on rocker arm shaft. Note difference between intake and exhaust rocker arms. Intake rocker arms are identified by a

Chrysler

INBOARD ENGINES

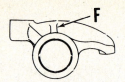

Fig. CH5-16 — Note location of fillet (F) to identify intake rocker arms.

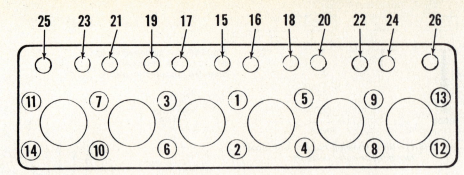

Fig. CH5-18 — Cylinder head bolt tightening sequence for MN6-33.

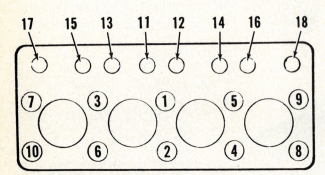

Fig. CH5-17 — Cylinder head bolt tightening sequence for MN4-33.

fillet between backbone and bore of rocker arm as shown in Fig. CH5-16. Short locating springs should be between intake rocker arms on rocker shaft with longer springs installed between exhaust rocker arms. See Fig. CH5-17 and CH5-18 for appropriate cylinder head bolt tightening sequence.

CONNECTING RODS AND PISTONS

Connecting rods and caps are numbered to indicate location in block. Be sure numbers on rod and cap are on the same side when bolted together. Install connecting rod in piston so when piston assembly is installed in block the numbers on connecting rod will be opposite camshaft side of engine and combustion chamber of piston will be towards injection pump side of engine as shown in Fig. CH5-19.

CRANKSHAFT

Model MN6-33 engines have a metal cone which secures the crankshaft pulley to the crankshaft. After removing pulley nut, cone may be removed by tapping evenly on face of pulley.

Gear train timing marks are shown in Fig. CH5-10. Gear backlash may be measured by inserting solder between gear teeth and rotating gears. Backlash should be 0.076-0.117 mm.

Main bearings have an oil groove and an oil hole in upper bearing half. Oil hole must be aligned with oil hole in block. Main bearing caps are stamped with an "F" which should be towards front of engine when installed. MN6-33 main bearing caps are also stamped with a number to indicate position of cap (cap at front of engine is "1").

OIL PUMP

A gear type oil pump is used on MN4-33 and MN6-33 engines. Gear-to-housing clearance should be 0.098-0.184 mm on MN4-33 and 0.074-0.150 mm on MN6-33. Gear backlash should be 0.3-0.4 mm. Place a straightedge across gears and housing as shown in Fig. CH5-20 and measure gap between gears and straightedge. On MN4-33 housing gasket must be on housing. Gap should be 0.040-0.11 mm on MN4-33 and 0.02-0.08 mm on MN6-33.

OIL JET

An oil jet is attached to front of cylinder block to lubricate crankshaft and

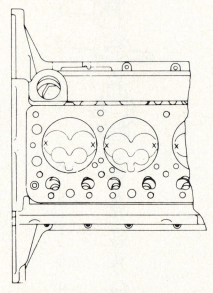

Fig. CH5-19 — View showing position of installed pistons. Flywheel end of engine is shown.

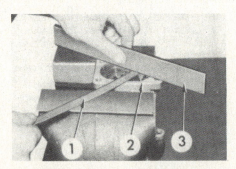

Fig. CH5-20 — Using a straightedge (3), measure gap between gears and housing (2).

camshaft gears as shown in Fig. CH5-10. Oil jet should be cleaned and checked for blockage. Install oil jet so outer oil hole is directed at idler gear and inner hole is directed toward contact area of crankshaft and camshaft gears.

INBOARD ENGINES — Chrysler

CHRYSLER
ENGINE SERVICE DATA
NOTE: Metric fasteners are used throughout engine.

ENGINE MODEL	CM6-55
General	
Number of Cylinders	6
Bore	98 mm
Stroke	120 mm
Displacement	5430 cc
Compression Ratio	19:1
Firing Order	1-5-3-6-2-4
Cylinder Numbering System, from flywheel	6-5-4-3-2-1
Maximum Angle of Installation	15°
Main Bearings, Number of	7
Tune-Up	
Oil Capacity:	
Level Installation	9.53 liter
15° Installation	8.58 liter
Coolant Capacity	19.0 liter
Low Idle Speed	580-620 rpm
High No-Load Speed	3400 rpm
Oil Pressure:	
Idle	87.0 kPa
1200 rpm	294-392 kPa
Fuel Injection Timing	17° BTDC
Fuel Injection Pressure	10.78-12.74 MPa
Compression Pressure	2.55 MPa
Valve Timing:	
Intake	
Opens	30° BTDC
Closes	66° ABDC
Exhaust	
Opens	66° BBDC
Closes	30° ATDC
Valve Clearance (Cold)	0.3 mm
Oil Pump Volume @ 1000 rpm	32.0 liter min.
Water Pump Volume @ 3000 rpm	100 liter min.
Sizes — Capacities — Clearances	
Injection Pump	Bosch ND-PES6A80B
Injection Nozzle:	
Holder Type	Bosch ND-KD58SD
Tip Type	Throttle Type ND-DN4SD
Precombustion Chamber Recess	0.1-0.5 mm
Valve Seat Angle	45°
Valve Depth	1.1 mm
Valve Seat Width:	
Intake	1.4 mm
Exhaust	2.8 mm
Valve Margin	1.5 mm
Valve Guide Protrusion	22.5 mm
Valve Seat Interference Fit	0.050-0.080 mm
Valve Stem to Guide Clearance:	
Intake	0.055-0.085 mm
Exhaust	0.07-0.1 mm

ENGINE MODEL	CM6-55
Sizes — Capacities — Clearances (Cont.)	
Valve Spring Free Length:	
Inner	51.2 mm
Outer	55.4 mm
Valve Spring Pressure @ Installed Height:	
Inner	136.7 kPa @ 42.3 mm
Outer	348.0 kPa @ 47.0 mm
Rocker Arm Bushing to Shaft Clearance	0.020-0.051 mm
Valve Lifter to Lifter Bore Clearance	0.015-0.066 mm
Camshaft Journal to Bearing Clearance	0.04-0.09 mm
Camshaft End Play	0.10-0.25 mm
Camshaft Lobe Height	45.615-46.715 mm
Camshaft Runout	0.00-0.05 mm
Idler Gear Bushing to Shaft Clearance	0.025-0.075 mm
Idler Gear End Play	0.05-0.15 mm
Crank Gear to Idler Gear Backlash	0.09-0.19 mm
Idler Gear to Camshaft Gear Backlash	0.1-0.2 mm
Idler Gear to Injection Pump Gear Backlash	0.1-0.2 mm
Oil Pump Gear Backlash	0.08-0.20 mm
Piston Diameter:	
Size	
A	97.865-97.874 mm
B	97.875-97.885 mm
C	97.886-97.895 mm
Piston Ring to Groove Clearance:	
Top Ring	0.04-0.08 mm
Second Ring	0.025-0.065 mm
Oil Control Ring	0.025-0.065 mm
Piston Ring Side Clearance	0.3-0.5 mm
Piston Ring End Gap	0.3-0.5 mm
Piston Pin to Piston Bore Clearance	0.0-0.017 mm
Piston Pin to Connecting Rod Bushing Bore Clearance	0.020-0.052 mm
Connecting Rod Bearing to Journal Clearance	0.035-0.100 mm
Crankshaft Main Bearing to Journal Clearance	0.036-0.098 mm
Crankshaft End-Play	0.100-0.198 mm
Crankshaft Runout	0.0-0.05 mm
Cylinder Liner ID:	
Size	
A	98.000-98.011 mm
B	98.011-98.023 mm
C	98.023-98.035 mm
Cylinder Liner Protrusion	0.11-0.20 mm

Illustration courtesy Chrysler

Chrysler

INBOARD ENGINES

Sizes — Capacities — Clearances (Cont.)

Oil Pump Gear to Housing Clearance	0.11-0.18 mm
Oil Pump Gear to Cover Clearance	0.20-0.04 mm

Tightening Torques

(All values are in newton meters.)

Camshaft Gear Bolt	34.3
Camshaft Thrust Plate	20.58
Connecting Rod Nut	93.1
Crankshaft Pulley Nut	392.0
Cylinder Head Bolt:	
NA models	176.4
TI & TW models	196.0
Exhaust Manifold	
Bolt	41.2
Nut	34.4

Tightening Torques (Cont.)

Flywheel Bolt:	
Marked F	88.2
Marked H	107.8
Flywheel Housing Bolt	53.9
Glow Plug	81.3
Idler Shaft Bolt	34.3
Injection Nozzle Nut	58.8-78.4
Injection Pump Delivery Valve Holder	24.5-34.3
Main Bearing Bolt:	
14 flange head	138.2
16 flange head	157.2
Injection Nozzle	78.4-98.0
Precombustion Chamber Retaining Screw	392.0
Rocker Arm Cover Nut	19.6
Rocker Shaft Bracket Bolt	41.8

MAINTENANCE

CM6-55 engines feature indirect injection and precombustion chambers with glow plugs. Engines are produced in naturally aspirated (NA) and turbocharged (TI and TW) versions. Both are built around the same base 5430 cc engine and are fresh-water cooled.

Turbocharged engines have intercooling between turbocharger and the intake manifold for increased engine life and efficiency. A wet turbocharger (TW model) is also in use.

LUBRICATION

Engine oil and filter should be changed after first 25 hours of operation on a new or rebuilt engine, and after every 100 hours or seasonally thereafter. Extreme operating conditions (hot or cold), short runs or poor quality fuel may require more frequent changes.

Use of a high quality API specification CD oil is recommended. Use SAE 30 for temperatures from 0°C to 10°C, and SAE 40 for temperatures above 10°C.

FUEL SYSTEM

BLEED SYSTEM. To bleed fuel system unscrew bleed screw (1–Fig. CH6-1) and operate priming pump (1–Fig. CH6-2) until air-free fuel flows then tighten fuel filter bleed screw. Next unscrew injection pump bleed screw (2–Fig. CH6-2) and again operate priming pump until air-free fuel flows and tighten bleed screw. Unscrew injection pump bleed screw (3) and operate priming pump (1) until air-free fuel flows and tighten bleed screw (3). Finally, place throttle lever in full speed position and crank engine, with switch in stop position, for 10 seconds to bleed injector lines.

FUEL INJECTION TIMING. Use the following procedure to adjust injection timing. Rotate engine so number 1 cylinder is at 15° BTDC on compression by aligning timing mark on flywheel with reference mark on flywheel housing as shown in Fig. CH6-3. Disconnect number 1 cylinder fuel line from delivery valve holder on injection pump. Loosen four nuts which secure pump to engine. Rotate top of injection pump away from engine. Operate priming pump while rotating pump towards engine. Stop rotation when fuel ceases to flow from

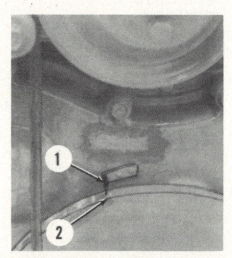

Fig. CH6-3 — View of timing pointer (1) and timing marks (2), which are located on crankshaft vibration damper.

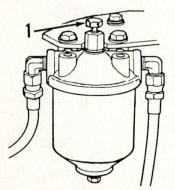

Fig. CH6-1 — To bleed secondary fuel filter unscrew bleed screw (1) and operate priming pump until air-free fuel flows then tighten bleed screw.

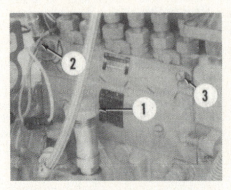

Fig. CH6-2 — Injection pump is bled by first opening bleed screw (2) and operating priming pump (1) until air-free fuel flows; repeat operation after unscrewing bleed screw (3).

Fig. CH6-4 — Injection pump timing is adjusted using marks on pump flange and index mark (T) on flange plate. See text for fuel injection pump timing procedure.

INBOARD ENGINES — Chrysler

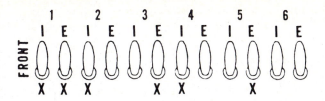

Fig. CH6-5 — With number 1 piston at TDC on compression valves marked (X) may be adjusted. With number 6 piston at TDC on compression remaining valves may be adjusted.

delivery valve holder (H). Injection to number 1 cylinder would begin at this time and timing marks on injection pump flange (Fig. CH6-4) should indicate 15 crankshaft degrees (one injection pump degree mark equals six crankshaft degrees). Tighten pump retaining nuts being careful not to disturb pump position. Connect number 1 cylinder fuel line.

VALVE ADJUSTMENT

Valve clearance should be checked and adjusted after every 250 hours of operation or seasonally, whichever is more frequent. Remove rocker arm cover and bring number 1 piston to TDC on compression and adjust valves indicated by an X in Fig. CH6-5, by loosening adjusting screw locknut and turning adjusting screw until a feeler gage of the proper thickness will just slide between top of valve stem and rocker arm. On turbocharged engines set intake valves at 0.3 mm and exhaust valves at 0.38 mm. On naturally aspirated engines set both intake and exhaust valves to 0.3 mm. After completing above procedure position number 6 piston at TDC on compression and adjust remaining valves in a similar manner.

BELT TENSION

FRESH-WATER PUMP. Fresh-water pump/alternator drive belt tension is correct when a force of 10 pounds causes belt to deflect ½-inch at a point mid-way between fresh-water pump pulley and alternator pulley. Belt tension is adjusted by loosening alternator mounting bolts and rotating alternator away from engine.

RAW-WATER PUMP. Raw-water pump belt tension is correct when a force of 10 pounds causes belt to deflect ½-inch at a point halfway between crankshaft pulley and raw-water pump pulley. To adjust belt tension loosen raw water pump mounting bolts and slide pump straight away from engine on adjusting brackets then tighten mounting bolts.

TURBOCHARGER AND INTERCOOLER

After every 100 hours of operation or seasonally, turbocharger and intercooler must be cleaned to ensure proper operation. With boat underway and engine at normal operating temperature, bring engine speed to 2700-2800 rpm. Remove foam air cleaner element but not expanded metal air cleaner frame.

CAUTION: Do not place hands or fingers near turbocharger inlet while engine is running. Vacuum at this point can draw fingers into compressor resulting in serious injury. Using a hand pump type spray atomizer, spray 2 ounces of clean diesel fuel into turbocharger intake at a rate of 1 ounce per minute. This is done to eliminate any carbon build up in the compressor housing or intercooler which can restrict intake air flow. Replace foam air filter insert and retainer.

REPAIR

COOLING SYSTEM

RAW-WATER PUMP. To disassemble raw-water pump first remove pump pulley and separate pump housing (20 — Fig. CH6-6) from pump body (7) by removing three ¼-20 hex head bolts. Remove impeller (17) and end plate (16) then remove key (15) and snap ring (14) from shaft (13). Next remove snap ring (11) and key (12) from drive end of shaft (13). Remove snap ring (2), then using a suitable press force shaft (13) with bearings (3 and 5) from body (7). Press shaft (13) out of bearings (3 and 5) and spacer (4). Remove snap ring (6) from body (7) and press seat (9) from body (7). Finally remove screw (21) from housing (20) and lift shoe (18) out of housing.

Inspect all parts for deterioration and wear and renew as necessary. Assemble pump in opposite order of disassembly using all new "O" rings and seals. When installing impeller (17) into housing (20) coat impeller vanes with petroleum jelly to avoid impeller damage on initial start-up.

FRESH-WATER PUMP. After removing pump from engine, remove flange nut (1 – Fig. CH6-7) and washer (2) from pump shaft (7), then remove pump cover (14) from back of pump housing (10). Remove snap ring (4) from pump housing and unscrew impeller (13) from shaft (7). Using a suitable press remove shaft (7) along with bearings (5 and 8) from pump housing (10). Detach snap ring (9) from shaft (7) and press bearings (5 and 8) individually from shaft. Press seal and seat assembly (12) from pump housing (10).

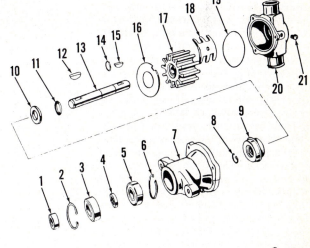

Fig. CH6-6 — Exploded view of raw-water pump used on CM6-55 engines.

1. Pulley spacer
2. Snap ring
3. Front bearing
4. Spacer
5. Rear bearing
6. Snap ring
7. Body
8. Snap ring
9. Seal
10. Seal seat
11. Thrust washer
12. Pulley key
13. Shaft
14. Snap ring
15. Impeller key
16. End plate
17. Impeller
18. Shoe
19. "O" ring
20. Housing
21. Shoe retaining screw

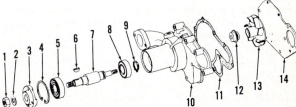

Fig. CH6-7 — Exploded view of fresh-water pump used on CM6-55 engines.

1. Nut
2. Washer
3. Flange
4. Snap ring
5. Front shaft bearing
6. Key
7. Shaft
8. Rear shaft bearing
9. Snap ring
10. Housing
11. Gasket
12. Seal
13. Impeller
14. Cover plate

Illustration courtesy Chrysler

Chrysler — INBOARD ENGINES

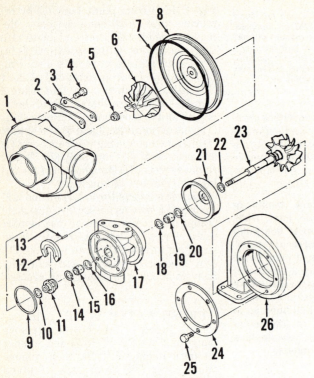

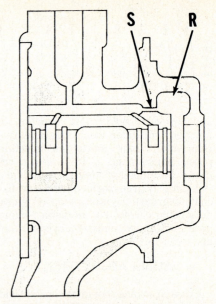

Fig. CH6-8 — Exploded view of turbocharger unit used on CM6-55 engines.

1. Compressor housing
2. Clamp
3. Lockplate
4. Screw
5. Locknut
6. Compressor wheel
7. "O" ring
8. Backplate
9. Seal ring
10. Piston ring
11. Thrust collar
12. Thrust bearing
13. Alignment pin
14. Snap ring
15. Bearing
16. Snap ring
17. Center housing
18. Snap ring
19. Bearing
20. Snap ring
21. Wheel shroud
22. Piston ring
23. Turbine wheel & shaft assy.
24. Housing clamp
25. Screw
26. Turbine housing

Fig. CH6-9 — When inspecting and cleaning turbocharger center housing be sure to clean all old oil and carbon out of spray hole (S) and oil reservoir (R).

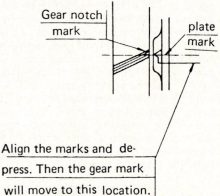

Fig. CH6-9A — View of marks on injection pump gear and pump mounting plate.

Inspect all parts for deterioration and wear; renew parts as necessary. Assemble pump in opposite order of disassembly using new seals and gasket.

TURBOCHARGER

R&R AND OVERHAUL. Before disassembly clean exterior of turbocharger housing with a suitable solvent to prevent any dirt from contaminating the interior moving parts. Match mark compressor housing (1–Fig. CH6-8), turbine housing (26), and center housing (17) with a punch or scribe to assure correct assembly. Bend tabs of lockplates (3), remove screws (4), lockplates (3), clamp (2) and housings (1 and 26). **Use care when removing compressor housing to avoid damage to compressor wheel blades.** Clamp a ¾-inch socket vertically in a vise and place hex end of turbine wheel assembly (23) in the socket. Use a double universal socket wrench, to avoid placing bending loads on turbine wheel shaft, and remove locknut (5). Lift compressor wheel (6) from shaft of turbine wheel assembly (23). Remove turbine wheel assembly with piston ring (22) from center housing (17). Remove piston ring from turbine wheel assembly. Remove backplate assembly (8) from center housing.

NOTE: Do not remove spring that is pressed into backplate center bore or locating pins (13) that are pressed into center housing.

Before cleaning parts, inspect for burning, rubbing, or other damage that might not be evident after cleaning. Clean all parts in a non-caustic cleaning solution. Use a soft bristle brush, a plastic blade scraper, and dry compressed air to completely remove all deposits. Do not use abrasive cleaning methods which might damage or destroy machined surfaces. Carefully check turbine end of center housing and remove all carbonized oil. If center housing incorporates an oil squirt hole (Fig. CH6-9) make sure hole is free of carbonized oil through the use of a cleaning wire the same size as the hole. Do not enlarge the diameter of the squirt hole in the cleaning process.

Thoroughly inspect all parts and renew as necessary. Reassemble turbocharger in reverse order of disassembly while observing the following: Fill piston ring groove in turbine wheel assembly (23–Fig. CH6-8) with high vacuum silicon grease, then install piston ring (22) on turbine wheel assembly. **Do not force piston ring into center housing bore as this part is easily broken.** With piston ring and wheel shroud (21) installed on turbine wheel assembly, carefully guide turbine wheel assembly through bearings (15 and 19) to avoid damage to bearing bores. Install piston ring (10) on thrust collar (11) and start thrust collar (11) on shaft of turbine wheel assembly. Install thrust bearing (12) in groove of collar and slide assembled parts down against center housing so pins (13) engage holes in thrust bearing. Install backplate assembly (8) over shaft of turbine wheel assembly and carefully guide piston ring (22) into backplate bore, this can be easily accomplished if ring gap is started into bore first. Tighten backplate to center housing bolts to 75-90 in.-lbs. Install compressor wheel (6) on shaft of turbine wheel assembly using a double universal joint to avoid applying a bending load to turbine wheel assembly shaft (23). Install locknut (5) on shaft and tighten to 18-20 in.-lbs. above drag torque required to bottom locknut. After nut has been torqued it must be tightened an additional 90 degrees; this stretches shaft (23) 0.1397-0.1651 mm for proper installation of compressor wheel. Apply high temperature anti-seize compound to screws (25) before installation. Tighten screws (4 and 25) to 100-130 in.-lbs.

INBOARD ENGINES

After assembly of turbocharger is complete pour 4 ounces of engine oil into oil inlet port and turn compressor wheel by hand a minimum of 10 revolutions, then pour out excess oil.

FUEL INJECTION PUMP

R&R AND OVERHAUL. Starter must be removed to remove injection pump. Disconnect fuel supply and injection lines from injection pump. Disconnect throttle linkage, stop solenoid wire and linkage, aneroid hose, and rear mounting brackets. Remove upper retaining nuts from timing gear case, unscrew injection pump flange bolts and slide injection pump rearward out of timing gear case.

If governor, automatic timing device, fuel pump or fuel injection pump are faulty, tear down of injection pump is required. Injection pump should be tested and repaired in a shop that specializes in injection pump repair.

To reinstall pump, number 1 piston must be at TDC on compression. Align mark on pump gear with mark on pump mounting plate as shown in Fig. CH6-9A, then install pump assembly. Note that gear mark will move as shown in Fig. CH6-9A when gears mesh.

INJECTION NOZZLES

REMOVE AND REINSTALL. Before removing injection nozzles thoroughly clean nozzles and surrounding cylinder head area using clean fuel and compressed air. Disconnect fuel injection and return lines. Unscrew nozzles from precombustion chambers and remove gasket from precombustion chamber. Cover all open fuel lines and precombustion chamber to prevent any dirt from entering cylinder.

Install a new copper gasket on end of nozzle nut and screw nozzle holder into precombustion chamber then tighten to 78.4-98.0 N·m. Install fuel injection and return lines. Bleed fuel system as previously outlined.

TESTING. A complete job of testing and adjusting injection nozzles requires use of special testing equipment. Only clean testing oil should be used to test nozzles. Nozzle should be tested for opening pressure, seat leakage and spray pattern.

When operating properly during test, nozzle will emit a buzzing sound and cut off quickly with no fluid leakage at seat.

Before conducting test, operate tester lever until test oil flows, then attach nozzle. Close valve to tester gage and pump tester lever a few quick strokes to be sure nozzle valve is not stuck, which would indicate that nozzle may be ser-

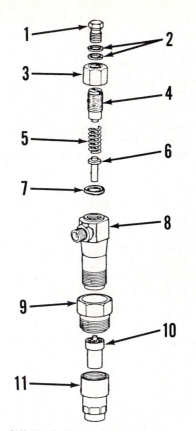

Fig. CH6-10 — Exploded view of injection nozzle used on CM6-55 engines.

1. Hollow screw
2. Washer
3. Nut
4. Adjusting screw
5. Spring
6. Pin
7. Washer
8. Body
9. Nozzle holder
10. Nozzle and valve
11. Nozzle nut

viceable without disassembly.

WARNING: Fuel emerges from nozzle with sufficient force to penetrate skin. When testing nozzle, keep yourself clear of nozzle spray.

OPENING PRESSURE. Operate pump at a rate of 60 strokes per minute and note opening pressure of nozzle. Opening pressure should be 10.78-12.74 MPa. If pressure is not correct, adjust pressure by turning adjusting screw (4 – Fig. CH6-10).

SEAT LEAKAGE. Slowly raise tester pressure to 10.29 MPa and check nozzle tip for any signs of wetness or dripping. Nozzle tip should remain dry at this pressure for at least 30 seconds.

SPRAY PATTERN. The type of nozzle used in CM6-55 engines produces two kinds of spray: "throttle injection" and "main injection". Throttle injection is first, smaller in volume and is made up of narrow streams of large particles of fuel. Main injection follows with a sudden increase in volume and wider streams of fine particles of fuel. Both kinds of spray patterns should be tested.

Chrysler

Test throttle injection spray pattern by operating tester handle at a rate of one stroke per second. Fuel should emerge in steady smooth pulses while making a hissing sound. Fuel spray does not have to break off cleanly during throttle injection phase. Spray should come out in line with nozzle and be slightly conical in shape.

Test main injection spray pattern by operating tester lever at a rate of 4-6 strokes per second. Spray should emerge from nozzle in a 4° wide pattern in line with nozzle tip. Spray should be highly atomized and break off cleanly between strokes. Nozzle tip should not become wet between strokes.

OVERHAUL. Hard or sharp tools, emery cloth, grinding compound or other than approved solvents or lapping compounds must never be used. An approved nozzle cleaning kit is available through a number of specialized sources.

Wipe all dirt and loose carbon from exterior of nozzle and holder assembly. Refer to Fig. CH6-10 for exploded view and proceed as follows:

Place body (8) in a vise and loosen nut (11). Remove nozzle (10) with needle valve. Remove holder (9). Remove cap nut (3) and adjusting screw (4). Take body (8) out of vise and carefully remove pressure spring (5), pin (6) and washer (7).

Remove carbon from all parts by soaking them in a suitable carbon solvent and using a scraper made of soft wood. Check that needle valve will slide smoothly in and out of nozzle tip and that it fits well. Inspect body (8) for wear with a magnifying glass. Check pin (6) for wear. Inspect pressure spring (5) for cracks, damage or sagging. Inspect contact surfaces of pin (6) and needle valve for wear.

Reassemble nozzle as follows: Place body (8) in a vise and install washer (7), pressure pin (6) and pressure spring (5). Install adjusting screw (4) finger tight and install cap nut (3). Turn assembly upside down and install cylinder screw (9). Place nozzle (10) and needle valve in nozzle nut (11) and install them onto body (8). Tighten nozzle nut (11) to 58.8-78.4 N·m while making sure that assembly is centered.

CYLINDER HEAD

ROCKER ARMS AND SHAFT ASSEMBLY. Before loosening bolts holding rocker arm shaft brackets to cylinder head, coolant must be drained from cylinder block as these bolts pass through coolant passages and also act as cylinder head bolts. When removing rocker arm shaft bracket bolts follow

Chrysler INBOARD ENGINES

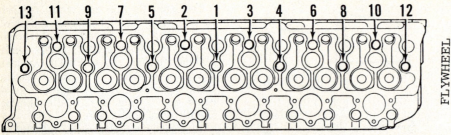

Fig. CH6-11 – Loosen cylinder head bolts in sequence shown when removing rocker arm shaft and brackets.

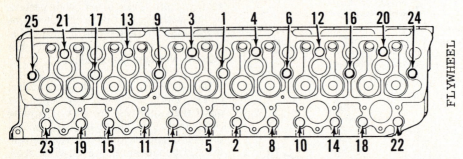

Fig. CH6-12 – Use bolt tightening sequence shown when installing cylinder head on crankcase or rocker arm shaft and brackets on cylinder head. When removing cylinder head from crankcase, loosen cylinder head bolts in same order as they are tightened.

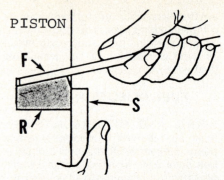

Fig. CH6-14 – To properly check side clearance of top, keystone type compression ring (R), hold ring face flush with side of piston using a straightedge (S). Then insert a feeler gage (F) of the proper thickness between top of ring and top of piston ring groove as shown.

removal sequence shown in Fig. CH6-11. After lifting rocker arm shaft and arms from cylinder head, remove bolts securing rocker shaft supports to rocker shaft and slide components from shaft and place in order of removal for ease in assembly.

Inspect all parts for wear and renew as necessary. Renew any push rods that are bent more than 0.4 mm. Assemble rocker arm shaft and brackets in opposite order of disassembly. Place rocker assembly on cylinder head and insert cylinder head bolts. Tighten head bolts in sequence shown in Fig. CH6-12. On NA models torque head bolts to 176.4-194.0 N·m. On TI and TW engines torque cylinder head bolts to 196.0-202.8 N·m. Tighten all bolts as shown; not just those removed. Adjust all valve clearances as previously outlined.

WATER DIRECTORS. Water passages at bottom of cylinder head contain flow-directors which aim coolant around exhaust ports and bridge between valves. Renew director if it shows any sign of wear. Place new part in cylinder head and aim director at bridge between intake and exhaust valve as shown in Fig. CH6-13.

VALVE GUIDES. Intake and exhaust valve stem-to-guide clearance should be 0.55-0.85 mm. If clearance is excessive renew valve guide by driving old guide out of cylinder head from gasket side and pressing a new guide in from top of cylinder head. Measure valve guide protrusion from valve spring seat to top of valve guide which should be 22.5 mm.

VALVE SEATS. If valve seat requires refacing, check to see that sufficient stock remains. If valve seat is less than 1.35 mm thick or loose in cylinder head it must be renewed. To renew valve seat, reduce thickness of valve seat to 0.5-1.0 mm, using an end mill or valve seat cutter and pry remaining part of seat from cylinder head. Measure ID of valve seat cavity, if ID exceeds 46.025 mm for intake valve seats or 39.025 mm for exhaust valve seats an oversize seat must be used. Valve seat to cylinder head fit is an interference of 0.5-0.8 mm. Place new seat in dry ice while heating cylinder head to 100° C. Insert cooled seat into cylinder head and let temperature stabilize before cutting valve seat or staking seat into head.

CAUTION: Do not handle cooled valve seat with bare hands as severe burns will result.

PISTONS

Pistons are available in standard size, 0.50 mm, 0.75 mm, and 1.0 mm oversizes. Standard bore pistons and liners are a select fit and classified A, B or C. To determine class of standard size piston, measure piston diameter 77.0 mm down from top and at right angles to the piston pin bore. Class A pistons measure 97.865-97.874 mm; class B pistons measure 97.875-97.885 mm; class C pistons measure 97.886-97.895 mm.

Pistons must match each other in weight. Weight difference must not exceed 5 grams from heaviest to lightest piston.

Piston pin is free floating and retained by snap rings at each end. To remove or install piston pin, heat piston in water to 100° C.

Top compression ring is keystone type on TI and TW models and semi-keystone type on NA engines. Ring end gap should be 0.3-0.5 mm with a maximum allowable gap of 1.5 mm when installed in a standard liner, and not less than 12.5 mm when free. A free gap of less than 12.5 mm indicates lost tension or ring set. When checking top ring side clearance hold ring in groove with a straightedge and check side clearance with a feeler gage as shown in Fig. CH6-14. Top ring side clearance must be 0.04-0.08 mm.

Second compression ring and oil control ring installed end gap must be 0.3-0.5 mm. Maximum allowable installed

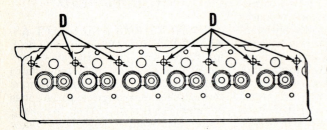

Fig. CH6-13 – When installing new water flow directors (D) in cylinder head be sure they are pointed in direction indicated by arrows.

Illustration courtesy Chrysler

INBOARD ENGINES

Chrysler

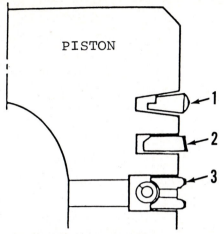

Fig. CH6-15—Install top compression ring (1), keystone type, with notch facing up. Second compression ring (2) is installed with bevel facing top of piston. Oil control ring (3) is installed in third groove.

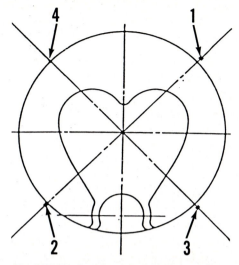

Fig. CH6-16—Position ring end gaps as shown.

1. Top compression ring end gap
2. Second compression ring end gap
3. Oil control ring rail gaps
4. Oil control ring expander gap

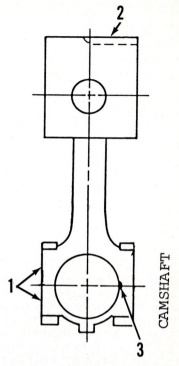

Fig. CH6-17—Install piston on connecting rod so precombustion chamber (2) is located opposite connecting rod weight markings (1). Install piston and rod assembly in crankcase so connecting rod weight markings (1) are opposite camshaft.

end gap is 1.5 mm. Second compression ring free gap must not be less than 12.5 mm. Side clearance for both second compression ring and oil control ring must be 0.025-0.065 mm.

Install piston rings on piston as shown in Fig. CH6-15 with ring gaps located as illustrated in Fig. CH6-16. Piston should be installed on connecting rod so weight stamped side of connecting rod is opposite precombustion chamber in piston crown. See Fig. CH6-17. Install piston and connecting rod assembly in engine so weight stamp on rod is opposite camshaft.

CONNECTING RODS

Connecting rod weights must be checked. When renewing a connecting rod, use a new rod that matches remaining connecting rods in weight. Connecting rods are marked by weight as follows:

Mark	Weight
A	1753-1772 grams
B	1733-1752 grams
C	1713-1732 grams
W	1833-1852 grams
X	1813-1832 grams
Y	1793-1812 grams
Z	1773-1792 grams

CAMSHAFT

Check camshaft lobes, oil pump drive gear and bearing surfaces for scratches, uneven wear and damage. Surface scratches may be burnished. Do not grind or alter cam lobes. Calculate camshaft lobe height by subtracting lobe width measurement (W—Fig. CH6-18) from height measurement (H). Difference must be 6.690-7.189 mm. If lobe height is less than 6.690 mm renew camshaft.

CRANKSHAFT

Inspection of crankshaft is primarily dimensional checking of crankshaft journals and checking for straightness. Obvious wear or damage should be checked first to see if crankshaft is repairable. When checking crankshaft for straightness, support crankshaft on V-blocks at front and rear main bearing journals. Use a dial indicator to measure runout of center main bearing journal. A reading of 0.00-0.05 mm is acceptable; 0.05-0.07 mm is repairable. A reading in excess of 0.07 mm is not repairable and crankshaft must be renewed.

CYLINDER LINERS

Cylinder liners are renewable or may be rebored to 0.50 mm, 0.75 mm or 1.00 mm oversize. Replacement liners are matched to the original bore size of 98.0 mm. New standard cylinder liners are classified as A, B or C and only same letter classification pistons may be used. To determine standard cylinder liner class, measure liner inside diameter 90 mm down from top of liner and compare this measurement to the following table:

Class	Liner Diameter
A	98.000-98.011 mm
B	98.012-98.023 mm
C	98.024-98.035 mm

Before installing cylinder liners in cylinder block thoroughly clean block bore. Lubricate new liner "O" rings in soapy water and install them on liner. Align notch in liner with left side of cylinder

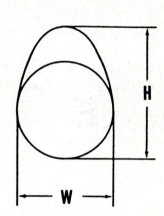

Fig. CH6-18—To determine camshaft lobe height, measure lobe width (W) and height (H) and refer to text.

block, grasp liner with both hands and gently push liner into block without any twisting motion. Use a soft mallet and gently tap around top of liner to seat "O" rings. Measure liner protrusion using a dial indicator; liner should protrude 0.11-0.20 mm.

OIL PUMP

R&R AND OVERHAUL. Oil pump is camshaft driven at one half crankshaft speed and externally mounted on right side of engine. To remove oil pump, re-

Chrysler — INBOARD ENGINES

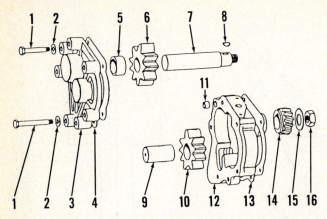

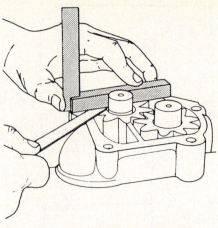

Fig. CH6-19 — Exploded view of externally mounted oil pump used on CM6-55 engines.

1. Cover bolts
2. Washers
3. Cover
4. Cover gasket
5. Drive shaft bushing
6. Drive gear
7. Drive shaft
8. Key
9. Driven shaft
10. Driven gear
11. Alignment pin
12. Housing
13. Gasket
14. Camshaft driven gear
15. Washer
16. Nut

Fig. CH6-21 — If oil pump gear to cover clearance is greater than 0.15 mm, gears and/or housing must be renewed.

move screw and retainer plate securing oil cooler lines to top of pump, then remove five screws retaining pump to side of engine block. Lift oil cooler lines from top of pump and separate pump from crankcase. Turn pump to left far enough to remove line leading to relief valve and pull pump from engine.

Disassemble pump (Fig. CH6-19) and inspect parts for defects and wear. Put gears back in pump body and measure clearance between gear teeth and body as shown in Fig. CH6-20. Clearance should be 0.11-0.20 mm. Measure clearance between gear face and pump body as shown in Fig. CH6-21. This clearance should be 0.02-0.15 mm. Gear width should be 32.019-32.040 mm. Oil pump drive shaft diameter should be 19.9-20.0 mm and shaft to bushing clearance must be 0.04-0.15 mm.

Check oil cooler bypass valve opening pressure. Valve should open at 166.6-225.4 kPa. Pressure is adjusted by adding or removing shims (2 – Fig. CH6-22). A 1 mm change in shim thickness will alter valve opening pressure 17.34 kPa.

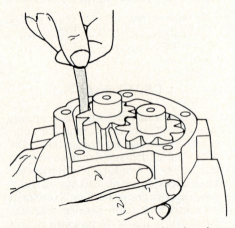

Fig. CH6-20 — If oil pump gear to housing clearance is greater than 0.20 mm, gears and/or housing must be renewed.

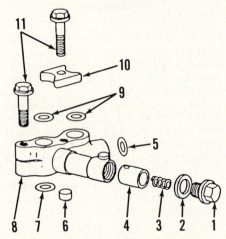

Fig. CH6-22 — Exploded view of pressure relief valve used on CM6-55 engine oil pump.

1. Cap nut
2. Shim
3. Spring
4. Valve
5. Gasket
6. Alignment pin
7. Gasket
8. Housing
9. Gaskets
10. Bridge
11. Mounting bolts

INBOARD ENGINES   Crusader

CRUSADER

THERMO ELECTRON ENGINE CORP.
7100 East 15 Mile Road
Sterling Heights, Michigan 48077

ENGINE SERVICE DATA

ENGINE MODEL	185
General	
Cylinders	6
Bore	3.87 in.
Stroke	4.12 in.
Displacement—Cu. In.	292
Compression Ratio	7.8:1
Compression Pressure at Cranking Speed	140 psi
Main Bearings, Number Of	7
Firing Order:*	
RH Rotation	1-4-2-6-3-5
LH Rotation	1-5-3-6-2-4
Numbering System (Front to Rear)	1-2-3-4-5-6

*RH rotation is clockwise at output end of engine while LH rotation is counterclockwise.

Tune-Up	
Valve Lifter Type	Hydraulic
Valve lash	¾ Turn Down From Zero Lash
Valve Seat Angle	46°
Valve Face Angle	45°
Valve Seat Width:	
Intake	1/32-1/16 inch
Exhaust	1/16-3/32 inch
Valve Spring Length	1.90
Installed Spring Height	1-21/32 inches
Valve Stem Clearance:	
Intake	0.0010-0.0027 in.
Exhaust	0.0015-0.0032 in.
Timing Mark Location	Crankshaft Pulley
Ignition Timing	10° BTDC
Cam Angle (Dwell)	31°-34°
Breaker Point Gap	0.018 in.
Spark Plug Type	RBL-8
Spark Plug Gap	0.035 in.
Carburetor Type	Rochester 2G
Float Level	⅝-inch
Float Drop	1-31/32 inches
Engine Idle Speed	550-650 rpm

Sizes — Capacities — Clearances	
Crankshaft Journal Diameter	2.2983-2.2993 in.
Main Bearing Clearance	0.0035 Max.
Crankpin Diameter	1.999-2.000 in.

ENGINE MODEL	185
Sizes — Capacities — Clearances (Cont.)	
Rod Bearing Clearance	0.0035 Max.
Rod Side Clearance	0.008-0.014 in.
Crankshaft End Play	0.002-0.006 in.
Piston Pin Diameter	0.9270-0.9273 in.
Pin Clearance In Piston	0.001 Max.
Pin Clearance In Rod	Interference
Piston Clearance	0.0025-0.0045 in.
Piston Ring End Gap	0.010-0.020 in.
Ring Side Clearance:	
Top Comp.	0.0012-0.0032 in.
2nd Comp.	0.0012-0.0027 in.
Oil	0.005 in.
Camshaft Journal Diameter	1.8682-1.8692 in.
Camshaft Runout	0.0015 in. Max.
Crankcase Capacity W/Filter	6 Qts.
Oil Pressure at 2000 rpm	30-45 psi
Fuel Pump Pressure	4-7 psi
Fuel Required	Leaded 93 Octane Research

Tightening Torques
(All values are in foot pounds.)

	Torque Rating
Camshaft Thrust Plate	80 in.-lbs.
Connecting Rod Cap	35
Crankshaft Front Cover	80 in.-lbs.
Crankshaft Pulley	60
Cylinder Head	95
Distributor Clamp	20
Exhaust to Inlet Manifold	25
Flywheel	60
Flywheel Housing Pan	80 in.-lbs.
Main Bearing Caps	65
Manifold Clamps	20-25
Oil Pan to Crankcase:	
4-20 Screws	80 in.-lbs.
5/16-18 Screws	75 in.-lbs.
Oil Pan to Front Cover	50 in.-lbs.
Oil Pump	115 in.-lbs.
Oil Pump Cover	70 in.-lbs.
Push Rod Cover	50 in.-lbs.
Rocker Arm Cover	45 in.-lbs.
Spark Plugs	15
Temperature Sending Unit	20
Thermostat Housing	15
Water Pump	15

MAINTENANCE

CARBURETOR

Rochester 2G

IDLE MIXTURE. Turn idle mixture screws clockwise to lean mixture.

FLOAT ADJUSTMENT. Carburetor float level should be ⅝ inch. Invert air horn assembly and measure distance from edge of float seam to air horn gasket surface as shown in Fig. CR1-1. Bend float arm as shown in Fig. CR1-1 to adjust float level.

Float drop should be 1-31/32 inch. Hold air horn assembly in its installed position and measure distance between air horn gasket surface and bottom of float as shown in Fig. CR1-2. Bend float arm tang to adjust float drop.

ACCELERATOR PUMP. To check accelerator pump action, be sure pump

Illustration courtesy Thermo Electron

Crusader — INBOARD ENGINES

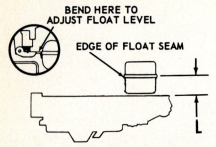

Fig. CR1-1 – Adjust carburetor float level as shown above. Float level (L) should be 5/8-inch.

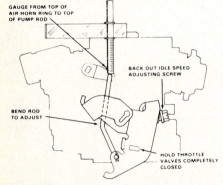

Fig. CR1-2 – Adjust float drop as shown above. Float drop (D) should be 1-31/32 inches.

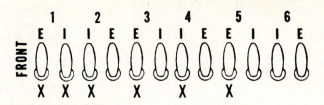

Fig. CR1-4 – Adjust valves statically on left hand rotating engines as explained in text. Valves marked "X" should be adjusted when No. 1 piston is at TDC on compression.

rod is in outer hole of pump arm, backout idle speed screw until throttle valves are closed, and measure from top of air horn next to pump plunger to top of pump rod. Measurement should be 1 5/8 inch as shown in Fig. CR1-3. Bend pump rod to adjust.

REPAIR

VALVE ADJUSTMENT

The valves may be adjusted with engine stopped. Turn crankshaft until number 1 (front) piston is at TDC on compression stroke and adjust valves indicated by "X" in Figs. CR1-4 or CR1-5. Rotate crankshaft exactly one turn, again align TDC marks on crankshaft pulley and pointer, and adjust the remaining valves. Second crankshaft setting locates the crankshaft at TDC with number 6 piston on compression stroke.

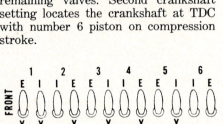

Fig. CR1-5 – Valves marked "X" on right hand rotating engines should be adjusted statically when No. 1 piston is at TDC on compression. See text.

Fig. CR1-6 – Use sequence shown when tightening cylinder head bolts.

PISTONS

Notch cast into top of piston should be toward front of engine. Compression rings are marked with letters which should be toward top of piston. See Fig. CR1-6 for cylinder head bolt tightening sequence.

CAMSHAFT

Camshaft end play should be 0.001-0.005 inch. Maximum camshaft gear runout is 0.003 inch. Camshaft gear backlash is 0.004-0.006 inch. Note location of timing marks in Fig. CR1-7.

Fig. CR1-7 – View of timing marks on camshaft and crankshaft gears.

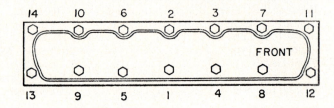

Illustration courtesy Thermo Electron

INBOARD ENGINES   Crusader

CRUSADER

ENGINE SERVICE DATA

ENGINE MODEL	CH220	CH270	CH350
General			
Cylinders	V8	V8	V8
Bore	*3.74 in.	4.00 in.	4.25 in.
Stroke	*3.48 in.	3.48 in.	4.00 in.
Displacement – Cu. In.	*305	350	454
Compression Ratio	8.4:1	8.8:1	8.6:1
Compression Pressure at Cranking Speed	←———— 150 psi ————→		
Main Bearings, Number Of	←———————— 5 ————————→		
Numbering System (Front to Rear)			
Port Bank	←———— 1-3-5-7 ————→		
Starboard Bank	←———— 2-4-6-8 ————→		
Firing Order:#			
RH Rotation	←———— 1-2-7-5-6-3-4-8 ————→		
LH Rotation	←———— 1-8-4-3-6-5-7-2 ————→		

*Model CH220 prior to Sept. 1975 has 3.87 in. bore, 3.27 in. stroke and 307 cu. in. displacement.
#RH rotation is clockwise at output end of engine while LH rotation is counterclockwise.

Tune-Up			
Valve Lifter Type	←———————— Hydraulic ————————→		
Valve Lash	←———— ¾ Turn Down From Zero Lash ————→		
Valve Seat Angle	←———————— 46° ————————→		
Valve Face Angle	←———————— 45° ————————→		
Valve Seat Width:			
Intake	←———— 1/32-1/16 in. ————→		
Exhaust	←———— 1/16-3/32 in. ————→		
Valve Spring Length	2.08 in.	2.08 in.	2.09 in.
Installed Spring height	1.656 in.	1.656 in.	1.875 in.
Valve Spring Pressure:			
Closed (lbs. @ in.)	76-84 at 1.70	76-84 at 1.70	74-86 at 1.88
Open (lbs. @ in.)	194-206 at 1.25	194-206 at 1.25	288-312 at 1.38
Valve Stem Clearance:			
Intake	←———— 0.0010-0.0027 in. ————→		
Exhaust	←———— 0.0015-0.0032 in. ————→		
Timing Mark Location	←———— Crankshaft Pulley ————→		
Ignition Timing	←———— 10° BTDC ————→		
Cam Angle (Dwell)	←———— 28°-31° ————→		
Breaker Point Gap	←———— 0.016 in. ————→		
Spark Plug Type	←———— RBL-8 ————→		
Spark Plug Gap	←———— 0.035 in. ————→		
Carburetor Type	←———— Rochester 4MV ————→		
Float Level	←———— ¼-inch ————→		
Engine Idle Speed	←———— 550-650 rpm ————→		

Sizes – Capacities – Clearances			
Crankshaft Journal Diameter:			
No. 1	2.4484-2.4493 in.	2.4484-2.4493 in.	2.7485-2.7494 in.
Nos. 2-4	2.4481-2.4491 in.	2.4481-2.4491 in.	2.7481-2.7490 in.
No. 5	2.4479-2.4488 in.	2.4479-2.4488 in.	2.7478-2.7488 in.
Main Bearing Clearance – Max.	0.0035 in.	0.0035 in.	0.0035 in.
Crankpin Diameter	2.099-2.100 in.	2.099-2.100 in.	2.199-2.200 in.
Rod Bearing Clearance – Max.	0.0035 in.	0.0035 in.	0.0035 in.
Rod Side Clearance	0.008-0.014 in.	0.008-0.014 in.	0.013-0.021 in.
Crankshaft End Play	0.002-0.006 in.	0.002-0.006 in.	0.006-0.010 in.
Piston Pin Diameter	0.9270-0.9273 in.	0.9270-0.9273 in.	0.9895-0.9898 in.
Pin Clearance in Piston – Max.	0.001 in.	0.001 in.	0.001 in.
Pin Clearance in Rod	Interference	Interference	Interference

Illustration courtesy Thermo Electron

Crusader — INBOARD ENGINES

ENGINE SERVICE DATA CONT.

ENGINE MODEL	CH220	CH270	CH350
Sizes — Capacities — Cleaarances (Cont.)			
Piston Clearance	0.0036-0.0042 in.	0.0034-0.0049 in.	0.0034-0.0049 in.
Piston Ring End Gap	0.010-0.020 in.	0.010-0.020 in.	0.010-0.020 in.
Ring Side Clearance:			
Top Comp.	0.0012-0.0032 in.	0.0012-0.0032 in.	0.0017-0.0032 in.
2nd Comp.	0.0012-0.0027 in.	0.0012-0.0027 in.	0.0017-0.0032 in.
Camshaft Journal Diameter	1.8682-1.8692 in.	1.8682-1.8692 in.	1.9482-1.9492 in.
Camshaft Runout — Max.	0.0015 in.	0.0015 in.	0.0015 in.
Crankcase Capacity W/Filter	6 qts.	6 qts.	6-7 qts.
Oil Pressure at 2000 rpm	30-45 psi		
Fuel Pump Pressure	4-7 psi		
Fuel Required	Leaded 93 Octane Research		

Tightening Torques
(All values are in foot pounds.)

ENGINE MODEL	CH220, CH270	CH350
Camshaft Sprocket	20	20
Connecting Rod Cap	45	50
Crankshaft Damper	60	85
Cylinder Head	65	80
Exhaust Manifold	20	20
Flywheel	60	65
Flywheel Housing to Block	25	25
Flywheel Cover to Housing	80 in.-lbs.	80 in.-lbs.
Intake Manifold	30	30
Main Bearing Cap	75	105
Oil Pump	65	65
Oil Pump Cover	80 in.-lbs.	80 in.-lbs.
Rocker Arm Cover	45 in.-lbs.	50 in.-lbs.
Spark Plug	15	15
Timing Case Cover	80 in.-lbs.	80 in.-lbs.
Water Pump	30	30

MAINTENANCE

CARBURETOR

Rochester 4MV

IDLE MIXTURE. Turning idle mixture screws clockwise leans idle mixture.

FLOAT ADJUSTMENTS. Remove air horn assembly. Gently but firmly push float and needle assembly down into needle seat and measure distance from fuel bowl gasket surface to toe of float. Measurement should be ¼ inch. See Fig. CR2-1. Bend float up or down to adjust.

ACCELERATOR PUMP. To check accelerator pump adjustment, throttle valves must be completely closed and pump rod must be in inner hole of pump lever. Measure from top of choke valve wall, next to vent stack, to top of pump stem as shown in Fig. CR2-2. Dimension should be 9/32 inch. Bend pump rod to adjust.

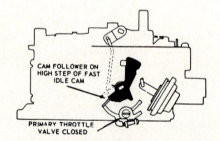

Fig. CR2-3 — To adjust fast idle, turn fast idle screw in two turns after screw is fully seated. Primary valves must be completely open and cam follower on high step to fast idle cam when making adjustment.

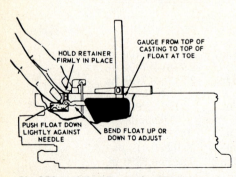

Fig. CR2-1 — Adjust Rochester 4MV float level as shown above. Float level should be ¼-inch.

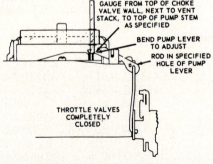

Fig. CR2-2 — There must be 9/32-inch between top of accelerator pump stem and top of choke valve wall next to vent stack for correct accelerator pump action. Bend pump rod to adjust.

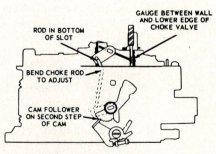

Fig. CR2-4 — Adjust choke rod as outlined in text.

Illustration courtesy Thermo Electron

INBOARD ENGINES

Crusader

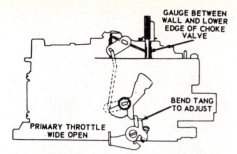

Fig. CR2-5 — Refer to text for adjusting the choke unloader on Rochester 4MV carburetors.

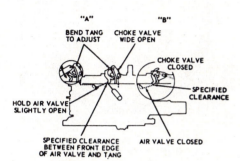

Fig. CR2-6 — Check lockout clearance as shown. Recommended clearance is less than 0.015 inch, but parts should not touch.

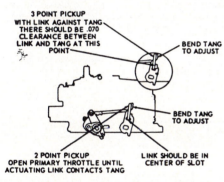

Fig. CR2-7 — Secondary opening should be checked and adjusted for 2- or 3-point pickup as shown.

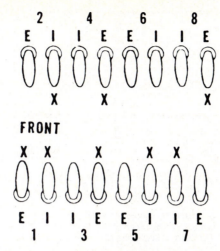

Fig. CR2-9 — Valves marked "X" can be adjusted on left hand rotating models with No. 1 piston at TDC on compression stroke. Adjust remaining valves with No. 6 piston at TDC on compression stroke.

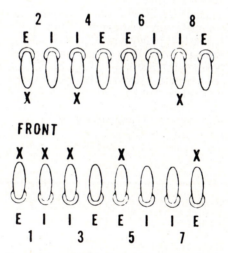

Fig. CR2-10 — Valves marked "X" can be adjusted on right hand rotation models with No. 1 piston at TDC on compression stroke.

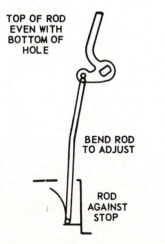

Fig. CR2-8 — Adjust choke coil rod as outlined in text.

FAST IDLE. To adjust fast idle primary valves must be completely closed and cam follower must be on high step of fast idle cam as shown in Fig. CR2-3. Turn fast idle screw in two turns after screw contacts the cam. After adjusting fast idle, check choke rod adjustment. Place cam follower on second step of fast idle cam and against high step. Rotate choke valve towards closed position by pushing down on vacuum break lever. Measure between lower edge of choke valve, at choke lever end and carburetor bore (Fig. CR2-4). Dimension should be 0.100 inch.

VACUUM BREAK. To adjust vacuum break, rotate choke valve towards closed position by pushing down on vacuum break lever and seat the vacuum diaphragm using an outside vacuum source. Measure the distance between lower edge of choke valve and air horn wall using a 0.150 inch gage. Bend choke lever tang to adjust.

CHOKE UNLOADER. To check choke unloader adjustment, hold choke valve closed using a rubber band on the vacuum break lever. Move the primary throttle to wide open position and measure choke valve opening. See Fig. CR2-5. Clearance between lower edge of choke valve and air horn wall should be 0.300 inch. Bend tang on fast idle lever to adjust.

SECONDARY ADJUSTMENTS. Check the secondary lockout clearance as shown in Fig. CR2-6. Clearance should be less than 0.015 inch but the parts should not be touching. Refer to Fig. CR2-7 for secondary opening adjustment. Open the carburetor primary throttle when checking.

CHOKE ADJUSTMENT. To adjust choke coil rod, completely close choke valve and position choke rod in bottom

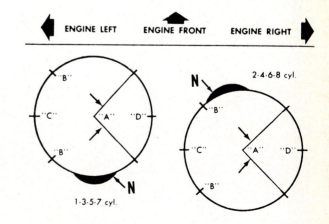

Fig. CR2-11 — Arrange piston ring end gaps as shown. Note location of cylinder block notches (N) on CH350.

A. Oil ring spacer gap (within arc)
B. Oil ring rail gaps
C. 2nd compression ring gap
D. Top compression ring gap

Illustration courtesy Thermo Electron

Crusader

INBOARD ENGINES

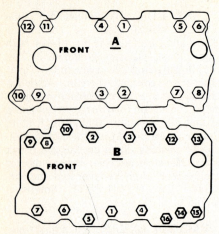

Fig. CR2-12 — Intake manifold tightening sequence. Use sequence (A) for Models CH220 and CH270 and sequence (B) for Model CH350.

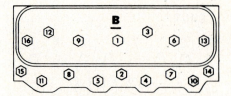

Fig. CR2-13 — Cylinder head tightening sequence. Use sequence (A) for Models CH220 and CH270 and sequence (B) for Model CH350.

Fig. CR2-14 — View showing camshaft and crankshaft sprocket timing marks (T).

of choke lever slot. Pull up on choke coil rod to end of travel. Bend choke coil rod until top of rod is even with bottom of hole in vacuum break lever as shown in Fig. CR2-8.

REPAIR

VALVE ADJUSTMENT

Valves may be adjusted with engine not running, by turning the crankshaft until the number 1 piston is at TDC on compression stroke. The valves marked "X" in Fig. CR2-9 or CR2-10 can be adjusted with number 1 piston on compression stroke. Rotate the crankshaft one complete turn and again align mark on crankshaft pulley with TDC "O" mark on timing plate. This second setting will position the number 6 piston at TDC on compression stroke. The valve not marked in Fig. CR2-9 or CR2-10 can be adjusted with crankshaft at second setting (number 6 piston at TDC on compression).

PISTONS

Compression rings should be installed with marked side of ring toward top of piston. Refer to Fig. CR2-11. Install pistons with notch in piston crown towards front of engine. Oil hole in connecting rod big end must be towards camshaft.

INBOARD ENGINES FORD

FORD

FORD INDUSTRIAL ENGINES OPERATIONS
300 Renaissance Center
Detroit, Michigan 48243

ENGINE SERVICE DATA

ENGINE MODEL	YSD-424	YSD-635
General		
Cylinders	4	6
Bore	3.68 in.	
Stroke	3.36 in.	
Displacement – Cu. In.	144	216
Compression Ratio	21.5:1	
Engine Type	In-Line, 22½°	Inclined to Left
Firing Order	1-2-4-3	1-5-3-6-2-4
Numbering System (Front to Rear)	1-2-3-4	1-2-3-4-5-6
Main Bearings, Number of	5	7
Idle Speed	600-650 rpm	
Tune-Up		
Valve Clearance (Hot):		
Inlet	0.013-0.015 in.	
Exhaust	0.013-0.015 in.	
Valve Lift:		
Inlet	0.384 in.	
Exhaust	0.413 in.	
Camshaft Lobe Lift:		
Inlet	0.256 in.	
Exhaust	0.275 in.	
Oil Pressure (Min.)	15 psi	
Oil Capacity	5¾ qts.	9¾ qts.
Injection Timing	12° BTDC	
Fuel Injector Opening Pressure:		
CAV Micromec	2575 psi	
CAV Minimec	2130 psi	
BOSCH	2575 psi	
Sizes – Clearances		
Valve Guide:		
Internal Diameter –		
Production	0.3539-0.3556 in.	
Service	0.3535-0.3550 in.	
Outside Diameter	0.5795-0.580 in.	
Length	2.42 in.	
Valve Guide Protrusion (Inlet)	0.768 in.	
Valve Seat Insert Recess Diameter:		
Inlet	1.7995-1.8102 in.	
Exhaust	1.4945-1.4960 in.	
Valve Seat Insert Recess Depth:		
Inlet	0.371-0.383 in.	
Exhaust	0.371-0.383 in.	
Valve Seat Angle:		
Inlet	45°-45°30′	
Exhaust	30°-30°30′	

Illustration courtesy Ford

FORD INBOARD ENGINES

ENGINE SERVICE DATA (CONT.)

ENGINE MODEL	YSD-424	YSD-635

Sizes — Clearances (Cont.)

	YSD-424 / YSD-635
Valve Stem Diameter:	
Inlet	0.3520-0.3530 in.
Exhaust	0.3513-0.3523 in.
Valve head Diameter:	
Inlet	1.736-1.748 in.
Exhaust	1.421-1.433 in.
Valve Face Angle:	
Inlet	44°30'-45°
Exhaust	29°30'-30°
Stem Guide Clearance:	
Inlet	0.0006-0.0028 in.
Exhaust	0.0013-0.0035 in.
Valve Margin Minimum	0.008 in.
Valve Spring Free Length:	
Outer Exhaust	2.024 in.
Inner Exhaust	1.854 in.
Inlet	1.765 in.
Push Rod Diameter	0.304-0.316 in.
Push Rod Length	6.08-6.12 in.
Valve Lifter Diameter	0.6288-0.6293 in.
Valve Lifter to Lifter Bore Clearance	0.0006-0.002 in.
Valve Spring Assembled Height (Pad to Retainer):	
Inlet	1.59 in.
Exhaust	1.73 in.
Valve Lifter Length	2.442 in.
Camshaft Journal Diameter	2.205-2.2030 in.
Camshaft End Play	0.002-0.008 in.
Camshaft Journal to Bearing Clearance	0.002-0.0055 in.
Nominal Valve Timing @ 0.021 in. Clearance:	
Inlet Opens	10° BTDC
Inlet Closes	30° ABDC
Exhaust Opens	54° BBDC
Exhaust Closes	10° ATDC
Rocker Shaft Diameter	0.7430 in. / 0.7442 in.
Clearance Between Rocker Arm and Shaft	0.0008-0.003 in.
Main Bearing Journal Diameter:	
Rear	3.0267-3.0275 in.
All Others	2.7550-2.7560 in.
Crankshaft Journals (All)	
Out-of-Round (Max.)	0.0004-0.0002 in. in 90°
Taper (Max.)	0.0003 in. per inch
Connecting Rod Journal Diameter	2.3617-2.3622 in.
Connecting Rod Journal Length	1.2709-1.2748 in.
Connecting Rod Journal Clearance	0.0015-0.0035 in.
Crankshaft End Play	0.002-0.010 in.
Main Bearing Clearance	0.0020-0.0034 in.
Main Journal Length:	
Front	1.100-1.120 in.
Intermediate	1.3402-1.3505 in.
Rear	1.185-1.215 in.
Connecting Rod Piston Pin Bushing ID	1.1421-1.1426 in.
Connecting Rod Big End Diameter	2.500-2.504 in.

Rocker Shaft Diameter: YSD-424 = 0.7430 in.; YSD-635 = 0.7442 in.

Illustration courtesy Ford

INBOARD ENGINES

Ford

ENGINE SERVICE DATA (CONT.)

ENGINE MODEL	YSD-424	YSD-635

Sizes -- Clearances (Cont.)

Connecting Rod Bearing Clearance	0.0014-0.0035 in.
Connecting Rod Piston Pin Clearance	0.0005-0.0013 in.
Connecting Rod Length: Center-to-Center	6.065-6.066 in.
Piston Ring Groove Width:	
Compression	0.0951-0.0965 in.
Oil Control	0.188-0.189 in.
Piston-to-Cylinder Clearance	0.0045-0.0084 in.
Piston Diameter: Grade –	
1.	3.6814-3.6819 in.
2.	3.6819-3.6824 in.
3.	3.6824-3.6829 in.
4.	3.6829-3.6834 in.
Piston and Rod Weight Variation	18 Grams
Piston Pin Type	Full Floating
Piston Pin Diameter	1.1413-1.1416 in.
Piston Pin Length	2.923-2.933 in.
Piston Pin-to-Piston Clearance at 70°F	0.0000-0.0002 in.
Piston Ring End Cap:	
1st and 2nd	0.010-0.020 in.
Oil Control	0.010-0.023 in.
Piston Ring-to-Groove Clearance:	
1st and 2nd	0.0016-0.0035 in.
Oil Control	0.0015-0.0030 in.
Cylinder Bore Diameter Measured 3.50 in. from Top of Liner: Grade –	
1.	3.6869-3.6874 in.
2.	3.6874-3.6879 in.
3.	3.6879-3.6884 in.
4.	3.6884-3.6889 in.
Oil Pump Type	Centrifugal
Oil Pump Rotor Assembly End Clearance (Assembled)	0.006 in.
Oil Pump Inner-to-Outer Rotor Clearance	0.0007-0.012 in.

Tightening Torques

(All values are in ft.-lbs.)

Camshaft Gear	55-70
Camshaft Thrust Plate	18-22
Connecting Rod Nuts:	
1st Stage	35-45
2nd Stage	45-55
Cylinder Head Bolts	100-110
Damper or Pulley	230-250
Exhaust Manifold	30-37
Flywheel	43-47
Front Cover	18-22
Front Housing Cylinder Block Bolts:	
1 to 9	20-23
10	15-18
Fuel Pump	12-15
Injection Pump Bolts	15-20
Injection Pump Timing Gear	11-15

Illustration courtesy Ford

Ford INBOARD ENGINES

ENGINE SERVICE DATA (CONT.)

ENGINE MODEL	YSD-424	YSD-635

Tightening Torques (Cont.)
- Injector Leak Off Pipe .... ——— 11-15 ———
- Injector Nozzle Nut .... ——— 43-58 ———
- Injector Retaining Bolt .... ——— 11-14.5 ———
- Intake Manifold .... ——— 8-10 ———
- Oil Pan .... ——— 10-15 ———
- Oil Pump Cover .... ——— 10-15 ———
- Rocker Shaft Bolts:
    - M10 .... ——— 48-51 ———
    - M8 .... ——— 12-15 ———
- Water Pump .... ——— 10-15 ———

Alternator Service Data

BOSCH
- DC Output @ 12 v .... ——— 35 amps ———
- Stator Winding Resistance .... ——— 3.4 ohms ———
- Exciter Winding Resistance .... ——— 4.0 ohms ———
- Slip Ring Runout (max.) .... ——— 0.001 in. ———
- Rotor Pole Wheel Runout (max.) .... ——— 0.002 in. ———
- Carbon Brush Length (min.) .... ——— 0.563 in. ———
- Brush Spring Pressure .... ——— 10.7-14.1 oz. ———
- Slip Ring Diameter (min.) .... ——— 1.25 in. ———

LUCAS
- DC Output @ 12 v .... ——— 36 amps ———
- Alternator Controlled Voltage .... ——— 13.6-14.4 volts ———
- Max. Permissible Speed .... ——— 15,000 rpm ———
- Rotor Field Winding Resistance:
    - Pink Windings .... ——— 4.2 ohms ———
    - Green Windings .... ——— 3.2 ohms ———
- Brush Spring Pressure .... ——— 9-13 oz. ———
- Brush Length:
    - New .... ——— 0.5 in. ———
    - Minimum .... ——— 0.03 in. ———

MAINTENANCE

LUBRICATION

Under normal operating conditions it is recommended that engine oil and filter be changed after every 100 hours of operation or seasonally, whichever is more frequent. Use a high quality API specification SF or SE oil. See Fig. F1-1 for viscosity recommendations.

FUEL SYSTEM

BLEED FUEL SYSTEM. Fig. F1-2 shows a diagram of fuel system. To bleed fuel system open fuel filter bleed screw (1—Fig. F1-3) and operate fuel pump priming lever (L—Fig. F1-4) until air-free fuel appears, then close fuel

Fig. F1-1 — Use chart shown to determine correct oil viscosity for ambient temperature.

SINGLE VISCOSITY OILS

When Outside Temperature is Consistently	Use SAE Viscosity Number
−10°F. to +60°F.	*10W
+10°F. to +90°F.	20W-20
Above +32°F.	30
Above +50°F.	40

MULTI VISCOSITY OILS

When Outside Temperature is Consistently	Use SAE Viscosity Number
Below +14°F.	*5W-20
Below +60°F.	5W-30
−10°F. to 90°F.	10W-30
Above −10°F.	10W-40 or 10W-50
Above +20°F.	20W-40 or 20W-50

*Not recommended for severe service — including high RPM operation.

Illustration courtesy Ford

INBOARD ENGINES

Ford

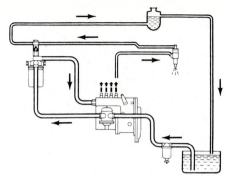

Fig. F1-2—Diagram of YSD engine series fuel system.

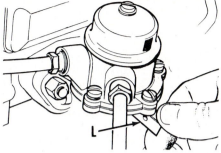

Fig. F1-4—Illustration showing location of fuel system priming pump lever (L).

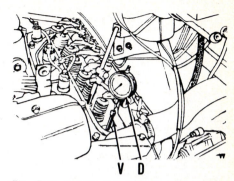

Fig. F1-6—Install dial indicator (D) against number 1 cylinder exhaust valve stem (V) and check fuel injection pump timing as outlined in text.

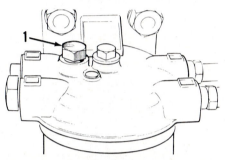

Fig. F1-3—Illustration showing location of fuel filter bleed screw (1).

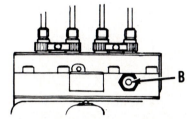

Fig. F1-5—Illustration showing location of fuel injection pump bleed screw (B).

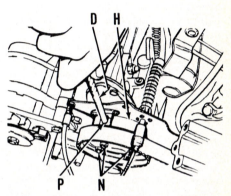

Fig. F1-7—Use a ¼-inch drift (D) to check alignment of fuel injection pump housing (H) and timing plate (P). Loosen nuts (N) and turn housing (H) to time fuel injection pump as outlined in text.

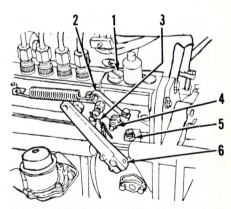

Fig. F1-8—Illustration showing location of injection pump controls and adjustment points.

1. Oil filler plug
2. Stop control lever
3. Maximum speed stop screw
4. Excess fuel device
5. Idle stop screw
6. Engine speed control lever

filter bleed screw. Unscrew fuel injection pump bleed screw (B—Fig. F1-5) and operate priming lever as before until air-free fuel appears, then tighten injection pump bleed screw. If fuel priming lever appears inoperative rotate engine until lever becomes effective.

FUEL PUMP. Fuel lift pump is located on injection pump and is injection pump camshaft operated. Pump incorporates a fuel priming lever (L—Fig. F1-4) which is used to bleed fuel system. With engine running at idle, fuel pump should produce a vacuum of 8½-inches Mercury. Pump should also produce 5 to 8 psi of fuel pressure throughout engine's operating speed range.

INJECTION PUMP TIMING. To check or set injection pump timing, position number 1 piston at TDC on compression stroke and align timing marks on flywheel and bellhousing. Remove timing belt cover and rocker shaft cover. Loosen number 1 cylinder exhaust valve rocker arm and turn it sideways clear of valve stem. Using a suitable valve spring compressor remove valve spring from number 1 cylinder exhaust valve. Remove circlip and oil seal from valve guide and allow valve to gently drop down onto top of number 1 piston.

NOTE: It is suggested that a small "O" ring be temporarily installed on upper part of valve stem to prevent valve from accidentally falling into cylinder if piston is lowered. Be sure that this "O" ring, used as a safety stop, does not interfere with measurements and that it is removed before assembling valve seal and spring.

Install a dial indicator and holding fixture so gage anvil is pressing on end of valve stem as shown in Fig. F1-6. Using dial indicator, rock crankshaft first backward then forward to accurately establish number 1 piston TDC. Zero dial indicator and slowly turn crankshaft backward until dial indicator shows a reading of minus 0.039 inch, this is exactly 11° BTDC on number 1 piston. Using a suitable punch permanently mark flywheel for future reference. It should now be possible to insert a ¼-inch diameter drift through hole in injection pump timing plate and into injection pump flange as shown by (D—Fig. F1-7). If drift cannot be inserted, loosen injection pump timing gear nuts and turn injection pump shaft until drift can be properly inserted. Tighten nuts to 11-15 ft.-lbs. and check that piston is still at 11° BTDC.

NOTE: If injection pump cannot be set properly, because injection pump shaft studs have reached the end of their slots in pump drive gear, it will be necessary to remove the timing belt. See TIMING BELT section.

Remove timing belt and turn pump shaft and gear until the ¼-inch diameter drift can be properly inserted as shown in Fig. F1-7. Center pump shaft studs in gear slots and tighten gear nuts to 11-15 ft.-lbs. then reinstall timing belt.

Remove dial indicator, install oil seal and circlip, valve spring and valve cap. Adjust valve for proper clearance. Install rocker shaft cover and timing cover.

ENGINE SPEED ADJUSTMENTS

IDLE SPEED. Idle speed is adjusted by turning idle speed stop screw (5—Fig. F1-8), see ENGINE SERVICE DATA for specification. Note that a

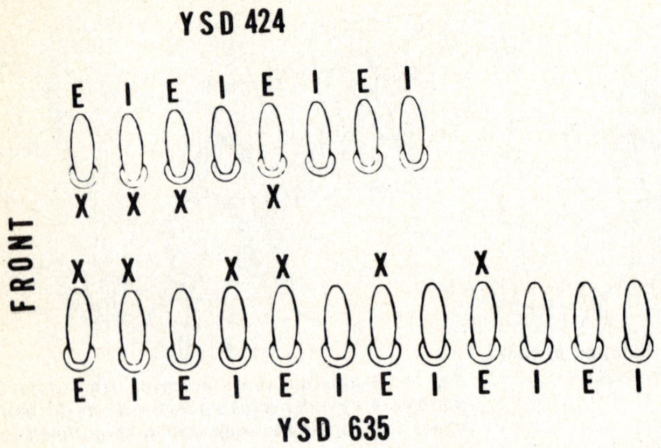

Ford

INBOARD ENGINES

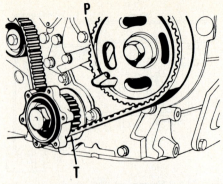

Fig. F1-9 – With number 1 piston on compression adjust valves marked (X). Rotate engine exactly one revolution and adjust remaining valves.

Fig. F1-10 – Illustration showing location of crankshaft gear timing mark (T) and correct installation of camshaft timing pin (P).

completely cold engine, with the correct idle speed adjustment, may stall but will run satisfactorily after a 30 second warm-up. It is recommended that you do not increase the idle speed to compensate for this cold engine stalling condition.

MAXIMUM ENGINE SPEED. Maximum engine speed is adjusted with engine running and at normal operating temperature. Remove lock wire and loosen locknut for maximum speed adjustment screw (3 – Fig. F1-8). With transmission in neutral, advance throttle to full speed position and adjust engine speed to 3600 rpm using screw (3). After correct maximum engine speed has been obtained tighten adjustment screw locknut and replace lock wire.

THROTTLE LINKAGE. Throttle linkage should be checked for correct length when making engine speed adjustments. Hand throttle should have ¼ to ½ inch dead travel before engine rpm starts to rise off idle. This dead travel is necessary to prevent activation of injection pump governor at low engine speeds.

With engine running set hand throttle to idle position and disconnect throttle linkage from injection pump speed control lever (6 – Fig. F1-8). Move injection pump speed control lever (6) to its idle stop position and adjust throttle linkage as necessary to ensure speed control lever (6) is always allowed to return to its full idle position. After adjustment check for sufficient dead travel of hand throttle lever.

VALVE ADJUSTMENT

With engine at normal operating temperature valves should be adjusted statically to specification shown in ENGINE SERVICE DATA section. Bring number 1 piston to TDC on compression and adjust valves marked (X – Fig. F1-9). Rotate engine exactly one revolution and adjust remaining valves.

REPAIR

FUEL INJECTION PUMP

To remove fuel injection pump, position number 1 piston at TDC on compression stroke and remove timing belt cover. Install camshaft locking pin as shown in Fig. F1-10 and remove timing belt as outlined in TIMING BELT section. Disconnect all control cables from injection pump, remove and cap all fuel injection, supply and return lines. Remove injection pump drive gear, pump retaining bolts and mounting bracket then remove injection pump.

The injection pump should be tested and repaired by a shop qualified in diesel injection pump repair.

When installing injection pump be sure to fill pump with ½ pint of engine oil. Install pump on front cover and tighten retaining bolts. Install drive gear and plate and tighten nuts finger tight. Time injection pump as outlined in INJECTION PUMP TIMING section. Check to be sure crankshaft timing marks are properly aligned and camshaft timing pin is correctly installed, then install timing belt and tensioner. Remove camshaft and injection pump timing pins. Install timing belt cover and tighten bolts to 18-22 ft.-lbs.

INJECTORS

Before removing injector for service or renewal always clean area around injector and cap open fuel lines. If heat shield comes out with injector a new heat shield to cylinder head washer must be installed. Clean injector thoroughly using clean fuel and a brass wire brush. Using an appropriate tester, test nozzle for proper opening pressure as specified in ENGINE SERVICE DATA. Be sure to keep nozzle pointed in a safe direction away from hands and eyes.

To adjust opening pressure remove cap nut (1 – Fig. F1-11) and turn adjusting nut (2) to obtain correct pressure.

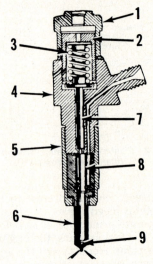

Fig. F1-11 – Cross-sectional drawing of fuel injection nozzle.

1. Cap nut
2. Adjusting nut
3. Spring
4. Nozzle holder
5. Nozzle nut
6. Nozzle
7. Spindle
8. Needle valve
9. Valve seat

Check spray pattern by pumping tester lever at a rate of 6 to 8 strokes per second and observing that all four nozzle holes are producing a similar pattern 90 degrees apart and that fuel is well atomized.

To test nozzle seat leakage, wipe nozzle tip dry with blotting paper and apply 2520 to 2594 psi pressure for one minute. Touch blotting paper to nozzle tip, the resulting stain should not be larger than ½-inch in diameter.

Check nozzle leak back by applying 2200 psi pressure to CAV injections or 1500 psi pressure to BOSCH injectors and measure the amount of time it takes for pressure to fall off to 1500 psi for CAV injectors or 1150 psi for BOSCH injectors. This pressure loss should take at least 10 seconds in CAV injectors and 6 to 22 seconds in BOSCH injectors.

If injector does not pass all of the above tests it is recommended that it be sent to a repair facility which specializes in diesel injection equipment repair.

Illustration courtesy Ford

INBOARD ENGINES

Ford

TIMING BELT

The timing belt drives the camshaft and the injection pump. It is important that the belt be correctly installed so injection and valve opening will be correct in relation to the crankshaft (and piston) position. If the timing belt has broken with engine running, it is possible that some valve damage may have occurred. Extreme care should be exercised if camshaft or crankshaft is rotated independently, because valves may be damaged by contacting the pistons. It is suggested that rocker arms (or preferably that cylinder head) be removed while timing the camshaft.

Remove the timing belt cover and rotate the crankshaft until timing mark on crankshaft is aligned with mark cast at (T–F1-10). Loosen belt tensioner, remove belt and inspect the condition of the cogged pulleys on injection pump, camshaft and crankshaft. Install new pulley or smooth any sharp edges which could damage drive belt.

Turn camshaft until timing pin, Ford special tool number 21-016 can be inserted through camshaft pulley and into hole as shown at (P). Insert a ¼ inch diameter drift (D–Fig. F1-7) to correctly position injection pump. Use a dial indicator on piston (or exhaust valve as described in INJECTION PUMP TIMING section) to position the crankshaft at exactly 11 degrees BTDC as indicated by piston position 0.039 inch Before Top Dead Center. Install timing belt and tensioner being careful that injection pump, camshaft and crankshaft are all still correctly positioned. Remove timing pins from camshaft and injection pump, rotate crankshaft two complete revolutions, then position crankshaft at 11 degrees BTDC. Dowel rod (D–Fig. F1-7) should slide easily into place. Small changes in injection pump timing may be accomplished by loosening nuts (N) and moving shaft. If pump can not be moved enough in slots to provide correct ignition timing, it will be necessary to loosen the belt and turn the pump shaft without moving the crankshaft or camshaft. Turn pump shaft and gear until ¼-inch drift can be properly inserted in timing hole and studs are centered in gear slots. Tighten gear stud nuts and install timing belt. Install timing belt cover and tighten bolts to 18-22 ft.-lbs.

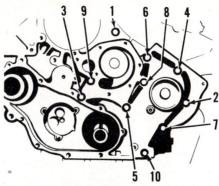

Fig. F1-13—When installing engine front plate be sure oil seal is centered on camshaft and tighten retaining screws in sequence shown. Tighten screws (1 through 9) to 20-23 ft.-lbs., and screw (10) to 15-18 ft.-lbs.

TIMING GEARS

REMOVE AND REINSTALL. Drain cooling system, and remove water pump belt, alternator belt, water pump pulley and crankshaft pulley. Remove timing belt cover and turn crankshaft until number 1 piston is at TDC on compression stroke and crankshaft timing marks are aligned as shown by (T–Fig. F1-10).

NOTE: Crankshaft is not originally provided with timing marks for injection pump to crankshaft timing. Before removing timing belt, turn crankshaft backwards until a ¼-inch diameter drift can be inserted through hole in injection pump timing plate and into injection pump flange as shown in Fig. F1-7. Using a suitable punch, mark crankshaft or flywheel for future reference.

Lock crankshaft into place by using Ford special tool number 21-018 (1–Fig. F1-12) and remove crankshaft center bolt (4). Remove belt tensioner (3), timing belt (5) and crankshaft hub. Lock camshaft into place by inserting timing pin, Ford special tool number 21-016, through hole in camshaft gear and into machined hole in front of cylinder block. Unbolt and remove camshaft gear (6). Unbolt and remove injection pump gear (2).

If engine front plate was removed, use Ford special tool number 21-017 to center front plate oil seal around camshaft and install retaining screws finger tight. Tighten front plate retaining screws to torque specified in ENGINE SERVICE DATA section in the sequence shown in Fig. F1-13. Tighten camshaft gear retaining bolt to specified torque using timing pin, Ford special tool number 21-016, to lock gear in place. Install spacer and timing belt drive gear onto crankshaft, tightening drive gear retaining bolts to 230-250 ft.-lbs. Install injection pump drive gear and tighten retaining bolts finger tight.

With crankshaft timing marks aligned and timing pin installed in camshaft gear, install timing belt and tensioner assembly. Remove timing pin from camshaft gear and turn crankshaft backwards until injection pump timing punch marks on crankshaft are aligned. (If crankshaft was not marked before timing belt was removed, refer to INJECTION PUMP TIMING section for outline of pump timing procedure.) Remove timing belt and turn injection pump gear until drift (D–Fig. F1-7) can be installed in pump flange timing hole, then reinstall timing belt and tighten pump gear retaining screws. Rotate crankshaft two revolutions, resetting it on TDC marks, and make sure timing pin can be installed in camshaft gear. Use Ford special tool number 21-025 to renew crankshaft oil seal in timing belt cover and to center seal and cover around crankshaft. Tighten cover retaining screws to 18-22 ft.-lbs.

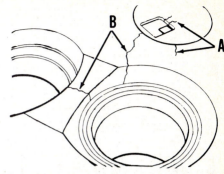

Fig. F1-14—Hair-line cracking (A) around combustion chamber insert is acceptable, while cracking in any other area of cylinder head (B) will require cylinder head renewal.

CYLINDER HEAD

No more than 0.010 inch should be removed from cylinder head gasket surface. Valve guides and seats are renewable and are a press fit using commonly accepted methods.

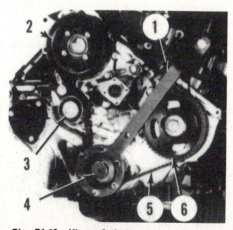

Fig. F1-12—View of timing gears and timing belt. Ford special tool number 21-018 (1) is used to hold crankshaft while removing and installing crankshaft hub bolt (4).

1. Ford special tool 21-018
2. Injection pump drive gear
3. Belt tensioner
4. Hub bolt
5. Timing belt
6. Camshaft gear

Illustration courtesy Ford

Ford   INBOARD ENGINES

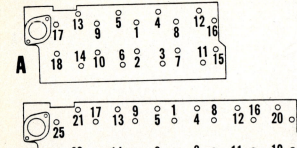

Fig. F1-15—Tighten cylinder head bolts in sequence (A) for YSD-424 or sequence (B) for YSD-635.

Fig. F1-17—Install thrust washer tang (T) in center main bearing cap groove.

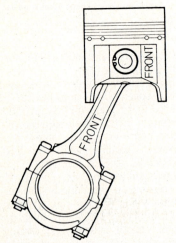

Fig. F1-16—View of piston and rod assembly showing location of "FRONT" markings.

Ford special tool 21-021 automatically sets correct valve guide protrusion when face of tool just touches cylinder head. However it is not mandatory that this tool be used.

After renewing either valve guides or valve seats it is necessary to grind the valve seat to insure correct alignment. When refacing valve stems no more than 0.010 inch should be removed. Also measure valve head recess below cylinder head surface. Valve head should be flush but not more than 0.008 inch recessed below head surface.

Slight cracking of cylinder head around combustion chamber insert (Fig. F1-14) is acceptable. Cracks cannot be more than 0.156 inch in length and should be hairline in appearance. Any other cracking of cylinder head is unacceptable and requires cylinder head renewal. Cylinder head bolt tightening sequence is shown in Fig. F1-15.

CAMSHAFT AND BEARINGS

To remove camshaft, first remove camshaft gear as outlined in TIMING GEARS section. Remove rocker cover, rocker arm assembly and push rods. Raise and secure tappets in uppermost position using magnetic holders or other suitable means. Unbolt camshaft front retainer plate and carefully withdraw camshaft.

Camshaft bushings can be renewed using Ford special tool 21-022, or other suitable tool. Flywheel housing must be removed when renewing bushings. Bushings are pre-sized and require no machining after installation. Be sure to align tang on front bushing with slot in bore, then bend tang into the slot. See ENGINE SERVICE DATA section for camshaft and bearing sizes and clearances.

Reinstall in reverse order of removal. Be sure oil gallery sealing balls are in each end of camshaft. Renew seal in front housing using Ford special tool 21-017 to install seal and center front plate around camshaft. Tighten the ten front plate retaining screws to the specified torque and in the sequence shown in Fig. F1-13. Time gears as outlined in TIMING GEARS section.

PISTONS

Pistons are graded by weight either "H" (heavy) or "L" (light) and stamped on piston crown accordingly. When renewing pistons be sure to use a like weight piston. A maximum weight variation for all piston and rod assemblies of 18 grams is allowed.

Inspect piston crown, thrust surfaces, pin bosses and ring grooves for damage and excessive wear. Also inspect piston for signs of a bent or twisted connecting rod.

CONNECTING RODS

Connecting rod and piston are assembled so the "FRONT" markings face the same direction as shown in Fig. F1-16. Inspect piston pin bushing for wear. Always use a new snap ring when assembling piston and rod. See ENGINE SERVICE DATA section for specifications. Inspect rod for wear, damage and straightness.

CRANKSHAFT

Crankshaft main and rod bearing journals may be ground undersize, however, care must be taken that the fillet radii be maintained and free from chatter marks. Center main bearing journal length may be increased provided an equal amount is machined from each face and corresponding oversize thrust washers are installed. Crankshaft thrust and end play is controlled by thrust washers located on either side of center main bearing. Thrust washers are in two halves with lower half having a tang (T—Fig. F1-17) which locates in a slot in bearing cap to prevent washers from turning. See ENGINE SERVICE DATA for specifications.

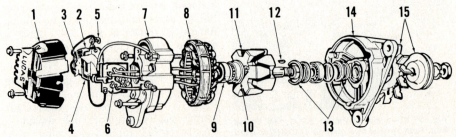

Fig. F1-18—Exploded view of Lucas 17ACR alternator.

1. Cover
2. Brush and regulator assy.
3. Output regulator
4. Brush and spring assy.
5. Regulator grounding screw
6. Rectifier
7. End bracket
8. Stator
9. Slip ring
10. Rear bushing
11. Rotor
12. Woodruff key
13. Front bearing assy.
14. Drive-end bracket
15. Fan assy.

Illustration courtesy Ford

INBOARD ENGINES

ELECTRICAL SYSTEM

ALTERNATORS

Engines may be equipped with either a Lucas or Motorola alternator. Refer to ENGINE SERVICE DATA section for service specifications. Lucas 17ACR 36 amp alternator, Fig. F1-18, incorporates a special avalanche-diode for voltage surge protection. It is located on outer face of slip ring bracket and connected between "IND" terminal and frame. Do not confuse this diode with noise supression capacitor which is located on drive-end bracket.

BOSCH 35 amp alternator, Fig. F1-19, is also used interchangeably on YSD engines. Diagnosis and testing of all three type alternators is quite similar with little variation from generally accepted shop practices.

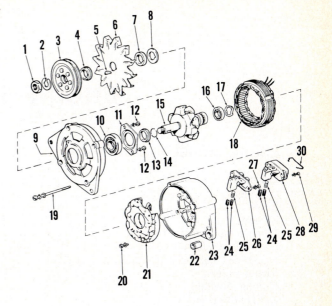

Fig. F1-19—Exploded view of Bosch alternator.

1. Nut
2. Lockwasher
3. Pulley
4. Spacer
5. Woodruff key
6. Fan
7. Spacer
8. Washer
9. Drive-end plate
10. Bearing
11. Bearing retainer
12. Screws
13. Spacer
14. Slip ring
15. Rotor
16. Bearing
17. Wave washer
18. Stator
19. Through bolt
20. Screw
21. Rectifier
22. Bushing
23. Housing
24. Brushes
25. Brush springs
26. Brush holder
27. Screw
28. Regulator & brush holder
29. Regulator
30. Terminal clip

Ford INBOARD ENGINES

FORD

ENGINE SERVICE DATA

ENGINE MODEL	SSD-437	SSD-655	SSD-681
General			
Cylinders	4	6	6
Bore	←——— 4.05 in. ———→		4.53 in.
Stroke	←——— 4.33 in. ———→		5.12 in.
Displacement – Cu. In.	224	335	495
Compression Ratio	←——————— 17:1 ———————→		
SSD-681 Turbocharged	......	......	15.5:1
Firing Order	1-3-4-2	←——— 1-5-3-6-2-4 ———→	
Number System (Front to Rear)	1-2-3-4	←——— 1-2-3-4-5-6 ———→	
Main Bearings, Number of	5	←——— 7 ———→	
Idle Speed	650 rpm	←——— 600-650 rpm ———→	
Maximum Speed:			
No Load	←——————— 3520 rpm ———————→		2850 rpm
Full Load	......	......	2600 rpm
Tune-Up			
Valve Clearance (Cold):			
Intake	←——— 0.010 in. ———→		0.012 in.
Exhaust	←——— 0.014 in. ———→		0.020 in.
Valve Lift	←——— 0.394 in. ———→		0.0236 in.
Camshaft Lobe Lift			
Intake	←——— 0.366 in. ———→		0.289 in.
Exhaust	←——— 0.420 in. ———→		0.289 in.
Oil Pressure (Warm):			
Idle	←——— 10 psi ———→		21 psi
Governed Speed	←——— 43-56 psi ———→		71 psi
Oil Relief Opening Pressure	←——————— 51.2 psi ———————→		
Oil Capacity with Filter	12 qts.	16 qts.	12 qts.
Injection Timing	←——————— See Text ———————→		
Injection Pump	Rotary	←——— In-Line ———→	
Pump Rotation At Drive End	Counterclockwise	←——— Clockwise ———→	
Injectors	←——— 3-hole Nozzles ———→		4-hole Nozzles
Nozzles Opening Pressure	←——— 3200-3342 psi ———→		2774-2915 psi
Engine Cranking Speed @ 70°F	←——— 155 rpm ———→		110 rpm
Starter Current Draw:			
Normal Load	←——— 500-600 amps ———→		730-830 amps
Sizes – Clearances			
Injector Protrusion	←——— 0.04-0.06 in. ———→		0.1122-0.1398 in.
Valve Stem Clearance	←——— 0.0009-0.0021 in. ———→		0.0012-0.0026 in.
Valve Guide Bore Diameter	←——— 0.549-0.550 in. ———→		0.5512-0.5519 in.
Valve Guide ID	←——— 0.3158-0.3160 in. ———→		0.3146-0.3154 in.
Valve Guide OD:			
Standard	←——— 0.5507-0.5518 in. ———→		0.5523-0.5527 in.
Oversize	←——— 0.5586-0.5596 in. ———→		0.5554-0.5558 in.
Valve Guide Interference Fit	←——— 0.0002-0.002 in. ———→		0.0004-0.0197 in.
Exhaust Valve Seat Bore Diameter	......	......	1.6921-1.6937 in.
Exhaust Valve Seat OD	......	......	1.6988-1.6996 in.

Illustration courtesy Ford

INBOARD ENGINES   **Ford**

ENGINE SERVICE DATA (CONT.)

ENGINE MODEL	SSD-437	SSD-655	SSD-681
Sizes — Clearances (Cont.)			
Exhaust Valve Seat Interference Fit	......	......	0.0051-0.0075 in.
Valve Guide Protrusion:			
Intake	......	......	0.551 in.
Exhaust	......	......	0.827 in.
Valve Seat Angle	——— 45° ± 5' ———		45°15'
Valve Seat Width	——— 0.0625-0.09375 in. ———		
Valve Seat Runout:			
Intake	——— 0.0012 in. ———		0.0039-0.0197 in.
Exhaust	——— 0.0016 in. ———		0.0157-0.0315 in.
Valve Head Depth:			
Intake	——— 0.0002-0.002 in. ———		0.0004-0.0197 in.
Exhaust	——— 0.0002-0.002 in. ———		0.0157-0.0315 in.
Valve Stem Diameter	——— 0.314-0.315 in. ———		0.3127-0.3134 in.
Valve Head Diameter:			
Intake	——— 1.7224-1.7323 in. ———		......
Exhaust	——— 1.4469-1.4567 in. ———		......
Valve Face Angle	——— 45°23'-45°37' ———		45°20'
Valve Spring Free Height:			
Inner	——— 2.008 in. ———		......
Outer	——— 2.48 in. ———		1.941 in.
Valve Spring Pressure (Lbs. @ Specified Length):			
Inner Open	34.0-36.8 lbs. @ 1.055-1.134 in.		......
Inner Closed	14.4-16.6 lbs. @ 1.476-1.516 in.		......
Outer Open	80.2-86.8 lbs. @ 1.17-1.25 in.		141.75 lbs. @ 1.161 in.
Outer Closed	42.5-47.8 lbs. @ 1.59-1.63 in.		52.25 lbs. @ 1.655 in.
Valve Spring Out of Square	——— 0.078 in. ———		
Rocker Shaft Diameter	——— 0.7079-0.7087 in. ———		0.8274-0.8282 in.
Rocker Shaft Bracket Bore Diameter	——— 0.7087-0.7103 in. ———		0.8283-0.8292 in.
Rocker Shaft to Bracket Clearance	——— 0.000-0.0024 in. ———		0.0002-0.0018 in.
Rocker Shaft to Rocker Clearance	——— 0.0006-0.0020 in. ———		0.0002-0.0181 in.
Rocker Arm Bushing OD	——— 0.8270-0.8280 in. ———		......
Rocker Arm Bushing Interference Fit	——— 0.0013-0.0036 in. ———		0.0005-0.0026 in.
Rocker Arm Bushing ID	——— 0.7092-0.7100 in. ———		......
Rocker Arm Bore Diameter	——— 0.8243-0.8256 in. ———		0.8287-0.8299 in.
Rocker Arm Side Clearance	——— 0.0025 in. ———		......
Valve Lifter to Bore Clearance	——— 0.0012-0.0027 in. ———		0.0016-0.0037 in.
Camshaft Journal Diameter:			
Front	2.006-2.007 in.	2.026-2.027 in.	1.9272-1.9281 in.
Front Intermediate	1.987-1.988 in.	2.006-2.007 in.	1.9272-1.9281 in.
Rear Intermediate	......	1.987-1.988 in.	......
Rear	1.067-1.968 in.	1.967-1.968 in.	1.9272-1.9281 in.
Camshaft Bushing ID:			
Front	2.011-2.012 in.	2.031-2.033 in.	1.9313-1.9327 in.
Front Intermediate	1.991-1.993 in.	2.011-2.012 in.	1.9313-1.9327 in.
Rear Intermediate	......	1.991-1.993 in.	......
Rear	1.971-1.973 in.	1.971-1.973 in.	1.9313-1.9327 in.
Camshaft Bushing OD:			
Front	2.160-2.163 in.	2.180-2.182 in.	2.0511-2.0526 in.
Front Intermediate	2.140-2.142 in.	2.160-2.163 in.	2.0511-2.0526 in.
Rear Intermediate	......	2.140-2.142 in.	......
Rear	2.121-2.123 in.	2.121-2.123 in.	2.0511-2.0526 in.
Camshaft Bushing Bore Diameter	......	......	2.0472-2.0482 in.

Illustration courtesy Ford

Ford
INBOARD ENGINE
ENGINE SERVICE DATA (CONT.)

ENGINE MODEL	SSD-437	SSD-655	SSD-681
Sizes — Clearances (Cont.)			
Camshaft to Bushing Bore			
Interference Fit	———	0.0027-0.0059 in. ———	0.0029-0.0054 in.
Camshaft End Play	———	0.002-0.023 in. ———	......
Camshaft Bearing Clearance	———	0.0032-0.0063 in. ———	0.0031-0.0055 in.
Idler Gear Shaft Diameter	———	1.2588-1.2598 in. ———	......
Idler Gear Bushing			
Bore Diameter	———	1.2617-1.2627 in. ———	......
Idler Shaft to Bushing			
Clearance	———	0.0020-0.040 in. ———	......
Idler Gear Thrust			
Washer Clearance	———	0.057-0.059 in. ———	......
Idler Gear to Bushing			
Interference Fit	———	0.0025-0.0055 in. ———	......
Lifter Bore Diameter	———	0.5512-0.5519 in. ———	1.0630-1.0643 in.
Block Cylinder Bore:			
Standard	———	4.2082-4.2102 in. ———	4.8031-4.8047 in.
Oversize 0.008 in.	———	4.2161-4.2181 in. ———	......
Cylinder Liner ID	......	......	4.5276-4.5284 in.
Cylinder Liner OD:			
Standard	———	4.2133-4.2145 in. ———	......
Oversize 0.008 in.	———	4.2212-4.2224 in. ———	......
Cylinder Liner Interference Fit	———	0.0031-0.0063 in. ———	......
Cylinder Liner Fitted Clearance	......	......	0.0012-0.0047 in.
Cylinder Liner Pilot Diameter	......	......	4.8000-4.8029 in.
Cylinder Liner Height Above Block	......	......	0.0051-0.0063 in.
Cylinder Liner Misalignment			
Top (Max.)	......	......	0.0012 in.
Piston Diameter:			
Standard	———	4.0477-4.0482 in. ———	4.5210-4.5215 in.
0.008 in. OS	———	4.0556-4.0561 in. ———	......
0.016 in. OS	———	4.0635-4.0639 in. ———	......
0.020 in. OS	———	4.0713-4.0718 in. ———	......
0.032 in. OS	———	4.0792-4.0797 in. ———	......
Piston to Cylinder Clearance	———	0.0068-0.0080 in. ———	0.0060-0.0074 in.
Piston Protrusion	———	0.018-0.030 in. ———	......
Piston Ring Groove Width:			
Top	———	0.1016-0.1024 in. ———	0.1008-0.1016 in.
Second	———————————	0.1000-1.1008 in.	———————————
Oil Control	———————————	0.1587-0.1594 in.	———————————
Piston Ring Side Clearance:			
Top	———	0.0035-0.0048 in. ———	0.0028-0.0040 in.
Second	———————————	0.0020-0.0032 in.	———————————
Oil Control	———————————	0.0016-0.0028 in.	———————————
Piston Ring Gap:			
Top	———	0.014-0.022 in. ———	0.0157-0.0236 in.
Second	———	0.012-0.020 in. ———	0.0157-0.0236 in.
Oil Control	———	0.012-0.018 in. ———	0.0118-0.0177 in.
Piston Pin Diameter:			
Standard	———	1.3379-1.3381 in. ———	1.6535-1.6538 in.
0.008 in. OS	———	1.3457-1.3460 in. ———	......
Piston Pin Bore Diameter:			
Standard	———	1.3383-1.3385 in. ———	1.6539-1.6541 in.
0.008 in. OS	———	1.3461-1.3464 in. ———	......
Piston Pin to Piston Clearance	———————————	0.0001-0.0006 in.	———————————
Piston Pin to Rod Clearance	———	0.0006-0.0011 in. ———	0.0007-0.0014 in.
Total Piston Weight			
Variation (Max.)	———————————	10 grams	———————————

INBOARD ENGINES — Ford

ENGINE SERVICE DATA (CONT.)

ENGINE MODEL	SSD-437	SSD-655	SSD-681
Sizes — Clearances (Cont.)			
Piston Pin Bushing ID:			
Standard	—	1.3387-1.3390 in.	1.6545-1.6549 in.
0.005 in. OS	—	1.3438-1.3441 in.	......
Piston Pin Bushing Bore ID	—	1.490-1.4915 in.	1.8089-1.8099 in.
Piston Pin Bushing OD	—	1.4952-1.4967 in.	1.8137-1.8157 in.
Piston Pin Bushing to Bore Interference Fit	—	0.0037-0.0067 in.	0.0039-0.0069 in.
Main Bearing Journal Diameter	—	2.9994-3.0000 in.	3.1410-3.1417 in.
Connecting Rod Journal Diameter	—	2.3121-2.3126 in.	2.8536-2.8543 in.
Main Bearing Thickness	—	0.0853-0.0855 in.	0.0854-0.0857 in.
Connecting Rod Bearing Thickness	—	0.0715-0.0717 in.	0.0811-0.0815 in.
Main Bearing Clearance	—	0.0016-0.0035 in.	0.0020-0.0042 in.
Rod Bearing Clearance	—	0.008-0.0023 in.	0.0023-0.0044 in.
Main Bearing Journal Runout	—	0.002 in.	0.0039 in.
Crankshaft End Play	—	0.003-0.013 in.	0.0027-0.0106 in.
Main and Connecting Rod Journal Out-of-Round	—	0.0003 in.	0.0002 in.
Thrust Washer Thickness	—	0.1330-0.1350 in.	—
Cylinder Block Main Bearing Bore Diameter	—	3.1727-3.1735 in.	3.3152-3.3160 in.
Oil Pump Driving Shaft Diameter	......	0.7082-0.7086 in.	—
Oil Pump Driving Shaft Bushing ID	......	0.7092-0.7109 in.	—
Oil Pump Driving Shaft to Bushing Clearance	0.0006-0.0021 in.	0.0006-0.0027 in.	—
Oil Pump Driving Shaft Bushing Interference Fit	......	0.0013-0.0036 in.	—
Oil Pump Driven Gear Shaft Interference Fit	......	0.0004-0.0019 in.	—
Oil Pump Driven Gear Shaft Diameter	......	0.5901-0.5905 in.	—
Oil Pump Driven Gear Shaft Bushing ID	......	0.5911-0.5922 in.	—
Oil Pump Driven Gear Shaft Clearance	......	0.0006-0.0021 in.	—
Oil Pump Gear Tooth Backlash	—	0.004 in.	—
Oil Pump Gear End Play	0.001-0.005 in.	0.0006-0.0042 in.	—
Oil Pump Relief Valve Spring:			
Free Length	—	1.772 in.	—
Pressure (Length @ Lbs.)	—	1.48 in. @ 10.1-11 Lbs.	1.083 in. @ 23.6-25.5 Lbs.
	—	1.20 in. @ 20-21 Lbs.	

DYNAMIC BALANCER SPECIFICATIONS (SSD-437)

Idler Shaft in Bore Interference Fit	0.0004-0.0029 in.
Idler and Drive Gear Bushing Interference Fit	0.0025-0.0055 in.
Idler and Drive Gear Shaft-to-Bushing Clearance	0.0020-0.0039 in.
Drive Shaft-to-Splined Sleeve Clearance	0.0011-0.0041 in.
Drive Gear Bushing-to-Balancer Housing Interference Fit	0.0025-0.0055 in.
Drive Gear Bushing-to-End Support Interference Fit	0.0015-0.0039 in.
Balancer Weight Drive Gear Bushing-to-Hub Clearance	0.0020-0.0039 in.
Bushing-to-Balancer Weight Interference Fit	0.0016-0.0039 in.
Balancer Weight Bushing ID	0.9851-0.9867 in.
Balancer Weight Shaft-to-Bushing Clearance	0.0008-0.0029 in.
Weight Drive Idler Gear Shaft-to-Housing Bore Interference Fit	0.0003-0.0024 in.

ENGINE SERVICE DATA (CONT.)

DYNAMIC BALANCER SPECIFICATIONS (CONT.)

Bushing-to-Weight Drive Idler Gear Interference Fit	0.0015-0.0039 in.
Weight Drive Idler Gear Bushing ID	0.9848-0.9859 in.
Idler Gear Shaft-to-Bushing Clearance	0.0005-0.0024 in.
Gear Tooth Backlash	0.0031 in.

AUTOMATIC ADVANCE VARIATOR (SSD-655 and SSD-681)

Type	Flyweight Type
Max. Angular Variation at Max. Governed Speed	6° to Pump Shaft

Tightening Torques (Ft.-Lbs.)	SSD-437	SSD-655	SSD-681
Advance Device	……	18	……
Balancer	110	……	……
Camshaft Thrust Plate	……	……	36
Connecting Rod Cap	81	81	87
Crankshaft Pulley Bolts	36	36	……
Crankshaft Pulley Hub	220	220	412
Cylinder Head	110	110	159
Exhaust Manifold	……	……	36
Flywheel	88	88	203
Injection Pump to Support	……	……	36
Injection Pump	17	17	18
Intake Manifold	……	……	65
Main Bearing Cap	110	110	152
Oil Pressure Valve Body	17	17	……
Oil Pump	17	17	18
Oil Pump Cover	17	17	18
Rear Seal Cover	……	……	10
Rocker Arm Shaft Bolts	17	17	36
Rocker Arm Shaft Nuts	17	17	36

MAINTENANCE

LUBRICATION

Engine oil and filter(s) should be changed after every 200 hours of operation or seasonally whichever is more frequent. For a new or rebuilt engine change oil and filter(s) after first 50 hours of operation. Do not leave oil filter(s) in service longer than recommended as oil filter system incorporates a by-pass which will circulate unfiltered oil if filter(s) become plugged.

On naturally aspirated Model SSD-437 and SSD-655 engines, API specification SE/SF/CC single or multi-viscosity oils should be used. Oil viscosity for these engines should be matched to the ambient temperature range expected in the next 200 hours of operation. See Fig. F2-1 for single viscosity oil recommendations or Fig. F2-2 for multi-viscosity oil recommendations.

Only single viscosity oils meeting API specification CD should be used in turbocharged version of Model SSD-655 and either the naturally aspirated or turbocharged Model SSD-681 engines. See Fig. F2-1 for oil viscosity recommendations.

When Outside Temperature is Consistently	Use SAE Viscosity Number
Below 5°F (-15°C)	SAE 10W
5°F to 32°F (-15° to 0°C)	SAE 20W
32°F to 95°F (0° to 35°C)	SAE 30
Above 95°F (35°C)	SAE 40

Fig. F2-1 — Refer to adjacent chart when selecting a single viscosity oil.

When Outside Temperature is Consistently	Use SAE Viscosity Number
Below +10°F (-12°C)	5W-20
Below +60°F (15°C)	5W-30
-10°F to 90°F (-23° to 32°C)	10W-30
Above -10°F (-23°C)	10W-40 or 10W-50
Above +20°F (-6°C)	20W-40 or 20W-50

Fig. F2-2 — Refer to adjacent chart when selecting a multi-viscosity oil.

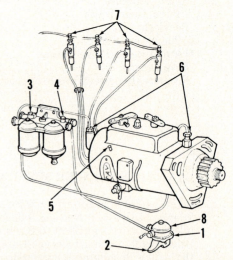

Fig. F2-3 — Illustration of Model SSD-437 fuel system.

1. Fuel lift pump
2. Priming lever
3. Fuel filter bleed screw
4. Fuel filter bleed screw
5. Injection pump bleed screw
6. Fuel return line nuts
7. Injector fuel return lines
8. Fuel lift pump cover

Illustration courtesy Ford

INBOARD ENGINES

Ford

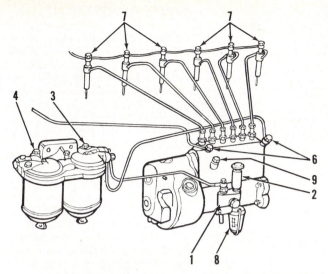

Fig. F2-4 — Illustration of Model SSD-655 and SSD-681 fuel system.

1. Fuel lift pump
2. Priming pump
3. Fuel filter bleed screw
4. Fuel filter bleed screw
6. Fuel return lines
7. Injector return lines
8. Sediment bowl
9. Injection pump fill plug

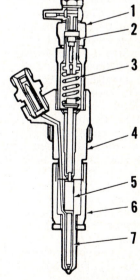

Fig. F2-6 — View showing adjustment points for Model SSD-655 and SSD-681 fuel injection pump.

1. Locknut
2. Idle speed screw
3. Maximum speed screw
T. Throttle lever
M. Timing marks

FUEL SYSTEM

FUEL FILTER. On Model SSD-437 and SSD-655 engines fuel filters should be drained to remove any water from the system after every 200 hours of operation. Loosen bottom screw of first fuel filter and operate fuel lift pump priming lever (2 – Fig. F2-3) until all water is removed. Tighten fuel filter bottom screw and bleed rest of fuel injection system.

SEDIMENT FILTER. After every 200 hours of operation sediment filter should be removed and cleaned in fresh diesel fuel.

On Model SSD-437 engine, sediment filter is a screen located under lift pump cover (8 – Fig. F2-3). Remove and clean or renew screen as required.

Model SSD-655 and SSD-681 engines are equipped with a cup type sediment filter (8 – Fig. F2-4). Remove bowl and clean both bowl and filter element in fresh diesel fuel.

Bleed complete fuel injection system after cleaning or renewal of sediment filter.

BLEED FUEL SYSTEM. Location of bleed points and fuel system components is shown in Fig. F2-3 for Model SSD-437 and Fig. F2-4 for Models SSD-655 and SSD-681. Refer to appropriate Figure when performing the following fuel system bleeding procedure.

Loosen fuel filter bleed screw (3) and operate priming pump lever or plunger (2) until air-free fuel flows from around bleed screw. Tighten bleed screw (3) and loosen fuel filter bleed screw (4) and operate priming lever or plunger (2) until no more air bubbles appear. Tighten bleed screw (4). Loosen injection pump bleed screw (5) on Model SSD-437 only, and injection pump return line unions (6) on all models. Operate priming pump lever or plunger (2) until air-free fuel appears then tighten bleed screw (5) and fittings (6). On Model SSD-437 only, loosen injector lines (7) completely and, using starter, turn engine over until air-free fuel appears. Tighten injector lines (7). Start engine and check for fuel leaks.

ENGINE SPEED ADJUSTMENT

IDLE SPEED. Engine should be at normal operating temperature before making idle speed adjustment. With engine idling loosen idle speed locknut (1 – Fig. F2-5 or F2-6). Turn idle speed screw (2) until engine idles at speed specified in ENGINE SERVICE DATA section. Turning idle speed screw clockwise will increase engine rpm. Tighten locknut (1) and increase engine speed and return it to idle several times to check adjustment.

MAXIMUM SPEED ADJUSTMENT. Engine should be allowed to reach normal operating temperature before making maximum no-load adjustment.

NOTE: The maximum no-load engine speed adjustment screw is factory sealed. After making adjustment be sure to reseal adjustment screw.

With transmission in neutral, increase engine speed to maximum rpm. Turn maximum speed adjustment screw (3 – Fig. F2-5 or F2-6) to adjust engine speed to specification given in ENGINE SERVICE DATA section.

INJECTION PUMP TIMING

Model SSD-437

Model SSD-437 C.A.V. rotary injection pump is internally timed. If injection pump timing is suspect, pump must be removed and sent to a shop which

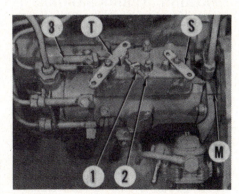

Fig. F2-5 — View showing adjustment points for Model SSD-437 fuel injection pump.

1. Locknut
2. Idle speed screw
3. Maximum speed screw
T. Throttle lever
S. Stop lever
M. Timing reference marks

Fig. F2-7 — Illustration of injection nozzle.

1. Cap nut
2. Adjusting screw
3. Spring
4. Nozzle holder
5. Nozzle valve
6. Nozzle nut
7. Nozzle

Illustration courtesy Ford

Ford

INBOARD ENGINES

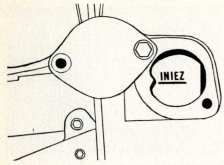

Fig. F2-8 – Illustration of fuel injection timing mark alignment on Model SSD-655 and SSD-681 flywheel.

specializes in diesel injection equipment repair. Pump is correctly installed when assembly mark on pump flange is aligned with mark (M – Fig. F2-5) on timing gear housing.

Model SSD-655 and SSD-681

To check or adjust fuel injection pump timing on Model SSD-655 and SSD-681 position number 1 piston at TDC on compression stroke and check that "INIEZ" mark on flywheel and pointer on flywheel housing are aligned as shown in Fig. F2-8.

Remove injection pump tappet cover, number 1 cylinder injector line (1 – Fig. F2-9) and delivery valve holder (2). Lift out delivery valve, spring, and reducer plug then reinstall delivery valve holder.

Place throttle lever in full speed position and fill engine fuel system using priming pump (3). Turn crankshaft counterclockwise until number 1 cylinder injection pump tappet (4) is down and at start of stroke. Use priming pump to be sure fuel flows out of pressure outlet. Turn crankshaft slowly clockwise until fuel flow from number 1 cylinder pressure outlet stops but remains flush with top of pressure outlet. This point is the beginning of fuel injection for number 1 cylinder. "INIEZ" mark on flywheel should be aligned with pointer on flywheel housing (Fig. F2-8), if not turn flywheel until marks are aligned. Loosen injection pump mounting bolts and rotate injection pump towards engine until fuel again flows out of number 1 cylinder delivery valve holder (2 – Fig. F2-9). Slowly rotate injection pump away from engine until fuel flow just stops and tighten injection pump mounting bolts. Injection pump timing is now correct.

Using an appropriate chisel or punch, lightly mark pump flange and timing gear case as shown in Fig. F2-6 for future reference.

Reinstall number 1 cylinder reducer plug, spring, and delivery valve. Reconnect injector fuel supply line and bleed

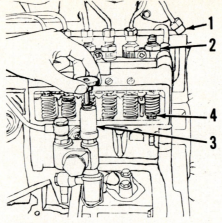

Fig. F2-9 – Operate priming pump (3) when checking fuel injection pump timing as outlined in text.

1. Injection line to number 1 cylinder
2. Pressure outlet
3. Priming pump
4. Number 1 injection pump tappet

fuel system as outlined in BLEED FUEL SYSTEM section. Start engine and check for fuel leaks. Adjust idle speed and maximum engine speed as previously outlined.

TURBOCHARGER

All Models So Equipped

STARTING. Before starting, turbocharger equipped engines should be cranked for a minimum of 15 seconds with throttle control lever in stop position. If during this cranking period oil pressure is indicated on oil gage or warning light goes out it is safe to start engine. At all times, even immediately after starting, turbocharger equipped engines should be allowed to idle for two minutes before stopping engine to avoid damage to turbocharger unit.

PRIMING TURBOCHARGER. If during 15-second cranking period with throttle lever in stop position, no oil pressure is indicated on oil gage or warning light does not go out, turbocharger unit must be manually primed with engine oil.

Disconnect oil feed pipe from turbocharger and fill turbocharger with engine oil. Reconnect oil feed pipe. Remove a plug from engine oil gallery and using a syringe, force at least 4 pints of engine oil into engine. Reinstall oil gallery plug and start engine. Allow engine to run at idle for two minutes checking oil pressure gage or warning light for adequate oil pressure. Stop engine and check oil level. Add or remove engine oil as required to bring level to full mark on dipstick.

VALVE ADJUSTMENT

Valve adjustment should only be made on a cold engine. See ENGINE SERVICE DATA section for specifications.

Valves are adjusted in companion cylinder sequence. On Model SSD-437 engines companion cylinders are 1 and 4, 3 and 2. On Model SSD-655 and SSD-681 engines companion cylinders are 1 and 6, 2 and 5, 3 and 4.

Remove rocker arm cover and loosen injectors to relieve compression. Rotate crankshaft in normal direction until both valves of number 1 cylinder are open an equal amount (overlap), then adjust both valves of the companion cylinder. Rotate crankshaft until valves of companion cylinder are open an equal amount and then adjust valve clearance on number 1 cylinder. Repeat this procedure on remaining groups of companion cylinders. Renew rocker arm cover gasket and reinstall rocker arm cover. Tighten injector hold down nuts to specification given in ENGINE SERVICE DATA section.

REPAIR

INJECTORS

CAUTION: When testing fuel injection nozzles keep nozzle tip pointed in a safe direction away from hands and eyes. Fuel spray will penetrate skin due to high pressure and atomization.

A complete job of testing and adjusting injectors requires use of special test equipment. Only clean, approved testing oil should be used to test injectors. Injector nozzle should be tested for opening pressure, leak-back, seat leakage and spray pattern.

Fuel injection nozzles from four different sources are used on SSD series engines. Care should be taken not to intermix injection nozzle types on any one engine. Injection nozzles should be cleaned and tested after every 400 hours of operation.

To remove injector from cylinder head first clean injector and adjacent cylinder head area using compressed air and a suitable solvent. Remove and cap fuel return and supply lines. Remove injector retaining nuts and washers. Remove retaining collar and injector along with outer sealing ring.

Clean carbon deposits from nozzle tip using a brass brush and clean diesel fuel. Check nozzle spray holes for obstructions.

Before conducting tests, operate tester lever until test oil flows, then attach injector. To check nozzle opening pressure, pump tester several strokes to obtain an accurate reading and ensure

INBOARD ENGINES

Ford

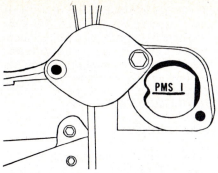

Fig. F2-10 – Illustration of fuel injection timing mark alignment on Model SSD-437 flywheel.

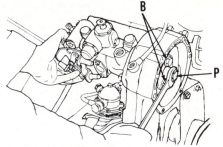

Fig. F2-11 – Loosen flange bolts (B) then unscrew pump shaft nut (P) for injection pump removal. See text.

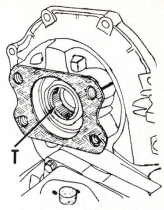

Fig. F2-13 – Injection pump drive gear master spline (T) on Model SSD-655 and SSD-681 engines must engage pump shaft master spline (G – Fig. F2-14).

nozzle valve is not stuck. See ENGINE SERVICE DATA for opening pressure specifications. If opening pressure is incorrect, remove cap nut (1 – Fig. F2-7) and turn adjusting screw (2) until opening pressure is correct.

To test nozzle leak-back on Model SSD-437 and SSD-655 engines, apply 2800 psi pressure to injector and check amount of time it takes pressure to fall off to 2100 psi. This pressure drop should take between 10 and 40 seconds. Test Model SSD-681 injectors in the same manner using a starting pressure of 2500 psi and watching for drop in pressure to 1500 psi in the same 10 to 40 second time period.

After checking nozzle leak-back check for nozzle seat leakage. On Model SSD-437 and SSD-655 injectors wipe nozzle tip dry with blotting paper and apply a pressure of 3000-3142 psi. After one minute touch nozzle tip with blotting paper and measure resulting stain. Stain should not be larger than ½-inch in diameter. Test Model SSD-681 injectors in a similar manner starting with a pressure of 2500 psi.

Injectors used on Model SSD-437 and SSD-655 engines have a three-hole nozzle tip while injectors used on Model SSD-681 engines have a four-hole nozzle tip. Pump tester handle at a rate of 6 to 8 strokes per second to check spray pattern. Spray from each nozzle tip hole must be similar, with no visible streaks or distortion. Each spray must be fully atomized and form a cone.

If injector passes all four tests it can be returned to service. If injector fails any test it should be renewed or repaired by a shop which specializes in diesel injection equipment repair.

Before installing injector check injector bore in cylinder head to be sure it is free from any dirt or carbon deposits. Use care to prevent any carbon deposits from falling down into cylinder when cleaning injector bore. Install outer ring on injector and fully insert injector into cylinder head. Install retaining collar, washers and nuts. Tighten nuts to specification shown in ENGINE SERVICE DATA section. Install fuel inlet and return lines. Start engine and carefully check for any fuel leaks.

INJECTION PUMP

Model SSD-437

REMOVE AND REINSTALL. Model SSD-437 engines are equipped with a C.A.V. rotary injection pump. To remove injection pump, rotate engine until number 1 piston is on compression stroke and align PMS 1 mark on flywheel with pointer on flywheel housing. See Fig. F2-10. Disconnect throttle linkage, fuel and injector lines. Remove inspection cover from timing gear case. Remove injection pump mounting nuts and washers. Loosen retaining flange bolts (B – Fig. F2-11) and unscrew pump shaft nut (P) while supporting pump with free hand as shown in Fig. F2-11. Carefully pull pump out of drive gear. Injection pump drive gear is now loose and may fall out of place if bumped or jarred.

Fuel injection pump should be serviced by a shop qualified in diesel injection equipment repair.

Fig. F2-12 – View showing correct timing gear alignment for Model SSD-437 engine. See text for gear timing procedure.

C. Crankshaft timing gear
F. Fuel lift pump drive gear
I. Idler gear
P. Injection pump drive gear
T. Pto drive gear
V. Camshaft drive gear

When reinstalling injection pump be sure "PMS 1" mark on flywheel and pointer on flywheel housing are aligned as shown in Fig. F2-10. If pump drive gear was removed or has fallen out of place, align timing mark "4" on pump gear with mark "4" on lift pump drive gear as shown in Fig. F2-12.

Line up key in injection pump shaft and keyway in drive gear and slide pump into position. Install pump mounting nuts and washers hand tight. Install pump shaft nut (P – Fig. F2-11) using it as a puller to fully seat pump drive gear onto pump shaft. Tighten retaining flange bolts to specification given in ENGINE SERVICE DATA section. Rotate injection pump housing until assembly marks on pump flange and timing gear case are aligned as shown in (M – Fig. F2-5). Install inspection cover, throttle cable, fuel and injector lines. Bleed fuel system, adjust idle and maximum speed as previously outlined.

Models SSD-655 and SSD-681

REMOVE AND REINSTALL. To remove in-line injection pump from Model SSD-655 and SSD-681 engines rotate crankshaft so number 1 piston is on compression stroke and align "INIEZ" mark on flywheel with pointer on flywheel housing. See Fig. F2-8. Disconnect fuel line, oil line, throttle linkage and injector lines from injection pump. Remove mounting bolts while supporting pump with free hand and remove pump.

To install injection pump, check that number 1 piston is on compression stroke and "INIEZ" mark on flywheel is aligned with pointer on flywheel housing. See Fig. F2-8. Align master splines on pump drive gear (Fig. F2-13) and pump shaft (Fig. F2-14) and slide pump into place. Install pump mounting bolts finger tight. Align marks (M – Fig. F2-6)

Illustration courtesy Ford

Ford
INBOARD ENGINES

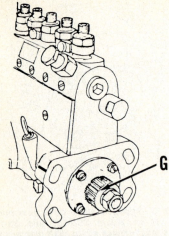

Fig. F2-14—Injection pump shaft master spline (G) on Model SSD-655 and SSD-681 engines must engage drive gear master spline (T—Fig. F2-13).

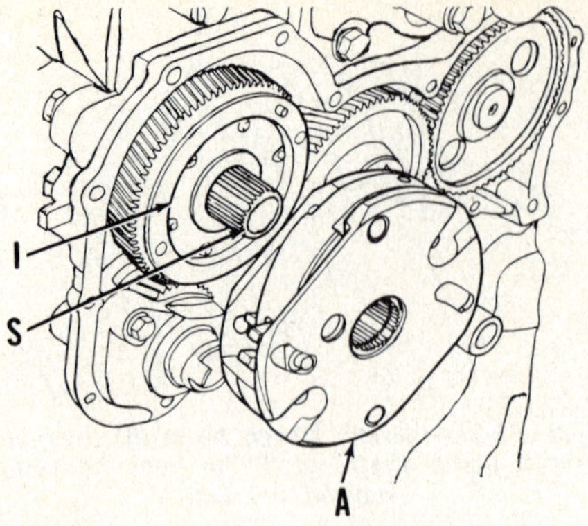

Fig. F2-16—Illustration showing installation of automatic advance variator on Model SSD-655 and SSD-681 engines.

A. Automatic advance variator
I. Injection pump drive gear
S. Injection pump splined shaft

on pump flange and timing gear case and tighten mounting bolts to specification shown in ENGINE SERVICE DATA section.

NOTE: If assembly marks are not present refer to INJECTION PUMP TIMING section to establish correct fuel injection timing.

Remove fuel injection pump filler plug (9–Fig. F2-4) and add 8 ounces of engine oil. This must be done any time injection pump is removed from engine. Connect oil line, throttle linkage, fuel and injector lines. Bleed fuel system, adjust idle speed and maximum engine speed as previously outlined.

TIMING GEARS

Model SSD-437

Use the following procedure to install and phase timing gears. See ENGINE SERVICE DATA section for torque specifications.

Fig. F2-15—View showing correct timing gear alignment for Model SSD-655 and SSD-681 engines. See text for gear timing procedure.

C. Crankshaft timing gear
I. Idler gear
P. Injection pump drive gear
T. Pto drive gear
V. Camshaft drive gear

Install injection pump and tighten retaining nuts finger tight. Install injection pump drive gear (P–Fig. F2-12) as outlined in INJECTION PUMP TIMING section. Install fuel lift pump shaft and drive gear (F) while aligning "4" on lift pump drive gear with "4" on injection pump drive gear. Install fuel lift pump and support housing. Install pto drive gear (T), which is not stamped and may be installed in any position, in mesh with fuel lift pump drive gear (F). Install thrust washers and idler gear (I) on idler gear shaft. Align "3" on idler gear with "3" on lift pump drive gear; align "2" on idler gear with "2" on camshaft drive gear (V); align "1" on idler gear with (1) on crankshaft gear (C). When all marks are aligned and teeth of idler gear are in mesh with teeth of other gears, slide idler gear fully onto idler gear shaft and install idler gear retaining snap ring. Install timing gear case cover. Time injection pump as outlined in INJECTION PUMP TIMING section. Install injection pump drive gear inspection cover.

Model SSD-655

Proceed as follows to install and phase timing gears. See ENGINE SERVICE DATA section for tightening torque specifications.

Install fuel injection pump and drive gear (P–Fig. F2-15) as outlined in INJECTION PUMP section while leaving pump mounting bolts finger tight. Install pto drive gear (T) in mesh with injection pump drive gear. Pto drive gear is not marked and can be installed in any position. Install camshaft (V) and crankshaft (C) gears if they have been removed. Install thrust washers and idler gear (I) on idler gear shaft and align "1" on idler gear with "1" on crankshaft gear; align "2" on idler gear with "2" on camshaft gear; align "3" on idler gear

with "3" on injection pump drive gear. Install Automatic Advance Variator (A–Fig. F2-16) by firmly pushing it onto injection pump drive sleeve and fastening it to injection pump drive gear. Install timing gear case cover. Time fuel injection pump as outlined in INJECTION PUMP TIMING section.

Model SSD-681

Gear alignment and installation on Model SSD-681 engines is identical to that on Model SSD-655 engines with the exception that, if still installed, oil pump drive gear must be removed before attempting to install idler gear. After timing gears have been properly installed and phased, reinstall oil pump drive gear and complete timing process as outlined for Model SSD-655 engine.

CYLINDER HEAD

Model SSD-437 and SSD-655 cylinder heads have renewable valve guides and integral valve seats. Model SSD-681 cylinder head intake valve seats are integral while exhaust valve seats are renewable. Model SSD-681 intake valves incorporate deflector vanes integral with valve head. To position these vanes correctly in valve ports, and prevent them from rotating out of position, a flat is ground on each intake valve stem, which is engaged by a flat on each intake valve spring lower seat. Lower spring seats are held in position by alignment pins in cylinder head spring seat faces so intake valves can only be installed in one position and are not free to rotate.

Oversize valve guides are available. Valve seat refacing should be closely coordinated with valve guide renewal or reaming and valve refacing. Grind all valves and valve seats to a true 45° angle. Finished valve seat should contact center of valve face. If after refacing, finished valve edge is less than 1/32 inch thick, valve should be renewed as it

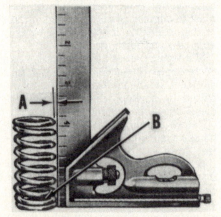

Fig. F2-17—Valve spring out-of-square (A) should not exceed 0.078 inch. Install spring with closed coil (B) down.

INBOARD ENGINES
Ford

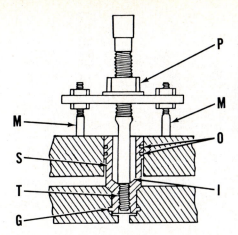

Fig. F2-18—Diagram showing proper installation of injector sleeve removal tool. Tap sleeve section (T) with suitable threads prior to installing puller.

G. Compression seal seat
I. Injector seat
M. Injector retaining studs
O. Injector sleeve "O" ring seals
P. Injector sleeve puller
S. Injector sleeve

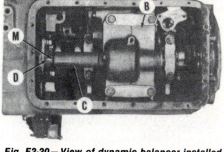

Fig. F2-20—View of dynamic balancer installed in crankcase of Model SSD-437 engine.

B. Dynamic balancer
C. Coupling shaft
D. Drive pinion
M. Timing marks on coupling sleeve and drive pinion

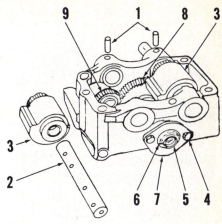

Fig. F2-21—Exploded view of dynamic balancer used on Model SSD-437 engine.

1. Roll pins
2. Flyweight shaft
3. Flyweight
4. Bolts
5. Snap ring
6. Thrust washer
7. Drive gear flange
8. Drive gear
9. Idler gear

will run too hot. Do not lap valve and seat.

Check each valve spring for squareness as shown in Fig. F2-17. Rotate valve spring slowly and measure maximum distance (A). Any spring exceeding 0.078 inch should be renewed.

If any injector sleeve is found to be leaking compression or coolant, or if injector protrusion is too deep, injector sleeve must be renewed. To properly remove and reinstall injector sleeves the following Ford special tools are necessary: tool number 7586 Sleeve Puller; tool number 7587 Injector Sleeve Burnishing Tool; tool number 7588 Tool Set to tap old sleeve for removal and cut injector seat in new sleeve; or tool number 4203 30 seat cutter for Model SSD-681 injector seat.

Using guide supplied with burnishing tool, tap injector sleeve and using sleeve puller remove injector sleeve from cylinder head as shown in Fig. F2-18. Carefully clean groove (G) at bottom of cylinder head bore to remove remaining pieces of old sleeve. Install new "O" rings (O) on new injector sleeve (S) and press sleeve into cylinder head until it is fully seated. Use burnishing tool to force sleeve outward and reestablish compression seal (G). Ream injector seat (I) with special casing reamer to establish correct injector protrusion. See ENGINE SERVICE DATA section for specifications.

Cylinder head should not be planed more than 0.020 inch. Install cylinder head gasket with letters "ALTO" facing up. See Fig. F2-19 for appropriate cylinder head bolt tightening sequence. See ENGINE SERVICE DATA section for torque specifications.

PISTONS

Oversize piston pins are available for Model SSD-437 and SSD-655 engines. Manufacturer recommends that when reaming connecting rod and piston pin bores that only a machine driven reamer be used. Oversize piston pins are not available for Model SSD-681 engines; if necessary piston and/or connecting rod bushing must be renewed. Piston pin should be a thumb push fit at room temperature.

Standard size, 0.008, 0.016, 0.020 and 0.032-inch oversize pistons and rings are available for Model SSD-437 and SSD-655 engines. Oversize pistons and rings are not available for Model SSD-681 engines. Install piston rings with ring gaps 120° apart. Total piston weight variation should not exceed 0.34 ounces.

CRANKSHAFT

Main and connecting rod journals of naturally-aspirated engine crankshafts may be ground undersize if necessary. Manufacturer advises against grinding crankshaft journals of turbocharged engines unless heat-treating facilities are available to restore surface hardness. When grinding crankshaft be sure to maintain fillet radii. Both grinding and polishing of crankshaft journals should be against direction of rotation.

DYNAMIC BALANCER

Model SSD-437

To remove dynamic balancer assembly, remove bolts holding balancer to its support. Lift balancer (B—Fig. F2-20) and move it towards flywheel end of engine while disengaging coupling sleeve (C) from splined drive pinion (D).

To overhaul dynamic balancer, remove roll pins (1—Fig. F2-21), drive flyweight shafts (2) out of housing and lift out flyweights (3). Remove flyweight flange retaining bolts (4), snap ring (5) and thrust washer (6). Remove drive

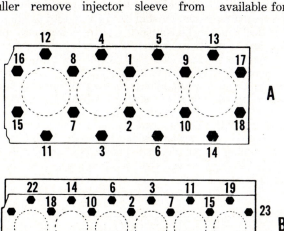

Fig. F2-19—Tighten cylinder head bolts in sequence shown to specification given in ENGINE SERVICE DATA section.

A. SSD-437
B. SSD-655 and SSD-681

Ford — INBOARD ENGINES

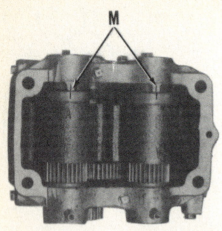

Fig. F2-22—View showing correct alignment of dynamic balancer flyweight timing marks (M).

Fig. F2-23—View showing correct alignment of dynamic balancer drive pinion timing mark (M). Note drift (D) used to lock flyweights in position.

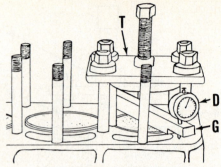

Fig. F2-24—Illustration showing use of special cylinder liner seating tool (T), dial indicator (D) and gage plate (G) to check cylinder liner protrusion on Model SSD-681 engines.

gear flange (7) and drive gear (8). Remove flyweight idler gear snap ring, idler gear (9) and shaft. Renew all worn or damaged parts which do not meet specifications given in ENGINE SERVICE DATA section.

If new bushings are to be installed in flyweights (3), first heat flyweights in oil at 283°-320°F. before pressing in new bushings. After installation ream bushings to proper size.

Reassemble balancer by reversing disassembly procedure. When installing flyweight idler gear (9) make sure longer end faces housing wall. Always use new roll pins to secure flyweight shafts in balancer housing. During reassembly align shaft and flange timing marks (M–Fig. F2-23) then install flyweights with marks aligned as shown in Fig. F2-22.

To install balancer, secure flyweights in place with a suitable drift as shown in Fig. F2-23. Align drive pinion timing marks (M–Fig. F2-20) and mesh master spline on coupling sleeve (C) with master spline of drive pinion. Slide balancer assembly forward onto coupling sleeve (C) until it rests on its supports. Secure balancer assembly, torqueing bolts to specification given in ENGINE SERVICE DATA section. Be sure to remove drift used to secure flyweights in balancer housing.

CYLINDER LINERS

Models SSD-437 and SSD-655

Cylinder liners can be rebored if necessary to correct for excessive wear, taper or out-of-round. If liner is to be replaced proceed as follows:

Press old liner out from bottom of block using a hydraulic press and suitable press plate. Check block bore and new liner O.D. for proper interference fit as specified in ENGINE SERVICE DATA section. Coat liner O.D. and cylinder block bore with engine oil. Press liner in 2¾ to 3½ inches and check that press pressure does not exceed 3,300 lbs. Continue to press liner to a point ⅜ inch before liner is seated. Press loading at this point should be 7,937 to 14,330 lbs. If press loading does not fall within these limits, remove liner and install another. Press liner into block until plate bottoms on block surface. Machine liner top even with block if necessary. After installation of new liner, bore and hone liner to standard as specified in ENGINE SERVICE DATA section. Before boring and refinishing any liner install all main bearing caps to prevent distortion of crankshaft bearing bores.

Model SSD-681

If bore wear, taper or out-of-round exceeds 0.006 inch cylinder sleeve must be renewed as boring is not practical and oversize pistons and rings are not available. If seated height or squareness is out of limits, sleeve seat spacer shim must be renewed and sleeve seat counterbore in block may have to be refaced.

Install Ford special tool, number 2798, as shown in Fig. F2-24, and torque preloading screw to 10-12 ft.-lbs. to simulate cylinder head loading. Use dial indicator and gage plate to check cylinder sleeve standout in several places around sleeve. Standout should be 0.0051 to 0.0063 inch and uniform at all points checked within 0.0012 inch. Cylinder sleeve standout must be uniform for all cylinders, and within specification limits for cylinder head to properly seat them. Spacer shims in eight thicknesses, in steps of 0.0012 inch, to correct sleeve protrusion are available.

Cylinder sleeves should be numbered and be marked to show their original orientation within the cylinder block. Keep sleeve shims with their original sleeve. Lift out sleeve and check sleeve seat and bore for corrosion or evidence of leakage. As necessary true up sleeve seats to correct for mis-alignment or to remove corrosion.

A special hand operated milling device, available from Ford, is used to recondition cylinder sleeve seats. Follow tool manufacturers instructions carefully and remove no more material than necessary from counterbore to true up and clean seats. An entire set of sleeve shim spans a range of just over 0.008 inch so there is very little room for material removal before cylinder block must be renewed.

After cylinder sleeve seat is true and clean, install sleeve and original shim in cylinder block and measure sleeve protrusion and squareness as previously outlined. Add shim thickness as indicated to bring protrusion within specification limits. If sleeve is out-of-square, cylinder sleeve re-seating operation must be repeated to correct condition. This operation is crucial to a successful overhaul of a wet sleeve engine, since cylinder head must bear evenly on all sleeves at all points to form a leak proof assembly.

INBOARD ENGINES Ford

FORD

ENGINE SERVICE DATA

ENGINE MODEL	254	362	363	380
General				
Cylinders	4	←——————— 6 ———————→		
Bore	4.22 in.	←—— 4.125 in. ——→		4.22 in.
Stroke	←————————— 5.52 in. —————————→			
Displacement	254 cu. in.	362 cu. in.	363 cu. in.	380 cu. in.
Firing Order	1-2-4-3	←———— 1-5-3-6-2-4 ————→		
Number System (Front to Rear)	1-2-3-4	←———— 1-2-3-4-5-6 ————→		
Main Bearings, Number of	5	←——————— 7 ———————→		
Idle Speed	←————————— 500-600 rpm —————————→			
Compression Ratio	16:1	←—— 15.7:1 ——→		16:1
Tune-Up				
Valve Clearance (Hot):		9½ qts.		
		12½ qts.		
Inlet and Exhaust—				
Naturally Aspirated	←————————— 0.015 in. —————————→			
Turbocharged	←————————— 0.018 in. —————————→			
Valve Clearance (Cold):				
Inlet	←————————— 0.014-0.018 in. —————————→			
Exhaust	←————————— 0.010-0.014 in. —————————→			
Valve Lift	←————————— 0.395 in. —————————→			
Camshaft Lobe Lift	←————————— 0.303 in. —————————→			
Oil Pressure (Hot)	←————————— 45-50 psi @ 2000 rpm —————————→			
Oil Capacity with Filter:				
Front or Rear Sump	9½ qts	←———— 14½ qts. ————→		
High Inclination Sump	12½ qts.	←———— 21 qts. ————→		
Injection Timing:				
Naturally Aspirated	←————————— 22° BTDC —————————→			
Naturally Aspirated with				
Auto Advance	←————————— 18° BTDC —————————→			
Turbocharged	←————————— 23° BTDC —————————→			
Injection Pump Type	←————————— SIMMS Minimec —————————→			
Nozzle Opening Pressure:				
Naturally Aspirated	←————————— 2700-2750 psi —————————→			
Turbocharged	←————————— 2975-3050 psi —————————→			
Engine Cranking Speed	170 rpm	130 rpm	120 rpm	130 rpm
Starter Current Draw (amps)	←—— 420 ——→		480	420
Starter Brush Wear Limit	←————————— 5/16 in. —————————→			
Starter Brush Spring Tension	←————————— 42 oz. —————————→			
Fuel Pump Static Pressure	←————————— 5-8 psi —————————→			
Fuel Pump Volume @ 1000 Rpm	←————————— 1 pt/20 sec. —————————→			
Fuel Pump Inlet Vacuum	←————————— 8½ in. Mercury —————————→			
Fuel Oil:				
Summer above 20°F.	←————————— #2 Diesel —————————→			
Winter below 20°F.	←————————— #1 Diesel —————————→			
Sizes — Clearances				
Valve Stem Diameter:				
Inlet	←————————— 0.3730-0.3740 in. —————————→			
Exhaust	←————————— 0.3723-0.3733 in. —————————→			
Valve Head Diameter:				
Inlet	←————————— 1.770-1.780 in. —————————→			
Exhaust	←————————— 1.533-1.543 in. —————————→			
Valve Face Angle	←————————— 29°15'-29°30' —————————→			
Valve Stem Clearance:				
Inlet	←————————— 0.0011-0.0033 in. —————————→			
Exhaust	←————————— 0.0018-0.004 in. —————————→			
Valve Margin (Minimum)	←————————— 1/32 in. —————————→			
Valve Seat Width	←————————— 1/16-3/32 in. —————————→			

Illustration courtesy Ford

Ford INBOARD ENGINES

ENGINE SERVICE DATA (CONT.)

ENGINE MODEL	254	362	363	380
Sizes — Clearances (Cont.)				
Valve Head Diameter:				
Inlet	←————————	1.770-1.780 in.	————————→	
Exhaust	←————————	1.533-1.543 in.	————————→	
Valve Face Runout	←————————	0.0015-1.543 in.	————————→	
Valve Spring Free Length	←————————	2.31 in.	————————→	
Valve Spring Out-of-Square (Maximum)	←————————	5/64 in.	————————→	
Valve Spring Assembled Height	←————————	1.97 in.	————————→	
Valve Spring Pressure	←————————	62-68 lb. @ 1.97 in.	————————→	
	←————————	157-169 lb. @ 1.56 in.	————————→	
Diameter of Push Rods	←————————	0.315-0.325 in.	————————→	
Valve Lifter Diameter	←————————	0.6080-0.6085 in.	————————→	
Valve Lifter Clearance	←————————	0.005-0.020 in.	————————→	
Valve Lifter Length	←————————	2.417-2.437 in.	————————→	
Push Rod Length	←————————	11.88-11.92 in.	————————→	
Rotator Cap Clearance	←————————	0.001-0.005 in.	————————→	
Valve Guide:				
Internal Diameter	←————————	0.3751-0.3761 in.	————————→	
Outside Diameter	←————————	0.6257-0.6262 in.	————————→	
Valve Guide Length	←————————	3.00 in.	————————→	
Valve Guide Protrusion (Inlet)	←————————	0.72 in.	————————→	
Valve Seat Insert Recess Diameter:				
Inlet	←————————	1.94-1.948 in.	————————→	
Exhaust	←————————	1.699-1.700 in.	————————→	
Valve Seat Insert Recess Depth:				
Inlet	←————————	0.291-0.296 in.	————————→	
Exhaust	←————————	0.298-0.309 in.	————————→	
Valve Seat Angle	←————————	30°-30°30'	————————→	
Valve Seat Width	←————————	1/16-3/32 in.	————————→	
Valve Seat Runout	←————————	0.0015 in.	————————→	
Inlet Valve Opens	←————————	13° BTDC	————————→	
Inlet Valve Closes	←————————	48°49'12" ATDC	————————→	
Exhaust Valve Opens	←————————	48°49'12" BBDC	————————→	
Exhaust Valve Closes	←————————	12° ATDC	————————→	
Rocker Shaft Diameter	0.744-0.745 in.	←————	0.743-0.744 in.	————→
Rocker Arm to Shaft Clearance	←————————	0.001-0.003 in.	————————→	
Camshaft Journal Diameter	←————————	2.1845-2.185 in.	————————→	
Camshaft Journal Runout	←————————	0.005 in.	————————→	
Camshaft Journal Out-of-Round	←————————	0.0005 in.	————————→	
Camshaft End Play	←————————	0.002-0.023 in.	————————→	
Camshaft Gear Backlash	←————————	0.001-0.0127 in.	————————→	
Camshaft Lobe Lift	←————————	0.303 in.	————————→	
Camshaft Bearing Clearance:				
Front	0.002-0.0035 in.	←————	0.0015-0.0025 in.	————→
Intermediate and Rear	0.002-0.0035 in.	←————	0.001-0.002 in.	————→
Camshaft Gear Clearance Fit	←————————	0.001 in.	————————→	
Piston Ring Groove Width:				
Upper Compression Ring—				
Naturally Aspirated	←————————	0.0958-0.0968 in.	————————→	
Turbocharged (Wedge Type)	←————————	0.127-0.129 in.	————————→	
Intermediate Ring	←————————	0.0962-0.0972 in.	————————→	
Lower Compression Ring—				
Naturally Aspirated	←————————	0.0952-0.0962 in.	————————→	
Turbocharged	←————————	0.0962-0.0972 in.	————————→	
Oil Control Ring	←————————	0.180-0.190 in.	————————→	
Piston to Bore Clearance	←———	0.0058-0.0068 in. ———→	0.0068-0.0078 in.	0.0058-0.0068 in.
Piston Diameter:				
Grade 1	4.2137-4.2142 in.	4.1248-4.1253 in.	4.1175-4.1180 in.	4.2137-4.2142 in.
Grade 2	4.2142-4.2147 in.	4.1253-4.1258 in.	4.1180-4.1185 in.	4.2142-4.2147 in.
Grade 3	4.2147-4.2152 in.	4.1258-4.1263 in.	4.1185-4.1190 in.	4.2147-4.2152 in.
Grade 4	4.2152-4.2157 in.	4.1263-4.1268 in.	4.1190-4.1195 in.	4.2152-4.2157 in.
Piston Protrusion	←————————	0.006 in. below to 0.016 in. above block surface	————————→	
Piston Ring Groove Clearance:				
Top Ring—				
Naturally Aspirated	←————————	0.0023-0.0038 in.	————————→	
Turbocharged	←————————	0.0025-0.0060 in.	————————→	

Illustration courtesy Ford

INBOARD ENGINES   **Ford**

ENGINE SERVICE DATA (CONT.)

ENGINE MODEL	254	362	363	380
Sizes — Clearances (Cont.)				
Piston Ring Clearance (Cont.):				
Second Ring		0.0027-0.0042 in.		
Third Ring—				
Naturally Aspirated		0.0017-0.0032 in.		
Turbocharged		0.0027-0.0042 in.		
Oil Control Ring		0.0025-0.0040 in.		
Piston Ring End Gap:				
Top Ring—				
Naturally Aspirated		0.013-0.023 in.		
Turbocharged		0.017-0.025 in.		
Second and Third Ring		0.013-0.023 in.		
Oil Control Ring		0.013-0.028 in.		
Piston Pin Diameter		1.3751-1.3754 in.		
Piston Pin Length		3.531-3.546 in.		
Piston Pin to Piston Clearance		0-0.0002 in.		
Piston Weight Variation		1.0582 oz.		
Piston Pin Bushing ID		1.3751-1.3754 in.		
Connecting Rod Big End Diameter	2.7905-2.7910 in.	2.6460-2.6465 in.		2.7905-2.7910 in.
Connecting Rod Bearing Width		1.33-1.34 in.		
Connecting Rod Bearing Thickness	0.08150-0.08175 in.	0.0715-0.07175 in.		0.08150-0.08175 in.
Connecting Rod Bearing Clearance		0.002-0.0038 in.		
Piston Pin to Bushing Clearance		0.0001-0.0007 in.		
Connecting Rod Length				
Center to Center		7.998-8.002 in.		
Connecting Rod Side Clearance		0.003-0.009 in.		
Main Bearing Journal Diameter		3.0002-3.0010 in.		
Main Bearing Journal Runout		0.002 in.		
Main and Rod Bearing Journal:				
Out-of-Round (Max.)		0.00025 in.		
Taper (Max.)		0.0005 in.		
Connecting Rod Journal Diameter	2.6242-2.6250 in.	2.4997-2.5005 in.		2.6242-2.6250 in.
Connecting Rod Journal Length		1.660-1.664 in.		
Crankshaft End Play		0.002-0.010 in.		
Main Bearing Clearance		0.002-0.0041 in.		
Main Journal Length:				
Front		1.295-1.305 in.		
Intermediate		1.395-1.405 in.		
Rear		1.831-1.841 in.		
Main and Rod Journal Fillet Radii		0.17-0.19 in.		
Main Bearing Thickness		0.08150-0.08175 in.		
Cylinder Bore:				
Grade 1	4.2200-4.2205	4.1248-4.1253 in.		4.2200-4.2205 in.
Grade 2	4.2205-4.2210	4.1253-4.1258 in.		4.2205-4.2210 in.
Grade 3	4.2210-4.2215	4.1258-4.1264 in.		4.2210-4.2215 in.
Grade 4	4.2215-4.2220	4.1264-4.1268 in.		4.2215-4.2220 in.
Cylinder Liner Bore:				
Turbocharged Model 363	....	....	4.2812-4.2832 in.	....
Cylinder Liner Protrusion	....	....	0.020-0.025 in.	....
Cylinder Liner Interference Fit:				
Cast Iron	....	....	0.0035-0.0055 in.	....
Cromard	....	0.0015 in. clearance to 0.0005 in. interference		....
Valve Lifter to Bore Clearance		0.001-0.002 in.		
Oil Pump Rotor Assembly:				
End Clearance		0.005 in.		
Inner to Outer Rotor				
Clearance		0.006 in.		

Tightening Torques (All values are in ft.-lbs.)

Alternator Adjusting Bolt	12-15	Connecting Rod Bolts	85-90
Alternator Support Bracket Bolts	12-15	Connecting Rod Nuts	55-60
Camshaft Gear Retaining Bolt	150-155	Crankshaft Damper	240

Illustration courtesy Ford

Ford — INBOARD ENGINES

ENGINE SERVICE DATA (CONT.)

Tightening Torques (Cont.)

Cylinder Head Bolts:	
Step 1	80-85
Step 2	90-95
Step 3	
Model 254	105-110
Turbocharged engines built before 5-1-76	105-110
Turbocharged engines built after 5-1-76	120-125
Exhaust Manifold Bolts	17-22
Flywheel Retaining Bolts	80-90
Front Cover Bolts	6-8
Front Housing Bolts	25-30
Fuel Filter Bleed Screws	5-7
Fuel Filter Bracket Bolts	12-15
Fuel Filter Element Retaining Bolts	12-15
Fuel Lift Pump Cover Bolt	45-55
Fuel Lift Pump Mounting Bolts	12-15
Injection Pump Bleed Screws	3-5
Injection Pump	
Filler Plug	3-5
Level Plug	3-5
Drain Plug	3-5
Injection Pump Retaining Bolts	22-27
Injection Pump Timing Gear Retaining Nuts	46
Injector Cap Nut	37-43
Injector Inlet Adapter	16-20
Injector Leak-Off Pipe Banjo Connection	12-15
Injector Leak-Off Pipe To Injector Retaining Bolt	12-15
Injector Nozzle Nut	60-75
Injector Pipe Union Nut	16-20
Injector Retaining Bolts	12-15
Intake Manifold Bolts	17-22
Main Bearing Cap Bolts	115-120
Oil Filter Retaining Bolt	7-10
Oil Pan Bolts	22-24
Oil Pan Drain Plug	35-40
Oil Pick-up Tube Support Bolts	3-4
Oil Pump Cover Plate Bolts	12-15
Oil Pump Pick-up Tube to Oil Pump Bolts	55-65
Rocker Shaft Bracket Bolts	17-22
Timing Scale Bolts	25-30
Valve Rocker Arm Cover Bolts	12-18
Water Outlet Housing	12-15
Water Pump to Cylinder Block	12-15

MAINTENANCE

LUBRICATION

OIL AND FILTER. Engine oil and filter should be changed after every 100 hours of operation or seasonally, whichever is more frequent. For naturally aspirated engines use only high quality oils meeting API specifications SE or SE/CC. For turbocharged engines use a high quality oil which meets API specification CD only. See Fig. F3-1 for a chart which recommends oil viscosity based on expected average ambient temperatures for next 100 hours of operation.

FUEL INJECTION PUMP. Fuel injection pump lubricating oil should be changed after every 100 hours of engine operation. Oil is drained from injection pump by removing plug (3–Fig. F3-2). Use same grade and quality of oil as used in engine crankcase and fill injection pump through plug hole (1) to level of plug hole (2).

ENGINE SPEED ADJUSTMENTS

IDLE SPEED ADJUSTMENT. Idle speed is adjusted by turning idle speed stop screw (5–Fig. F3-3), see ENGINE SERVICE DATA section for specification. Note that a completely cold engine with the correct idle speed adjustment may stall but will run satisfactorily after a 30 second warm-up. It is recommended that you do not increase the idle speed to compensate for this cold engine stalling condition.

MAXIMUM ENGINE SPEED ADJUSTMENT. Maximum engine speed is adjusted with engine running and at normal operating temperature. With transmission in forward and vessel underway, advance throttle to the full speed position. Adjust maximum speed stop screw (3–Fig. F3-3) until an engine speed of 2500 rpm has been achieved for all model engines except turbocharged 363 which should be set at 2400 rpm. Be careful when making this adjustment that engine is not allowed to overspeed as serious damage could result.

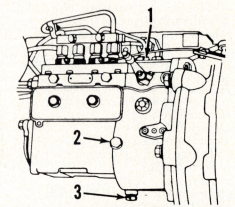

Fig. F3-2 – Injection pump oil fill plug (1), oil level plug (2) and oil drain plug (3) are located as shown.

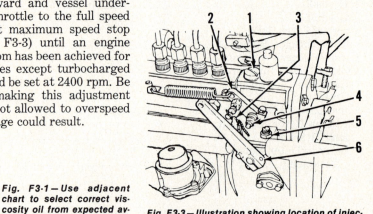

Fig. F3-1 – Use adjacent chart to select correct viscosity oil from expected average ambient temperature for next 100 hours of engine operation.

Fig. F3-3 – Illustration showing location of injection pump adjustment points.

1. Oil filler plug
2. Stop control lever
3. Maximum speed stop screw
4. Excess fuel device
5. Idle stop screw
6. Engine speed control lever

SINGLE VISCOSITY OILS	
When Outside Temperature is Consistently	Use SAE Viscosity Number
10°F. to +32F.	(†)10W
+10°F. to +60°F.	20W-20
+32°F. to +90°F.	30
Above 60°F.	40

MULTI-VISCOSITY OILS	
When Outside Temperature is Consistently	Use SAE Viscosity Number
Below +32°F.	(†) 5W-30
10°F. to +90°F.	10W-30
10°F. to +90°F. (or above)	10W-40
Above +10°F.	20W40

(†) Where sustained high RPM operation is anticipated, use 20W20.

INBOARD ENGINES

Ford

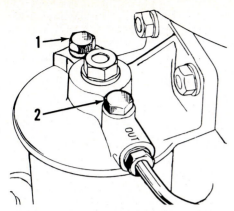

Fig. F3-4 — Illustration showing location of fuel filter inlet bleed screw (1) and outlet bleed screw (2).

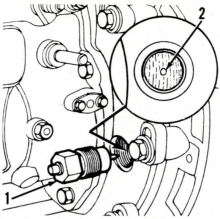

Fig. F3-6 — Remove plug from injection pump mounting flange and install Ford special tool number C9077 (1) as outlined in text. Tool tip must engage timing mark dimple (2) in camshaft gear.

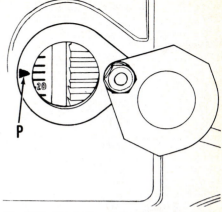

Fig. F3-7 — Illustration of flywheel timing marks and pointer (P) on flywheel housing.

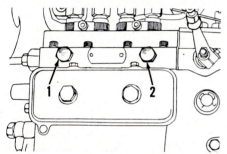

Fig. F3-5 — Illustration showing location of injection pump inlet bleed screw (1) and outlet bleed screw (2).

THROTTLE LINKAGE ADJUSTMENT. Throttle linkage should be checked for correct length when making engine speed adjustments. Hand throttle should have ¼ to ½ inch dead travel before engine rpm starts to rise off idle. This dead travel is necessary to prevent activation of injection pump governor at low engine speeds.

With engine running set hand throttle to idle position and disconnect throttle linkage from injection pump speed control lever (6 – Fig. F3-3). Move injection pump speed control lever (6) to its stop idle position and adjust throttle linkage as necessary to ensure speed control lever is always allowed to return to its full idle position. After adjustment check for sufficient dead travel of hand throttle lever.

FUEL SYSTEM

BLEED SYSTEM. To bleed fuel system loosen bleed screws shown in Fig. F3-4 on top of fuel filter and operate fuel lift pump priming lever until air-free fuel appears. Tighten inlet side bleed screw (1) first then outlet bleed screw (2) while continuing to operate priming lever. Next loosen bleed screws on injection pump (Fig. F3-5), and operate priming lever as before until air-free fuel appears. Tighten inlet side bleed screw (1) first then outlet bleed screw (2).

INJECTION PUMP TIMING. To check injection pump timing insert Ford special timing tool number C9077 (1 – Fig. F3-6) into aperature in injection pump mounting flange and rotate engine until spring-loaded plunger indexes in center punch mark (2) in rear of camshaft gear. At this point, correct timing mark, as specified in ENGINE SERVICE DATA section, should be aligned with pointer in flywheel cover. See Fig. F3-7. If any doubt exists as to accuracy of timing marks, proceed as follows to spill time injection pump to engine. Rotate crankshaft until number 1 piston is starting its compression stroke and then align specified BTDC timing mark on flywheel with pointer on flywheel cover as shown in Fig. F3-7. See ENGINE SERVICE DATA section for timing specification. Remove number 1 injector delivery valve holder volume reducer, delivery valve and spring. Reinstall delivery valve holder and install spill tube. Loosen mounting flange bolts and fully retard pump. Fill injection pump using priming pump; fuel should spill out of delivery valve holder. Slowly advance injection pump until fuel just stops flowing from spill tube and immediately tighten mounting flange bolts. Injection pump is now correctly timed to engine. Reinstall delivery valve, spring and volume reducer.

TURBOCHARGER

STARTING. Before starting, turbocharger equipped engines should be cranked for a minimum of 15 seconds with throttle control lever in stop position. If during this cranking period oil pressure is indicated on oil gage or warning light goes out it is safe to start engine. At all times, even after starting, turbocharger equipped engines should be allowed to idle for two minutes before stopping engine to avoid damage to turbocharger unit.

PRIMING TURBOCHARGER. If during 15-second cranking period, with throttle in stop position, no oil pressure is indicated on oil gage or oil warning light does not go out, turbocharger unit must be manually primed with engine oil.

Disconnect oil feed pipe to turbocharger unit and fill housing with engine oil. Reconnect oil feed pipe. Using a suitable syringe, inject a minimum of 4 pints of clean engine oil into oil gage pressure supply fitting of engine, then reinstall oil gage fitting. Start engine and allow to run at idle for two minutes while checking oil pressure gage or warning light for adequate oil pressure. Stop engine and check oil level. Add or remove engine oil as required to bring oil level to full mark on dipstick.

VALVE ADJUSTMENT

Adjust valves to specifications given in ENGINE SERVICE DATA section with engine at normal operating temperature. To check valve clearances, rotate crankshaft and adjust valves indicated in the following table (valves are numbered from timing gear end of engine):

FOUR-CYLINDER MODELS

Valves Open	Adjust Valves
1 and 6	3 and 8
2 and 4	5 and 7
3 and 8	1 and 6
5 and 7	2 and 4

SIX-CYLINDER MODELS

Valves Open	Adjust Valves
1 and 4	9 and 12
8 and 10	3 and 5
2 and 6	7 and 11
9 and 12	1 and 4
3 and 5	8 and 10
7 and 11	2 and 6

Illustration courtesy Ford

Ford   INBOARD ENGINES

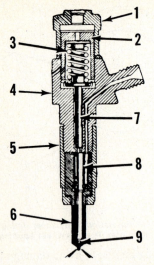

Fig. F3-8 — Cutaway drawing of fuel injection nozzle.

1. Cap nut
2. Adjusting screw
3. Spring
4. Nozzle holder
5. Nozzle nut
6. Nozzle
7. Spindle
8. Needle valve
9. Valve seat

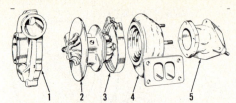

Fig. F3-9 — Exploded view of major turbocharger components.

1. Compressor housing
2. Center core
3. "V" Clamp
4. Turbine housing
5. Exhaust adapter and mounting bracket

REPAIRS

INJECTORS

CAUTION: When testing fuel injection nozzles keep nozzle tip pointed in a safe direction away from hands and eyes. Fuel spray will penetrate skin due to high pressure and atomization.

A complete job of testing and adjusting injectors requires use of special test equipment. Only clean, approved testing oil should be used to test injectors. Injector should be tested for opening pressure, leak-back, seat leakage and spray pattern.

Before removing injector from cylinder head first clean injector and adjacent cylinder head area with compressed air and a suitable solvent. Remove and cap fuel return and supply lines. Remove two retaining bolts and lift out injector. Remove copper sealing washer from cylinder head unless it was removed with injector.

Before conducting tests, clean carbon deposits from nozzle tip using a brass brush and clean diesel fuel. Check nozzle spray holes for obstructions. Operate tester lever until fuel flows then attach injector. To check nozzle opening pressure, pump tester several strokes to obtain an accurate reading and ensure nozzle valve is not stuck. See ENGINE SERVICE DATA section for opening pressure specifications. If opening pressure is not correct, loosen cap nut (1 — Fig. F3-8), insert a screwdriver through hole in leak-off pipe connection and turn adjusting screw (2) until opening pressure is correct.

To check nozzle leak-back apply 2200 psi to injector and check amount of time it takes pressure to fall off to 1500 psi. This pressure drop should take between 6 and 10 seconds.

After checking nozzle leak-back check for nozzle seat leakage. Wipe nozzle tip dry with blotting paper and apply a pressure of 2500 psi. After one minute touch nozzle tip with blotting paper and measure the resulting stain. Stain should not be larger than ½ inch in diameter.

Next, pump tester handle at a rate of 6 to 8 strokes per second to check spray pattern. Spray from each nozzle tip hole should be similar, with no visible streaks or distortions. Each spray must be fully atomized and form a cone.

If injector passes all four tests it can be returned to service. If injector fails any test it should be renewed or repaired by a shop which specializes in diesel injection equipment repair.

Before installing injector check injector bore in cylinder head to be sure it is free from any dirt or carbon deposits. Use care to prevent any carbon deposits from falling down into cylinder when cleaning injector bore. Install a new copper sealing ring and insert injector, connect injector lines and tighten injector bolts evenly to specification given in ENGINE SERVICE DATA section.

NOTE: Injector mounting bolts are of very high tensile steel and are installed without lockwashers. It is important that only correct type bolts are used.

INJECTION PUMP

To remove injection pump, disconnect throttle control cable, stop control cable, injector lines from delivery valve holders, fuel delivery line from rear of injection pump and pump drain pipe. Remove mounting bolts and nut. Remove pump and drive gear.

Fuel injection pump should be serviced by a shop qualified in diesel injection equipment repair.

To install injection pump, rotate crankshaft until number 1 piston is on compression stroke and notch in flywheel housing is in line with injection timing mark specified in ENGINE SERVICE DATA. See Fig. F3-7. A timing mark (2 — Fig. F3-6) on rear face of camshaft gear will be visible through injection pump opening when engine is on correct stroke. Remove plug in injection pump mounting flange and insert Ford special timing tool number C9077. Rotate injection pump drive gear until spring-loaded plunger drops into center punch mark on rear face of gear. Back out tool and rotate camshaft gear ⅝ inch counterclockwise. Install "O" ring on face of injection pump and install pump and gear into engine while keeping the mounting stud centered in slotted hole. Install mounting bolts and nut hand-tight. Screw special tool into plug hole and rotate pump until spring-loaded plunger in Ford special tool again engages center punch mark in camshaft gear and torque mounting bolts and nut to specification given in ENGINE SERVICE DATA section. Remove special timing tool, and reinstall plug in injection pump flange. Install pump drain line, injector lines, fuel supply line, throttle and stop control cables. Bleed fuel system and adjust idle and maximum engine speed as previously outlined.

If engine surges at any point in its speed range be sure injection pump oil level and grade of lubrication are correct; refer to LUBRICATION section.

TURBOCHARGER

NOTE: Turbine wheel rotates at 80,000 to 90,000 rpm when operating at maximum speed. Care and cleanliness are very important when repairing turbocharger.

To remove turbocharger disconnect oil supply line, drain line, exhaust pipe and air intake pipe. Remove nuts securing turbocharger to exhaust manifold.

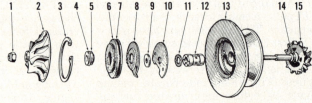

Fig. F3-10 — Exploded view of center core assembly.

1. Locknut
2. Compressor wheel
3. Snap ring
4. Piston ring
5. Spacer sleeve
6. Insert
7. "O" ring
8. Oil deflector
9. Thrust ring
10. Thrust plate
11. Thrust washer
12. Bearing
13. Bearing housing
14. Piston ring
15. Turbine wheel & shaft assy.

Illustration courtesy Ford

INBOARD ENGINES — Ford

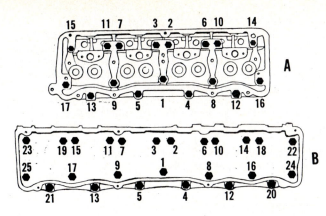

Fig. F3-11 – Follow cylinder head bolt tightening sequence in adjacent drawing when installing Model 254 cylinder head (A) or Models 362, 363 and 380 cylinder head (B).

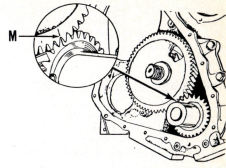

Fig. F3-12 – Illustration of correct camshaft to crankshaft gear timing marks (M).

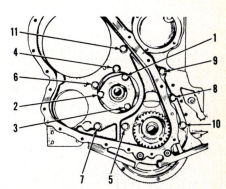

Fig. F3-13 – Tighten timing case cover screws using tightening sequence shown.

Remove mounting bracket retaining bolts and lift off turbocharger unit.

To disassemble turbocharger unit, clamp turbine inlet flange (4 – Fig. F3-9) in a vise. Remove oil inlet and drain tubes. Mark compressor housing (1), center core (2), turbine housing (4) and mounting bracket (5) to ensure correct alignment when reassembling unit. Remove bolts and lockwashers securing compressor housing (1) to center core (2) and remove housing. Unscrew "V" clamp locknut, detach "V" clamp (3) and separate turbine housing (4) from center core.

To disassemble center core, remove compressor wheel (2 – Fig. F3-10), snap ring (3) and lift out insert (6) from bearing housing (13) using two screwdrivers as levers. Remove spacer sleeve (5) by gently pushing it through insert (6). Remove "O" ring (7) from insert (6). Remove oil deflector (8), thrust ring (9), thrust plate (10) and thrust washer (11) from bearing housing (13). Remove turbine wheel and shaft (15), and bearing (12) from bearing housing (13). Remove piston rings (4) from spacer sleeve (5) and piston rings (14) from turbine wheel and shaft assembly (15).

Clean all parts by soaking them in a non-caustic metal cleaner and scrubbing with a plastic bristle brush. Blow out all drilled passages using compressed air.

Inspect bearing journals and piston groove walls for scratches and excessive wear. Check for cracked, bent or damaged turbine and compressor wheel blades. **DO NOT ATTEMPT TO STRAIGHTEN BLADES.**

Before reassembly lubricate all parts with clean engine oil. Install new piston rings (4 and 14 Fig. F3-10) on spacer sleeve (5) and turbine wheel shaft (15). Install turbine wheel and shaft assembly (10) into bearing housing (13). Install thrust washer (11) and thrust plate (10) into bearing housing (13); be sure holes in thrust plate engage dowels in bearing housing. Install thrust ring (9), and oil deflector plate (8) in bearing housing (13); be sure holes in deflector plate engage dowels in bearing housing and bent portion of plate is towards oil gallery in housing. Install new "O" rings on insert (6) and gently push spacer sleeve (5) into insert (6) from inside with stepped end of spacer pointing away from insert. Install insert and spacer sleeve assembly into bearing housing, install snap ring (3) with beveled side facing outward. Install compressor wheel (2) using a new locknut (1) torqued to 13 ft.-lbs.

Connect oil supply and drain tubes and tighten securely. Align turbine housing (4 – Fig. F3-9) and center core (2) assembly marks and secure together using "V" clamp (3); torque locknut to 10 ft.-lbs. Align compressor housing (1) and center core (2) assembly marks and secure together using bolts and lockwashers; torque bolts to 5 ft.-lbs. Rotate turbine shaft by hand and check for free operation. Install mounting bracket (5) on turbine housing (4) using assembly marks for alignment. Complete rest of installation in opposite order of removal. It is essential that turbocharger housing and oil supply line be filled with oil prior to starting engine as outlined in PRIMING TURBOCHARGER section.

CYLINDER HEAD

Intake and exhaust valve guides are renewable and identical. When renewing valve guides set intake valve guide protrusion at 0.72 inch and exhaust valve guide protrusion at 1.10 inch. Replacement valve seat inserts are available. Where inserts have not been installed previously, it will be necessary to machine a recess in cylinder head for replacement insert. Do not plane or grind more than 0.010 inch from cylinder head gasket surface. Valves and valve seats should not be lapped. Do not remove more than 0.010 inch from end of valve stem. If valve head margin is less than 1/32 inch thick after grinding valve must be renewed. Cylinder head bolt tightening sequence is shown in Fig. F3-11. See ENGINE SERVICE DATA section for torque specifications. Retighten cylinder head bolts after engine is at operating temperature and after 100 hours of operation.

PISTONS

During manufacture pistons and cylinder bores are graded. Piston grade letter is stamped on piston head and each cylinder bore grade letter is stamped on push rod side of cylinder block. See ENGINE SERVICE DATA section for specifications. Piston skirt is oval so piston skirt diameter must be measured at right angles to piston pin and 1 inch from bottom of skirt. Install piston on connecting rod so notch on piston dome and word "FRONT" on connecting rod face in same direction and are installed facing front of engine.

CRANKSHAFT

Crankshaft used in turbocharged engine is dimensionally identical to naturally aspirated engine, but material specification is different so they are not interchangeable. Crankshaft main and rod bearing journals may be ground undersize. Original fillet radii must be maintained and fillet must be smooth and free from chatter marks. Center main journal length can be increased provided an equal amount of material is removed from each face and oversize thrust washers are used. Grinding and

Ford INBOARD ENGINES

polishing should both be against direction of normal crankshaft rotation. See Fig. F3-12 for illustration of correct crankshaft to camshaft timing mark alignment.

CYLINDER BLOCK AND LINERS

In all engines except turbocharged Model 363, pistons are in direct contact with cylinder block. Boring and honing of cylinder bores to correct for wear, damage or incorrect piston fit is permissible. See ENGINE SERVICE DATA section for piston and cylinder bore specifications.

Late production turbocharged Model 363 marine engines incorporate a dry-type "Cromard" cylinder liner which protrudes above cylinder block surface to reduce the dead air space between cylinder head and gasket. Cylinder blocks designed for turbocharger equipped engines are identified by a "T" stamped on rear of cylinder block pad.

"Cromard" cylinder liners are pre-finished and should not be resurfaced in any way. At time of installation cylinder liner protrusion should be 0.020-0.025 inch, however once having been in service it is permissible for cylinder liners to drop a maximum of 0.060 inch below cylinder block surface.

See Fig. F3-13 for illustration of tightening sequence of timing gear housing retaining bolts.

INBOARD ENGINES Ford

FORD

ENGINE SERVICE DATA

ENGINE MODEL	CSG-850M	WSG-858M	LSG-875M
General			
Displacement – Cu. In.	302	351	460
Number of Cylinders	←——————— 8 ———————→		
Bore	4.00 in.	4.00 in.	4.36 in.
Stroke	3.00 in.	3.50 in.	3.85 in.
Cylinder Numbering (front to rear)			
Right Bank	←——————— 1-2-3-4 ———————→		
Left Bank	←——————— 5-6-7-8 ———————→		
Firing Order:			
Standard Rotation	←——— 1-3-7-2-6-5-4-8 ———→		1-5-4-2-6-3-7-8
Reverse Rotation	←——— 1-8-4-5-6-2-7-3 ———→		1-8-7-3-6-2-4-5
Oil Capacity with Filter	←——————— 5 qts. ———————→		
Number of Main Bearings	←——————— 5 ———————→		

*CSG-850M low output engine firing order is same as LSG-875M engine.

	CSG-850M	WSG-858M	LSG-875M
Tune-up			
Idle Speed	←——————— 550-575 rpm ———————→		
Fast Idle Speed	←——————— 1500 rpm ———————→		
Ignition Timing	←——— 6° BTDC ———→		10° BTDC
Breaker Point Gap:			
GPD	←——————— 0.014-0.019 in. ———————→		
Mallory	←——————— 0.019-0.021 in. ———————→		
Prestolite	←——————— 0.014-0.019 in. ———————→		
Spark Plug Gap	←——————— 0.035 in. ———————→		
Dwell Angle at Idle:			
GPD	←——————— 26° ———————→		
Mallory	←——————— 26° ———————→		
Prestolite	←——————— 31° ———————→		
Centrifugal Advance:			
0-550 rpm	←——————— 0° ———————→		....
750 rpm	←——————— 4°-6½° ———————→		....
900 rpm	......	......	8°
1000 rpm	←——— 9½° ———→		....
1500 rpm	←——— 11½° ———→		....
2000 rpm	←——— 13½° ———→		15°
Hydraulic Lifter Collapsed Gap:			
Desired	0.096-0.165 in.	0.123-0.173 in.	0.100-0.150 in.
Allowable	0.071-0.193 in.	0.098-0.198 in.	0.075-0.175 in.
Fuel Pump Pressure			
@500 rpm	←——— 5-7 psi ———→		5.5-7.7 psi
Fuel Pump Volume			
@500 rpm	←——————— 1 pint/20 sec. ———————→		
Thermostat:			
Low Temperature –			
Opens	←——————— 157°-164°F ———————→		
Fully Open	←——————— 184°F ———————→		
High Temperature –			
Opens	←——————— 188°-195°F ———————→		
Fully Open	←——————— 212°F ———————→		
Belt Tension:			
New	←——————— 140 ft.-lbs. ———————→		
Used	←——— 110 ft.-lbs. ———→		100 ft.-lbs.
Oil Pressure (Hot)			
@2000 rpm	40-60 psi	40-65 psi	35-65 psi

Illustration courtesy Ford

Ford — INBOARD ENGINES

ENGINE SERVICE DATA (CONT.)

ENGINE MODEL	CSG-850M	WSG-858M	LSG-875M

Tune-Up (Cont.)

Starter, Current Draw:
- 4-inch Diameter —
  - Normal Load .... 150-200 amps @ 180-250 rpm
  - Maximum Load .... 460 amps
  - No Load .... 70 amps
- 4½-inch Diameter —
  - Normal Load .... 150-180 amps @ 150-290 rpm
  - Maximum Load .... 670 amps
  - No Load .... 80 amps

Starter Brushes:
- New Length .... 0.50 in.
- Wear Limit .... 0.25 in.
- Spring Tension .... 40 oz.

Through-Bolt Torque .... 55-75 in.-lbs.
Mounting Bolt Torque .... 15-20 ft.-lbs.

Sizes — Clearances

Specification	CSG-850M	WSG-858M	LSG-875M
Combustion Chamber Volume	56.7-59.7 cc	58.9-61.9 cc	94.7-97.7 cc
Valve Guide Bore Diameter		0.3433-0.3443 in.	
Valve Seat Width		0.060-0.080 in.	
Valve Seat Angle		45°	
Valve Seat Runout		0.002 in.	
Rocker Arm Lift Ratio		1.61:1	1.73:1
Valve Push Rod Runout		0.015 in.	
Rocker Arm Stud Bore Diameter (standard)		0.3680-0.3695 in.	....
Rocker Arm Stud Diameter:			
Standard		0.3714-0.3721 in.	....
0.006 in. Oversize		0.3774-0.3781 in.	....
0.010 in. Oversize		0.3814-0.3821 in.	....
0.015 in. Oversize		0.3864-0.3871 in.	....
Hydraulic Lifter Leakdown Rate		5-50 sec. max. at 1/16 in. plunger travel	
Lifter Diameter		0.8740-0.8745 in.	
Lifter to Bore Clearance		0.0007-0.0027 in.	
Valve Stem Diameter:			
Intake —			
Standard		0.3416-0.3423 in.	
0.003 in. Oversize		0.3446-0.3453 in.	
0.015 in. Oversize		0.3566-0.3573 in.	
0.030 in. Oversize		0.3716-0.3723 in.	
Exhaust —			
Standard		0.34111-0.3418 in.	0.3416-0.3423 in.
0.003 in. Oversize		0.3441-0.3418 in.	0.3446-0.3453 in.
0.015 in. Oversize		0.3561-0.3568 in.	0.3566-0.3573 in.
0.030 in. Oversize		0.3711-0.3718 in.	0.3716-0.3723 in.
Valve Face Angle		44°	
Valve Stem Clearance:			
Intake		0.0010-0.0027 in.	
Exhaust		0.0015-0.0032 in.	0.0010-0.0027 in.
Valve Face Runout		0.0020 in.	
Valve Head Diameter:			
Intake		1.773-1.791 in.	2.075-2.090 in.
Exhaust		1.453-1.468 in.	1.6461-1.661 in.
Valve Spring Free Length:			
Intake	1.94 in.	2.06 in.	2.07 in.
Exhaust	1.87 in.	1.87 in.	2.07 in.
Valve Spring Out-of-Square		5/64 in.	
Valve Spring Pressure	76-84 lbs. @ 1.69 in.	71-79 lbs. @ 1.79 in.	76-85 lbs. @ 1.81 in.
Valve Spring Installed Height:			
Intake	1-21/32 – 1-23/32 in.	1-49/64 – 1-13/16 in.	1-51/64 – 1-53/64 in.
Exhaust		1-19/32 – 1-5/8 in.	1-51/64 – 1-53/64 in.

INBOARD ENGINES — Ford

ENGINE SERVICE DATA (CONT.)

ENGINE MODEL	CSG-850M	WSG-858M	LSG-875M
Sizes-Clearances (Cont.)			
Camshaft Journal Diameter:			
No. 1 Bearing	← 2.0805-2.0815 in. →		2.1238-2.1248 in.
No. 2 Bearing	← 2.0655-2.0665 in. →		2.1238-2.1248 in.
No. 3 Bearing	← 2.0505-2.0515 in. →		2.1238-2.1248 in.
No. 4 Bearing	← 2.0355-2.0365 in. →		2.1238-2.1248 in.
No. 5 Bearing	← 2.0205-2.0215 in. →		2.1238-2.1248 in.
Camshaft Journal Runout (Max.)	← 0.005 in. →		
Camshaft Journal Clearance	← 0.001-0.003 in. →		
Camshaft Journal Out-of-Round (Max.)	← 0.005 in. →		
Camshaft Lobe Lift:			
CSG-850M Low Output —			
Intake	0.2303 in.	......	......
Exhaust	0.238 in.	......	......
All Other Models —			
Intake	0.2600 in.	0.278 in.	0.2530 in.
Exhaust	0.278 in.	0.283 in.	0.2780 in.
Camshaft End Play	← 0.001-0.007 in. →		
Timing Chain Deflection	← 0.500 in. →		
Camshaft Bearing Inside Diameter:			
No. 1 Bearing	← 2.0825-2.0835 in. →		2.1258-2.1268 in.
No. 2 Bearing	← 2.0675-2.0685 in. →		2.1258-2.1268 in.
No. 3 Bearing	← 2.0525-2.0535 in. →		2.1258-2.1268 in.
No. 4 Bearing	← 2.0375-2.0385 in. →		2.1258-2.1268 in.
No. 5 Bearing	← 2.0205-2.0215 in. →		2.1258-2.1268 in.
Piston Diameter:			
Coded Red	3.9984-3.9990 in.	3.9978-3.9984 in.	4.3585-4.3591 in.
Coded Blue	3.9996-4.0002 in.	3.9990-3.9960 in.	4.3597-4.3603 in.
0.003 in. Oversize	4.0008-4.0014 in.	4.0002-4.0008 in.	4.3609-4.3615 in.
Piston Clearance	← 0.0018-0.0026 in. →		0.0022-0.0032 in.
Piston Pin Bore Diameter	0.9122-0.9126 in.	0.9124-0.9127 in.	1.0402-1.0405 in.
Piston Pin Diameter			
Standard	← 0.9120-0.9123 in. →		1.0398-1.0403 in.
0.001 in. Oversize	← 0.9130-0.0133 in. →		1.0410-1.0413 in.
0.002 in. Oversize	← 0.9140-0.9143 in. →		....
Piston Pin Length	← 3.010-3.040 in. →		3.290-3.320 in.
Piston Pin to Piston Clearance	0.0002-0.0004 in.	0.0003-0.0005 in.	0.0002-0.0004 in.
Piston Ring Groove Width:			
Top Ring	← 0.077-0.078 in. →		0.080-0.0815 in.
Second Ring	← 0.077-0.078 in. →		0.080-0.0815 in.
Oil Control Ring	← 0.1880-0.1890 in. →		0.180-0.190 in.
Piston Ring Width:			
Top Ring	← 0.077-0.078 in. →		
Second Ring	← 0.077-0.078 in. →		
Piston Ring Side Clearance:			
Top Ring	← 0.002-0.004 in. →		0.0025-0.0045 in.
Second Ring	← 0.002-0.004 in. →		0.0025-0.0045 in.
Piston Ring End Gap:			
Top Ring	← 0.010-0.020 in. →		
Second Ring	← 0.010-0.020 in. →		
Oil Control Ring	← 0.015-0.055 in. →		
Connecting Rod Piston Pin Bore Diameter	← 0.9096-0.9112 in. →		1.0386-1.0393 in.
Connecting Rod Big End Bore Diameter	2.2390-2.2398 in.	2.4265-2.4273 in.	2.6522-2.6530 in.
Connecting Rod Length Center-to-Center	5.0885-5.0915 in.	5.9545-5.9575 in.	6.6035-6.6065 in.
Connecting Rod Side Clearance	← 0.010-0.020 in. →		

Illustration courtesy Ford

Ford — Inboard Engines

ENGINE SERVICE DATA (CONT.)

ENGINE MODEL	CSG-850M	WSG-858M	LSG-875M

Sizes — Clearances (Cont.)

	CSG-850M	WSG-858M	LSG-875M
Connecting Rod Bearing Clearance			
Desired		0.0008-0.0015 in.	
Allowed		0.0008-0.0025 in.	
Main Bearing Journal Diameter	2.2482-2.2490 in.	2.9994-3.0002 in.	
Main Bearing Journal Runout		0.001 in.	0.002 in.
Main Bearing Journal Out-of-Round		0.0006 in.	
Main Bearing Journal Taper		0.0006 in.	
Connecting Rod Journal Diameter	2.1228-2.1236 in.	2.3103-2.3111 in.	2.4992-2.500 in.
Connecting Rod Journal Out-of-Round		0.0006 in.	
Connecting Rod Journal Taper		0.0006 in.	
Thrust Bearing Journal Length		1.137-1.139 in.	1.124-1.126 in.
Crankshaft End Play		0.004-0.008 in.	
Main Bearing Bore Diameter	2.4412-2.4420 in.	3.1922-3.1930 in.	
Main Bearing Clearance:			
No. 1 Bearing—			
Desired	0.0001-0.0015 in.	0.0008-0.0015 in.	
Allowed	0.0001-0.0020 in.	0.0005-0.0024 in.	0.0004-0.0020 in.
No. 2, 3, 4, 5—			
Desired	0.0005-0.0015 in.	0.0008-0.0015 in.	
Allowed	0.0005-0.0024 in.	0.0008-0.0026 in.	
Cylinder Bore Diameter	4.0004-4.0052 in.	4.0000-4.0048 in.	4.3600-4.3636 in.
Cylinder Bore Out-of-Round (Max.)		0.0015 in.	
Cylinder Bore Taper (Max.)		0.001 in.	
Lifter Bore Diameter		0.8752-0.8767 in.	
Distributor Shaft Bearing Bore Diameter	0.4525-0.4541 in.	0.5155-0.5171 in.	0.5160-0.5175 in.
Oil Pump Relief Valve Spring Tension	10.6-12.2 lbs. @ 1.704 in.	18.2-20.2 lbs. @ 2.49 in.	20.6-22.6 lbs. @ 2.490 in.
Oil Pump Drive Shaft to Bearing Clearance		0.0015-0.0029 in.	
Oil Pump Relief Valve Clearance		0.0015-0.0029 in.	
Oil Pump Rotor Assembly End Clearance		0.001-0.004 in.	
Oil Pump Outer Rotor to Housing Clearance		0.001-0.013 in.	

Tightening Torques
(All values are in ft.-lbs.)

	CSG-850M	WSG-858M	LSG-875M
Alternator Pivot Bolt		45-57	
Camshaft Sprocket		40-45	
Camshaft Thrust Plate		9-12	
Connecting Rod Nuts	10-24	40-45	
Cylinder Front Cover		12-18	
Cylinder Head Bolts:			
Step 1	50	90	70-80
Step 2	60	100	100-110
Step 3	65-70	112	130-140
Exhaust Manifold		18-24	28-33
Flywheel		75-85	
Fuel Pump		19-27	
Intake Manifold		23-25	22-32
Main Bearing Cap	60-70	95-105	

Illustration courtesy Ford

INBOARD ENGINES — Ford

ENGINE SERVICE DATA (CONT.)

ENGINE MODEL	CSG-850M	WSG-858M	LSG-875M

Tightening Torques (Cont.)

Oil Pan:
- 1/4-20 7-9
- 5/16-18 8-11
- Oil Pan Drain Plug 15-25
- Oil Pump 22-32
- Oil Pump Cover Plate 6-10
- Oil Pump Inlet Tube .... 10-15 ....
- Vibration Damper 70-90
- Water Outlet Housing 10-15
- Water Pump 12-18

CARBURETOR SPECIFICATIONS

CARBURETORS	D2JL C 302	D2JL E 351	D3JL S 302-351	D4JL F 302	D4JL G 351	D1FF TA 460	D4JL J 460
Carburetor Size							
Throttle Bore Diameter							
Primary —	1.5" (38.1mm)	1.5625"(39.7mm)	1.50" (38.1mm)	1.5" (38.1mm)	1.5625"(39.7mm)	1.687	1.686
Secondary —	1.5" (38.1mm)	1.5625"(39.7mm)	—	1.5" (38.1mm)	1.5625"(39.7mm)	1.687	1.686
Venturi Diameter							
Primary —	1.094" (27.8mm)	1.250"(31.8mm)	1.187"(30.15mm)	1.094" (27.8mm)	1.250"(31.8mm)	1.375	1.375
Secondary —	1.094" (27.8mm)	1.3125"(33.3mm)	—	1.094" (27.8mm)	1.3125"(33.3mm)	1.437	1.437
Fuel System							
Fuel Level (Wet)	①	①	③	③ ⑤	④ ⑤	①	③ ⑤
Float Level (Dry)	②	②	②	②	②	②	②
Main Metering System							
Main Jet							
Primary —	#58	#64	#60	#58	#622	#72	#722
Secondary —	N/A	N/A	—	N/A	#84	N/A	N/A
Power Valve Timing							
Inch/Hg	8.5" (215.9mm)	5.0" (127mm)	5" (127mm)	8.5" (215.9mm)	2.5" (63.5mm)	8.5" (215.9mm)	8.5" (215.9mm)
Idle Mixture (Preliminary Setting)	1½	1½	1½	1½	1½	1½	1½
Accelerator Pump System							
Capacity — cc/10 Strokes	21-31	25-35	25-35	21-31	22-32	18-22	17-27
Pump Rod Location	#2	#1	#1	#2	#2	#2	#2
Override Spring Adjustment	.015" (.381mm)	.015" (.381mm)	.015" (.381mm)	.015" (.381mm)	.015" (.381mm)	.015" (.381mm)	.015" (.381mm)
Pump Cam Color	Red	Pink	Pink	Red	Pink	Red	Red
Idle Speed							
Curb Idle RPM	550-575	550-575	550-575	550-575	550-575	550-575	550-575
Fast Idle RPM	1500	1500	1500	1500	1500	1500	1500
Choke Cover Setting	3 Lean	3 Lean	3 Lean	Index	Index	Index	Index
Dechoke	.300" (7.62mm)	.300" (7.62mm)	.300" (7.62mm)	.300" (7.62mm)	.270" (6.86mm)	.300" (7.62mm)	.300" (7.62mm)
Choke Qualifying	.140" (3.56mm)	.140" (3.56mm)	.140" (3.56mm)	.140" (3.56mm)	.120" (3.048mm)	.140" (3.56mm)	.140" (3.56mm)
Secondary Throttle Opening	¼-½	¼-½	—	¼-½	¼-½	¼-½	¼-½
Holley							
I.D. Number	6407	6576-A	7036	7159	7163	6361	7128
Carburetor Model	4160C	4160C	2300C	4160C	4160C	4150C	4160C

① Lower Edge of Sight Plug Hole.
② Parallel with Float Bowl Floor (bowl inverted).
③ ½" (12.70mm) Primary ⅝" (15.88mm) Secondary
④ ½" (12.70mm) Primary ¾" (19.05mm) Secondary
⑤ Use Kent Model Gauge #10193

MAINTENANCE

LUBRICATION. Engine oil and filter should be changed after every 100 hours of operation or seasonally whichever is more frequent. Use a good quality API specification SF, SE or SE/CC oil. Oil which also meets API specification CD is not recommended by manufacturer. See Fig. F4-1 for oil viscosity recommendations based on anticipated ambient temperature for next 100 hours of engine operation.

Illustration courtesy Ford

Ford

INBOARD ENGINES

SINGLE VISCOSITY OILS

When Outside Temperature is Consistently	Use SAE Viscosity Number
-10°F. to +60°F.	*10W
+10°F. to +90°F.	20W-20
Above +32°F.	30
Above +50°F.	40

MULTI VISCOSITY OILS

When Outside Temperature is Consistently	Use SAE Viscosity Number
Below +10°F.	*5W-20
Below +60°F.	5W-30
-10°F. to 90°F.	10W-30
Above -10°F.	10W-40
Above -10°F.	10W-50
Above +20°F.	20W-40
Above +20°F.	20W-50

*Not recommended for severe service — including high RPM operation.

Fig. F4-1 — Use adjacent chart in selecting the correct viscosity engine oil for the next 100 hours of operation.

threaded fittings to specifications shown in chart below:

	Torque (in.-lbs.)
Bowl Screws	25-30
Main Jet	30-40
Adjustable Needle and Seat Lockscrew	50-60
Manifold/Carburetor Flange nut	60-80
Fuel Inlet Valve Seats (5/16 in.)	60-80
Fuel Inlet Valve Seats (7/16 in.)	70-90
Power Valves, Spark Valves and Plugs	40-50
Fuel Inlet Fitting (9/16 in.)	175-200
Fuel Inlet Fitting (7/8 in.)	200-250

Refer to the following sections for carburetor adjustment.

CHOKE CONTROL QUALIFYING. DIVORCED CHOKE. To adjust choke on models using an intake manifold-mounted, bi-metal choke assembly, open throttle and manually close choke. With choke held closed release throttle. Measure distance (D – Fig. F4-3) from top of choke rod hole in choke control lever to base of carburetor. This measurement should be 1-15/32 to 1-19/32 inch with carburetor on bench. If carburetor is on engine, measurement should be taken from top of choke rod hole in choke control lever to top of intake manifold-mounted choke assembly. This measurement should be 2-23/32 to 2-25/32 inch. Bend choke rod at point shown in Fig. F4-3 to adjust choke.

INTEGRAL CHOKE EARLY PISTON DESIGN. To qualify choke with early design piston, bend a paper clip that is 0.030-0.036 inch in diameter to the shape shown in Fig. F4-4. The bent end must not be longer than 1/8 inch. Insert bent end of paper clip into piston bore so clip end hooks top end of bore slot. With paper clip in end of slot, slowly close choke valve until piston contacts paper clip. Bend piston lever adjusting tab as shown in Fig. F4-4 to adjust

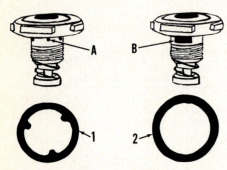

Fig. F4-2 — There are two different power valves (A and B) gaskets (1 and 2) used in Holley carburetors. Be sure to properly match piston and gasket. Gasket (1) must be installed on drilled power valve (A) while gasket (2) must be installed on rectangular-port power valve (B).

Water damage is a problem on carbureted marine engines. Never attempt to use a fuel bowl or carburetor body that has been damaged by water. Water damage is indicated when bottom of fuel bowl is covered by a white powder and the metal is etched. Water, gasoline and zinc combine to form a zinc oxide.

There are several things to watch on reassembly. Make certain the right parts are used and pay particular attention to gasket fit. Do not use old gaskets. There are two different power valve gaskets. Power valves with multiple fuel drillings (A – Fig. F4-2) use gasket (1). Power valves with two rectangular fuel openings (B) use gasket (2). Use of the wrong gasket will result in fuel leakage around power valve and poor performance. When installing balance tube on four-barrel carburetors, use new "O" rings and washers and be sure they are seated in recess on both primary and secondary sides; this is very important, otherwise fuel leakage will occur. Position balance tube so that only one inch extends beyond secondary metering body. Torque all screws and

CARBURETOR
(Holley Model 2300, 4150 and 4160)

OVERHAUL. The first digit of each model number designates the number of barrels (throttle bores) in the carburetor. Model 2300 is a two-barrel carburetor while Models 4150 and 4160 are four-barrel carburetors. The various systems and adjustments of the Model 2300 also apply to the primary side of Model 4150 and 4160 carburetors. Secondary side systems and adjustments apply only to Model 4150 and 4160 carburetors.

Before disassembling carburetor place it on a suitable stand or legs. Legs can be made from four two-inch cap screws and eight nuts. This will help prevent damage to throttle valves or shafts.

Inspection is a part of disassembly. If a part has a dark area or shiny area, check the fit. Check castings for trueness with a straightedge and for leakage.

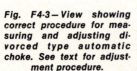

Fig. F4-3 — View showing correct procedure for measuring and adjusting divorced type automatic choke. See text for adjustment procedure.

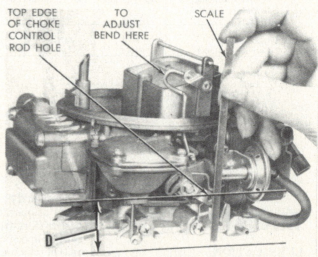

Illustration courtesy Ford

INBOARD ENGINES

Ford

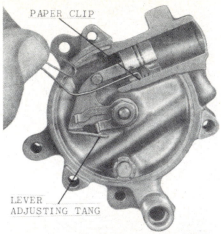

Fig. F4-4—Choke adjustment of early model integral type automatic chokes is achieved by using a paper clip that has been bent and inserted into choke housing as shown. See text for choke adjustment procedure.

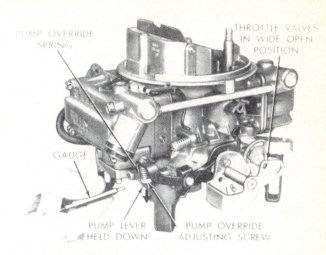

Fig. F4-6—Perform accelerator pump adjustment with throttles held wide open and pump lever held down. Adjust pump override screw so there is a clearance of 0.015-0.062 inch between pump lever and screw.

Fig. F4-5—Late model integral chokes are adjusted using adjusting screw to limit piston travel. See text for choke adjustment procedure.

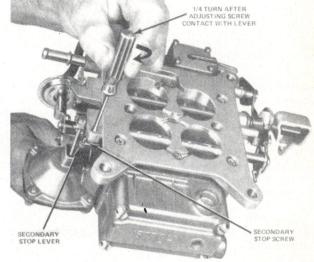

Fig. F4-7—Turn secondary stop screw in until it just touches stop on throttle lever, then turn secondary stop screw in an additional ¼ turn.

Fig. F4-8—Bowl vent valve clearance should be 0.015 inch and is adjusted by bending actuating rod.

choke qualifying opening (distance between choke valve and air horn wall) to specification given in carburetor table of ENGINE SERVICE DATA section.

INTEGRAL CHOKE LATE PISTON DESIGN. Use a paper clip to push piston against adjustable stop screw (Fig. F4-5). While holding piston against stop screw gently push choke valve closed until all linkage free play is removed. The resulting choke qualifying setting (distance from choke valve to air horn wall) is adjusted by turning stop screw. See carburetor chart in ENGINE SERVICE DATA section for specification. Be careful not to back adjusting screw out so far that piston will partially pass screw as screw will then damage piston during inward adjustment.

ACCELERATOR PUMP ADJUSTMENT. Hold throttle valves wide open and accelerator pump lever down. Adjust pump override screw until a clearance of 0.015-0.062 inch has been achieved. See Fig. F4-6. There must be no free play of accelerator pump lever when throttle valves are closed. Accelerator pump linkage for secondary side of carburetor is adjusted in the same manner.

SECONDARY THROTTLE STOP. Back out secondary throttle stop screw (Fig. F4-7) until secondary throttle valves are completely closed. Turn

Illustration courtesy Ford

Ford   INBOARD ENGINES

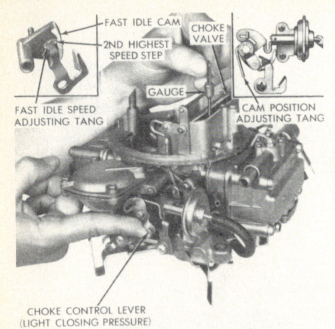

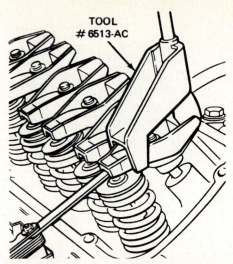

Fig. F4-9 – Fast idle cam is adjusted as shown using a 0.060-0.065 inch gage. See text for adjustment procedure.

Fig. F4-12 – Use tool number 6513-AC to collapse hydraulic lifter and measure gap as outlined in text.

throttle stop screw in until it just touches stop on throttle lever, then turn stop screw in an additional ¼ turn.

BOWL VENT VALVE CLEARANCE. With throttle valves closed it should be possible to insert a 0.015 inch gage between bowl vent stem and operating rod (on earlier models gage is inserted between rubber valve and bowl surface). To adjust clearance, bend operating rod to change point of contact with throttle lever. See Fig. F4-8.

FAST IDLE CAM POSITION. With fast idle speed adjusting tang on second highest step of fast idle cam and choke valve gently held in its closed position, it should be possible to insert a 0.060-0.065 inch gage between top edge of choke valve and air horn wall. Bend choke control lever adjusting tang until correct choke valve opening has been obtained. See Fig. F4-9.

IDLE MIXTURE ADJUSTMENT. To properly adjust idle mixture engine must be at normal operating temperature with air cleaner properly installed. Do not idle engine more than three minutes at one time without raising engine speed to 2000 rpm for 1 minute. With engine running adjust idle mixture screws (M – Fig. F4-10) to obtain "lean best idle" at specified idle rpm. See carburetor chart in ENGINE SERVICE DATA section for specifications. Lean best idle is the point at which engine speed drops 10 rpm due to leanness.

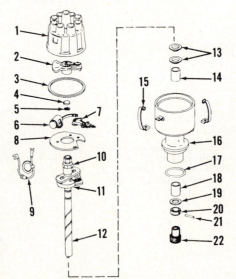

Fig. F4-11 – Exploded view of Prestolite distributor used in Ford marine engines.

1. Distributor cap
2. Rotor
3. Cap gasket
4. Lubricating wick
5. Retainer
6. Condenser
7. Breaker points
8. Breaker subplate
9. Primary wire
10. Cam assy.
11. Centrifugal advance assy.
12. Shaft
13. Thrust washers
14. Upper bushing
15. Clamp
16. Housing
17. Oil seal
18. Lower bushing
19. Thrust washer
20. Collar
21. Pin
22. Drive gear

Fig. F4-10 – Adjust idle mixture using screw (M), and idle mixture screw on opposite side of carburetor. Idle speed is adjusted by turning screw (S).

IDLE SPEED. To properly adjust idle speed engine must be at normal operating temperature. Idle speed is adjusted by turning idle screw (S – Fig. F4-10), turning idle speed screw clockwise will increase engine speed.

FAST IDLE ADJUSTMENT. With engine off and at normal operating temperature open throttle and close choke valve. Close throttle, then release choke, to place fast idle screw on highest step of fast idle cam. Move fast idle cam until screw drops down to second step and is against first step shoulder. Without touching accelerator, start engine and allow speed to stabilize. Adjust fast idle screw, which is located on opposite side of carburetor from idle speed adjustment screw, as necessary to obtain engine speed specified in carburetor chart of ENGINE SERVICE DATA section.

DISTRIBUTOR

All models use a Prestolite distributor. Shaft (12 – Fig. F4-11) and drive gear (22) are renewed as an assembly; do not renew separately.

When installing a new distributor shaft (12) holes for pins (21) must be located and drilled. Insert a 0.024 inch feeler gage between collar (20) and distributor housing (15) base. Slide shaft (12) through collar (20). While holding collar (20) in place against distributor housing (16) base, drill a ⅛ inch hole through shaft (12) using hole in collar (20) as a pilot. Place distributor housing (15) and shaft (12) on a press using a support plate so all shaft (12) end play has been removed. Place drive gear (22) on end of shaft (12) and press drive gear (22) onto shaft (12) to a point where dis-

INBOARD ENGINES

Ford

tance from bottom of drive gear (22) face is 4.031 to 4.038 inches from bottom face of distributor mounting flange. Drill a 1/8 inch hole through shaft (12) using hole in drive gear (22) as a pilot. Remove distributor housing (15) from press and install retaining pins (21) through collar (20) and drive gear (22).

VALVE ADJUSTMENT

No valve clearance adjustment is required. Push rods that are 0.060 inch shorter or longer than standard length are available to compensate for wear or dimensional variances. If noise appears to come from valve train components and is not easily diagnosed (as a collapsed hydraulic valve lifter), check for wear in valve train as follows:

Remove rocker arm covers and observing firing order (ENGINE SERVICE DATA), move each piston in turn to top dead center after compression stroke and apply pressure, using Ford special tool 6513AC, to each push rod as shown in Fig. F4-12. When pressure has caused lifter to bleed down completely, check valve stem to rocker arm gap using a narrow (under 3/8-inch) feeler gage. Note desired clearance in ENGINE SERVICE DATA and install a shorter push rod if clearance is insufficient, or install a longer push rod if clearance is excessive. Disassembly and renewal of worn valve train parts, including hydraulic lifters, is necessary if clearance is incorrect.

REPAIR

INTAKE MANIFOLD

Tighten intake manifold bolts in appropriate sequence in Fig. F4-13, F4-14

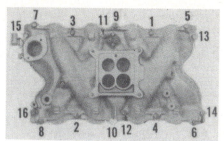

Fig. F4-15 — Use bolt tightening sequence shown when installing intake manifold on Model LSG-875 engines.

or Fig. F4-15 to specification given in ENGINE SERVICE DATA section. After completion on intake manifold installation run engine until it reaches normal operating temperature and again torque bolts to specification.

FRONT OIL SEAL

On engines built prior to 1979 front oil seal can only be renewed after removing cylinder front cover. Front oil seal is installed from rear of cylinder front cover and should be driven into its bore until it is fully seated in recess. On engines after 1978 the front oil seal is installed from front, therefore, cylinder front cover does not have to be removed.

CYLINDER HEAD AND VALVES

Do not plane or grind more than 0.010 inch from cylinder head gasket surface.

If it becomes necessary to ream a valve guide always reface valve seat and use a suitable scraper to break sharp corner (ID) at top of valve guide. Refacing of valve seat should be closely coordinated with grinding valve face. Grind valve seat to a true 45 degree angle and valve face to a true 44 degree angle to maintain specified interference fit. To raise valve seats of all engines use a 60 degree angle grinding wheel to remove stock from bottom of seat. Use a 30 degree angle grinding wheel to remove stock from top of valve seat to lower seat. Finished valve seat should contact approximate center of valve face. Under no circumstances should aluminized intake valves be ground or lapped as this will remove diffused aluminum coating and reduce valves heat and wear resistance. If aluminized valve faces are worn or pitted it will be necessary to renew valve. Manufacturer recommends that valve and seat not be lapped. Do not remove more than 0.010 inch from end of valve stem. Use tightening sequence shown in Fig. F4-16 when installing cylinder head bolts.

PISTONS AND PISTON RINGS

Fig. F4-17 shows proper installed location of compression and oil control ring end gaps. If new piston rings are installed, cylinder bore glaze must be removed using a suitable cylinder hone. Oil piston rings, pistons and cylinder bores with engine oil. Be sure to install pistons in cylinders from which they

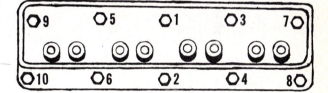

Fig. F4-16 — Use bolt tightening sequence shown when installing cylinder head.

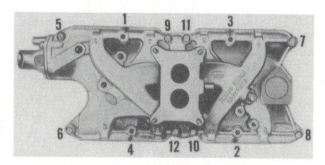

Fig. F4-13 — Use bolt tightening sequence shown when installing intake manifold on Model CSG-850M engines.

Fig. F4-14 — Use bolt tightening sequence shown when installing intake manifold on Model WSG-858M engines.

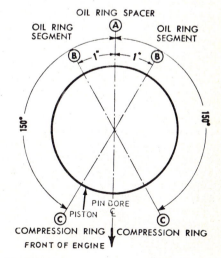

Fig. F4-17 — Position piston ring end gaps as shown before installing piston in cylinder bore.

Illustration courtesy Ford

Ford   INBOARD ENGINES

were removed or to which they were fitted. Notch in piston crown must be towards front of engine when piston is installed. See Fig. F4-18.

CONNECTING RODS

Connecting rods and caps are numbered from 1 to 4 on right bank and 5 to 8 on left bank, beginning at front of engine. Number on connecting rod and cap must be on same side when installed in cylinder bore. See Fig. F4-18 for correct piston-to-rod relationship. See ENGINE SERVICE DATA section for torque specifications.

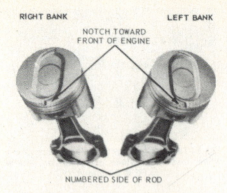

Fig. F4-18—Install pistons on rods as shown. Notch in piston crown should be pointing towards front of engine when installed.

Fig. F4-19—View of crankshaft and camshaft sprocket timing marks (M).

INBOARD ENGINES — Mercruiser

MERCRUISER

**MERCURY MARINE
DIVISION OF BRUNSWICK CORP.
Fon du Lac, Wisconsin 54935**

ENGINE SERVICE DATA

ENGINE MODEL	233	255	350
General			
Cylinders	V8	V8	V8
Bore	4.00 in.	4.00 in.	4.25 in.
Stroke	3.5 in.	3.48 in.	4.0 in.
Displacement – Cu. In.	351	350	454
Compression Ratio	8.0:1	8.5:1	8.5:1
Compression Pressure at Cranking Speed	150 psi	150 psi	150 psi
Main Bearings, Number Of	5	5	5
Firing Order	*	**	**
Numbering System (Front-to-Rear):			
Port Bank	5-6-7-8	1-3-5-7	1-3-5-7
Starboard Bank	1-2-3-4	2-4-6-8	2-4-6-8
Tune-Up			
Valve Lifter Type	Hydraulic	Hydraulic	Hydraulic
Valve Lash	N.A.	¾ Turn Down From Zero Lash	¾ Turn Down From Zero Lash
Valve Seat Angle	45°	46°	46°
Valve Face Angle	44°	45°	45°
Valve Seat Width:			
Intake	0.080 in.	0.0312-0.0625 in.	0.0312-0.0625 in.
Exhaust	0.080 in.	0.0625-0.0938 in.	0.0625-0.0938 in.
Valve Spring Length	2.07 in.	2.08 in.	2.10 in.
Installed Spring Height	1.75-1.81 in.	1.656 in.	1.88 in.
Valve Spring Pressure – Lbs. at In.:			
Closed	71-79 at 1.79	74-86 at 1.88	74-86 at 1.88
Open	190-210 at 134	288-312 at 1.38	288-312 at 1.38
Valve Stem Clearance:			
Intake	0.0010-0.0027	0.0010-0.0035 in.	0.0010-0.0035 in.
Exhaust	0.0015-0.0032	0.0012-0.0037 in.	0.0012-0.0037 in.
Timing Mark Location	Crankshaft damper	Crankshaft damper	Crankshaft damper
Ignition Timing	10° BTDC	6° BTDC	10° BTDC
Cam Angle (Dwell)	26°-31°	28°-30°	Breakerless
Breaker Point Gap	0.017	0.017	Breakerless
Spark Plug Type	AC-C83T Champ.-F10	AC-MR43T Champ.-RBL8	AC-M41T
Spark Plug Gap	0.030 in.	0.035 in.	0.035 in.
Carburetor Type	Roch. 2GC	Roch. 4MV	Roch. 4MV
Float Level	⅝-in.	¼-in.	¼-in.
Float Drop	1-29/32 in.	......	......
Engine Idle Speed	550-600 rpm	550-660 rpm	550-660 rpm
Sizes — Capacities — Clearances			
Crankshaft Journal Diameter:			
No. 1	2.9994-3.0002 in.	2.4484-2.4493 in.	2.7475-2.7484 in.
Nos. 2-4	2.9994-3.0002 in.	2.4481-2.4491 in.	2.7481-2.7490 in.
No. 5	2.9994-3.0002 in.	2.4479-2.4488 in.	2.7468-2.7478 in.
Main Bearing Clearance:			
No. 1	0.0008-0.0026 in.	0.0008-0.0024 in.	0.0019-0.0031 in.
Nos. 2-4	0.0008-0.0026 in.	0.0008-0.0024 in.	0.0019-0.0031 in.
No. 5	0.0008-0.0026 in.	0.0010-0.0026 in.	0.0024-0.0040 in.
Crankpin Diameter	2.3103-2.3111 in.	2.100 in.	2.1985-2.1995 in.

Illustration courtesy Mercury Marine

Mercruiser — INBOARD ENGINES

ENGINE MODEL	233	255	350
Sizes — Capacities — Clearances (Cont.)			
Rod Bearing Clearance	0.0008-0.0026 in.	0.0007-0.0028 in.	0.0014-0.0035 in.
Rod Side Clearance	0.010-0.020 in.	0.019-0.025 in.	0.019-0.027 in.
Crankshaft End Play	0.004-0.008 in.	0.003-0.011 in.	0.006-0.010 in.
Piston Pin Diameter	0.9119-0.9124 in.	0.9270-0.9273 in.	0.9895-0.9898 in.
Pin Clearance in Piston	0.0008 in. Max.	0.001 in. Max.	0.001 in. Max.
Pin Clearance In Rod	——— 0.0008-0.0016 in. Interference ———		
Piston Clearance	0.0018-0.0026 in.	0.0016-0.0026 in.	0.004-0.005 in.
Piston Ring End Gap	0.010-0.020 in.	0.010-0.020 in.	0.010-0.020 in.
Ring Side Clearance:			
Top Comp	0.002-0.004 in.	0.0012-0.0042 in.	0.0017-0.0042 in.
2nd Comp	0.002-0.004 in.	0.0012-0.0037 in.	0.0017-0.0042 in.
Oil	Snug	0.000-0.006 in.	0.0011-0.0075 in.
Camshaft Journal Diameter:			
No. 1	2.0805-2.0815 in.	1.8682-1.8692 in.	1.9487-1.9497 in.
No. 2	2.0655-2.0665 in.	1.8682-1.8692 in.	1.9487-1.9497 in.
No. 3	2.0505-2.0515 in.	1.8682-1.8692 in.	1.9487-1.9497 in.
No. 4	2.0355-2.0365 in.	1.8682-1.9692 in.	1.9487-1.9497 in.
No. 5	2.0205-2.0215 in.	1.8682-1.8692 in.	1.9487-1.9497 in.
Camshaft Runout	0.005 in. Max.	0.0015 in. Max.	0.0015 in. Max.
Crankcase Capacity W/Filter	7 qts.	7 qts.	7 qts.
Oil Pressure At 2000 rpm	40-70 psi	30-55 psi	30-70 psi
Fuel Pump Pressure	3-6 psi	4-7 psi	4-7 psi
Fuel Required	——— 93 Research Octane Min. W/Lead ———		

*Firing order: L.H. Rotation – 1-3-7-2-6-5-4-8; R.H. Rotation – 1-8-4-5-6-2-7-3.
**Firing order: L.H. Rotation – 1-8-4-3-6-5-7-2; R.H. Rotation – 1-2-7-5-6-3-4-8.

TIGHTENING TORQUES
(All values are in foot pounds.)

Model 233	Torque Rating
Camshaft Sprocket	43
Connecting Rod Nut	40
Cylinder Head Bolt	108
Flywheel Bolt	80
Main Bearing Cap Bolt	100
Intake Manifold Screw	25
Oil Pump Mounting Bolt	25
Rocker Arm Cover Screw	4
Spark Plug	15
Timing Chain Cover Bolt	13
Vibration Damper	80
Water Pump Bolt	14

Models 255, 350	Torque Rating
Camshaft Sprocket	20
Connecting Rod:	
255	45
350	50
Cylinder Head:	
255	65
350	80
Exhaust Manifold	20
Flywheel:	
255	60
350	65
Intake Manifold	30
Main Bearing Cap:	
255	75
350	110
Oil Pump Mounting	65
Timing Chain Cover	6
Vibration Damper:	
255	60
350	85
Water Pump	30

MAINTENANCE

CARBURETOR

Rochester 2GC

FLOAT LEVEL/FLOAT DROP. Refer to ENGINE SERVICE DATA for float level and float drop specifications. Refer to Figs. M1-1 and M1-2 for methods of float measurement.

ACCELERATOR PUMP. To adjust accelerator pump action, back out idle speed screw until throttle valves are closed and measure from top of air horn next to pump plunger to top of pump rod. Measurement should be 1 1/8 inches as shown in Fig. M1-3. Bend pump rod to adjust.

CHOKE. Choke should have scribed mark on cover in line with long case

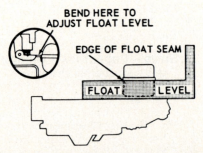

Fig. M1-1 – Adjust Rochester 2GC carburetor float level as shown above. Float level should be 5/8-inch.

Illustration courtesy Mercury Marine

INBOARD ENGINES
Mercruiser

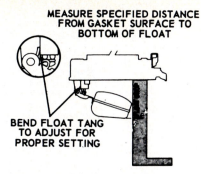

Fig. M1-2 — Adjust float drop as shown above for 2GC carburetors.

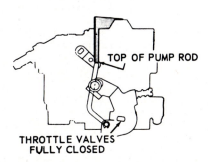

Fig. M1-3 — For correct accelerator pump action, distance from air horn to top of pump rod should be 1⅛ inches.

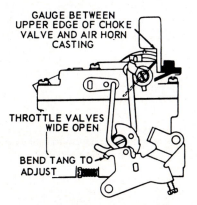

Fig. M1-4 — Open throttle valves fully and measure between choke valve and carburetor bore to check choke unloader setting. Refer to text for measurement. Bend throttle lever tang to adjust.

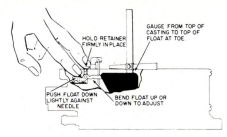

Fig. M1-5 — Adjust float level on Rochester 4MV as shown above. Float level should be ¼-inch.

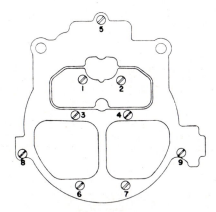

Fig. M1-6 — Tightening sequence for Rochester 4MV air horn screws.

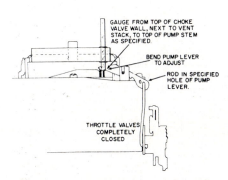

Fig. M1-7 — There must be 9/32-inch between top of accelerator pump stem and top of choke valve wall next to vent stack for correct accelerator pump action. Bend pump rod to adjust.

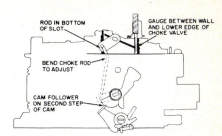

Fig. M1-8 — Adjust choke rod as outlined in text.

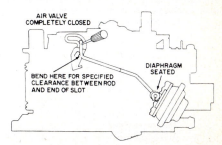

Fig. M1-9 — Adjustment of air valve dashpot. Note placement of 0.030 inch wire gage under rod in slot of valve lever.

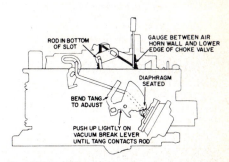

Fig. M1-10 — Vacuum break adjustment procedure. See text.

mark on choke housing. Place throttle valves in wide open position and measure choke unloader setting between choke valve and carburetor bore as shown in Fig. M1-4. Setting should be 0.080 inch for carburetors with tag numbers 7025188 and 7026088 or 0.160 inch for carburetors with tag numbers 7028086 and 7020993. Bend tang of throttle lever to adjust.

Rochester 4MV

FLOAT LEVEL. Refer to ENGINE SERVICE DATA for idle speed and float setting. Adjust float level as shown in Fig. M1-5. Note tightening sequence of carburetor M1-6.

ACCELERATOR PUMP. To check accelerator pump adjustment, throttle valves must be completely closed and pump rod in inner hole of pump lever. Measure from top of choke valve wall, next to vent stack, to top of pump stem as shown in Fig. M1-7. Dimension should be 9/32-inch. Blend pump rod to adjust.

FAST IDLE. To adjust fast idle, primary valves must be completely closed and cam follower on high step of fast idle cam. Turn fast idle screw in two turns after screw is fully seated.

CHOKE ROD. After adjusting fast idle, check choke rod adjustment. Place cam follower on second step of fast idle cam and against high step. Rotate choke valve towards closed position by pushing down on vacuum break lever. Measure between lower edge of choke valve, at choke lever end, and carburetor bore (Fig. M1-8). Dimension should be 0.100 inch.

AIR VALVE DASHPOT. Adjust air valve dashpot by pushing down on the vacuum break lever shown in Fig. M1-8 and seat the vacuum diaphragm using an outside vacuum source. Bend rod as shown in Fig. M1-9 to obtain a clearance of 0.030 inch (use a wire gage) between dashpot rod and end of slot in air valve lever.

VACUUM BREAK. To adjust vacuum break, rotate choke valve toward closed position by pushing down on the vacuum break lever and seat the vacuum diaphragm using an outside vacuum source. Measure the distance between lower edge of choke valve and air horn wall using a 0.150 inch gage (Fig. M1-10). Bend choke lever tang to adjust.

Illustration courtesy Mercury Marine

Mercruiser

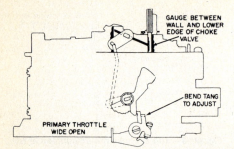

Fig. M1-11 – Adjustment procedure for setting choke unloader. Be sure to hold toward closed position while setting.

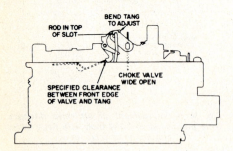

Fig. M1-12 – Air valve lockout adjustment points. See text.

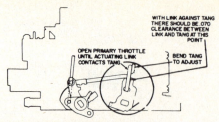

Fig. M1-13 – Adjustment of secondary throttle opening point. Follow procedure outlined in text.

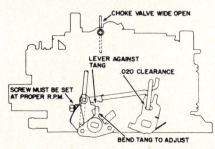

Fig. M1-14 – Adjustment of secondary throttle closing point. Engine idle speed must be set first.

CHOKE UNLOADER. To check the choke unloader adjustment, hold choke valve closed using a rubber band on the vacuum break lever. Move the primary throttle to wide open position and measure choke valve opening (Fig. M1-11). Clearance between lower edge of the choke valve and air horn wall should be 0.300 inch. Bend the tang on fast idle lever to adjust.

AIR VALVE LOCKOUT. Check the air valve lockout clearance as shown in Fig. M1-12. Clearance should be less than 0.015 inch but the parts should not be touching.

SECONDARY THROTTLE. Refer to Fig. M1-13 for adjusting secondary opening. Open the carburetor primary throttle when checking. Refer to Fig. 1-14 to adjust secondary throttle closing. Start engine and set idle speed at 500-600 rpm. Refer to Fig. M1-14 and check for 0.020-inch clearance (No. 76 drill) between secondary link and forward end of secondary lever slot when primary throttle lever tang just contacts link lever. Bend primary throttle lever tang to set clearance.

CHOKE COIL ROD. Adjust choke coil rod as follows: Completely close choke valve and position choke rod in bottom of choke lever slot. Pull up on choke coil rod to end of travel. Bend choke coil rod until top of rod is even with bottom of hole in vacuum break lever as shown in Fig. M1-15.

THUNDERBOLT IGNITION SYSTEM

Model 255

Model 255 is equipped with a breakerless, capacitive discharge ignition system. Important safety precautions are as follows:
1. Do not touch any part of the ignition system with engine running. Do not disconnect any part of ignition system with key switch "ON" or with battery cables connected.
2. Never reverse cable connections (polarity) at battery terminals. This is a negative (−) ground system.
3. Do not "flash" or spark battery posts with cable connectors to determine polarity of battery.
4. Never disconnect cables at battery while engine is running.
5. Do not use test or service equipment except that recommended here or in manufacturer's service literature. Conventional ignition service tools (except timing light) cannot be used in this system.
6. Observe troubleshooting sequence in exact order shown for each test operation.

Failure to follow these instructions can easily result in personal injury or damage to the system. Required test equipment is as follows:

Voltmeter. Minimum range: 0-15 VDC.
Ohmmeter. MerCruiser C-91-52751 Volt-Ohm-Ampere Tester (VOA) or equivalent.
Jumper lead 10-15 inches insulated wire with test clips having ¾-inch jaw

INBOARD ENGINES

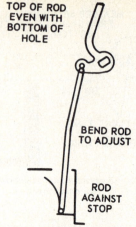

Fig. M1-15 – Bend choke coil rod so top of rod is even with bottom of hole.

opening.
Trigger – new.
Ignition coil – new.
Switch box assembly – new.

TROUBLESHOOTING

Engine Misfiring Or Running Roughly

CHECK SPARK PLUG LEADS. Modify a conventional (not polar gap) spark plug by removal of side (ground) electrode, and connect modified plug to any plug lead to be checked. Use jumper lead to ground shell of modified plug to engine and crank engine. Observe for spark from center electrode to shell while cranking. Renew individual plug leads or entire set if defective. Test by running engine. If results are not satisfactory, proceed to next check.

DISTRIBUTOR CAP AND ROTOR. Thoroughly inspect distributor cap and rotor for cracks or damage. Renew if defects appear.

Fig. M1-16 – Coil should be satisfactory if ignition spark will bridge ½-inch gap to ground.

Illustration courtesy Mercury Marine

INBOARD ENGINES

Mercruiser

NOTE: High secondary voltages "flash over" tracks in bakelite where current goes to ground by following hairline cracks in material.

Engine Will Not Start Or Run

CHECK SPARK AT COIL. Check as preceding for spark at any plug lead. If spark is normal, check for fuel supply to carburetor. If no spark, check at coil by removing secondary lead at center well of distributor cap and performing cable to ground check as in Fig. M1-16. If spark appears with sufficient intensity to jump ½-inch air gap, then check distributor cap, rotor and spark plug cables as covered in preceding paragraphs. If there is still no spark, proceed as follows:

CHECK WIRING AND CONNECTIONS. Connect voltmeter positive (+) lead to switch box terminal to which red wire is connected. See Fig. M1-17 or system schematic, Fig. M1-19. Ignition switch if "OFF." When voltmeter negative (−) lead is grounded on engine, battery voltage should indicate on meter scale. If reading is below battery voltage or does not register, disconnect battery positive cable, isolate red wire, and check with ohmmeter for open circuit or high resistance. If either of these condi-

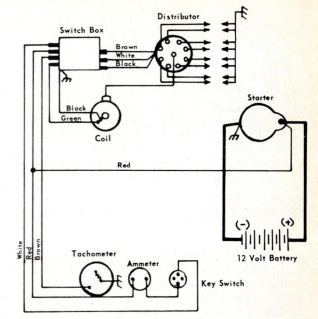

Fig. M1-19 — Thunderbolt ignition system schematic.

tions appear, renew red wire. If normal battery voltage shows on meter, proceed as follows: Change positive voltmeter test lead to switch box lug to which white wire is connected, Fig. M1-17, with negative voltmeter lead grounded on engine. With battery positive cable connected and ignition key switch "ON,"

battery voltage should be indicated. As a quick check of ignition switch and its wiring, turn key "ON" and "OFF" a few times observing meter dial. If meter shows erratic response, it is possible there is a faulty connection or key switch contacts are defective which may cause intermittent failure to function.

NOTE: Whenever ohmmeter-continuity checks are made, it is advisable to pull and stretch wiring or device under test in a manner similar to normal mechanical stresses of operation so hidden defects such as broken conductors, concealed by insulating material, loose or stripped terminals or worn or broken contacts will appear at this time, when repair or renewal is more convenient.

If these voltmeter tests indicated constant battery voltage, turn key "Off" and proceed:

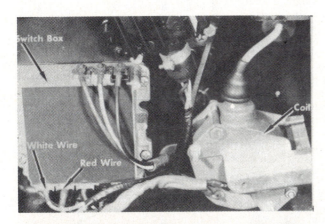

Fig. M1-17 — View of Thunderbolt ignition system test connection points for voltmeter. Refer to text for hookup procedure.

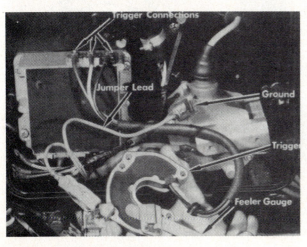

Fig. M1-18 — View of trigger test connections. Note that new trigger is connected to switch box terminals and that jumper wire is used to ground body of trigger during test.

TRIGGER CHECK. Disconnect brown, white and black trigger leads from switch box, see Fig. 1-18 or schematic, Fig. M1-19, and connect same color leads from new trigger assembly to proper switch box terminals. Ground trigger body, using jumper wire as in Fig. M1-18 to coil bracket or other suitable ground. Set ½-inch gap to ground in high voltage coil to distributor lead as in Fig. M1-16, turn key switch "ON" and pass a feeler gage blade or other thin metal strip between trigger inductance coils as shown, observing coil wire gap to ground. If spark jumps air gap, original trigger is defective and must be renewed. If no spark appears, but a clicking noise sounds from coil, then coil has an internal short (or open) and must be renewed. If there is NO

Illustration courtesy Mercury Marine

115

Mercruiser
INBOARD ENGINES

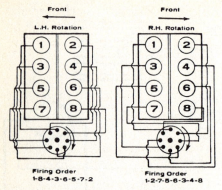

Fig. M1-20—Cylinder numbering arrangement and firing orders (L & R rotation) for 255 and 350 models.

click from coil and NO spark at air gap, install a new switch box. Reconnect all wiring, observing color coding as in Fig. M1-19, with original trigger and coil assemblies in place, then recheck for spark at spark plug lead. If no spark is observed, then reinstall original switch box and renew ignition coil. System should now operate normally.

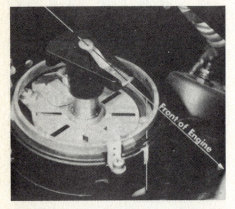

Fig. M1-21—Line-up of distributor adapter and rotor to static engine timing. See IGNITION TIMING in text.

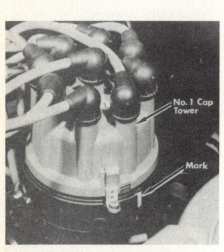

Fig. M1-22—Mark distributor housing adapter for disassembly. See text.

SET IGNITION TIMING. This is the only adjustment which applies to Thunderbolt Ignition. Refer to Fig. M1-20 or to ENGINE SERVICE DATA for cylinder numbering arrangement and locate number 1 piston at Top Dead Center. If necessary, remove rocker arm cover from left-hand cylinder head to identify compression stroke by observation of valve rockers while rotating engine by hand. Line up timing mark on crankshaft damper with TDC mark on timing tab. This takes about 1/3 turn after number 1 intake valve closes. Install distributor pilot body with pilot mark and rotor lined up toward front of engine as shown in Fig. M1-21. Install distributor cap, reconnect all wiring and start engine. With timing light connected to number 1 spark plug lead, engine idling at 550-600 rpm, aim timing light at timing tab and shift distributor body rotation until marks align properly.

R&R AND OVERHAUL. Disconnect battery positive (+) cable and remove electrical panel cover. Disconnect trigger lead, brown, white and black, from switch box terminal lugs and pull out through panel grommets. Mark distributor housing below number 1 plug lead well as shown in Fig. M1-22 and remove distributor cap. Rotate engine manually until distributor rotor is aligned with mark on adaptor housing as in Fig. M1-21, and crankshaft pulley timing mark and TDC line of timing tap are aligned. Disconnect distributor body ground wire, remove hold-down clamp cap screw and lift distributor from engine. Renew distributor body gasket whenever distributor has been removed.

To disassemble distributor, matchmark adaptor housing and distributor pilot for ease of reassembly. If rotor is

Fig. M1-23—Collapse hydraulic valve lifter on Model 233 using tool number 6513AC and insert a narrow feeler gage as outlined in text.

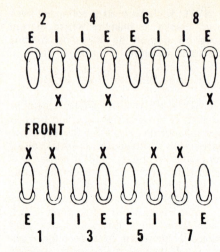

Fig. M1-24—Valves marked "X" can be adjusted statically on left-hand rotation Models 255 and 350 with number 1 piston at TDC on compression stroke. Adjust remaining valves with number 6 piston at TDC on compression stroke.

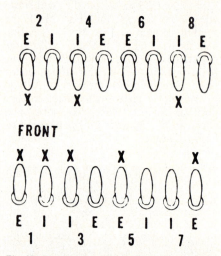

Fig. M1-25—Valves marked "X" can be adjusted statically on right-hand rotation Models 255 and 350 with number 1 piston at TDC on compression stroke. Adjust remaining valves with number 6 piston at TDC on compression stroke.

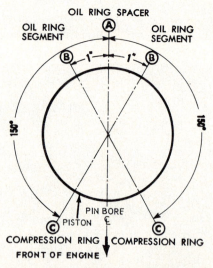

Fig. M1-26—View showing arrangement of piston ring end gaps on Model 233 piston.

INBOARD ENGINES

Mercruiser

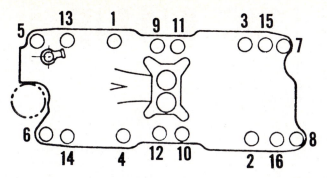

Fig. M1-27—Use sequence shown above to tighten intake manifold fasteners on Model 233.

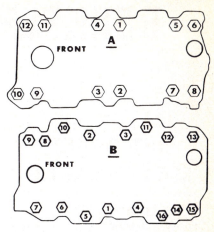

Fig. M1-30—Intake manifold tightening sequence. View A is Model 255; view B is Model 350.

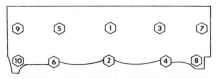

Fig. M1-28—Cylinder head bolts on Model 233 should be tightened using sequence shown above.

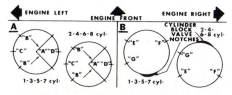

Fig. M1-29—Arrangement of piston ring end gaps. View A is Model 255; view B is Model 350.

A. Oil ring spacer gap (within arc)
B. Oil ring rail gaps
C. 2nd compression ring gap
D. Top compression ring gap
E. Oil ring end gap
F. 2nd compression ring gap
G. Top compression ring gap

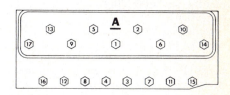
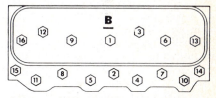

Fig. M1-31—Cylinder head tightening sequence. View A is Model 255; view B is Model 350.

not damaged or defective, removal from shaft end is unnecessary. Rotor is secured to shaft with "Loctite" A. Remove with care to prevent damage to shaft or slotted disc.

Four screws with lockwashers secure adaptor housing to pilot assembly. Remove these from underside of pilot, followed by four mounting screws which retain trigger assembly. Carefully slide trigger from its base on distributor pilot so as not to damage slotted timer disc.

Distributor drive gear is removed for renewal by driving out roll pin which is fitted through gear hub and lower end of shaft. No further disassembly of distributor shaft and pilot is recommended. Timer disc, pilot and shaft are not available as individual parts, and special assembly fixtures are required. Reassemble distributor by reversal of disassembly steps. Use four drops of "Loctite" A (C-92-32609) in rotor hub to hold rotor in place on shaft end.

VALVE LIFTER

Model 233

ADJUSTMENT. No valve clearance adjustment is required. If noise indicative of damage or defect appears to come from valve train components which is not easily diagnosed (as a collapsed hydraulic valve lifter), check for wear in valve train as follows:

Remove rocker arm covers and observing firing order (ENGINE SERVICE DATA), move each piston in turn to Top Dead Center after compression stroke and apply pressure (tool 6513AC) to each push rod as shown in Fig. M1-23. When pressure has caused lifter to bleed down completely, check valve stem to rocker arm gap using a narrow (under ⅜-in.) feeler gage. Clearance should be 0.083-0.183 inch. If not to specification, disassembly and renewal of worn valve train parts, including hydraulic lifters, is indicated.

Models 255 And 350

ADJUSTMENT. Valves may be adjusted with engine not running. Turn crankshaft until number 1 piston is at TDC on compression stroke. The valves marked "X" in Fig. M1-24 or M1-25 can be adjusted with number 1 piston at TDC on compression stroke. Rotate crankshaft one complete turn and again align mark on crankshaft damper with TDC ("O") mark on timing plate. This second setting will position number 6 piston at TDC on compression stroke.

The valves not marked in Fig. M1-24 or M1-25 can be adjusted with crankshaft at the second setting (number 6 piston at TDC on compression stroke).

REPAIRS

PISTON AND ROD UNITS

All Models

Assemble connecting rods and pistons so notch or arrow in piston crown will be towards front and numbered side of rod is towards outside of engine. Arrange piston rings so end gaps are located as shown in Fig. M1-26 or M1-29.

Illustration courtesy Mercury Marine

BERKELEY 12JB, 12JC & 12JE

BERKELEY PUMP COMPANY
829 Bancroft Way
Berkeley, California 94710

JET DRIVE MAINTENANCE

LUBRICATION

Lubricate impeller shaft ball bearing through grease fitting (G—Fig. 1-1) with Shell Alvania #2 or equivalent. Bearing should be lubricated every two months or after every 100 hours of operation.

Lubricate bowl bushings every two months or after every 100 hours of operation. Remove two 1/8-inch pipe plugs (P—Fig. 1-1) on bowl and insert nozzle of oil gun into one of the plug openings. Force oil into the bowl until clean oil is ejected from the other opening. Good quality EP90 gear oil should be used.

Impeller shaft universal joints should be lubricated through grease fittings with a good quality multi-purpose grease every two months or after every 100 hours of operation.

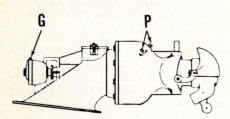

Fig. 1-1—View showing lubrication points. Refer to text.

PACKING SEALS

Packing seals (8—Fig. 1-2 or 1-3) must be kept tight around impeller shaft to prevent air and water leaks. Loose packing will allow air to be sucked into impeller housing at low speeds and water to leak out of impeller housing at high speeds. Tighten gland (7) nuts one-half turn each until gland is tight then back off each nut one-half turn. If leakage occurs after gland has been tightened, renew packing seals. Gland and packing seals may be removed without removing impeller shaft.

ADJUSTMENT

Position steering wheel for straight running and note direction of nozzle. Adjust steering mechanism so steering wheel position and nozzle direction are correct.

Reverse bucket (34—Fig. 1-2 or 1-3) must fit tightly over nozzle (30) for reverse direction but it must not obstruct water jet stream or forward movement will be impaired. With unit shifted to reverse, it should not be possible to move reverse bucket more than 1/4-inch and it should be under tension. To adjust reverse bucket movement, shorten or lengthen effective length of shifter cable using adjustment points at cable ends. Be sure cable housing is fastened securely or reverse bucket will function improperly due to excessive cable slack.

JET DRIVE SERVICE

REVERSE BUCKET

R&R AND OVERHAUL Disconnect shift cable from reverse bucket (34—Fig. 1-2 or 1-3). Unscrew Allen screws (33), drive out pivot pins (31) and remove reverse bucket. Inspect Nyliner bushings (32) and pivot pins (31) and renew any component which is excessively worn or damaged. Apply Loctite to Allen screws (33) during assembly.

NOZZLE

R&R AND OVERHAUL. To remove nozzle, detach steering and shift cables from jet drive unit. Unscrew set screw (35—Fig. 1-2 or 1-3) and remove steering arm from pivot pin (27). Tap pivot pin down until access to lower Woodruff key in pivot pin is obtained and remove key. Drive pivot pin (27) up and out of nozzle. Unscrew capscrew (36) and drive lower pivot pin (29) into center of nozzle and remove pin. Separate nozzle (30) from bowl (23). Inspect Nyliner bushings (28) and pivot pins for damage and excessive wear.

Reverse disassembly procedure for reassembly. Apply "Loctite" to cap screw (36). Align counterbore in upper pivot pin (27) with set screw (35) hole. Apply "Loctite" to set screw (35).

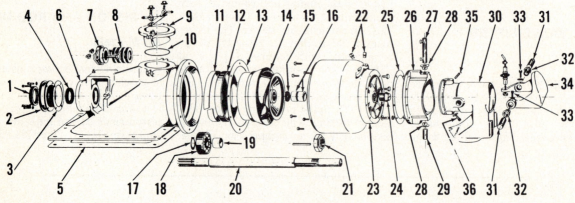

Fig. 1-2—Exploded view of Models 12JA and 12JB.

1. Seal
2. Bearing cap
3. Gasket
4. Seal
5. Gasket
6. Impeller housing
7. Gland
8. Packing seal rings
9. Inspection cover
10. "O" ring
11. Insulator
12. Wear ring
13. Gasket
14. Impeller
15. Seal
16. Bushings
17. Snap ring
18. Ball bearing
19. Sleeve
20. Impeller shaft
21. Nut
22. Lubrication plugs
23. Bowl
24. Plug
25. Gasket
26. Nozzle housing
27. Upper pivot pin
28. Nyliner bushing
29. Lower pivot pin
30. Nozzle
31. Bucket pivot pin
32. Nyliner bushing
33. Allen screw
34. Reverse bucket
35. Set screw
36. Capscrew

DRIVES

Berkeley

NOZZLE HOUSING

Models 12JA and 12JB

To remove nozzle housing (26—Fig. 1-2), disconnect steering and shift cables from drive unit and unscrew housing retaining nuts and screws. Note that two cap screws are located adjacent to reverse bucket lever.

BOWL

R&R AND OVERHAUL. To remove bowl, disconnect steering and shift cables from drive unit. Unscrew bowl retaining screws and tap bowl with a soft hammer to free bowl from impeller housing. It may be necessary to install long screws in screw holes of bowl and tap screws to loosen bowl. Withdraw bowl and hold bowl with big end up to keep oil in bowl.

Inspect bowl vanes and impeller shaft bushings (16). To remove bushings, unscrew end plug (24) and drive out bushings and seal (15). Install bushings so ends of bushings are flush with shoulders in bore of bowl. Apply "Loctite" Fit-All sealant or other equivalent sealant to end plug (24) threads. Install seal (15) with lip towards impeller. Lubricate "O" ring around bowl on all models except 12JE before installing bowl. Be sure "O" ring is not dislodged. Impeller shaft must turn freely after bowl installation. Lubricate bowl bushings as outlined in LUBRICATION section.

IMPELLER

R&R AND OVERHAUL. Remove bowl as previously outlined, secure forward end of impeller shaft and remove impeller nut (21—Fig. 1-2 or 1-3). Using a suitable puller, withdraw impeller (14) from impeller shaft. Care must be taken when using puller to prevent damage to impeller. Use a suitable pry bar to remove wear ring (12). Insulator (11) may be removed with wear ring or pulled out later.

Inspect wear ring and impeller. Outer wear surface of impeller should be machined if there are grooves greater than 1/8-inch wide over more than half the wear surface. Taper should not exceed 0.005 inch for the one-inch wear surface width. Minimum wear surface diameter of impeller is 7.175 inches. Impeller is still useable even though machining may not remove all imperfections. Impeller to wear ring clearance should be 0.025-0.030 inch. Standard inner diameter of wear ring is 7.250 inches. Wear rings are available with undersizes of 0.005, 0.010, 0.015, 0.020, 0.025, 0.030 and 0.045 inch. A new wear ring insulator (11—Fig. 1-2 or 1-3) should be installed with a new wear ring.

Impeller housing wear ring surface must be clean and smooth. Install wear ring insulator (11—Fig. 1-2 or 1-3) with "L" shaped lip inserted first and wear ring (12) with beveled edge towards impeller housing. Tap evenly around edge of wear ring until it is positioned in housing. Do not fold or wrinkle insulator (11) when installing wear ring. Protect wear ring edges while rapping wear ring sharply to firmly seat wear ring in impeller housing.

Install impeller key in impeller shaft (20—Fig. 1-2 or 1-3) with blunt end of key towards impeller housing (6). Be sure impeller shaft and impeller bore are clean, then apply "Loctite" Fit-All sealant or equivalent to shaft and impeller bore. Drive impeller (14) on shaft so impeller contacts impeller shaft shoulder.

NOTE: A buck must be placed behind splined end of impeller shaft to protect bearing (18) when driving impeller on shaft.

IMPELLER HOUSING AND SHAFT

R&R AND OVERHAUL. Impeller shaft must be removed through front of impeller housing which requires that either engine or impeller housing be removed from boat for access to impeller shaft.

To remove impeller housing on all models except Model 12JE, disconnect shift and steering cables and water hoses from drive unit and transom adapter. On models so equipped, remove inspection cover (9—Fig. 1-2 or 1-3) extension. Unscrew transom adapter mounting screws and screws securing impeller housing (6) to water intake housing. Separate impeller housing from intake housing and remove impeller housing through opening in transom.

To remove impeller housing on Model 12JE, disconnect steering and shift cables and water hose from drive unit. Support drive unit and unscrew impeller housing mounting bolts located in transom and bottom of boat.

Proceed as follows to remove impeller shaft on all models: Remove impeller wear ring as previously outlined. Remove bearing cap (2—Fig. 1-2 or 1-3) and drive impeller shaft (20) out through forward end of impeller housing. Remove snap ring (17) and press ball bearing (18) off impeller shaft. Inspect seals (1 & 4) and packing rings (8) and renew if necessary.

Install packing rings (8) so ring ends are installed 180 degrees from adjacent ring. Install seals (1 & 4) with lips toward bearing. Slide sleeve (19) on impeller shaft with beveled edge next to shaft shoulder and press bearing on impeller shaft so bearing is tight against sleeve (19). Install snap ring (17) and wrap threaded end of shaft with protective tape to prevent damage to seals. Install shaft and bearing assembly in impeller housing so bearing is seated. Install bearing cap (2) and lubricate bearing as outlined in LUBRICATION section. Lubricate "O" ring around bowl and transom housing when installing transom housing on all models except 12JE. Be sure "O" ring is not dislodged. Refer to PACKING SEAL section after unit has been run.

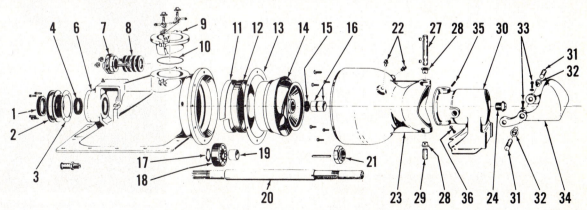

Fig. 1-3—Exploded view of Model 12JC. Model 12JE is similar but drive unit is attached to outside of transom rather than inside boat as on other models. Refer to Fig. 1-2 for parts identification.

Illustration courtesy Chrysler

CHRYSLER

CHRYSLER CORPORATION
P.O. Box 1
Marysville, Mich. 48040

Refer to Chrysler engine sections for engine service data.

JET DRIVE SERVICE

LUBRICATION

Drive shaft bearings are lubricated by an oil bath. Remove dipstick (9—Fig. 1-4) to check oil level. Add oil through dipstick hole until oil reaches full mark on dipstick. Recommended oil is SAE 30, service SE automotive oil. A suction pump is recommended to remove oil through dipstick hole as there is limited access to drain plug (5).

DOORS AND DOOR FRAME

R&R AND OVERHAUL. Detach cover (2—Fig. 1-1) by unscrewing Allen screws at front and rear underside of cover. Detach steering link (17) from port door (20) and shift link from cam (9). Remove inner "E" ring (12) and withdraw cam rod (11). Remove cam (9) and cam rollers (13 and 19). Unscrew plugs (14), drive out hinge pins (15) and remove doors (16 and 20). Drive out pin (8) and pin (7) and remove door frame (10).

Inspect pin bushings in doors and bushings (5). Inspect bushings in cam (9). Reassemble by reversing disassembly procedure.

NOZZLE

R&R AND OVERHAUL. To remove nozzle, remove cover (2—Fig. 1-1) by unscrewing Allen screws at front and rear underside of cover. Disconnect steering link (17) and shift link (13—Fig. 1-4). Support nozzle (3—Fig. 1-1), unscrew nozzle mounting screws and separate nozzle assembly from pump housing (10—Fig. 1-4). To remove stator, drive out roll pin (P—Fig. 1-2) then drive stator retaining pin (R) towards center of stator and separate stator from nozzle. If stator or nozzle is renewed, stator-to-impeller clearance should be checked as outlined in following section.

IMPELLER AND LINER

R&R AND OVERHAUL. To remove impeller, separate nozzle from pump housing as outlined in previous section. Unscrew nut (19—Fig. 1-3) and using a suitable puller withdraw impeller from pump housing. Unscrew liner set screw (11—Fig. 1-4) and pull liner out of pump housing using tool CM-103 shown in Fig. 1-5. Inspect impeller and liner for damage. Be sure groove in liner is aligned with set screw (11—Fig. 1-4) before tightening set screw. Liner should be flush with or inside face of pump housing. Install washer (18—Fig. 1-3) with rubber side adjacent to impeller.

If pump housing, impeller, drive shaft or bearings have been renewed, check stator-to-impeller clearance as follows: Install impeller without shims (10—Fig. 1-3) and tighten nut (19) to 70 ft.-lbs. Place a straight edge across face of pump housing and measure gap between straightedge and round surface of impeller. Be sure straightedge is against housing face and not liner. Liner should be flush with or inside housing face. Install sufficient shims

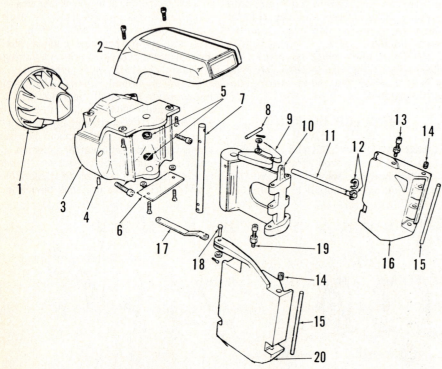

Fig. 1-1—Exploded view of nozzle and door assembly.

1. Stator
2. Cover
3. Nozzle
4. Pin
5. Bushing
6. Anode plate
7. Pin
8. Pin
9. Cam
10. Door frame
11. Cam rod
12. "E" rings
13. Cam roller
14. Plug
15. Hinge pin
16. Right door
17. Steering link
18. Pin
19. Cam roller
20. Left door

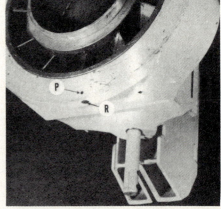

Fig. 1-2—Roll pin (P) and stator retaining pin (R) must be driven out before stator can be removed.

DRIVES

Chrysler

(10) to obtain a gap of 0.005-0.010 inch between straight edge and impeller.

WATER SEAL

REMOVE AND REINSTALL. Remove impeller as previously outlined and remove washer (14—Fig. 1-3), spring (13) and outer seal half (12). Using a suitable tool, work ceramic center out of seal (11) and then pull outer rubber portion out of housing bore. Use a suitable lubricant when installing new seal.

DRIVE SHAFT

R&R AND OVERHAUL. Engine and jet drive must be separated so there is access to front of pump housing. Remove impeller as previously outlined. Remove front bearing retainer (2—Fig. 1-4). Remove nut retainer (16—Fig. 1-3), unscrew nut (15) and remove water seal components (12, 13 & 14). Tap on impeller end of drive shaft to force front bearing cup (1) out front of pump housing and withdraw drive shaft and bearings from front. Using a suitable tool inserted through pump housing, drive rear bearing cup (5), oil seal (6) and seal retainer (8) out rear of pump housing. Inspect components and renew any showing signs of excessive wear or damage.

To adjust bearing preload, install drive shaft and bearing assembly, rear seal (6) and seal retainer (8). Install front bearing retainer (2—Fig. 1-4), "O" ring (3) and seal (4). Tighten nut (15—Fig. 1-3) until 50 in.-lbs. is required to turn drive shaft while lightly tapping end of drive shaft to be sure bearings are seating properly. Back off nut (15) until 10-15 in.-lbs. is required to turn drive shaft and line up a slot in nut with nut retainer (16). With water seal and impeller installed, 15-35 in.-lbs.

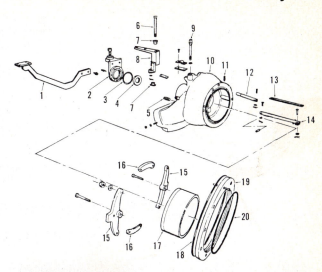

Fig. 1-4—Exploded view of pump housing.

1. Cable support
2. Front bearing retainer
3. "O" ring
4. Oil seal
5. Drain plug
6. Pivot bolt
7. Bushing
8. Bellcrank
9. Dip stick
10. Pump housing
11. Set screw
12. Shift plunger
13. Shift link
14. Steering plunger
15. Mount plate
16. Mount plate
17. Impeller liner
18. Seal
19. Mount ring
20. "O" ring

Fig. 1-5—Use Chrysler tool CM-103 to remove impeller lining from pump housing.

Fig. 1-6—Exploded view of drive coupling to engine.

1. Universal joint
2. Shield
3. Flywheel housing
4. Shield
5. Adapter
6. Flywheel

torque should be required to turn drive shaft.

Refer to IMPELLER AND LINER section and check clearance between impeller and stator.

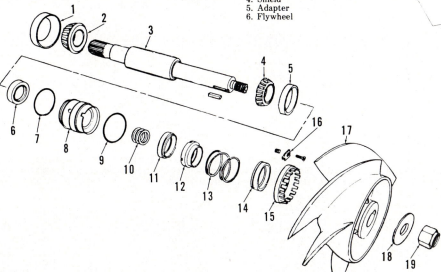

Fig. 1-3—Exploded view of impeller and drive shaft assemblies.

1. Front bearing cup
2. Bearing cone
3. Drive shaft
4. Bearing cone
5. Rear bearing cup
6. Oil seal
7. "O" ring
8. Seal retainer
9. "O" ring
10. Shims
11. Seal
12. Outer seal half
13. Spring
14. Washer
15. Nut
16. Nut retainer
17. Impeller
18. Washer
19. Nut

Illustration courtesy Chrysler

Hurth

DRIVES

HURTH

CARL HURTH
Maschinen-und Zahnradfabrik
Holzstrasse 19
D-8000 Munchen 5
West Germany

TRIGON MACHINERY
214 Brunswick Boulevard
Pointe Claire, Quebec Canada

MODELS HBW50, HBW100, HBW150, HBW150V & HBW220

OPERATION

All models except HBW150V are in-line type transmissions while Model HBW150V is a V-drive transmission. All models are equipped with a forward and a reverse gear which are engaged through multiple-disc clutches. Shifting and gear engagement is accomplished mechanically. Transmissions are available for either clockwise or counter-clockwise input shaft rotation.

A damper disc should be used to couple the transmission to the engine. Transmission input shaft runout when coupled to engine must not exceed 0.1 mm.

Maximum allowable fore-to-aft transmission inclination is 20 degrees.

NOTE: If boat is sailing or being towed with engine stopped then gearbox shift lever must be in neutral or in gear opposite direction of boat travel. For instance, if boat is sailing forward then gearbox must be in neutral or reverse

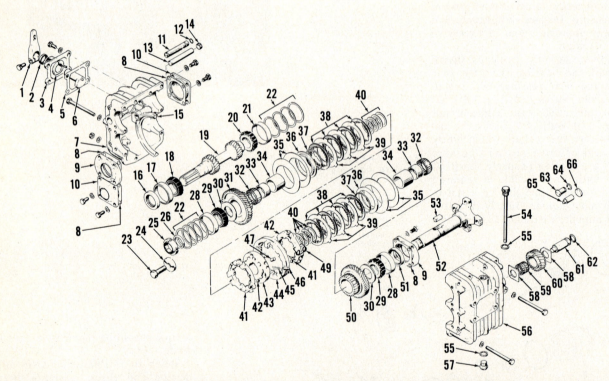

Fig. 1.1 – Exploded view of Hurth inline transmission. Shift shaft (11), "O" ring (12), cap screw (23) and washer (24) are used on Model HBW50 in place of components (13, 14, 25 and 26). Intermediate shaft (61) and "O" ring (62) are used on Model HBW100; intermediate shaft (63) and snap ring (64) are used on Model HBW50; intermediate shaft (65) and plug (66) are used on Model HBW220.

1. Shift lever
2. Seal
3. Shift cover
4. Dowel pin
5. Gasket
6. Shift cam
7. Gearcase half
8. Gasket
9. Seal housing
10. End cap
11. Shift shaft (HBW50)
12. "O" ring (HBW50)
13. Shift shaft (Except HBW50)
14. Plug (Except HBW50)
15. Shift fork
16. Seal
17. Bearing cup
18. Bearing cone
19. Input shaft
20. Bearing cone
21. Bearing cup
22. Shims
23. Cap screw (HBW50)
24. Washer (HBW50)
25. Slotted nut (Except HBW50)
26. Washer (Except HBW50)
27. Bearing cup
28. Bearing cup
29. Bearing cone
30. Thrust washer
31. Gear
32. Roller bearing
33. Inner race
34. Spacer
35. Belleville springs
36. Spring retainer
37. Snap ring
38. Friction clutch discs
39. Steel clutch plates
40. Shims
41. Drive collar
42. Steel balls (6)
43. Drive hub
44. Shift collar
45. Spring (3)
46. Detent pin (3)
47. Drive pin (3)
48. Return spring (3)
49. Return spring (3)
50. Gear
51. Seal
52. Output shaft
53. Drive key
54. Dipstick
55. Gasket
56. Gearcase half
57. Drain plug
58. Thrust plate
59. Roller bearing
60. Intermediate gear
61. Shaft (HBW100)
62. "O" ring (HBW100)
63. Shaft (HBW50)
64. Snap ring (HBW50)
65. Shaft (HBW220)
66. Plug (HBW220)

DRIVES | Hurth

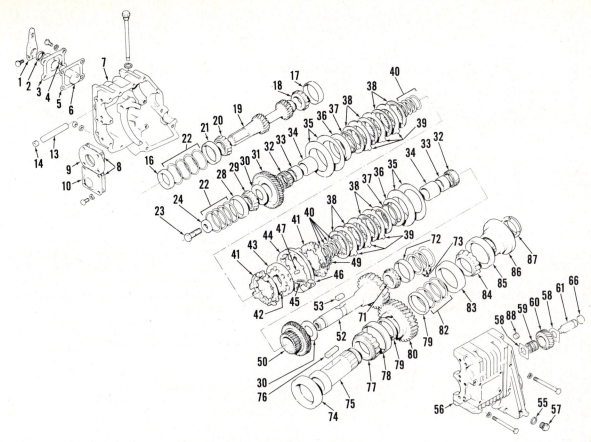

Fig. 1-2 — Exploded view of Model HBW150V V-drive transmission.

1. Shift lever
2. Seal
3. Shift cover
4. Dowel pin
5. Gasket
6. Shift cam
7. Gearcase half
8. Gasket
9. Seal housing
10. End cap
13. Shift shaft
14. Plug
15. Shift fork
16. Seal
17. Bearing cup
18. Bearing cone
19. Input shaft
20. Bearing cone
21. Bearing cup
22. Shims
23. Cap screw
24. Washer
28. Bearing cup
29. Bearing cone
30. Thrust washer
31. Gear
32. Roller bearing
33. Inner race
34. Spacer
35. Belleville springs
36. Spring retainer
37. Snap ring
38. Friction clutch discs
39. Steel clutch plates
40. Shims
41. Drive collar
42. Steel balls (6)
43. Drive hub
44. Shift collar
45. Spring (3)
46. Detent pin (3)
47. Drive pin (3)
48. Return spring (3)
50. Gear
52. Output shaft
53. Drive key
54. Dipstick
55. Gasket
56. Gearcase half
57. Drain plug
58. Thrust plate
59. Roller bearing
60. Intermediate gear
61. Shaft
66. Plug
71. Bearing cone
72. Bearing cup
73. Shims
74. Seal
75. Quill shaft
76. Drive key
77. Bearing cone
78. Bearing cup
79. Spacer
80. Gear
82. Shims
83. Bearing cup
84. Bearing cone
85. Seal
86. Coupling
87. Slotted nut
88. Plug

gear. If propeller must be locked in position, engage gearbox in gear opposite to direction of boat travel.

LUBRICATION

All models are lubricated by oil contained in the transmission case. Recommended transmission oil is automatic transmission fluid (ATF) type A. To check oil level, unscrew dipstick then insert dipstick into gearcase just so dipstick threads contact gearcase; do not screw dipstick into gearcase to check oil level. Oil level is correct when oil reaches groove on dipstick. Dipstick may be used to check oil level if transmission is inclined less than 20 degrees fore and aft. Transmission oil capacity is 300 mL for Model HBW50, 350 mL for Model HBW100, 550 mL for Model HBW150, 1.0 L for Model HBW150V and 750 mL for Model HBW220.

Transmission oil should be changed after first 25 hours of operation and annually thereafter. Manufacturer recommends filling transmission full of oil if transmission is to be inactive for more than one year.

Transmission oil temperature should not exceed 130°C (266°F). A cooling unit may be attached to the side of the transmission so fresh water may reduce transmission gearcase temperature thereby reducing oil temperature.

OVERHAUL

With transmission removed from boat, detach cooling unit from side of transmission, on models so equipped, and drain transmission lubricant. Refer to Fig. 1-1 for an exploded view of inline transmission models and to Fig. 1-2 for an exploded view of Model HBW150V transmission.

With shift lever in neutral position, unscrew then remove shift cover (3) and shift components. If required, disassemble shift lever assembly for access to seal (2) and to inspect components.

Detach seal housings (9) and end caps (10). Remove cap screws securing transmission case halves together, then tap shift side case half (7) off opposite case half (56). Before removing shaft assemblies from case half, note location and thickness of all shims so they may be reinstalled in their original position if allowed. Remove shaft assemblies. Heat case half (56) to approximately 80°C before driving out intermediate shaft (61). Unscrew plug (14) on models so equipped, and on all models pull shift shaft (11 or 13) out of case then remove shift fork (15).

To disassemble input shaft assembly, remove bearing cups (17 and 21) then drive or press bearing cones (18 and 20) off shaft. To disassemble output shaft

Illustration courtesy Hurth

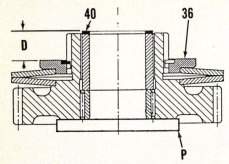

Fig. 1-3—To determine thickness of shims (40), support gear hub on a surface plate (P) as shown and measure distance (D) as outlined in text.

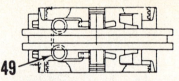

Fig. 1-4—Install return springs (49) between drive hub and shift collar so spring ends engage holes in drive collars.

assembly, unscrew slotted nut (25) or cap screw (23). Press against gear (50) and force output shaft components off shaft while identifying parts as they are removed so they can be returned to their original position. Remove drive key (Model HBW220 uses four keys while all other models use two drive keys). Remove thrust washer (30), roller bearing (32), inner race (33) and spacer (34) by pressing against thrust washer. Press bearing (29) off shaft. Remove clutch discs (38 and 39) from gears. Use a suitable tool against spring retainer (36) to compress Belleville springs (35), then remove snap ring (37), spring retainer and Belleville springs.

Disassemble drive hub assembly while being careful not to lose balls, pins or springs.

To disassemble quill shaft assembly on Model HBW150V, unscrew slotted nut (87) and remove seal (85) and coupling (86). Press components (80 through 84) off shaft, remove key (76) and spacer (79) then press bearing (77) off shaft.

Inspect all components for damage and excessive wear. Renew thrust washers (30) if worn more than 0.25 mm. Renew shift fork (15) if worn more than 0.2 mm on contact surfaces. Renew splined discs (38) if sintered metal coating is worn.

To assemble transmission, proceed as follows: Heat gearcase half (56) to approximately 100°C and install intermediate gear (60) and shaft assembly. Note that thrust plates (58) must be installed so cut-off corner of innermost plate points towards output shaft and outermost plate cut-off corner points towards input shaft. Models HBW150V and HBW220 are equipped with a plug (66) which must be sealed when installed. Install shift fork (15) in gearcase half (7) so long fork arm is pointing down and insert shift rail (11 or 13). Apply sealer to plug (14) on models so equipped and install plug while being sure there is approximately 0.5 mm clearance between end of plug and shift shaft.

Install Belleville springs (35) and spring retainer (36) on gears (31 and 50) so concave spring sides are together. Using a suitable tool compress Belleville springs and install snap ring (37). Place gear on a surface plate so only gear hub contacts plate as shown in Fig. 1-3. Install roller bearing (32–Fig. 1-1 or 1-2), inner race (33), spacer (34) and shims (40) then measure distance (D–Fig. 1-3) from spring retainer (36) to shims. Select shims (40) so distance (D) is 7.9-8.0 mm on Model HBW50, 12.9-13.0 mm on Model HBW100, 13.1-13.2 mm on Models HBW150 and HBW150V, and 16.1-16.2 mm on Model HBW220. Set aside shims for later installation.

On all models except HBW150V, install seal (51–Fig. 1-1) in seal housing so lip is towards inside of housing then install seal housing on output shaft (52). Press bearing cone (71–Fig. 1-2) on output shaft (70) of Model HBW150V; on all other models, press bearing cone (29–Fig. 1-1) with cup (28) on output shaft (52). On all models, install thrust washer (30–Fig. 1-1 or 1-2) so sintered side (brown) faces away from bearing. Press clutch inner race (33) onto shaft so it bottoms against thrust washer. Install bearing (32) and previously assembled gear (50) and spring assembly. Install clutch discs (38 and 39) alternately so fiber discs are installed first and last. Install spacer (34) and previously selected shims (40).

Assemble shift hub as follows: Install drive pins (47), springs (45) and detent pins (46) in drive hub (43), then press drive hub into shift collar (44) so hub is centered in collar (a click will be heard). Position balls (42) in ball grooves, mate drive collars (41) with drive hub (43) and install return springs (49) between shift hub and shift collar so spring ends engage holes in drive collars as shown in Fig. 1-4.

Install drive keys (53–Fig. 1-1 or 1-2) on output shaft; Model HBW220 has four drive keys while all other models have two drive keys. Install assembled drive hub assembly on output shaft while engaging tabs on steel plates (39) with slots in drive collar (41). Install previously selected shims (40) and spacer (34) of remaining gear on output shaft, then press inner bearing race (33) onto shaft. Install clutch discs (37 and 38) and previously assembled gear (31) and Belleville spring assembly. Install thrust washer (30) with sintered side (brown) towards gear. Heat bearing cone (29) to 100°C then press on shaft (be sure no clearance exists between bearing and thrust washer after bearing cools). Install slotted nut (25) or cap screw (23) and washer (24) then tighten to 100 N·m on Model HBW150V, 150 N·m on Model HBW220, or to 95 N·m on all other models. Stake nut on models so equipped. Check for free gear rotation. Position bearing cups on bearing cones and install output shaft assembly with original shims in shift lever half (7) of gearcase.

Heat bearing cones (18 and 20) to 100°C then press onto input shaft (19); be sure no clearance exists between bearing and side of input shaft gear after bearing cools. Place bearing cups on bearing cones and install input shaft with original shims (22) in shift lever half (7) of gearcase.

Refer to Fig. 1-2 and assemble quill shaft components in order shown. Press bearing cones on shaft. Install original shims (82). Tighten slotted nut (87) to 95 N·m; do not stake nut to shaft. After assembly, install quill shaft in shift lever half (7) of gearcase. Check gear backlash between output shaft gear and quill shaft gear. Backlash should be 0.10-0.16 mm. Adjust backlash by grinding spacers (79) or adjusting shim (82) thickness.

Temporarily install gearcase half (56–Fig. 1-1 or 1-2) on assembled gearcase half (7) and secure halves together with four or five bolts tightened to 22 N·m. Be sure gearcase halves are properly mated. Install seal in seal housing then install seal housing (9), end caps (10) and gaskets (8); tighten screws to 14 N·m. Check end play of all shafts which should be 0.03-0.07 mm. Output shaft end play on Model HBW150V is checked by unscrewing plug (88) and inserting a dial indicator. To adjust end play, remove end caps, seal housing and gearcase half (56), then change thickness of shims (22) to adjust input or output shaft end play or shims (82) to adjust quill shaft end play. After end play is adjusted, tighten nut (87) to 95 N·m and stake nut to shaft. Install seal (74). Apply sealant to gearcase half (56) then install on assembled gearcase half (7). Tighten gearcase bolts to 22 N·m. Install seal housing (9) and end caps (10) then tighten retaining screws to 14 N·m. Install shift cover (3) and shift components. Before tightening retaining screws, position shift cover so there is equal shift lever travel from neutral to forward and from neutral to reverse. Tighten shift cover screws to 14 N·m. Tighten shift lever clamp screw to 18 N·m. Fill transmission with fluid as outlined in LUBRICATION section. Check transmission operation.

JACUZZI 12YJ

JACUZZI BROS., INC.
11511 New Benton Highway
Little Rock, Arkansas 72203

JET DRIVE MAINTENANCE

LUBRICATION

Jet drive universal joints should be lubricated every six months or after 100 hours of operation. Lubricate impeller shaft thrust bearing with EP-2 lithium base grease through fitting shown in Fig. 1-1 every six months or after 100 hours of operation. Lubricate bowl bushings with EP-2 lithium base grease through fitting shown in Fig. 1-2. Once a season lubricate nozzle pivot pin bushings, inspection cap retaining bolts and all cables with a light oil.

ADJUSTMENT

Adjust steering mechanism by disconnecting steering cable from nozzle and centering nozzle and steering wheel. Adjust length of steering cable so that cable will reach nozzle with steering wheel and nozzle centered. Do not overtighten jam nut on cable tube as rubber grommet may be compressed thereby causing steering malfunction due to steering tube rigidity.

Jet drive direction is determined by position of reverse gate (G—Fig. 1-3). Jet drive direction is forward when reverse gate is up or reverse when reverse gate covers rear of nozzle as shown in Fig. 1-3. Before throttle opens, reverse gate should be fully open for forward or firmly seated on nozzle for reverse. Adjustment is provided at control end of shift cable. Minimum gap between bottom of reverse gate and top of nozzle with reverse gate in full open position is 1/16-inch. Inspect for worn parts if gap is less than 1/16-inch.

Jet drive trim is accomplished by loosening Allen screw (S—Fig. 1-3) and turning trim screw (T). Each turn and a half of trim screw changes nozzle angle one degree.

JET DRIVE SERVICE

NOZZLE

R&R AND OVERHAUL. Disconnect shift and steering cables. Unscrew retaining screws and using a suitable puller remove lower pivot pin (6—Fig. 1-4). Unscrew trim cap retaining screws and remove trim cap (8). Separate nozzle (22) from bowl (5). Unscrew retaining screws and use a suitable puller to remove reverse gate pivot pins (24). Inspect pivot pins and bushings for wear. Maximum clearance between nozzle pivot pins and bushings is 0.005 inch.

Apply a small amount of light oil to pivot pin bushings and locking compound to pivot pin retaining screws. Tighten reverse gate pivot pin retaining screws to 6 ft.-lbs. Tighten lower nozzle pivot pin retaining screw to 6 ft.-lbs. Apply sealant to trim cap gasket surface. Tighten trim cap retaining screws to 11 ft.-lbs.

BOWL

R&R AND OVERHAUL. To remove bowl, disconnect shift and steering cables and remove rudder (23—Fig. 1-4). Remove screws securing transom adapter (19) and remove adapter. Unscrew bowl retaining screws located on front of impeller housing flange. Care-

Fig. 1-1—View showing location of lubrication fitting for impeller housing bearing. Water leaking from water bleed hole (H) indicates failure of ceramic impeller shaft seal.

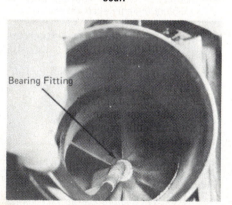

Fig. 1-2—View showing location of lubrication fitting for bowl bushings.

Fig. 1-3—Loosen Allen screw (S) and turn trim screw (T) to trim unit.

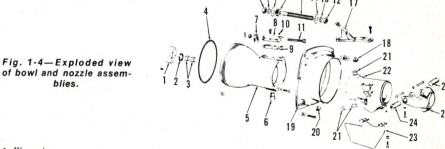

Fig. 1-4—Exploded view of bowl and nozzle assemblies.

1. Wear ring
2. Seal
3. Bushings
4. "O" ring
5. Bowl
6. Lower pivot pin
7. Upper pivot pin
8. Trim cap
9. Gasket
10. Allen screw
11. Trim screw
12. Nut
13. Lockwasher
14. Washer
15. Grommet
16. Steering tube
17. Tiller arm
18. Shift cable fitting
19. Transom adapter
20. Drain plug
21. Nylon bushing
22. Nozzle
23. Rudder
24. Reverse gate pivot pins
25. Reverse gate

Jacuzzi

DRIVES

fully separate bowl from impeller housing.

Maximum allowable diametral clearance between bowl bushings (3) and impeller shaft is 0.011 inch. Renew bushings if clearance is excessive or a new impeller shaft is installed. Use long end of Jacuzzi tool No. 50-0064-02 to install inner bushing and short end of tool to install outer bushing. Drive in bushings until flange on tool seats against lip seal shoulder in bowl. Install lip seal (2) with lips facing outward.

Diametral clearance between wear ring (1) and impeller hub should be 0.010-0.030 inch. Apply sealant to wear ring screws. Tighten screws to 24 in.-lbs.

Inspect bowl and vanes for cracks and chips. Remove small nicks from leading edges of vanes with a flat file. Apply sealant to bowl retaining screws and tighten screws to 20 ft.-lbs.

Apply Dow Corning 781 sealant or equivalent to flange of transom adapter (19). There should be no breaks in sealant bead. Be sure transom adapter is not cocked during installation as "O" ring (4) may be damaged. Inspect installation from inside boat to be sure "O" ring is in place and undamaged.

IMPELLER

R&R AND OVERHAUL. To remove impeller, remove bowl as outlined in previous section. Unscrew impeller nut (52—Fig. 1-5) and using a suitable puller detach impeller from shaft. Care should be used not to hit end of impeller shaft as seals and bearing may be damaged. Remove impeller wear ring (36).

Inspect impeller wear ring for damage and excessive wear. Inspect impeller for nicks, cracks or other damage to blades and hub. Do not attempt to weld cracked or broken blades.

Reverse disassembly to reinstall impeller. Align impeller wear ring with dowel pins in impeller housing. Install impeller nut with split side away from impeller. Tighten impeller nut to 20 ft.-lbs; do not overtighten. Measure clearance between impeller blade tips and wear ring. Clearance should be 0.001-0.010 inch and is adjusted with shims (28). Refer to IMPELLER SHAFT section for installation of shims.

IMPELLER HOUSING AND SHAFT

R&R AND OVERHAUL. Note that impeller shaft must be removed from front of impeller housing. If engine has been removed, impeller shaft may be removed without removing impeller housing from boat.

To remove impeller housing, remove impeller wear ring as outlined in previous section. Disconnect water line and ground strap. Remove inspection cap (34—Fig. 1-5) and bolts and unscrew ten bolts securing impeller housing (29) to grille housing (47). Remove impeller housing through hole in transom.

Remove bearing cap (27) and retain shims (28) for installation. Withdraw shaft from front of housing. Remove snap ring (38) and press bearing (39) off shaft. Remove remainder of components from shaft.

Inspect impeller shaft for excessive wear, roughness or other damage. Maximum runout with shaft placed in lathe centers is 0.003 inch. Minimum diameter of impeller end of shaft is 1.1218 inches. Be sure shaft shoulder for thrust washer (40) is square with shaft. Inspect seal components and discard components which are cracked or worn. Measure shoulder of ceramic seal (44) shown in Fig. 1-6 and renew seal if shoulder is less than 1/64-inch.

Reverse disassembly procedure for assembly. Install seal (41—Fig. 1-5) with lip in towards housing (42) and bottom the seal in housing. Compressing tools may be fabricated to compress ceramic seal (44) components for installation on shaft. Install bearing (39) with outer race snap ring towards front of shaft. Bearing must bottom against thrust washer (40). Install shaft so that bleed hole shown in Fig. 1-7 is towards bottom of impeller housing. Install seal (26—Fig. 1-5) with lips facing inwards. Seal should be flush to

Fig. 1-6—Measure shoulder of ceramic seal as shown and renew seal if shoulder height is less than 1/64-inch.

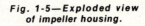

Fig. 1-7—Bleed hole in seal housing must face bottom of impeller housing when installing impeller shaft assembly.

Fig. 1-8—Install bearing cap so that lubrication relief hole (B) faces starboard side of impeller housing

Fig. 1-5—Exploded view of impeller housing.

26. Seal
27. Bearing cap
28. Shims
29. Impeller housing
30. Lubrication fitting
31. Spring pin
32. "O" ring
33. Bolt lock bar
34. Inspection cap
35. Water outlet
36. Wear ring
37. "O" ring
38. Snap ring
39. Bearing
40. Thrust washer
41. Seal
42. Seal housing
43. "O" ring
44. Ceramic seal
45. Snap ring
46. Gasket
47. Grill housing
48. Grill
49. Impeller shaft
50. Key
51. Impeller
52. Nut

DRIVES   Jacuzzi

1/16-inch below chamfer of bearing cap. Install bearing cap (27) with lubrication relief hole shown in Fig. 1-8 towards starboard side and with original shims. Install impeller as previously outlined and measure clearance between impeller blade tips and impeller wear ring. Clearance should be 0.001-0.010 inch. Adjust clearance by removing or installing shims (28—Fig. 1-5). Be sure shims are installed between snap ring on outer race of bearing (39) and impeller housing. Shims are 0.015 and 0.030 inch thick and will change clearance 0.005 and 0.010 inch respectively. Apply sealant to impeller housing and grille housing (47) gasket surfaces, install impeller housing on grille housing and tighten bolts to 20 ft.-lbs. Note that two rear bolts are two inches long.

OMC

OUTBOARD MARINE CORPORATION
100 Pershing Road
Waukegan, Illinois 60086

Refer to OMC engine sections for engine service data.

JET DRIVE MAINTENANCE

LUBRICATION

Jet drive universal joints should be lubricated every six months or after 100 hours of operation. Lubricate impeller shaft thrust bearing with OMC Sea-Lube Multi-Purpose Grease or equivalent through fitting shown in Fig. 1-1 every six months or after 100 hours of operation. Lubricate bowl bushings with OMC Sea-Lube Multi-Purpose grease or equivalent through fitting shown in Fig. 1-2. Once a season lubricate deflector pivot pin bushings, inspection cap retaining bolts and all cables with a suitable lubricant such as OMC Sea-Lube Anti-Corrosion lube.

ADJUSTMENT

Adjust steering mechanism by disconnecting steering cable from nozzle and centering nozzle and steering wheel. Adjust length of steering cable so that cable will reach nozzle with steering wheel and nozzle centered. Do not overtighten jam nut on cable tube as rubber grommet may be compressed thereby causing steering malfunction due to steering tube rigidity.

Jet drive direction is determined by position of reverse gate (G—Fig. 1-3). Jet drive direction is forward when reverse gate is up as shown in Fig. 1-3 or reverse when reverse gate covers rear of nozzle. Reverse gate should reach full open position or be firmly seated on nozzle in full closed position before throttle opens. Adjustment is provided at control end of shift cable. Minimum gap between reverse gate and nozzle with reverse gate in full open position is 1/16-inch. See Fig. 1-3. Inspect for worn parts if gap is less than 1/16-inch.

Jet drive trim is accomplished by loosening Allen screw located at (A—Fig. 1-3) and turning trim screw located at (B). Each turn and a half of trim screw changes nozzle angle one degree.

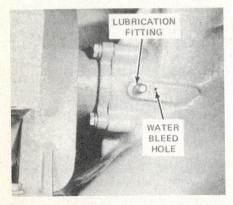

Fig. 1-1—View showing location of lubrication fitting for impeller housing bearing. Water leaking from water bleed hole indicates failure of ceramic impeller shaft seal.

Fig. 1-2—View showing location of lubrication fitting for bowl bushings.

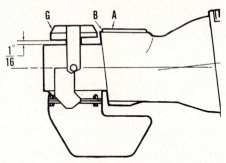

Fig. 1-3—Minimum gap between reverse gate and nozzle is 1/16-inch when jet drive is in forward drive. Loosen Allen screw located at (A) and turn trim screw located at (B) to trim unit.

JET DRIVE SERVICE

NOZZLE

R&R AND OVERHAUL. Disconnect shift and steering cables. Unscrew retaining screws and using a suitable puller remove lower pivot pin (40—Fig. 1-4). Unscrew trim cap retaining screws

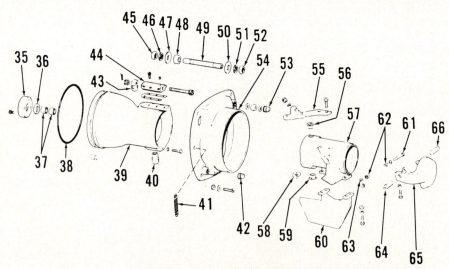

Fig. 1-4—Exploded view of nozzle and bowl assemblies.

35. Wear ring
36. Seal
37. Bushings
38. "O" ring
39. Bowl
40. Lower pivot pin
41. Ground strap
42. Drain plug
43. Upper pivot pin
44. Trim cap
45. Nut
46. Lockwasher
47. Washer
48. Grommet
49. Steering tube
50. Washer
51. Lockwasher
52. Nut
53. Plug
54. Transom adapter
55. Tiller arm
56. Nylon bushing
57. Nozzle
58. Nylon bushing
59. Nylon bushing
60. Rudder
61. Pin
62. Nylon bushing
63. "E" ring
64. Pivot pin
65. Reverse gate
66. Pivot pin

and remove trim cap (44). Separate nozzle (57) from bowl (39). Unscrew retaining screws and use a suitable puller to remove reverse gate pivot pins (64 and 66). Inspect pivot pins and bushings for wear. Maximum clearance between nozzle pivot pins and bushings is 0.005 inch.

Apply a small amount of OMC Sea-Lube Anti-Corrosion Lube or equivalent lubricant to pivot pin bushings and locking compound to pivot pin retaining screws. Tighten reverse gate pivot pin retaining screws to 8-12 ft.-lbs. Tighten lower nozzle pivot pin retaining screw to 11 ft.-lbs. Apply OMC Gasket Sealing Compound to trim cap gasket surface. Tighten trim cap retaining screws to 11 ft.-lbs.

BOWL

R&R AND OVERHAUL. To remove nozzle, disconnect shift and steering cables and remove rudder (60—Fig. 1-4). Remove screws securing transom adapter (54) and remove adapter. Unscrew bowl retaining screws located on front of impeller housing flange. Carefully separate bowl (39) from impeller housing.

Maximum allowable diametral clearance between bowl bushings (37) and impeller shaft is 0.011 inch. Renew bushings if clearance is excessive or a new impeller shaft is installed. Use long end of OMC tool No. 908374 to install inner bushing and short end of tool to install outer bushing. Drive in bushings until flange on tool seats against lip seal shoulder in bowl. Install lip seal (36) with lips facing out.

Diametral clearance between wear ring (35) and impeller hub should be 0.010-0.030 inch. Apply OMC Gasket Sealing Compound to wear ring screws. Tighten screws to 24 in.-lbs.

Inspect bowl and vanes for cracks and chips. Remove small nicks from leading edges of vanes with a flat file. Apply OMC Gasket Sealing Compound to nozzle retaining screws and tighten screws to 20 ft.-lbs.

Apply Dow Corning 791 sealant or equivalent to flange of transom adapter (54). There should be no breaks in sealant bead. Be sure transom adapter is not cocked during installation as "O" ring (38) may be damaged. Inspect installation from inside boat to be sure "O" ring is in place and undamaged.

IMPELLER

R&R AND OVERHAUL. To remove impeller, remove bowl as outlined in previous section. Unscrew impeller nut (31—Fig. 1-5) and using a suitable puller detach impeller (30) from shaft. Care should be used not to hit end of impeller shaft as seals and bearing may be damaged. Remove impeller wear ring (13).

Inspect impeller wear ring for damage and excessive wear. Renew impeller wear ring if thickness is less than 3/64-inch measured as shown in Fig. 1-6. Inspect impeller for nicks, cracks or other damage to blades and hub. Do not attempt to weld cracked or broken blades.

Reverse disassembly to reinstall impeller. Align impeller wear ring with dowel pins (12). Install impeller nut with split side away from impeller. Tighten impeller nut to 20 ft.-lbs. Measure clearance between impeller blade tips and wear ring. Clearance should be 0.005-0.015 inch and is adjusted with shims (4). Refer to IMPELLER SHAFT section for installation of shims.

IMPELLER HOUSING AND SHAFT

R&R AND OVERHAUL. Note that impeller shaft must be removed from front of impeller housing. If engine has been removed, impeller shaft may be removed without removing impeller housing from boat.

To remove impeller housing, remove impeller wear ring as outlined in previous section. Disconnect water line and ground strap. Remove inspection cap (9—Fig. 1-5) and bolts and unscrew ten bolts securing impeller housing (6) to grille housing (33). Remove impeller housing through hole in transom.

Remove bearing cap (3) and retain shims (4) for installation. Withdraw shaft from front of housing. Remove snap ring (15) and press bearing (16)

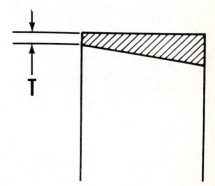

Fig. 1-6—Minimum thickness of wear ring is 3/64-inch (T).

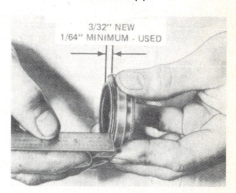

Fig. 1-7—Measure shoulder of ceramic seal as shown and renew seal if shoulder height is less than 1/64-inch.

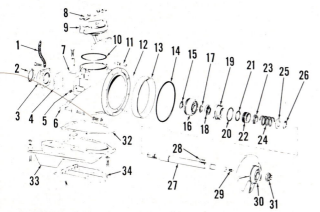

Fig. 1-5—Exploded view of impeller housing.

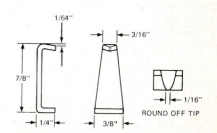

Fig. 1-8—Use the dimensions shown above to fabricate two seal compressing tools to aid during seal installation on shaft.

1. Ground strap
2. Seal
3. Bearing cap
4. Shims
5. Lubrication fitting
6. Impeller housing
7. Spring pin
8. Bolt lock bar
9. Inspection cap
10. "O" ring
11. Water outlet
12. Dowel pin
13. Wear ring
14. "O" ring
15. Snap ring
16. Bearing
17. Thrust washer
18. Seal
19. Seal housing
20. "O" ring
21. "O" ring
22. Ceramic seal
23. Seal ring
24. Spring
25. Spring cup
26. Snap ring
27. Impeller shaft
28. Key
29. Lubrication fitting
30. Impeller
31. Nut
32. Gasket
33. Grille housing
34. Grille

off shaft. Remove remainder of components from shaft.

Inspect impeller shaft for excessive wear, roughness or other damage. Maximum runout with shaft placed in lathe centers is 0.003 inch. Minimum diameter of impeller end of shaft is 1.1218 inches. Be sure shaft shoulder for thrust washer (17) is square with shaft. Inspect seal components and discard components which are cracked or worn. Measure shoulder of ceramic seal (22) shown in Fig. 1-7 and renew seal if shoulder is less than 1/64-inch.

Reverse disassembly procedure for assembly. Apply OMC Gasket Sealing Compound or equivalent to seal cavity in seal housing (19—Fig. 1-5) and install seal (18) with lips in towards housing. Bottom seal in seal housing. Apply OMC Gasket Sealing Compound or equivalent in seal housing (19) cavity for ceramic seal (22). Seal compressing tools may be fabricated using dimensions shown in Fig. 1-8 to compress seal components for installation on shaft. Install bearing (16—Fig. 1-5) with outer race snap ring towards front of shaft. Bearing must bottom against thrust washer (17). Install shaft so that bleed hole shown in Fig. 1-9 is towards bottom of impeller housing. Apply OMC Gasket Sealing Compound or equivalent to bearing cap (3—Fig. 1-5) cavity and install seal (2) with lips facing inwards. Seal should be flush to 1/16-inch below chamfer of bearing cap. Install bearing cap (3) with lubrication relief hole shown in Fig. 1-10 towards starboard side and with original shims. Install impeller as previously outlined and measure clearance between impeller blade tips and impeller wear ring. Clearance should be 0.005-0.015 inch. Adjust clearance by removing or installing shims (4—Fig. 1-5). Be sure shims are installed between snap ring on outer race of bearing (16) and impeller housing. Shims are 0.015 and 0.030 inch thick and will change clearance 0.005 and 0.010 inch respectively. Apply OMC Gasket Sealing Compound to gasket surfaces of impeller housing and grille housing (33), install impeller housing on grille housing and tighten bolts to 20 ft.-lbs. Note that two rear bolts are two inches long.

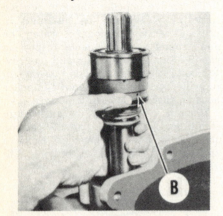

Fig. 1-9—Bleed hole (B) in seal housing must face bottom of impeller housing when installing impeller shaft assembly.

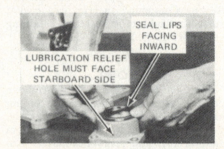

Fig. 1-10—Install bearing cap so that lubrication relief hole faces starboard side of impeller housing.

PANTHER JET 450E

JET DRIVE MAINTENANCE

LUBRICATION

Front bearings are lubricated by pouring EP 90 oil through oil fill tube into bearing cavity. Upper edge of oil fill tube (2—Fig. 1-1) should be even with impeller shaft centerline. Add oil until oil fill tube is full. Emission of oil from bearing cavity vent holes (V) indicates overfilling or a damaged rear oil seal. Emission of water from vent holes indicates a damaged water seal.

Bushing (30—Fig. 1-2) is greased during factory assembly of unit and should not require additional lubrication, however, fitting (F—Fig. 1-4) is provided to grease bushing should it run dry.

ADJUSTMENT

Steering and shift mechanisms must be adjusted to properly operate jet drive unit. Steering mechanism must have four inches of cable travel to turn jet drive nozzle desired ninety degrees from full left to full right. The shift mechanism must be adjusted so reverse gate is tilted forward out of jet stream when unit is in forward. Shift mechanism must also move reverse gate far enough down into jet stream to provide reverse thrust when unit is in reverse.

JET DRIVE SERVICE

NOZZLE AND REVERSE GATE

R&R AND OVERHAUL. Nozzle (38—Fig. 1-3) and reverse gate (39) may be removed after removing cover (41), disconnecting control cables and driving out pivot pins (34 and 37). Renew any pins or bushings (33 and 36) which are worn or damaged. Stainless steel shims should be used to remove any looseness between components.

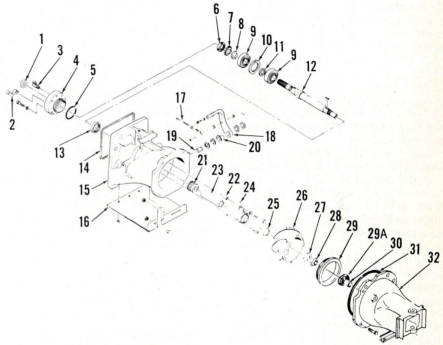

Fig. 1-2—Exploded view of impeller and stator housing assemblies.

1. Oil seal
2. Oil fill tube
3. Oil overflow cup
4. Bearing cap
5. "O" ring
6. Nut
7. Tab washer
8. Spacer
9. Bearings
10. Outer spacer
11. Inner spacer
12. Impeller shaft
13. Oil seal
14. Rubber seal
15. Impeller housing
16. Trim plate
17. Shift rod
18. Shift arm
19. Pivot pin
20. Bushing
21. Water seal
22. Spacer
23. Spacer
24. Fairing
25. Shims
26. Impeller
27. Washer
28. Nut
29. Seal
29A. Sand seal
30. Bushing
31. "O" ring
32. Stator housing

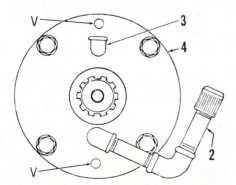

Fig. 1-1—View of bearing cap (4) showing location of oil fill tube (2) and oil overflow cup (3). Emission of oil or water from vent holes indicates overfilling or damaged seals.

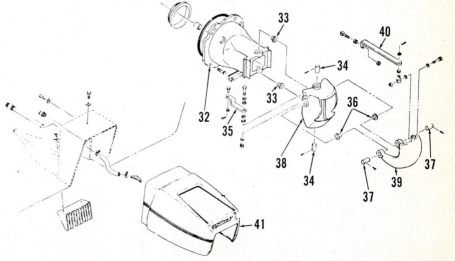

Fig. 1-3—Exploded view of stator housing, nozzle and reverse gate assembly.

32. Stator housing
33. Bushings
34. Pivot pins
35. Steering arm
36. Bushings
37. Pivot pins
38. Nozzle
39. Reverse gate
40. Shift link
41. Cover

Panther — DRIVES

STATOR HOUSING

R&R AND OVERHAUL. To remove stator housing (32—Fig. 1-3), remove cover (41) and disconnect control cables. Unbolt and separate stator housing (32—Fig. 1-2) from impeller housing (15). Self-lubricating bushing (30) must be renewed if excessively worn or damaged. Secure bushing with a suitable bushing cement. Early models are equipped with an aluminum sleeve which retains bushing (30). Renew sleeve if loose in stator housing. Note condition of sand seal (29A) and impeller shaft (12) bushing surface. Inspect stator blades in stator housing (32). Stator blades may be welded or repaired with epoxy putty to restore blades to original shape. Note that any portion of the stator housing that is welded or where bare metal is exposed must be painted with zinc chromate to prevent corrosion.

Note condition of aluminum seal (29). Radial fit between impeller (26) and seal (29) should be 0.015 inch. It may be necessary to stake or cement seal in place if it is loose in stator housing. Refer to IMPELLER section for radial clearance adjustment.

IMPELLER

R&R AND OVERHAUL. To remove impeller (26—Fig. 1-2), remove stator housing and unscrew nut (28). Using a suitable puller, detach impeller from shaft. Remove impeller key, shims (25), fairing (24), spacer (23) and water seal (21). Fairing (24) and spacer (23) are only used on early models.

File or grind leading edge of impeller blades if necessary to restore original contour. Bent blades may be returned to original shape by heating blade and bending. Blade heights may vary by approximately 1/8-inch. Impeller imbalance must not exceed 0.1 oz. per inch.

Inspect water seal (21). Seal must be renewed if ceramic or carbon sections are cracked or chipped. Rubber collar on seal must grip impeller shaft tightly.

Be sure fairing (24) is positioned so impeller shaft will rotate in center of fairing bore. Apply "Loctite" to fairing screw threads.

Axial clearance between impeller (26) and stator housing (32) should be 0.020-0.030 inch. To measure clearance, assemble jet drive without shims (25) and measure gap in several locations between impeller housing (15) and stator housing (32). Compute average gap between housings. Install shim pack (25) which is 0.020-0.030 inch thicker than average gap between housings.

IMPELLER SHAFT AND BEARINGS

R&R AND OVERHAUL. Remove impeller as outlined in previous section. Disconnect water line and remove impeller housing mounting bolts. Carefully detach impeller housing from boat. It may be necessary to gently pry against housing to break silicone seal bond between boat and housing. Remove fairing (24—Fig. 1-2) and spacer (23) on models so equipped. Remove water seal (21). Remove bearing cap (4) and press impeller shaft (12) and bearing assembly out of impeller housing (15). Unscrew bearing retainer nut (6) and press bearings (9) off impeller shaft. Note that outer spacer (10) has a gap which must be aligned with oil groove cast in top of impeller housing bearing cavity. Inspect oil seals (1 and 13) and renew if damaged. Grooves and gouges in impeller area of impeller housing which are deeper than 1/8-inch should be filled with epoxy putty and ground smooth. Areas of impeller housing which are repaired by welding or where bare metal is exposed should be painted with zinc chromate to prevent corrosion.

Silicone seal should be spread around edge of rubber seal (14) and around intake prior to installation of impeller housing in boat. Refer to LUBRICATION section.

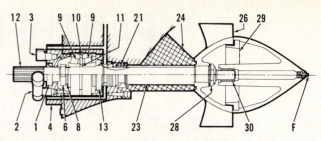

Fig. 1-4—Cross-section view of Panther jet. Rear bushing (30) may be greased through fitting (F). Refer to Fig. 1-2 for parts identification.

PARAGON

PARAGON POWER, INC.
7455 Tyler Blvd.
Mentor, Ohio 44060

SAO TRANSMISSION

OPERATION

A planetary gearset is used to provide forward and reverse direction. Refer to Figs. 1-1 and 1-1A for a cross-sectional view of the transmission or to Fig. 1-2 for an exploded view. Shift lever (32) actuates linkage to apply clutch pack for forward gear or tighten reverse band (33) around gear housing (12) for reverse gear. When shift lever is moved to engage forward gear, cone (28) moves away from planetary assembly thereby moving clutch levers (19) out which forces pressure plate (16) in to compress clutch plates. Transmission output shaft (29) and planetary assembly now rotate same direction as engine crankshaft. When shift lever (32) is moved for reverse gear, cone (28) moves towards planetary assembly which disengages clutch pack. Reverse cam (26—Fig. 1-3) moves against cam roller (R). Reverse band tightens around gear housing and transmission output shaft rotation is reverse of engine crankshaft rotation.

Some transmissions may be equipped with a reduction gear attached to the rear of the transmission and lubricated by transmission oil. Refer to Fig. 1-5 for an exploded view of reduction gear.

LUBRICATION

Recommended oil is SAE 30 automotive oil or automatic transmission fluid (ATF). Fill transmission until oil

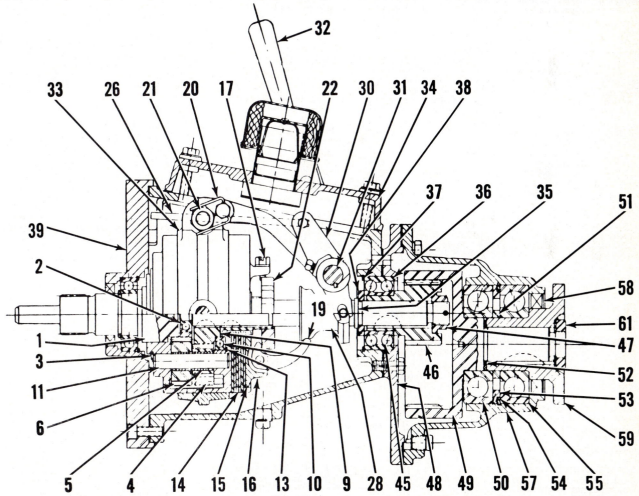

Fig. 1-1—Cross-sectional view of Paragon SA0 transmission and reduction gear. Refer to Fig. 1-1A for view of direct drive flange coupling assembly. Refer to Fig. 1-2 for exploded view of planetary gear assembly.

1. Input gear
2. Bearing
3. Snap ring
4. Long planetary gear shafts
5. Bushing
6. Short planetary gear
8. Spacer
9. Output gear
10. Bearing
11. Planetary gear shafts
12. Gearcase
13. Snap ring
14. Outer clutch plates
15. Inner clutch plates
16. Pressure plate
17. Lockscrew
19. Clutch levers
20. Lockspring
21. Nut
22. Collar
26. Cam
28. Shift cone
30. Shift yoke
31. Shift shaft
32. Shift lever
33. Reverse band
34. Cover
35. Snap ring
36. Bearing
37. Snap ring
38. Thrust washer
39. Front plate
46. Reduction pinion
47. Nut
48. Adapter
49. Ring gear
50. Bearing
51. Spacer
52. Spacer
53. Spacer
54. Snap ring
55. Bearing
56. Drain plug
57. Reduction housing
58. Oil seal
59. Flange coupling
60. Tab washer
61. Nut

Illustration courtesy Paragon

Paragon

DRIVES

reaches full mark indicated on dipstick. Oil should be changed after 100 hours of operation or every season.

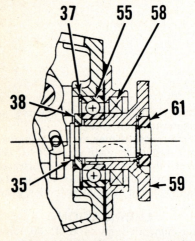

Fig. 1-1A—Cross-sectional view of flange coupling assembly used on direct drive transmissions. Refer to Fig. 1-1 for parts identification.

ADJUSTMENT

To adjust transmission, run engine and move gear selector to forward gear position. If slippage occurs in forward gear, move shift lever to neutral and stop engine. Remove transmission top cover, back out lockscrew (17—Fig. 1-1) and turn collar (22) clockwise one notch. Tighten lockscrew (17) and check operation of forward gear. Repeat procedure until slippage is removed.

To remove reverse gear slippage, remove transmission cover and turn adjusting nut (21—Fig. 1-3) clockwise two or three flats and check operation. If necessary, repeat adjustment until operation is satisfactory. Be sure lock spring (20) is in place.

TRANSMISSION OVERHAUL

Drain or pump oil from transmission. Separate transmission and reduction gear, if so equipped, from engine and remainder of drive train.

If transmission is equipped with a reduction gear, proceed as follows: Drain any oil remaining in reduction gear housing. Unscrew cap screws securing reduction gear housing to transmission housing and separate units. Remove nut (61—Fig. 1-5) and lockwasher (60) and use a suitable puller to remove coupling (59). Press output shaft (49) along with bearing (50) out of housing. If necessary, remove snap ring (54) and press out ball bearing (55). Unscrew nut (47) and remove reduction pinion (46). Refer to following paragraph for transmission disassembly.

To disassemble transmission, detach shift lever (32—Fig. 1-2) and remove cover (34—Fig. 1-1). Remove lock spring (20—Fig. 1-1 or 1-2), unscrew nut (21), detach cam (26) from shift yoke (30) and remove cam. Loosen the two screws retaining yoke (30) on shift shaft (31). Slide shift shaft out of transmission housing towards shift lever side of housing being careful not to damage shaft oil seal with keys in shaft. Remove brace (27—Fig. 1-2) and yoke (30).

Unbolt and remove front transmission plate (39—Fig. 1-1). Note on transmissions with reduction gear that planetary gear assembly can be removed if reduction pinion (46—Fig. 1-1 or 1-5) was previously removed. On all other transmissions, drive out roll pin (42—Fig. 1-4) and remove lockpin (43) securing reverse band to housing. Inspect lockpin "O" ring (41). Remove reverse band (33—Fig. 1-2). Unscrew nut securing flange coupling (61—Fig. 1-1A) or reduction pinion (46—Fig. 1-5)

Fig. 1-2—Exploded view of planetary gear assembly. Refer to Fig. 1-1 for parts identification except for:

7. Bushing	23. Spring	27. Brace	
18. Lever pins	24. Band tightening pin	29. Output shaft	
	25. Cam pin		

Fig. 1-3—Top view of reverse band and shift mechanism. When shift yoke (30) pulls cam (26), cam bears against cam pin (25) and roller (R) and pulls band tightening pin (24) to tighten reverse band around gearcase.

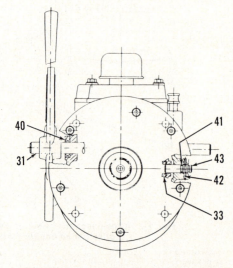

Fig. 1-4—Front cross-sectional view of transmission.

31. Shift shaft
33. Reverse band
40. Oil seal
41. "O" ring
42. Roll pin
43. Band lockpin

Illustration courtesy Paragon

DRIVES   Paragon

if not previously removed. Note some direct drive units have a splined output shaft and a flange coupling is not used. Support transmission housing while making provision to catch planetary gear assembly and press output shaft out towards front of transmission. Unscrew lockscrew (17—Fig. 1-1 or 1-2) and collar (22) while simultaneously removing cone (28) as collar (22) is unscrewed. Remove pressure plate (16) and clutch plates. Press output shaft (29—Fig. 1-2) out of output gear (9) and remove both shaft and gear. If necessary, remove planetary gears (4, 6 & 9) by removing snap ring (3) and pressing shafts towards front of gear housing.

Inspect components for excessive wear or damage. Renew reverse band (33—Fig. 1-1 or 1-2) if rivets have contacted gearcase (12). Brace (27—Fig. 1-2) and cam (26) should be flat. Shift cone (28) must move freely on output shaft (29).

To reassemble transmission and reduction gear, reverse disassembly procedure, while noting the following points: Steel and bronze clutch plates are installed alternately with first and last plates being bronze. Install thrust washer (38—Fig. 1-1A or 1-5) with counterbored side towards front of transmission. Refer to LUBRICATION and ADJUSTMENT paragraphs.

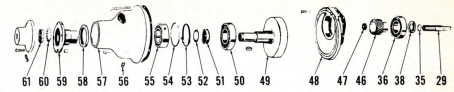

Fig. 1-5—Exploded view of reduction gear. Refer to Fig. 1-1 for parts identification except for:

29. Output shaft
56. Drain plug
60. Tab washer

PARAGON
SA1 TRANSMISSION

OPERATION

A planetary gearset is used to provide forward and reverse direction. Refer to Fig. 2-1, 2-2 or 2-3 for an exploded view of the transmission or to Fig. 2-4 for a cross-sectional view. The shift lever actuates linkage to apply clutch pack for forward gear or tighten reverse band (26—Fig. 2-2) around gear housing (11) for reverse gear. When shift lever is moved to engage forward gear, sleeve (23—Fig. 2-1) moves away from planetary assembly thereby moving clutch levers (24) out which forces pressure plate (19) in to compress clutch plates. Transmission output shaft and planetary assembly now rotate same direction as input shaft. When shift lever is moved for reverse gear, sleeve (23) moves toward planetary assembly which disengages clutch pack. Reverse link (38—Fig. 2-3) pulls reverse arms (36) when shift lever is moved to reverse. Pivot arm (34) tightens reverse band (26) around gear housing when reverse arm is pulled or loosens band when reverse arm is pushed away.

Some transmissions may be equipped with a reduction gear attached to the rear of the transmission. The reduction gear may be in-line as shown in Fig. 2-7 or drop-center. Both reduction gears are lubricated by transmission oil.

LUBRICATION

Recommended oil is SAE 30 automotive oil. Fill transmission until oil reaches full mark indicated on dipstick. Oil should be changed after 100 hours of operation or every season.

ADJUSTMENT

To adjust transmission, run engine and note if slippage occurs in either forward or reverse gear. Shift to neutral and stop engine. To correct forward gear slippage, remove transmission top cover and back out lockscrew (22—Fig. 2-5) until screw is withdrawn from hole in pressure plate (19). Turn collar (20) until lockscrew is aligned with next hole in pressure plate and retighten lockscrew (22). Be sure lockscrew properly engages hole in pressure plate. Check operation of forward gear. Transmission should not slip while in forward gear but excessive force should not be needed to shift transmission into gear. Additional adjustment is provided by unscrewing lockscrew (22) then installing lockscrew in an adjoining hole in collar.

To adjust reverse band, loosen nut (33—Fig. 2-6) and then tighten nut (35) against reverse band flange. Moderate force against shift lever should be

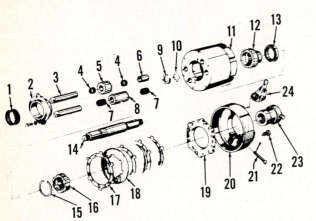

Fig. 2-1—Exploded view of planetary gear assembly used in SA1 transmission.

1. Roller bearing
2. Bearing carrier
3. Pinion shafts
4. Bushing
5. Short planetary gear
6. Spacer
7. Bushing
8. Long planetary gear
9. Nut
10. Tab washer
11. Gear housing
12. Output gear
13. Bearing
14. Output shaft
15. Snap ring
16. Clutch plate carrier
17. Outer clutch plate (5)
18. Inner clutch plates (4)
19. Pressure plate
20. Collar
21. Pin
22. Lockscrew
23. Clutch sleeve
24. Clutch lever

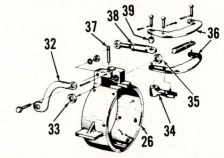

Fig. 2-3—Exploded view of reverse band tightening mechanism. Refer also to Fig. 2-2.

26. Reverse band
32. Brace
33. Nut
34. Pivot arm
35. Nut
36. Reverse arms
37. Pin
38. Reverse link
39. Ball joint

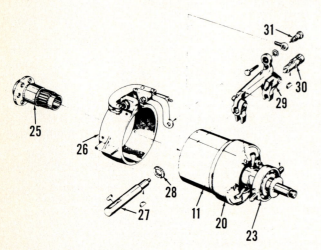

Fig. 2-2—View of shift mechanism. Also refer to Fig. 2-3. Note that two seals (28) are used on shafts (27 & 30).

11. Gear housing
20. Collar
23. Clutch sleeve
25. Input shaft
26. Reverse band
27. Left yoke shaft
28. Seal
29. Shift yoke
30. Right yoke shaft
31. Screw

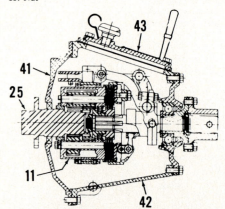

Fig. 2-4—Cross-sectional view of direct drive SA1 transmission. Refer to Fig. 2-7 for an exploded view of reduction gear which may be coupled to transmission.

11. Planetary gear assy.
25. Input shaft
41. Front cover
42. Transmission housing
43. Top cover

Illustration courtesy Paragon

DRIVES Paragon

needed to "overcenter" reverse band linkage thereby tightening reverse band around gear housing.

TRANSMISSION OVERHAUL

Drain or pump oil from transmission. Separate transmission and reduction gear, if so equipped, from engine and remainder of drive train.

If transmission is equipped with a reduction gear, proceed as follows: Drain any oil remaining in reduction gear housing. Unscrew cap screws securing reduction gear housing to transmission housing and separate units. Remove nut (50—Fig. 2-7) and lockwasher (51) and use a suitable puller to remove flange coupling (52). Press output shaft (62) along with bearing (61) out of housing. If necessary, remove snap ring (57) and press out ball bearing (56). Unscrew nut (64) and remove reduction pinion (65). Refer to following paragraph for transmission disassembly.

To disassemble transmission, remove shift lever and top cover (43—Fig. 2-4). Remove input shaft (25) and front cover (41). Remove screw (31—Fig. 2-2), loosen screws in shift yoke (29)

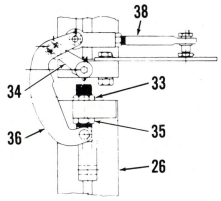

Fig. 2-6—View of reverse band tightening mechanism. Refer to text for adjustment. Refer to Fig. 2-3 for parts identification.

and remove shafts (27) and (30). Remove shift yoke (29) through cover opening and reverse band assembly through front of transmission. Unscrew flange coupling on direct drive models or reduction pinion nut on models equipped with reduction gear. Being careful to catch planetary gear assembly, press output shaft (14—Fig. 2-1) towards front of transmission and out of flange coupling or reduction pinion. Remove planetary gear assembly from transmission housing. Remove lockscrew (22) and shift sleeve (23). Unscrew collar (20) and remove pressure plate (19) and clutch plates. Unscrew nut (9) and press output shaft (14) out of output gear (12) and clutch plate carrier (16). Unbolt and remove bearing carrier (2). Remove planetary gears and shafts only if renewal is required.

Reassembly is accomplished by reversing disassembly procedure. Install thrust washer (67—Fig. 2-7) with counterbored side towards front of transmission. Refer to LUBRICATION and ADJUSTMENT sections.

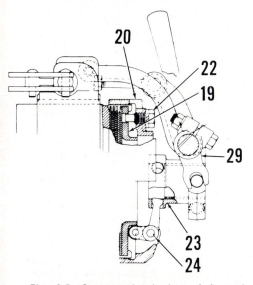

Fig. 2-5—Cross-sectional view of forward clutch application mechanism. Refer to previous captions for identification. Refer to text for adjustment.

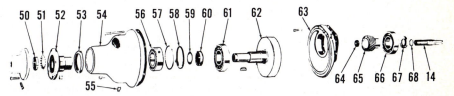

Fig. 2-7—Exploded view of in-line reduction gear. Drop center reduction gear is similar but gear (62) has external rather than internal gear teeth.

14. Trans. output shaft
50. Nut
51. Tab washer
52. Flange coupling
53. Oil seal
54. Reduction housing
55. Drain plug
56. Bearing
57. Snap ring
58. Spacer
59. Spacer
60. Spacer
61. Bearing
62. Output shaft & ring gear
63. Adapter
64. Nut
65. Reduction pinion
66. Bearing
67. Thrust washer
68. Snap ring

Illustration courtesy Paragon

PARAGON
P200, P300 & P400 TRANSMISSIONS

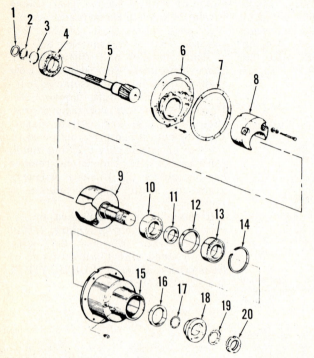

Fig. 3-1—Exploded view of reduction gear used with P200, P300 and P400 transmissions.

1. Bearing race
2. Thrust bearing
3. Snap ring
4. Bearing
5. Trans. output shaft & reduction pinion
6. Adapter
7. Gasket
8. Crescent
9. Ring gear & output shaft
10. Bearing
11. Inner spacer
12. Outer spacer
13. Bearing
14. Snap ring
15. Reduction gear housing
16. Oil seal
17. "O" ring
18. Flange coupling
19. Tab washer
20. Nut

MODEL IDENTIFICATION

First letter in model identification number is a "P" to denote Paragon Gear. The number following the letter "P" indicates the model series of the transmission. Number "2" indicates a P200 transmission; number "3" indicates a P300 transmission and number "4" indicates a P400 transmission. The next number in the model number indicates the reduction ratio. Number "1" indicates unit is direct drive while numbers "2" through "5" indicate unit is equipped with a reduction gear. Second letter in model identification number indicates direction input shaft must turn. Units with "R" in model number must have counter-clockwise rotating input shaft when viewed from front of transmission. Units with "L" must have clockwise rotating input shaft. For example, a transmission with model number "P31L" is a Paragon Gear P300 series transmission with direct drive which has a clockwise rotating input shaft as viewed from front of transmission.

NOTE: Transmissions coupled to a Paragon V-drive will have a "V" following the first letter "P," such as, "PV31L."

OPERATION

Shifting of all transmissions is accomplished hydraulically with oil pressurized by the gear type oil pump attached to front end plate (13—Fig. 3-3). Shift lever (1—Fig. 3-2) turns control valve (6) thereby redirecting pressurized oil and shifting transmission. Oil pressure directed behind servo piston (11) forces piston down against reverse band lever (16) which tightens reverse band (12—Fig. 3-3) around gear housing (43—Fig. 3-6). Rotation of input and output shafts is reversed. Forward gear is obtained when pressurized oil is directed by control valve (6—Fig. 3-2) through the transmission housing and collar (67—Fig. 3-6) to the cavity behind piston (64). Oil pressure applied behind piston forces piston forward thereby engaging clutch pack with planetary gear housing.

Transmission oil reservoir is located in bottom of transmission housing. Transmission oil is cooled by an external oil cooler. Recommended oil is Type "A" automatic transmission fluid (ATF). Fill transmission until oil reaches full mark on dipstick. Shift unit several times at idle speed to fill all oil circuits and oil cooler and recheck oil

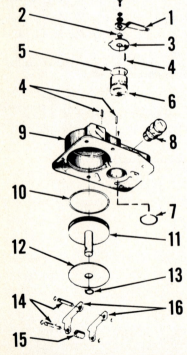

Fig. 3-2—Exploded view of control valve assembly. Detent assembly (8) is located on opposite side of housing (9) on early models.

1. Shift lever
2. Bushing
3. Lever pawl
4. Pins
5. "O" ring
6. Control valve
7. Snap ring
8. Detent assembly
9. Control valve housing
10. "O" ring
11. Reverse piston
12. Piston plate
13. "O" ring
14. Pins
15. Reverse band roller
16. Reverse band levers

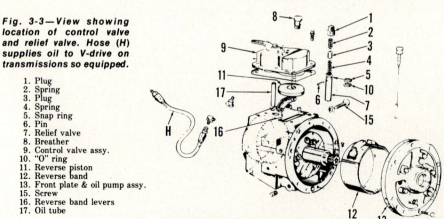

Fig. 3-3—View showing location of control valve and relief valve. Hose (H) supplies oil to V-drive on transmissions so equipped.

1. Plug
2. Spring
3. Plug
4. Spring
5. Snap ring
6. Pin
7. Relief valve
8. Breather
9. Control valve assy.
10. "O" ring
11. Reverse piston
12. Reverse band
13. Front plate & oil pump assy.
15. Screw
16. Reverse band levers
17. Oil tube

DRIVES
Paragon

level. Manufacturer recommends changing oil after every 100 hours of operation or each season. Change oil more frequently than recommended if operated under adverse conditions.

REDUCTION GEAR OVERHAUL

Drain or pump oil from transmission and reduction gear. Unscrew cap screws securing reduction gear housing (15—Fig. 3-1) to rear of transmission. Separate reduction gear housing from transmission by tapping on flange coupling (18) to break units apart. Unscrew nut (20) and using a suitable puller, remove flange coupling (18). Remove "O" ring (17) and then press ring gear and output shaft (9) out of housing. Remove snap ring (14) if bearing (13) removal is necessary. To remove transmission output shaft and pinion (5), remove crescent (8). Unscrew adapter plate (6) mounting bolts and separate adapter plate (6) and shaft (5) from transmission. Press shaft (5) and bearing (4) out of adapter plate (6). Remove snap ring (3) and press bearing (4) off shaft (5).

To reassemble reduction gear, reverse disassembly procedure while noting the following points: Bearing (4) must bottom against shoulder in adapter (6). Install ring gear and output shaft (9) so shoulder on shaft contacts bearing (10). Fill transmission with recommended lubricant.

TRANSMISSION OVERHAUL

Drain or pump oil from transmission. Remove adapter plate (6—Fig. 3-1) and shaft (5) on models equipped with reduction gear as outlined in previous section. Separate transmission from V-drive, if so equipped.

Unbolt and remove control valve housing (9—Fig. 3-2) by turning housing slightly while lifting. Back out screw (15—Fig. 3-3) approximately one inch and remove piston (11—Fig. 3-2) and reverse band lever (16). Unscrew detent assembly (8) and remove snap ring (7). Pull up on control lever (1) to remove control valve assembly from housing. Note position of control lever (1) on control valve (6) if lever and valve are to be separated. Unscrew plug (1—Fig. 3-3) for access to relief valve. Pin (6) must be driven out of valve body (7) to disassemble valve. Note chamfered side of piston plate (12—Fig. 3-2) must be next to bottom of piston (11) when reassembling control valve.

Detach front end plate (13—Fig. 3-3) from front of transmission. Remove oil pump cover (22—Fig. 3-4), mark oil pump gears for reassembly, and disassemble oil pump. Care should be taken not to damage port plate pins (19). Remove reverse band (12—Fig. 3-3). On transmission with reduction gear,

planetary gear assembly can now be removed. On direct drive models, unscrew bearing retainer (33—Fig. 3-5) screws. Tap retainer to break it loose from transmission housing and separate retainer (33) and output shaft (27) from

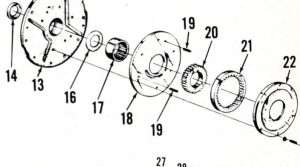

Fig. 3-4—Exploded view of front end plate and oil pump. Port plate (18) is not used on later models.

13. Front end plate
14. Oil seal
16. Thrust washer
17. Roller bearing
18. Port plate
19. Pins
20. Inner pump gear
21. Outer pump gear
22. Pump housing

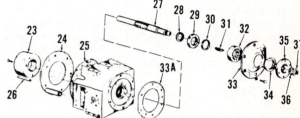

Fig. 3-5—View showing output shaft assembly on direct drive transmissions.

23. Baffle
24. Gasket
25. Transmission housing
26. Reverse band pin
27. Output shaft
28. Thrust washer
29. Seal washer
30. Thrust washer
31. Woodruff key
32. Bearing
33. Bearing retainer
33A. Gasket
34. Oil seal
35. Flange coupling
36. Tab washer
37. Nut

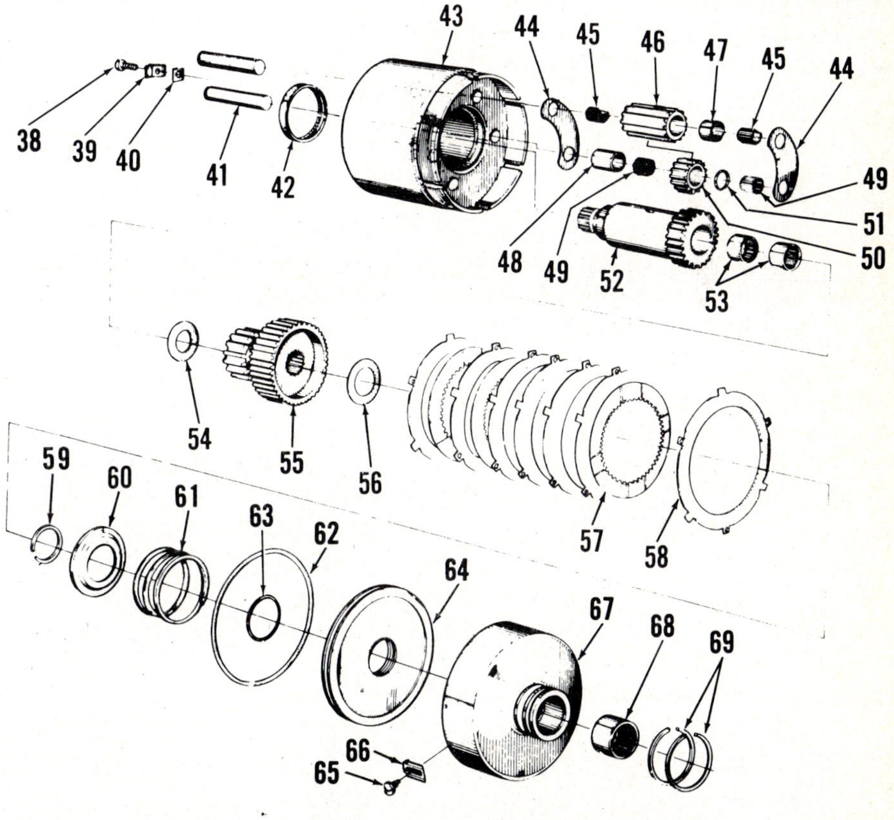

Fig. 3-6—Exploded view of planetary gear assembly.

38. Screws
39. Clips
40. Locking tab
41. Planetary gear shafts
42. Roller bearing
43. Gear housing
44. Thrust pads
45. Bearing rollers (32)
46. Long planetary gears
47. Spacer
48. Spacer
49. Bearing rollers (32)
50. Short planetary gears
51. Spacer
52. Input shaft
53. Roller bearings
54. Thrust washer
55. Output gear
56. Thrust washer
57. Bronze clutch plates
58. Steel clutch plates
59. Snap ring
60. Spring retainer
61. Spring
62. "O" ring
63. "O" ring
64. Piston
65. Lockscrew
66. Locking clip
67. Collar
68. Roller bearing
69. Seal rings

Illustration courtesy Paragon

Paragon

DRIVES

transmission housing. Planetary gear assembly can now be removed on direct drive models. Note that when disassembling output shaft and bearing retainer assembly on P400 models, that snap ring adjacent to bearing (32) must be removed before flange coupling (35) can be pressed out of bearing.

To disassemble planetary gear assembly, remove lockscrew (65—Fig. 3-6) and locking clip (66) and unscrew collar (67) from gear housing (43). Remove snap ring (59), spring retainer (60) and spring (61). Dislodge piston (64) from collar (67) by tapping collar on a soft surface. Note condition of "O" rings (62 and 63) and seal rings (69). Remove clutch plates, thrust washer (56), output gear (55) and thrust washer (54). Remove screws (38), clips (39) and locking tabs (40). Drive out shafts (41) for short pinions (50) and remove short pinions and spacers (48). Remove input shaft (52). Drive out shafts (41) for long pinions (46) and remove long pinions (46) and thrust pads (44).

When assembling transmission, note the following: There are 32 rollers in each row of bearings (45 and 49). Grease may be used to hold rollers in position during assembly. Thrust pads (44) should be installed so curvature of pads matches curvature of gear housing (43). Long planetary gears (46) are installed on outer row of shafts (41) while short planetary gears (50) are installed on inner row of shafts (41). Do not drive shafts (41) all the way in until all shafts and gears are in place. Install long gears (46), insert input shaft (52) and then install short gears (50). Press first of two bearings (53) 3½ inches into input gear (52) bore on P400 transmissions and 2-7/8 inches on P200 and P300 transmissions. Second of two bearings (53) should be installed flush with end of input gear (52). Turn shafts (41) so locking tabs (40) can be inserted into slots in ends of shafts. Alternate bronze (57) and steel (58) clutch plates with first and last plates being steel. Models P200 and P300 have six bronze plates and 7 steel plates while Model P400 has eight bronze plates and nine steel plates. Lubricate "O" rings before installation. Be sure "O" rings (62 and 63) are not damaged or do not roll out of grooves during piston (64) installation. Tighten collar (67) until threaded holes in collar are aligned with holes in gear housing (43) and install lockscrews (65) and locking tabs (66). Gaps of seal rings (69) should be in same position when installing planetary gear assembly in transmission housing. Note that gasket (24—Fig. 3-5) holds reverse band pin (26) in place.

PARAGON
PV300 & PV400 V-DRIVE

Service information for PV300 and PV400 V-drives was unavailable at time of publication. Refer to Figs. 4-1 and 4-2 for exploded views of V-drives.

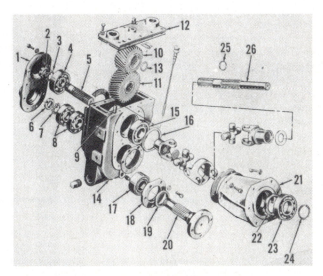

Fig. 4-1—Exploded view of early PV300 V-drive. Early Model PV400 V-drive is similar.

1. Cover
2. Nut
3. Tab washer
4. Bearing
5. Pinion shaft
6. Nut
7. Tab washer
8. Bearings
9. Dip stick tube
10. Pinion
11. Gear
12. Cover
13. Snap ring
14. Case
15. Bearing
16. Spacer
17. Bearing
18. Seal cap
19. Oil seal
20. Coupling
21. Angle housing
22. Oil seal
23. Bearing
24. Snap ring

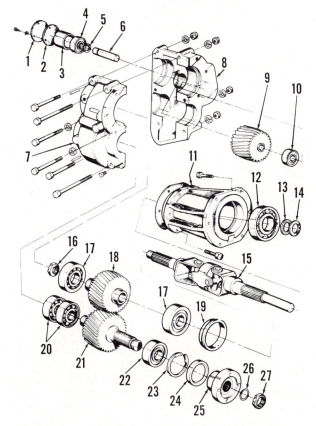

Fig. 4-2—Exploded view of late three gear PV300 V-drive. Two gear units are similar. Late Model PV400 V-drive is similar to PV300 V-drive.

1. Cover
2. Gasket
3. Spacer
4. Bearing
5. Snap ring
6. Idler shaft
7. Left housing
8. Right housing
9. Idler gear
10. Bearing
11. Angle housing
12. Bearing
13. Bearing
14. Bearing race
15. Universal joint
16. Nut
17. Bearing
18. Pinion
19. Spacer
20. Bearings
21. Gear
22. Bearing
23. Snap ring
24. Oil seal
25. Coupling
26. "O" ring
27. Nut

Illustration courtesy Paragon

PARAGON
SSR TRANSMISSION

OPERATION

The SSR transmission is designed and built for marine use. Gear reduction is 2:1. With shift lever mounted in normal position (lever pointing up), transmission is in forward when lever is moved towards the rear or reverse when shift lever is moved forward.

LUBRICATION

Transmission oil should be changed after every 500 hours of operation. Fill transmission to full mark on dipstick attached to fill plug. Recommended oil is a high quality SAE 30 automotive oil.

OVERHAUL

Proceed as follows to disassemble transmission: Remove raw-water pump (1 – Fig. 5-2), on models so equipped. Remove Woodruff key (2) from input shaft. Remove front cover (3) along with input shaft front bearing (4), snap ring (5), seal (6) and output shaft front bearing (7). Lift out input shaft (8) which has raw-water pump drive shaft (9) attached. Input shaft thrust bearing (10) and race (11) are now accessible. Remove output shaft thrust bearing (12), race (13), gear (14) along with bearing (15) and washer (16). Drive detent pin (17) into case using a flat punch. Rotate shift lever (18) to rear which will allow shift dog (19) to move forward and off of output shaft. Remove shift shoe (20) from shift shaft. Remove flange nut (21), washer (22), "O" ring (23), flange (24) and Woodruff key (25) from output shaft. Place transmission case (26) face down and press output shaft out of rear bearing (27). Remove snap ring (28) from output shaft. Remove thrust bearing (29), race (30), gear (31) containing bearing (32) and washer (33) from output shaft. Knock out pin (34) and remove shift lever (18). Slide shaft (35) into case and remove detent plate (36), springs (37) and spring washers (38). Drive pin (39) into idler gear shaft (40) using a flat punch. Remove idler gear shaft along with idler gear (41), thrust washer (42), thrust bearing (43), pin (44) and "O" ring (45).

Remove remaining snap rings, bearings and seals as necessary from case and front cover. When installing bearings and seals be sure to use a press; do not hammer bearings into place. Reassemble transmission in reverse order. Be sure to protect input and output shaft seals by covering Woodruff key slots with tape.

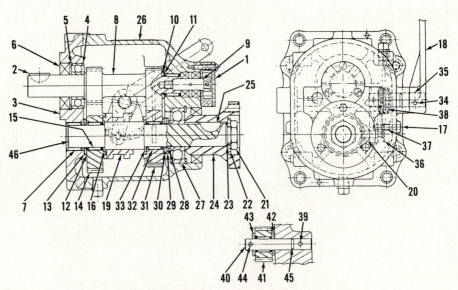

Fig. 5-1 – Exploded view of Paragon SSR transmission.

1. Raw-water pump
2. Input shaft Woodruff key
3. Front cover
4. Input shaft front bearing
5. Snap ring
6. Oil seal
7. Output shaft front bearing
8. Input shaft
9. Raw-water pump drive shaft
10. Thrust bearing
11. Race
12. Thrust bearing
13. Race
14. Gear
15. Bearing
16. Washer
17. Detent pin
18. Shift lever
19. Shift dog
20. Shift shoe
21. Flange nut
22. Washer
23. "O" ring
24. Flange
25. Output shaft Woodruff key
26. Transmission case
27. Output shaft rear bearing
28. Snap ring
29. Thrust bearing
30. Race
31. Gear
32. Bearing
33. Washer
34. Pin
35. Shifter shaft
36. Detent plate
37. Spring
38. Spring washer
39. Pin
40. Idler gear shaft
41. Idler gear
42. Thrust washer
43. Thrust bearing
44. Pin
45. "O" ring
46. Output shaft

DRIVES — Twin Disc

TWIN DISC
Racine, Wisconsin 53403

MG-502 IN-LINE & V-DRIVE TRANSMISSIONS

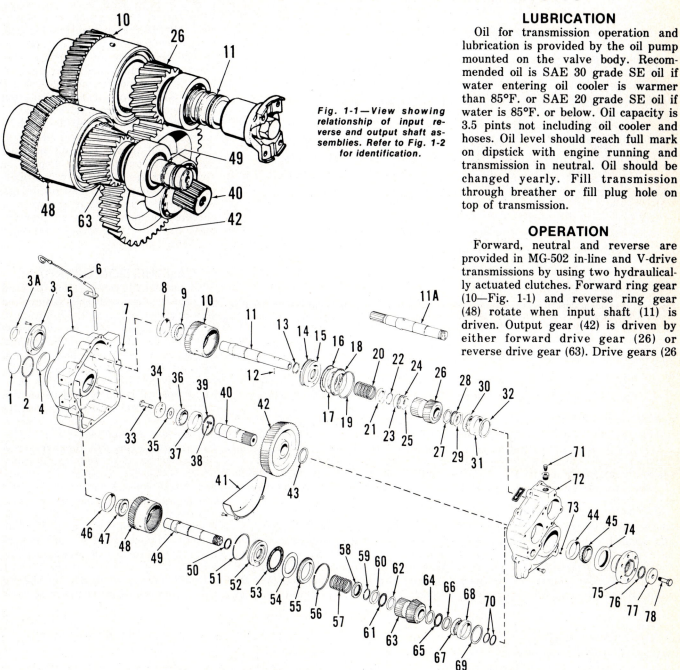

Fig. 1-1—View showing relationship of input reverse and output shaft assemblies. Refer to Fig. 1-2 for identification.

Fig. 1-2—Exploded view of V-drive input, reverse and output shaft assemblies. In-line transmissions are equipped with oil seal (3A) and input shaft (11A) is used in place of shaft (11). See text for clutch pack assembly.

LUBRICATION

Oil for transmission operation and lubrication is provided by the oil pump mounted on the valve body. Recommended oil is SAE 30 grade SE oil if water entering oil cooler is warmer than 85°F. or SAE 20 grade SE oil if water is 85°F. or below. Oil capacity is 3.5 pints not including oil cooler and hoses. Oil level should reach full mark on dipstick with engine running and transmission in neutral. Oil should be changed yearly. Fill transmission through breather or fill plug hole on top of transmission.

OPERATION

Forward, neutral and reverse are provided in MG-502 in-line and V-drive transmissions by using two hydraulically actuated clutches. Forward ring gear (10—Fig. 1-1) and reverse ring gear (48) rotate when input shaft (11) is driven. Output gear (42) is driven by either forward drive gear (26) or reverse drive gear (63). Drive gears (26

1. Expansion plug
2. Snap ring
3. Bearing retainer
3A. Oil seal
4. Expansion plug
5. Transmission case
6. Dip stick assy.
7. Dowel pin
8. Bearing cup
9. Bearing cone
10. Input ring gear
11. Input shaft
12. Roll pin
13. Inner piston ring
14. Outer piston ring
15. Piston
16. Fiber clutch plates
17. Steel clutch plates
18. Pressure plate
19. Snap ring
20. Spring
21. Spring retainer
22. Snap ring
23. Bearing race (0.123-0.126)
24. Thrust bearing
25. Bearing race (0.030-0.032)
26. Forward drive gear
27. Bearing race (0.030-0.032)
28. Bearing cone
29. Bearing race (0.154-0.157)
30. Bearing cone
31. Bearing cup
32. Shims
33. Cap screw
34. Washer
35. Shims
36. Bearing cone
37. Bearing cup
38. Roll pin
39. Snap ring
40. Output shaft
41. Gear pan
42. Output gear
43. Spacer
44. Bearing cup
45. Bearing cone
46. Bearing cup
47. Bearing cone
48. Ring gear
49. Reverse shaft
50. Inner piston ring
51. Outer piston ring
52. Piston
53. Fiber clutch plates
54. Steel clutch plates
55. Pressure plate
56. Snap ring
57. Spring
58. Spring retainer
59. Snap ring
60. Bearing race (0.123-0.126)
61. Thrust bearing
62. Bearing race (0.030-0.032)
63. Reverse drive gear
64. Bearing race (0.030-0.032)
65. Thrust bearing
66. Bearing race (0.154-0.157)
67. Bearing cone
68. Bearing cup
69. Shims
70. Shaft seal rings
71. Breather
72. Rear cover
73. Drain plug
74. Seal
75. Output flange
76. Seal ring
77. Washer
78. Cap screw

Illustration courtesy Twin Disc

Twin Disc

DRIVES

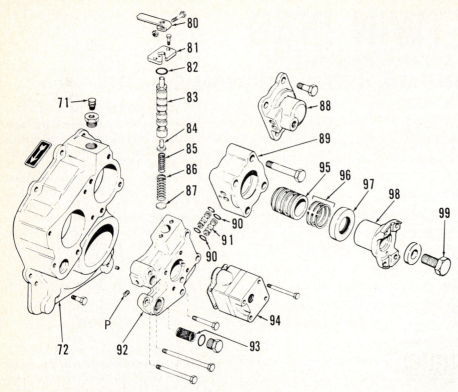

Fig. 1-3—Exploded view of valve body and collector assemblies. Collector (88) is used on in-line transmissions while collector (89) and components (95 through 99) are used on V-drives. Oil pump (94) components are not available separately.

P. Plug	83. Control valve	88. Collector (in-line)	94. Oil pump
71. Breather	84. Pressure regulator	89. Collector (V-drive)	95. Oil delivery sleeve
72. Rear cover	valve	90. "O" rings	96. Seal rings
80. Control lever	85. Inner spring	91. Oil tubes	97. Oil seal
81. Detent plate	86. Outer spring	92. Valve body	98. Input coupling
82. "O" ring	87. Spring plate	93. Oil screen	99. Cap screw

and 63) rotate with their ring gears (10 or 48) when the clutch in the ring gear is engaged. Clutches are engaged by oil directed to the desired clutch by the control valve shown in Fig. 1-3.

Two separate oil circuits from the control valve are used. Oil from oil pump (94—Fig. 1-3) is routed to an oil cooler then returned to valve body (92) and control valve (83). Oil is routed from the control valve to the desired clutch while a separate oil circuit from the control valve routes oil to gears and bearings. Reverse and input shafts have drilled oil passages for clutch actuation and lubrication. Pressure regulator valve (84) maintains oil pressure at 300 to 350 psi.

NOTE: Right and left hand rotation oil pumps are used. Be sure correct oil pump is installed.

TROUBLESHOOTING

Excessive transmission noise may be due to component failure or excessive gear backlash. Transmission overheating may be due to an inefficient oil cooler, improper oil, oil level too high or clutch slippage. Improper transmission operation may be due to incorrectly adjusted shift linkage or malfunctioning hydraulic circuit.

To check hydraulic circuit, unscrew plug (P—Fig. 1-3) and connect an oil pressure gage with 0-500 psi range. With normal transmission oil temperature (140°-180° F. at transmission inlet from cooler), transmission oil pressure should be 310-340 in all gears with transmission input shaft turning 1800 rpm. Transmission oil pressure should be 290-335 psi with transmission input shaft turning 600 rpm. No oil pressure may be due to low oil level, fully clogged oil strainer or a worn or damaged oil pump. Low oil pressure may result from a partially clogged oil strainer, stuck regulator valve, damaged input or reverse shaft seal rings, leaking clutch piston rings or a worn or damaged oil pump. High oil pressure may be due to a stuck pressure regulator valve.

TRANSMISSION OVERHAUL

To disassemble transmission, proceed as follows: drain oil and remove oil strainer (93—Fig. 1-3). Unbolt and remove oil pump (94). Remove screw (99) and yoke (98) on V-drive models. Unbolt and remove valve body (92) and collector (88 or 89) as a unit. Valve body and collector can now be separated from oil tubes (91). If necessary, withdraw control valve and pressure regulator components from valve body.

Remove expansion plugs (1 & 4—Fig. 1-2) and snap ring (2). Remove screw (33), washer (34) and shims (35). Unscrew bearing retainer (3) screws and install special tool T-16751 over bearing retainer using longer screws as shown in Fig. 1-4. Tool T-16751 may be fabricated using dimensions in Fig. 1-5. Unscrew cover (72—Fig. 1-2) screws and separate cover and case assemblies while turning jackscrew of tool T-16751 to force output shaft out of bearing (36). Remove forward and reverse shaft

Fig. 1-4—View of tool T-16751 used when separating case and cover. Refer to Fig. 1-5 for tool dimensions.

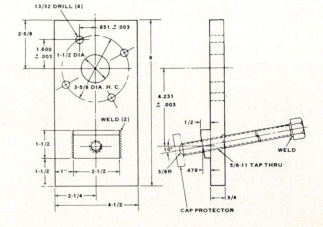

Fig. 1-5—Use dimensions shown to fabricate tool T-16751.

Illustration courtesy Twin Disc

DRIVES

Twin Disc

assemblies from case. Remove screw (78), washer (77) and seal (76) and pull flange (75) off output shaft. Remove gear pan (41) and using tool T-16753 or other suitable tool, pull output shaft (40) and gear (42) out of bearing (45). Save shims (35) for use during assembly. Disassembly of forward and reverse shaft assemblies is evident after inspection of units and referral to Figs. 1-2 and 1-3. Note that oil delivery sleeve (95—Fig. 1-3) is attached to input shaft with pin (12—Fig. 1-2). Snap rings (22 & 59) can be removed using spring compressor T-16752 or other suitable tool against spring retainers (21 & 58). Shims (32 & 69) should be saved for assembly.

Inspect components for damage and excessive wear. Clean all oil passages and orifices. Renew clutch plates if grooves in face are worn away or very shallow.

Before assembling transmission, all faced clutch plates should be submerged in transmission oil (see LUBRICATION section) for at least one hour. "Loctite" Fit All gasket sealer or equivalent should be used on all core plugs.

To assemble input and reverse shaft assemblies, reverse disassembly procedure. Note that there are nine steel clutch plates and ten faced clutch plates. Two of the faced clutch plates are faced on one side only and are installed as the first and last clutch plates in the clutch pack with the faced side towards the other plates. Note thickness of thrust washers in Fig. 1-2. Roll pin (12) must be installed so pin does not protrude into oil delivery sleeve (95—Fig. 1-3) groove.

If output gear (42—Fig. 1-2) and shaft (40) were separated, use the following procedure for assembly. Gear and shaft must mate along entire length of taper. Gear and shaft tapers must be free of surface irregularities and clean as possible to insure maximum metal-to-metal contact. Initial assembly of gear and shaft requires mating of gear and shaft with 500 lb. press. Measure distance from various points on shaft to nearest points on gear hub. Continue to press (approx. 32 tons required) gear on shaft until measured distances are increased 0.050-0.080 inch. For instance, if initial distance was 1.280 inch, gear will be located correctly when distance is 1.330-1.360 inch. Maximum runout from shaft centers to gear face is 0.005 inch.

Press bearing cup (44—Fig. 1-2) into cover (72) until cup is seated against shoulder. Install spacer (43) on shaft (40) and insert shaft and gear assembly into cover (72). Heat bearing cone (45) and install bearing on shaft so it butts against spacer (43). Install gear pan (41) and tighten screws to 15-17 ft.-lbs.

Install snap rings (2 & 39) in case (5) then press bearing cups (37 & 46) into case until they bottom against snap rings. Press bearing cups (31 & 68) into cover (72) so big end of cup is flush or just below machined surface for valve body and collector. Partially install bearing cup (8) and then install bearing retainer (3) to properly position bearing cup (8).

Install input and reverse shaft assemblies into case. Apply "Loctite" Fit All gasket sealer or equivalent to mating surfaces of case and cover and carefully mate case and cover. Tighten cover screws to 27-30 ft.-lbs. Apply "Loctite" Fit All gasket sealer or equivalent to mating surface of retainer (3) and install retainer. Tighten retainer screws to 27-30 ft.-lbs. Install components (74 through 78) and tighten flange screw (78) to 125-140 ft.-lbs.

End play of all shafts must be checked to insure correct bearing clearances. To check output shaft end play, measure thickness of original shim pack (35) then add 0.005 inch additional shim to make a trial shim pack. A trial shim pack 0.100 inches thick may be installed if original shim pack thickness is not known. Install trial shim pack (35) along with components (33, 34, 36 & 38). Tighten screw (33) to 125-140 ft.-lbs. Measure output shaft end play with a dial indicator positioned on output flange (75). Rotate output shaft while alternately pushing in shaft with 100-300 lbs. force then pulling out on shaft with same force. Remove shims (35) necessary to obtain 0.003-0.005 inch end play. Install expansion plug (4) after coating contact surface of plug with "Loctite" Fit All gasket sealer or equivalent.

Use procedure similar to checking output shaft end play to also check input or reverse shaft end play. Original shims (32 & 69) may be installed or trial shim packs may be used. To determine thickness of trial shim pack, measure depth of bearing cups (31 & 68) from machined surface of cover (72). Subtract height of pilot land on valve body (92—Fig. 1-3) from reverse shaft measurement. Subtract 0.003 inch from measurements for both shafts to obtain thickness of trial shim pack. Tighten collector (88 or 89—Fig. 1-3) screws to 61-68 ft.-lbs. and valve body (92) screws to 27-30 ft.-lbs. Be sure to rotate shafts when applying force to insure seating of bearings. Remove collector or valve body and install or remove shims necessary to obtain 0.003-0.005 inch end play.

NOTE: During final assembly, valve body (92—Fig. 1-3), oil tubes (91) and collector (88 or 89) must be installed as a unit.

Apply "Loctite" Fit All gasket sealer or equivalent to rear cover, valve body and collector mating surfaces. Tighten valve body screws to 27 ft.-lbs. and collector screws to 61-68 ft.-lbs. Tighten oil pump retaining screws to 15-17 ft.-lbs. Note on later models that breather is located in dipstick assembly (6—Fig. 1-2) and a plug is installed in place of breather (71).

Check for free rotation of transmission gears. Recheck bearing adjustments if transmission binds or turns hard.

TWIN DISC
MODELS MG-506L & MG-506R

IDENTIFICATION
Transmission model designation is located on identification plate attached to top of transmission. Arrows showing direction of input and output shaft rotation in forward gear are attached to transmission case and cover. Input and output shaft rotation on Model MG-506L is the same in forward gear while the input and output shafts on Model MG-506R rotate in opposite directions in forward gear. Model MG-506L and MG506R transmissions must be used with engines which rotate counter-clockwise at output end. A left hand propeller must be used with Model MG-506L while a right hand propeller must be used with Model MG-506R.

LUBRICATION
Oil for transmission operation and lubrication is provided by the oil pump mounted on rear cover and driven by reverse shaft. Recommended oil is SAE 30 grade CD oil if oil entering oil cooler is 150°-185° F. or SAE 40 grade CD oil if oil entering oil cooler is 175°-210°F. Transmission oil capacity is approximately 1.2 gallons without oil cooler and 1.6 gallons with oil cooler. Oil level should reach full mark on oil dipstick with engine running and transmission in neutral. Recheck oil level after shifting transmission several times. Fill transmission through breather hole in top of transmission. Oil should be changed after every 1,000 hours of operation or if transmission has been inoperative for three or more months.

OPERATION
Forward, neutral and reverse are provided in MG-506L and MG-506R transmissions by using two hydraulically actuated clutches. Input gear (12—Fig. 2-1) meshes with intermediate shaft ring gear (21) which meshes with countershaft ring gear (46). Input gear and both ring gears rotate when input shaft rotates. Intermediate shaft gear (34) and countershaft gear (47) constantly mesh with output gear (44). Hydraulically actuated clutches contained in ring gears transfer power from ring gear to intermediate shaft gear (34) or countershaft gear (44)

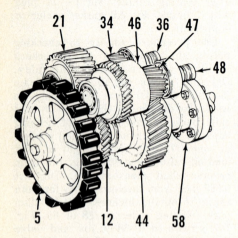

Fig. 2-1—View showing relationship of components in MG-506L transmission. MG-506R transmission is similar but tooth direction on gears (34, 37 & 44) is opposite to that shown. Refer to Fig. 2-2 for identification.

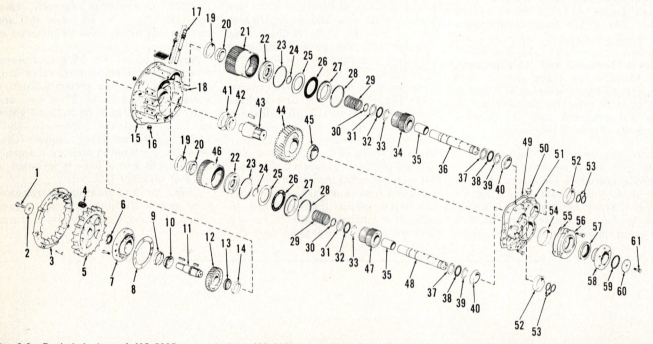

Fig. 2-2—Exploded view of MG-506R transmission. MG-506L is similar. Gear (34 or 47) and bushing (35) are not available separately.

1. Capscrew
2. Washer
3. Flywheel adapter
4. Rubber drive block (20)
5. Drive spider
6. Oil seal
7. Bearing retainer
8. Shims
9. Bearing cup
10. Bearing cone
11. Input shaft
12. Input gear
13. Bearing cone
14. Bearing cup
15. Transmission case
16. Drain plug
17. Dip stick assy.
18. Dowel pins (2)
19. Bearing cup
20. Bearing cone
21. Intermediate shaft ring gear
22. Piston
23. Outer piston ring
24. Inner piston ring
25. Steel clutch plate (8)
26. Faced clutch plate (9)
27. Pressure plate
28. Snap ring
29. Spring
30. Snap ring
31. Thrust race
32. Thrust bearing
33. Thrust race
34. Intermediate shaft gear
35. Bushing
36. Intermediate shaft
37. Thrust race
38. Thrust bearing
39. Thrust race
40. Bearing cone
41. Bearing cup
42. Bearing cone
43. Output shaft
44. Output gear
45. Bearing cone
46. Countershaft ring gear
47. Countershaft gear
48. Countershaft
49. Gasket
50. Breather
51. Rear cover
52. Bearing cup
53. Seal rings
54. Bearing cup
55. Shims
56. Bearing retainer
57. Oil seal
58. Output flange
59. Seal ring
60. Washer
61. Cap screw

DRIVES

Twin Disc

which results in output gear and shaft rotation. Clutches are actuated by oil directed to the desired clutch by the control valve shown in Fig. 2-3.

Two separate oil circuits from the control valve are used. Oil from oil pump (69—Fig. 2-3) is routed to an oil cooler then returned to valve body (81) and control valve (75). Oil is routed from the control valve to the desired clutch while a separate oil circuit from the control valve routes oil to gears and bearings. Intermediate shaft and countershaft have drilled oil passages for clutch actuation and lubrication. Pressure regulator valve (76) maintains oil pressure at 300 to 320 psi.

TROUBLESHOOTING

Excessive transmission noise may be due to component failure or excessive gear backlash. Transmission overheating may be due to an inefficient oil cooler, improper oil, oil level too high or clutch slippage. Improper transmission operation may be due to incorrectly adjusted shift linkage or malfunctioning hydraulic circuit.

To check hydraulic circuit, insert a tee in line from oil pressure gage with 0-500 psi range. Transmission oil pressure should be 300-320 psi at input shaft speed of 1800 rpm with oil entering oil cooler at 180°F. No oil pressure may be due to low oil level, fully clogged oil strainer or a worn or damaged oil pump. Low oil pressure may result from a partially clogged oil strainer, stuck regulator valve, damaged input or reverse shaft seal rings, leaking clutch piston rings or a worn or damaged oil pump. High oil pressure may be due to a stuck pressure regulator valve.

TRANSMISSION OVERHAUL

To disassemble transmission, proceed as follows: Drain oil and remove oil strainer (63—Fig. 2-3). Remove screw (61—Fig. 2-2) and detach output flange (58) from output shaft. Remove oil pump (69—Fig. 2-3). Unbolt and remove pump mount (67) and valve body (81) as a unit. Retain shims (66 & 80) for assembly. Valve body and pump mount can now be separated from oil tubes (71). If necessary, withdraw control valve and pressure regulator components from valve body. Unbolt bearing retainer (56—Fig. 2-2), remove retainer and save shims (55) for assembly. To separate rear cover (51) from case, unscrew rear cover screws and install two ½-13 screws in threaded holes near edge of rear cover. Tighten the two screws to force rear cover away from case.

With rear cover and case separated, remove output shaft (43—Fig. 2-2) assembly. Use a suitable press and attachments to separate bearing cones (42 & 45) and output gear (44) from output shaft.

Remove countershaft (48) and then intermediate shaft (36) assemblies from case (15). Due to components similarity, the following procedure may be used to disassemble intermediate shaft and countershaft assemblies. Remove and discard seal rings (53). Using a suitable puller, remove bearing cone (40) while being careful not to damage bearing races (37 or 39) or thrust bearing (38). Remove bearing races (37 & 39), thrust bearing (38), gear (34 or 47), bearing races (31 and 33) and thrust bearing (32). Remove snap ring (28), pressure plate (27) and all clutch plates. Compress clutch spring (29) and remove snap ring (30). Remove clutch spring and piston (22). Remove and discard seal rings (23 & 24). If necessary, use a suitable puller and remove bearing cone (20). Shaft and ring gear are available as a unit assembly only and should not be disassembled.

To remove input shaft, unscrew cap screw (1) and using a suitable puller drive spider (5) from input shaft. Unscrew bearing retainer (7) screws and install two 3/8-16 screws in threaded holes in retainer. Tighten the two screws against the transmission case to push bearing retainer (7) away from case. Save shims (8) for assembly. Remove input shaft (11) assembly and use a suitable press to disassemble input shaft, gear (12) and bearing cones (10 & 13).

Inspect components for damage and excessive wear. Clean all oil passages and orifices. Renew any cracked or broken rubber blocks (4). Renew excessively worn clutch plates. Components for the oil pump are not available separately but must be serviced as a unit assembly.

Before assembling transmission, all faced clutch plates should be submerged in transmission oil (see LUBRICATION section) for at least one hour. Bearing cones should be heated to 275° F. before installation.

Install input shaft assembly as follows: Heat input gear (12—Fig. 2-2) to 275° F. and press input shaft (11) into gear so "FRONT" on gear is towards shoulder on shaft and gear butts against shoulder. Bearing cones must be bottomed against shaft shoulders. Install oil seal (6) with lip towards inside of bearing retainer. To adjust input shaft end play, install original shims (8) and tighten bearing retainer (7) screws to 38 ft.-lbs. If original shims are not used, determine thickness of trial shim pack by installing input shaft assembly without shims and tightening three bearing retainer (7) screws just tight enough to remove end play from input shaft. Measure gap between retainer and case and add 0.004 inch to measured gap to obtain thickness of trial shim pack. Install trial shim pack and tighten all bearing retainer screws to 38 ft.-lbs. Measure input shaft end play by rotating shaft several revolutions while alternately pushing in and pulling out shaft with approximately 200 pounds force. Install shims (8) necessary to obtain 0.001-0.004 inch end

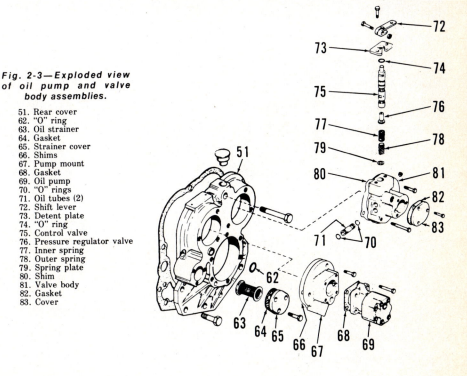

Fig. 2-3—Exploded view of oil pump and valve body assemblies.

51. Rear cover
62. "O" ring
63. Oil strainer
64. Gasket
65. Strainer cover
66. Shims
67. Pump mount
68. Gasket
69. Oil pump
70. "O" rings
71. Oil tubes (2)
72. Shift lever
73. Detent plate
74. "O" ring
75. Control valve
76. Pressure regulator valve
77. Inner spring
78. Outer spring
79. Spring plate
80. Shim
81. Valve body
82. Gasket
83. Cover

Illustration courtesy Twin Disc

Twin Disc — DRIVES

play. Place a 1/8 to 1/4-inch bead of "Loctite" Fit All Gasket sealer or equivalent around bearing retainer in corner between flange and pilot surfaces before final assembly. To check mating of drive spider (5) and input shaft, push drive spider on input shaft with 200-300 pounds force and mark location of spider on shaft. Install cap screw (1) and washer (2) and tighten cap screw to 175 ft.-lbs. Measure distance drive spider moved on input shaft. If movement was less than 0.011 inch, continue to tighten cap screw until 0.011 inch movement from original mark is obtained. If movement is greater than 0.018 inch, remove drive spider and inspect spider hub for cracks and hub and input shaft for damaged tapers.

To assemble intermediate shaft and countershaft assemblies, reverse disassembly procedure. First and last clutch plates should be faced plates with alternating steel and faced clutch plates in between. There are eight steel plates and nine faced clutch plates.

To assemble output shaft components, press bearing cone (42) on shaft until bottomed against shoulder. Push gear (44) on output shaft (43) using 200-300 pounds force and mark location of gear or position a dial indicator against gear. Press gear on shaft until gear has moved 0.026-0.038 inches farther on shaft. Press bearing cone (45) on output shaft so bearing bottoms against gear (44).

Install intermediate shaft, countershaft and output shaft assemblies in transmission case, position cover on case and tighten cover screws to 85 ft.-lbs. Use the following procedure to adjust intermediate shaft and countershaft end play. Install pump mount (67—Fig. 2-3) or valve body (81) and original shims (66 or 80) and tighten screws to 38 ft.-lbs. If original shims are not used, determine thickness of trial shim pack by installing pump mount or valve body without shims and tightening screws just tight enough to remove end play from intermediate shaft or countershaft. Measure gap between pump mount (67) and cover or valve body (81) and cover. Add 0.004 inch to measured gap to obtain thickness of trial shim pack. Install trial shim pack and tighten pump mount or valve body screws to 38 ft.-lbs. Measure intermediate shaft or countershaft end play by rotating shaft several revolutions while alternately pushing in and pulling out shaft with approximately 200 pounds force. Install shims (66 or 80) necessary to obtain 0.003-0.006 inch end play. Place a 1/8 to ¼-inch bead of "Loctite" Fit All Gasket sealer or equivalent around pump mount and valve body in corner between flange and pilot surfaces before final assembly. Pump mount (67), oil tubes (71) and valve body (81) must be installed as a unit. Tighten pump mount and valve body screws to 38 ft.-lbs.

To adjust output shaft end play, install bearing retainer (56—Fig. 2-2) and original shims (55) and tighten retainer screws to 85 ft.-lbs. If original shims are not used, determine thickness by installing bearing retainer (56) and tighten retainer screws finger tight. Install flange coupling (58), washer (60) and cap screw (61) and tighten cap screw to 175 ft.-lbs. Tighten bearing retainer screws just tight enough to remove output shaft end play and measure gap between bearing retainer and cover. Add 0.004 inch to measured gap to obtain thickness of trial shim pack. Install trial shim pack and tighten bearing retainer screws to 85 ft.-lbs. Install flange coupling (58), washer (60) and capscrew (61) and tighten cap screw to 175 ft.-lbs. Measure output shaft end play by rotating shaft several revolutions while alternately pushing in and pulling out shaft with approximately 200 pounds force. Install shims (55) necessary to obtain 0.001-0.004 inch end play. Place a 1/8 to ¼-inch bead of "Loctite" Fit All Gasket sealer or equivalent around bearing retainer in corner between flange and pilot surfaces before final assembly. Tighten retainer screws to 85 ft.-lbs. and coupling screw (61) to 175 ft.-lbs. during final assembly.

Be sure drive tang of oil pump (69—Fig. 2-3) properly engages slot in end of countershaft. Tighten oil pump mounting screws to 21 ft.-lbs. Refill transmission with oil noted in LUBRICATION section.

VELVET DRIVE 70, 71 & 72

**WARNER GEAR DIVISION
BORG-WARNER CORPORATION
P.O. Box 2688
Muncie, Indiana 47302**

MODEL IDENTIFICATION

An identification plate is attached to the side of the transmission and gives the model number and gear ratio. Refer to Fig. 1-1. Letters following model series number indicate input shaft rotation. The input shaft on "C" units turns clockwise when viewed from output coupling end of transmission. The input shaft on "CR" units turns counter-clockwise. Input shaft and output shaft turn in same direction when unit is in forward gear except on units with AS7 or AS17 model number prefix.

LUBRICATION

Recommended transmission oil is automatic transmission fluid type "A," suffix "A," Dexron or type "F." Oil capacity will vary according to inclination of transmission and oil capacity of oil cooler system. Oil level dipstick is attached to oil fill plug which is located just below gear selector lever. Oil level should be checked with engine running or just after engine is stopped before oil in cooler and oil lines can drain back into transmission. Clean oil screen thoroughly after draining oil. Oil should be changed every season.

OIL COOLER

NOTE: These transmissions require an oil cooler or bypass tube during operation or excessively high transmission oil pressure will result.

Transmission oil temperature in sump should be maintained between 140° F. and 190° F. Recommended maximum oil pressure rating of oil cooler should be 150 psi. Oil cooler line diameter should be at least 13/32-inch. Oil cooler must not be restrictive as transmission oil pressure will increase.

Oil cooler return line should be connected to hole at lower rear of V-drive on models so equipped. On all other models, connect oil cooler return line to hole (A—Fig. 1-2), if present. If a tapped hole does not exist at (A), connect oil cooler return hose to tapped hole at (B). If tapped holes do not exist at either (A or B), connect oil cooler

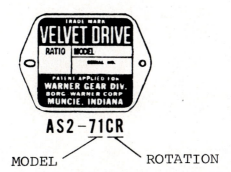

Fig. 1-1—View of identification plate on side of transmission. Model number shown is for a Model 71 transmission with counter clockwise rotating output shaft in forward gear.

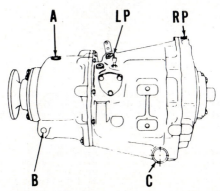

Fig. 1-2—Oil cooler return hose should be connected to lower rear of V-drive unit or to one of the above locations. Refer to text.

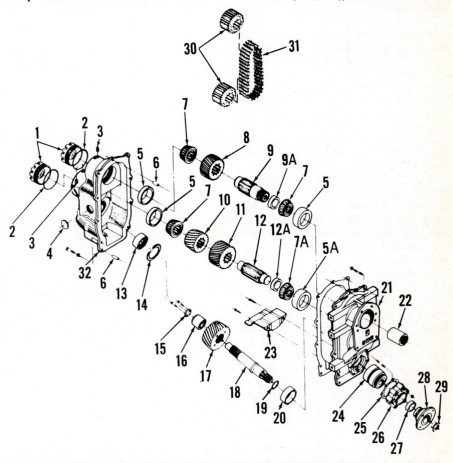

Fig. 1-3—Exploded view of V-drive. Sprockets (30) and chain (31) are used in place of gears (8 & 10) on chain drive models. Early models do not have expansion plug (4) or use shims (19). Spacers (9A & 12A) are used on later gear drive models.

1. Bearing caps
2. "O" rings
3. Spring pins
4. Expansion plug
5. Bearing cups
5A. Bearing cup
6. Taper pins
7. Bearing cones
7A. Bearing cone
8. Gear
9. Input shaft
9A. Spacer
10. Gear
11. Intermediate shaft gear
12. Intermediate shaft
12A. Spacer
13. Roller bearing
14. Snap ring
15. Race retainer
16. Inner bearing race
17. Output shaft gear
18. Output shaft
19. Shims
20. Oil baffle
21. Case
22. Coupling
23. Oil baffle
24. Bearing
25. Gasket
26. Bearing cap
27. Oil seal
28. Coupling
29. Nut
30. Chain sprockets
31. Chain
32. Cover

Illustration courtesy Borg-Warner

Velvet Drive

return hose to tapped hole at (C).

Tapped hole (C) has been manufactured with two different threads. An annular gasket must be used with bushing or drain plug if boss around hole has been machined as a gasket surface. If boss has not been machined, then hole (C) has been tapped with tapered pipe threads and a gasket is not required.

Screen (35—Fig. 1-5) may have an open or closed end. If hole (C—Fig. 1-2) is used as oil cooler return hole, screen (35—Fig. 1-5) must have an open end. If hole is used for drain plug only, screen may have open or closed end.

V-DRIVE

Velvet Drive V-drive Model 10-04 is mated with Velvet Drive transmission Model 71 while V-drive Model 10-05 is mated with transmission Model 72. Refer to following sections for transmission service.

V-drive may be equipped with all gear drive or gear and chain drive. Refer to Fig. 1-3 for exploded view of V-drive. Drive ratio may be changed by interchanging chain sprockets or input and intermediate shaft gears. Drive ratios are available from 0.96:1 to 3.14:1. Later models are equipped with longer input (9) and intermediate (12) shafts and a wider bearing cone (7A) and cup (5A) to accommodate 2½-inch chain (31) and sprockets (30) instead of earlier 2-inch chain and sprockets. Longer input and intermediate shafts and wider bearing are used on both chain and gear drive models. Spacers (9A and 12A) are used on later gear drive models with the longer input and intermediate shafts to properly position gears (8 and 11).

OVERHAUL

Drain transmission oil, unscrew retaining nuts and separate V-drive from transmission. Unscrew nut (29—Fig. 1-3), remove coupling (28), unscrew cover screws, drive out taper pins (6) and separate cover (32) from case. Remove baffle (23) on gear drive models. Bearings should be marked so they can be returned to their original positions if not renewed. Remove gears, shafts and bearings from case along with chain and sprockets on chain drive models. Do not lose shims (19) and note thickness for reassembly. Remove bearing cap (26) and bearing (24) being careful not to lose order of shims which were used on early models. If necessary, remove bearing caps (1) for access to bearing cups.

To reassemble V-drive, reverse disassembly procedure while noting the following points: Screw bearing caps (1) into cover so notched ends of caps are flush with cover (32). Position oil baffle on chain drive models but do not install screws until gears and shafts are installed. Bottom bearing cups (5) against bearing caps (1). Install output shaft gear (17) with taper away from threaded end of shaft. Press bearing race (16) on output shaft so race abuts gear (17). Install race retainer (15), tighten retainer screws to 42-45 ft.-lbs. and secure screws with safety wire. Bevel gear (10) must be installed with taper towards cover end of shaft. Be sure to install spacers (9A and 12A) on later gear drive models.

NOTE: Chain (31) and sprockets (30) must be assembled along with bevel gear (10) before bearings are pressed on shafts on chain drive units with a 23 tooth sprocket as sprocket has smaller diameter than bearing cones.

Coat bevel gears (10 & 17) with red lead to check tooth contact. Be sure to install oil baffle screws on chain drive models. Install taper pins (6) before tightening cover screws to 50-55 ft.-lbs.

Install shims in bearing (24) bore of case on early models not equipped with expansion plug (4). If original shims are not available, install a 0.025 inch trial shim pack. Install shims (19) on output shaft of models equipped with expansion plug (4). If original shims are not used, install a trial shim pack 0.025 inch thick. Install bearing (24) so bearing cone and outer race numbers with suffix "A" are on same side. Install bearing cap (26) and tighten

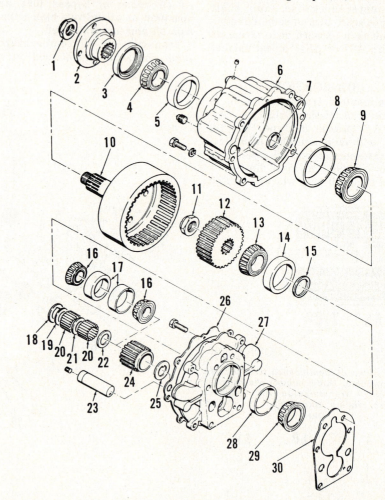

Fig. 1-4—Exploded view of CR2 drop center reduction gear. Note that component (25) is a shim on 1.58:1 and 2.03:1 units and a tab washer on other units. Bearings (16 & 17) are used on 1.58:1 and 2.03:1 units while washer (18), spacers (19, 21 & 22) and bearing rollers (20) are used on other units.

1. Nut
2. Coupling
3. Seal
4. Bearing cone
5. Bearing cup
6. Reduction gear housing
7. Shim
8. Bearing cup
9. Bearing cone
10. Ring gear & output shaft
11. Nut
12. Gear
13. Bearing cone
14. Bearing cup
15. Shim
16. Bearing cones
17. Bearing cups
18. Tab washer
19. Spacer
20. Bearing rollers (34-2.47:1) (52-2.93:1)
21. Spacer
22. Spacer
23. Idler gear shaft
24. Idler gear
25. Tab washer or shim
26. Gasket
27. Adapter
28. Bearing cup
29. Bearing cone
30. Gasket

DRIVES

Velvet Drive

fasteners to 50-55 ft.-lbs. Tighten bearing caps (1) until firmly bottomed against bearing cups then back cups out one notch to engage locking spring pins (3). This should provide 0.002-0.005 inch end play on input and intermediate shafts. Rotate input shaft two or three turns, remove expansion plug (4), on models so equipped, and note tooth contact pattern. On models not equipped with expansion plug, cover (32) must be removed to check contact pattern. Contact pattern should be centered in gear teeth. Shim (19) thickness on models equipped with expansion plug (4) is varied to adjust tooth contact pattern. Shims adjacent to bearing (24) must be varied on models not equipped with expansion plug to adjust tooth contact pattern. After tooth contact pattern has been adjusted on models not equipped with expansion plug, install bearing cap (26) on assembled unit and measure gap between case and bearing cap. Install shims between case (21) and bearing cap equal to gap plus 0.004-0.006 inch to prevent leakage.

REDUCTION GEAR

Two types of reduction gear units are used. Model CR2 drop-center reduction gear is shown in Fig. 1-4. Output shaft turns counter-clockwise in forward gear on all CR2 models. CR2 models can be identified by different centerlines for input and output shafts. All other reduction gear units use same centerline for input and output shafts and are identified for service purposes by gear ratio noted on transmission identification plate. Refer to Fig. 1-5 or 1-6 for an exploded view of inline reduction gear units. Output shaft rotation is indicated on transmission identification plate.

All gear reduction units are lubricated with transmission oil. Refer to LUBRICATION and OIL COOLER sections and to following overhaul sections.

R&R AND OVERHAUL

Model CR2

To disassemble reduction gear, unscrew coupling nut (1—Fig. 1-4), remove reduction housing retaining screws and separate reduction housing from transmission. Unscrew gear nut (11) and remove gear (12), bearing cone (13) and shim (15). Unscrew adapter screws and separate adapter (27) from transmission. Refer to exploded view in Fig. 1-4 and disassemble remainder of reduction gear components. Mark shims for reinstallation in their original positions.

To assemble reduction gear unit, proceed as follows: press bearing cups (14 & 28) into adapter, install adapter (27) on transmission and tighten adapter screws up to 73-83 ft.-lbs. Assemble components (12, 13 and 15) on trans-

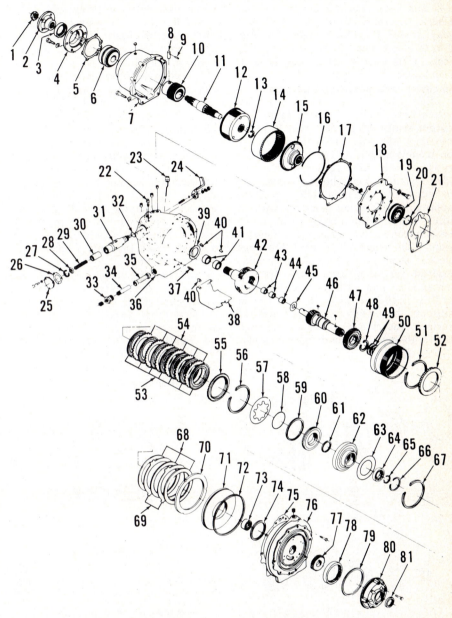

Fig. 1-5—Exploded view of Model 72C transmission with 1.52:1 gear reduction unit. Refer to Fig. 1-6 for exploded view of other gear reduction units.

1. Nut
2. Coupling
3. Oil seal
4. Bearing retainer
5. Gasket
6. Double tapered roller bearing
7. Reduction gear housing
8. Sun gear retaining pin
9. Spring pin
10. Sun gear
11. Output shaft
12. Planetary gears
13. Snap ring
14. Ring gear
15. Input gear
16. Snap ring
17. Gasket
18. Adapter
19. Bearing
20. Snap ring
21. Gasket
22. Breather
23. Dip stick
24. Shift lever
25. Valve cover
26. Gasket
27. Snap ring
28. Valve spring retainer
29. Valve spring
30. Pressure regulator valve
31. Shift control valve
32. "O" ring
33. Bushing
34. Oil return tube
35. Oil strainer
36. Transmission housing
37. Pressure plate spring
38. Oil baffle
39. Thrust washer
40. Dowel pins
41. Bushings
42. Planetary gears & output shaft
43. Bushings
44. Bushing
45. Thrust washer
46. Input shaft & gear
47. Forward clutch hub
48. Snap ring
49. Seal rings
50. Ring gear
51. Snap ring
52. Pressure plate
53. Inner forward clutch plates
54. Outer forward clutch plates
55. Pressure plate
56. Snap ring
57. Spring plate
58. Bearing ring
59. Piston seal ring
60. Forward clutch piston
61. Seal ring
62. Forward clutch cylinder
63. Thrust washer
64. Bearing
65. Snap ring
66. Snap ring
67. Snap ring
68. Inner reverse clutch plates
69. Outer reverse clutch plates
70. Pressure plate
71. Reverse clutch piston
72. Piston seal ring
73. Bearing
74. Seal ring
75. Gasket
76. Adapter
77. Pump drive gear
78. Outer pump gear
79. Gasket
80. Pump housing
81. Oil seal

Illustration courtesy Borg-Warner

Velvet Drive

DRIVES

mission output shaft and tighten nut (11) to 240 ft.-lbs. To hold transmission output shaft while tightening nut, direct compressed air (approximately 90 psi) into line pressure hole (LP—Fig. 1-2) and shift transmission to reverse. Check transmission output shaft end play. Install necessary shims (15—Fig. 1-4) to obtain end play of 0.0000-0.0018 inch. With correct shims installed it should require no more than 45 in.-lbs. to rotate transmission output shaft.

Idler gear (24) is used on models which have counter-rotating input and output shafts in forward gear. Tapered bearings (16) are used with idler gear on models with 1.58:1 and 2.03:1 gear ratios. Press bearing cups (17) into idler gear (24), place bearing cones (16) in cups and position idler gear in approximate running position without idler shaft. Measure gap between bearing cone and adapter boss. Select a shim (25) which is 0.001-0.002 inch thicker than measured gap to provide preload for idler gear bearings. To install idler gear with tapered bearings, drill a 5/16-inch hole in a bar and support bar above adapter gasket surface. Insert a ¼-20 screw through the 5/16-inch hole and thread screw into ¼-20 hole in adapter adjacent to idler shaft location. Gently tighten screw until idler gear (24), bearings and shim (25) can be inserted into position. Remove screw and rotate gear in bearings. Select another shim (25) if gear will spin or has excessive drag. Installation of idler gear shaft (23) should require a drive fit for last ¼-inch of travel.

To assemble idler gear on models with 2.47:1 or 2.93:1 gear ratio, install middle spacer (21) and bearing rollers (20) in idler gear (24). Two rows of 17 rollers are used on models with 2.47:1 gear ratio while two rows of 26 rollers are used on models with 2.93:1 gear ratio. Assemble spacers (19 and 22) and tab washers (18 and 25) with gear in adapter so tabs on washers engage recesses in adapter. Install idler gear shaft (23) being careful not to dislodge bearing rollers. It should be necessary to drive shaft into place during last ¼-inch of travel.

Press bearing cups (5 & 8) into housing (6) and bearing cone (9) onto output shaft (10). Using original shim (7) but without oil seal (3), temporarily assemble components (2 through 10) and tighten nut (1) to 240 ft.-lbs. Attach a torque wrench to output shaft and rotate shaft. Torque required to turn output shaft should be 1.5-39.0 in.-lbs. Adjust torque by changing size of shims (7). Apply suitable sealer between nut (1) and coupler (2) during final assembly to prevent leakage through splines. Tighten retainer housing screws to 73-83 ft.-lbs.

All Other Models

To disassemble in-line reduction gear units, disconnect oil cooler hose and unscrew reduction housing mounting screws. Disassembly of unit is self-evident after inspection and referral to exploded view in Figs. 1-5 and 1-6.

Four oil systems have been used to direct oil to reduction gear unit from the transmission. Original oil system returned oil from oil cooler to hole (B—Fig. 1-2). Original transmission housing can only be used with reduction case having tapped hole (B) and may be identified as shown in Fig. 1-7. Second and third type oil systems return oil from cooler to hole (C—Fig. 1-2). All transmission housings except original housing have oil passage (P—Fig. 1-7) which contains an orifice plug on second oil system. Original oil system adapter plate is flat while adapter plates used on all other systems have oil grooves shown in Fig. 1-8. Oil is routed around annular groove in outer bearing (19—Fig. 1-5) race in units with third oil system. A fourth oil system is used on later models with 2.10:1 gear ratio which has oil cooler return hose connected to hole (A—Fig. 1-2).

Repair kits are available to renew individual planetary gears. Dislodge snap ring on 1.91:1 units or remove oil collector ring on all other units for access to planetary gear shaft retaining pins. Remove shaft retaining pin and drive out gear shaft. Oil collector ring will be damaged during disassembly and must be discarded. Install outer row planetary gear shafts on 2.10:1 units with "O" in end of shaft away from retaining pin as shown in Fig. 1-9.

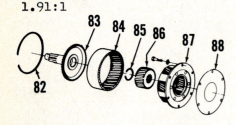

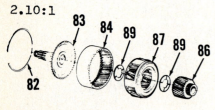

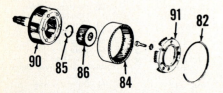

Fig. 1-6—Exploded view of planetary gear assemblies used on 1.91:1, 2.10:1, 2.57:1 and 2.91:1 gear reduction units. Components shown are used in place of components (8 through 16—Fig. 1-5).

82. Snap ring
83. Output shaft
84. Ring gear
85. Snap ring
86. Sun gear
87. Planetary gears
88. Oil strainer
89. Thrust washers
90. Planetary gears & output shaft
91. Gear plate

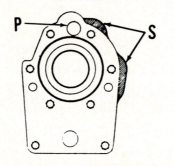

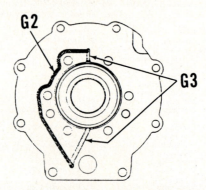

Fig. 1-7—Rear surface of transmission housing has been expanded to include areas (S) on all units except original. An orifice plug is used in oil passage (P) on units with second oil system outlined in text.

Fig. 1-8—Oil groove (G2) is present on adapter used in second oil system while groove (G3) is present on adapter used in third oil system.

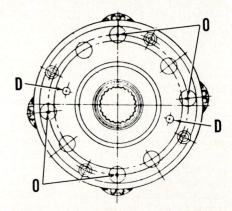

Fig. 1-9—Outer planetary gear shafts on 2.10:1 gear reduction units must be installed with (O) on end of shaft away from shaft retaining pin. Gear sets with dimples (D) must be used on units with clockwise "C" rotation.

DRIVES
Velvet Drive

To reassemble unit, reverse disassembly procedure. Assemble ring gear plate (91—Fig. 1-6), ring gear (84) and snap ring (82) on 2.57:1 and 2.91:1 units. Install six screws which hold ring gear assembly and adapter plate to transmission case and two lower reduction housing screws. Tighten screws to 42-50 ft.-lbs. then unscrew two reduction housing screws. Tighten adapter screws on all other units and two lower reduction housing screws to 42-50 ft.-lbs. then unscrew two reduction housing screws.

Two different planetary gear sets (87—Fig. 1-6) are used on 2.10:1 gear ratio units. Gear set identified by dimples (D—Fig. 1-9) must be used with clockwise rotating units while undimpled gear set must be used with counter-clockwise rotating units.

Output bearing (6—Fig. 1-5) is a double tapered roller bearing which must be assembled so bearing cone and bearing cup with "A" suffix in etched bearing number are matched. Install bearing retainer (4) so oil passages in retainer and reduction housing are aligned. Tighten bearing retainer screws to 42-50 ft.-lbs.

TRANSMISSION

This section covers Borg-Warner Velvet Drive marine transmissions Series 70, 71 and 72. Refer to previous sections for V-drive and reduction gear models used with these transmissions. Model identification, lubrication and oil cooler requirements are also outlined in previous sections.

OPERATION

Series 70, 71 and 72 transmissions are equipped with a planetary gear set which provides forward and reverse rotation of the transmission output shaft. Clutch packs (F & R—Fig. 1-10) control movement of ring gear (RG). Pressurized oil from the oil pump (P) is directed by rotary control valve (V) to the desired clutch piston. Forward gear (output shaft rotates same direction as input shaft) is obtained when pressurized oil is directed from the control valve to forward clutch pack (F) piston. The forward clutch pack (F) is compressed which forces ring gear (RG) to rotate with input shaft as planetary gear rotation is prevented. Reverse gear (output shaft rotation is reverse of input shaft) is obtained when pressurized oil is directed from the control valve to reverse clutch pack (R) piston. The reverse clutch pack (R) is compressed and ring gear (RG) is held stationary which allows planetary gear set to rotate and reverse output shaft rotation. Pressure relief valve (PR) returns pressurized oil to sump if pressure exceeds 200 psi. Oil is routed to bearings and planetary gear set in gear reduction housing on models so equipped.

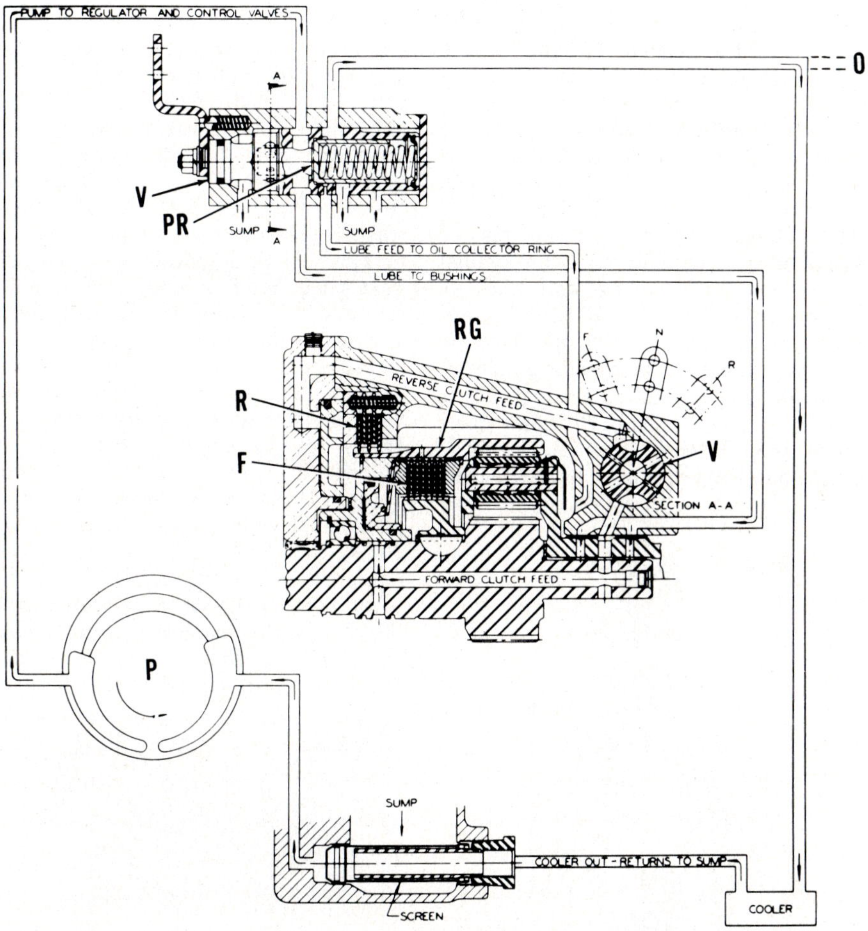

TROUBLESHOOTING

Noisy operation may be due to broken or chipped gear teeth. Note which gear (Forward or reverse) produces noise, disassemble transmission and inspect noisy gear teeth. A buzzing noise may be produced by an early style pressure relief valve which is not notched. Refer to OVERHAUL section to notch early style pressure relief valve.

Improper shifting of transmission may be due to incorrectly adjusted shift linkage or an internal malfunction. Shift control must be adjusted so transmission shift lever will completely engage shift detent ball in all gears. Failure to pull in gear may be due to broken or worn clutch plates, leaking clutch piston seal, oil leaks or damaged oil pump. Oil pressure may be checked by attaching a suitable oil pressure gage to holes at (LP and RP—Fig. 1-2). Oil pressure should be 110-150 psi at engine speed of 450-2000 rpm. Low oil temperature or high engine speed may raise oil pressure to 200-250 psi. Be sure transmission is properly filled with oil and connect gage to hole (LP) to check oil pump and forward gear. Low oil pressure in neutral may indicate oil leaks or a defective oil pump. If oil pressure drops after shifting to forward gear, oil leaks are present in oil circuit or forward clutch piston oil seal ring (59—Fig. 1-5) is leaking. Connect oil gage to hole (RP—Fig. 1-2) to check reverse gear. If oil pressure is not equal to neutral gear oil pressure, there are oil leaks in reverse gear oil circuit or reverse clutch piston oil seal ring (72—Fig. 1-5) is leaking.

OVERHAUL

Disconnect oil cooler and drain transmission oil. Separate reduction gear or V-drive, if so equipped, from transmission as previously outlined.

Drain oil from transmission. Remove oil pump (80—Fig. 1-5) bolts and detach oil pump from housing being careful not to damage oil seal (81) on input shaft splines. Pump gear (77) is keyed

Fig. 1-10—Sectional view of Model 72C transmission showing oil flow. Oil is directed from (0) to gear reduction unit. Refer to text.

Illustration courtesy Borg-Warner

Velvet Drive

to input shaft (46). Mark oil pump gears for proper mesh when reassembling.

Remove shift lever assembly. Be careful not to lose detent ball and poppet spring. Remove valve cover (25) and gasket (26) and tap gently on threaded end of transmission valve shaft (31). Pull out valve assembly. Depress valve spring retainer (28) to remove snap ring (27) and disassemble valve assembly.

Unscrew four cap screws and lift adapter (76) and reverse clutch piston (71) off housing. It may be necessary to tap gently on adapter.

NOTE: Pressure plate (70) may stick to piston (71). Do not allow pressure plate to drop as damage may result.

Use compressed air to remove reverse clutch piston (71) from adapter (76). Remove clutch pressure plate (70), springs (37) and dowel pins (40). Lift out input shaft and drive gear (46) and clutch assembly. Remove snap rings and tap on forward end of input shaft to separate input shaft unit (46) and clutch hub (47) from clutch assembly. Tap out bearing (64) and remove snap ring (67). Hold ring gear (50) and tap forward clutch cylinder (62) free from ring gear (50). Using compressed air, blow forward clutch piston (60) out of forward clutch cylinder (62). Remaining disassembly of ring and clutch assembly is self-evident.

Pull drive shaft coupler (2—Fig. 1-5) from output shaft. Remove bearing retainer (4) from rear of transmission housing. Place front of housing down with shop rags filling interior of housing. Press on end of output shaft (42) to free pinion cage and output shaft (42) from housing. Be sure there is a sufficient quantity of rags to prevent damage to pinion cage. Pull bearing from rear of housing.

Service kits are available to renew one or more planetary gears. The oil shield must be removed for access to gear shaft retaining pins. Oil shield will be damaged during removal and a new shield must be installed after overhauling planetary gear set.

Later type pressure regulator valves (30—Fig. 1-5) have a relief cut in perimeter of valve to prevent valve buzz. If regulator valve noise is present, install later type valve or cut a notch in older type valve as shown in Fig. 1-11.

To reassemble transmission, install oil baffle (38—Fig. 1-5) on Models 72, 72R, 72C and 72CR so two large holes in baffle are indexed on two round bosses adjacent to output shaft bore in housing. Install oil baffle on all other models so rectangular slots in baffle snap into bosses in inner walls of housing.

Transmission housings have been manufactured with or without bushings (41) in output shaft bore. Planetary gear and shaft assembly with oil grooves on shaft as shown in Fig. 1-12 must be used in transmission housings not equipped with bushings (41—Fig. 1-5), but may also be used in housings with bushings. Planetary gear and shaft assembly without oil grooves on shaft can only be used in housings equipped with bushings (41). Insert planetary gear and shaft assembly (42) in transmission. Support gear and shaft assembly and press bearing (19) into housing with groove in outer race towards rear of housing. Install oil seal in bearing retainer with lip towards transmission on models without a reduction gear of V-drive. Install bearing retainer, on models so equipped, and tighten screws to 42-50 ft.-lbs. Install flange coupling, on models so equipped, so coupling bottoms against inner race of bearing and tighten output shaft nut to 100-200 ft.-lbs. Output shaft end play should be zero with nut tightened to specified torque.

Install components (52 through 56) in ring gear (50). Series 70 units have three inner clutch plates (53), Series 71 units have five inner plates while Series 72 units have seven inner plates. Number of outer clutch plates is one less than number of inner clutch plates. Pressure plates (52 & 55) must be installed with flat surfaces towards clutch plates. Snap ring (56) is 0.090-0.093 inches thick and seats against shoulder of internal teeth in ring gear (50). Install spring (57) with concave side towards clutch plates. Use a suitable press or suitable tool to compress clutch pack and spring and hold forward clutch cylinder in position while installing snap ring (67). Snap ring (67) is 0.074-0.078 inch thick. On Models 72, 72R, 72C and 72CR, apply pressure to pressure plate (52) until clutch pack and spring are totally compressed, install snap ring (51) and measure gap between pressure plate (52) and snap ring. Gap should be 0.040-0.065 inch and may be obtained by installing one or more snap rings of the desired thickness. Snap ring (51) is color coded according to thickness and is available in the following thicknesses: green—0.050-0.054 inch; orange—0.074-0.078 inch; white—0.096-0.100 inch.

Press forward clutch hub (47) on input shaft (46) until hub bottoms against drive gear and groove for snap ring (48) is uncovered. Position seal rings (49) on input shaft being sure ring ends fit correctly. Mate ring gear and clutch pack with forward clutch hub and input shaft. Support input shaft and gear (46) and press bearing (64) into forward clutch cylinder (62). Install snap rings (65 & 66), thrust washer (45) and insert input shaft and forward clutch assembly into planetary gear set in housing being careful not to damage bushings in output shaft. Lubricate three dowel pins (40) and install in housing along with twelve springs (37). Springs and dowel pins must be firmly seated in clean holes. Install reverse clutch plates (68 & 69). Models 72, 72R, 72C and 72CR are equipped with two reverse clutch outer plates (69) while Models 70, 70R, 70B, 70BR, 71, 71R, 71C and 71CR are equipped with one outer plate (69) when combined with reduction gear or V-drive units. Reverse clutch outer plate (69) is absent on all other models. Install reverse clutch outer plates so

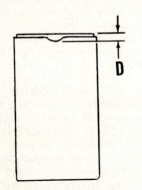

Fig. 1-11—Notch in edge of regulator valve should have 3/8-in. diameter and be 0.070-0.085 in. deep (D).

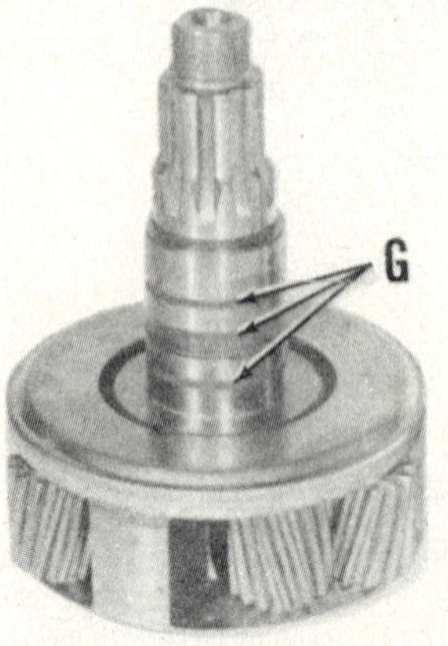

Fig. 1-12—View of oil grooves (G) in transmission output shaft. Refer to text.

Fig. 1-13—Install reverse clutch pressure plate so oil slot is aligned with housing oil passage as shown at (P).

DRIVES
Velvet Drive

odd shaped lug fits around dowel pin nearest bottom of transmission. Reverse clutch pressure plate (70) must be installed with slot in perimeter aligned with large oil hole in housing as shown in Fig. 1-13. Inspect and lubricate sealing surfaces of adapter (76—Fig. 1-5) and assemble components (71 through 76). Install adapter assembly on housing being sure oil passages are aligned and adapter fits squarely without binding. Tighten 12 four-point cap screws in a cross pattern to 27-37 ft.-lbs.

Note early style oil pump with backing plate shown in Fig. 1-14. Later style oil pump does not have a backing plate and must be used with adapter shown in Fig. 1-15. Early style oil pump may be used on later style adapter as long as drive key matches input shaft. Be sure to match marks on pump gears made during disassembly.

Pump housing (80—Fig. 1-5) must be installed to correspond to input shaft rotation or pump will not operate properly. Pump housing (80) is marked with two arrows and "TOP" adjacent to each arrow. See Fig. 1-16. The pump will operate properly if pump housing is positioned so arrow on pump housing which points in direction of input shaft rotation is near as possible to top of transmission. Tighten pump screws to 17-22 ft.-lbs.

Tighten valve cover screws to 12-14 ft.-lbs. With shift lever (24—Fig. 1-5) nut tightened to 12-16 ft.-lbs., it should be possible to move shift through gear positions with finger tip effort. Remove and inspect if unable to do so. If unit is equipped with a neutral switch, then tang on neutral switch cam must align with slot on valve as shown in Fig. 1-17. With switch cam properly installed, it should appear as shown in Fig. 1-18.

Fig. 1-14—View showing early oil pump backing plate (B).

Fig. 1-15—Later oil pump must be used with adapter having intake (I) and outlet (O) oil passages as shown above.

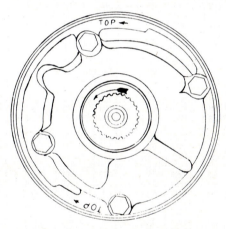

Fig. 1-16—Install pump housing so arrow on pump housing which points in input shaft direction is to top of transmission.

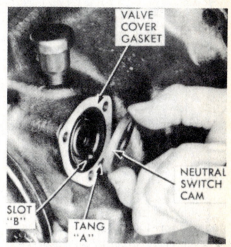

Fig. 1-17—Install neutral switch cam so tang "A" on cam fits slot "B" on valve.

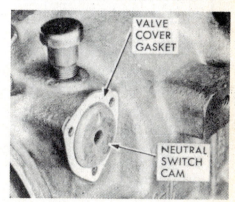

Fig. 1-18—With neutral switch cam properly installed, it should be in position shown above.

Illustration courtesy Borg-Warner

MM.	INCHES			MM.	INCHES			MM.	INCHES			MM.	INCHES			MM.	INCHES			MM.	INCHES			MM.	INCHES		
1	0.0394	1/32	+	51	2.0079	2.0	+	101	3.9764	3 31/32	+	151	5.9449	5 15/16	+	201	7.9134	7 29/32	+	251	9.8819	9 7/8	+				
2	0.0787	3/32	−	52	2.0472	2 1/16	−	102	4.0157	4 1/32	−	152	5.9842	5 31/32	+	202	7.9527	7 15/16	−	252	9.9212	9 29/32	+				
3	0.1181	1/8	−	53	2.0866	2 3/32	−	103	4.0551	4 1/16	−	153	6.0236	6 1/32	−	203	7.9921	8.0	−	253	9.9606	9 31/32	−				
4	0.1575	5/32	+	54	2.1260	2 1/8	+	104	4.0945	4 3/32	+	154	6.0630	6 1/16	+	204	8.0315	8 1/32	+	254	10.0000	10.0					
5	0.1969	3/16	+	55	2.1654	2 5/32	+	105	4.1339	4 1/8	+	155	6.1024	6 3/32	+	205	8.0709	8 1/16	+	255	10.0393	10 1/32	+				
6	0.2362	1/4	−	56	2.2047	2 7/32	−	106	4.1732	4 3/16	−	156	6.1417	6 5/32	−	206	8.1102	8 1/8	−	256	10.0787	10 3/32	−				
7	0.2756	9/32	−	57	2.2441	2 1/4	−	107	4.2126	4 7/32	−	157	6.1811	6 3/16	−	207	8.1496	8 5/32	−	257	10.1181	10 1/8	−				
8	0.3150	5/16	+	58	2.2835	2 9/32	+	108	4.2520	4 1/4	+	158	6.2205	6 7/32	+	208	8.1890	8 3/16	+	258	10.1575	10 5/32	+				
9	0.3543	11/32	+	59	2.3228	2 5/16	+	109	4.2913	4 9/32	+	159	6.2598	6 1/4	+	209	8.2283	8 7/32	+	259	10.1968	10 3/16	+				
10	0.3937	13/32	−	60	2.3622	2 3/8	−	110	4.3307	4 11/32	−	160	6.2992	6 5/16	−	210	8.2677	8 9/32	−	260	10.2362	10 1/4	−				
11	0.4331	7/16	−	61	2.4016	2 13/32	−	111	4.3701	4 3/8	−	161	6.3386	6 11/32	−	211	8.3071	8 5/16	−	261	10.2756	10 9/32	−				
12	0.4724	15/32	+	62	2.4409	2 7/16	+	112	4.4094	4 13/32	−	162	6.3779	6 3/8	+	212	8.3464	8 11/32	+	262	10.3149	10 5/16	+				
13	0.5118	1/2	+	63	2.4803	2 15/32	+	113	4.4488	4 7/16	+	163	6.4173	6 13/32	+	213	8.3858	8 3/8	+	263	10.3543	10 11/32	+				
14	0.5512	9/16	−	64	2.5197	2 17/32	−	114	4.4882	4 1/2	−	164	6.4567	6 15/32	−	214	8.4252	8 7/16	−	264	10.3937	10 13/32	−				
15	0.5906	19/32	−	65	2.5591	2 9/16	−	115	4.5276	4 17/32	−	165	6.4961	6 1/2	−	215	8.4646	8 15/32	−	265	10.4330	10 7/16	−				
16	0.6299	5/8	+	66	2.5984	2 19/32	+	116	4.5669	4 9/16	+	166	6.5354	6 17/32	+	216	8.5039	8 1/2	+	266	10.4724	10 15/32	+				
17	0.6693	21/32	+	67	2.6378	2 5/8	+	117	4.6063	4 19/32	+	167	6.5748	6 9/16	+	217	8.5433	8 17/32	+	267	10.5118	10 1/2	+				
18	0.7087	23/32	−	68	2.6772	2 11/16	−	118	4.6457	4 21/32	−	168	6.6142	6 5/8	−	218	8.5827	8 19/32	−	268	10.5512	10 9/16	−				
19	0.7480	3/4	−	69	2.7165	2 23/32	−	119	4.6850	4 11/16	−	169	6.6535	6 21/32	−	219	8.6220	8 5/8	−	269	10.5905	10 19/32	−				
20	0.7874	25/32	+	70	2.7559	2 3/4	+	120	4.7244	4 23/32	+	170	6.6929	6 11/16	+	220	8.6614	8 21/32	+	270	10.6299	10 5/8	+				
21	0.8268	13/16	+	71	2.7953	2 25/32	+	121	4.7638	4 3/4	+	171	6.7323	6 23/32	+	221	8.7008	8 11/16	+	271	10.6693	10 21/32	+				
22	0.8661	7/8	−	72	2.8346	2 27/32	−	122	4.8031	4 13/16	−	172	6.7716	6 25/32	−	222	8.7401	8 3/4	−	272	10.7086	10 23/32	−				
23	0.9055	29/32	−	73	2.8740	2 7/8	−	123	4.8425	4 27/32	−	173	6.8110	6 13/16	−	223	8.7795	8 25/32	−	273	10.7480	10 3/4	−				
24	0.9449	15/16	+	74	2.9134	2 29/32	+	124	4.8819	4 7/8	+	174	6.8504	6 27/32	+	224	8.8189	8 13/16	+	274	10.7874	10 25/32	+				
25	0.9843	31/32	+	75	2.9528	2 15/16	+	125	4.9213	4 29/32	+	175	6.8898	6 7/8	+	225	8.8583	8 27/32	+	275	10.8268	10 13/16	+				
26	1.0236	1 1/32	−	76	2.9921	3.0	−	126	4.9606	4 31/32	−	176	6.9291	6 15/16	−	226	8.8976	8 29/32	−	276	10.8661	10 7/8	−				
27	1.0630	1 1/16	+	77	3.0315	3 1/32	+	127	5.0000	5.0		177	6.9685	6 31/32	−	227	8.9370	8 15/16	−	277	10.9055	10 29/32	+				
28	1.1024	1 3/32	+	78	3.0709	3 1/16	+	128	5.0394	5 1/32	+	178	7.0079	7.0	+	228	8.9764	8 31/32	+	278	10.9449	10 15/16	+				
29	1.1417	1 5/32	−	79	3.1102	3 1/8	−	129	5.0787	5 5/64	−	179	7.0472	7 1/16	−	229	9.0157	9 1/32	−	279	10.9842	10 31/32	−				
30	1.1811	1 3/16	−	80	3.1496	3 5/32	−	130	5.1181	5 1/8	−	180	7.0866	7 3/32	−	230	9.0551	9 1/16	−	280	11.0236	11 1/32	−				
31	1.2205	1 7/32	+	81	3.1890	3 3/16	+	131	5.1575	5 5/32	+	181	7.1260	7 1/8	+	231	9.0945	9 3/32	+	281	11.0630	11 1/16	+				
32	1.2598	1 1/4	+	82	3.2283	3 7/32	+	132	5.1968	5 3/16	+	182	7.1653	7 5/32	+	232	9.1338	9 1/8	+	282	11.1023	11 3/32	+				
33	1.2992	1 9/32	−	83	3.2677	3 9/32	−	133	5.2362	5 1/4	−	183	7.2047	7 7/32	−	233	9.1732	9 5/32	−	283	11.1417	11 5/32	−				
34	1.3386	1 11/32	−	84	3.3071	3 5/16	−	134	5.2756	5 9/32	−	184	7.2441	7 1/4	−	234	9.2126	9 7/32	−	284	11.1811	11 3/16	−				
35	1.3780	1 3/8	+	85	3.3465	3 11/32	+	135	5.3150	5 5/16	+	185	7.2835	7 9/32	+	235	9.2520	9 1/4	+	285	11.2204	11 7/32	+				
36	1.4173	1 13/32	+	86	3.3858	3 3/8	+	136	5.3543	5 11/32	+	186	7.3228	7 5/16	+	236	9.2913	9 9/32	+	286	11.2598	11 1/4	+				
37	1.4567	1 15/32	−	87	3.4252	3 7/16	−	137	5.3937	5 13/32	−	187	7.3622	7 3/8	−	237	9.3307	9 11/32	−	287	11.2992	11 5/16	−				
38	1.4961	1 1/2	−	88	3.4646	3 15/32	−	138	5.4331	5 7/16	−	188	7.4016	7 13/32	−	238	9.3701	9 3/8	−	288	11.3386	11 11/32	−				
39	1.5354	1 17/32	+	89	3.5039	3 1/2	+	139	5.4724	5 15/32	+	189	7.4409	7 7/16	+	239	9.4094	9 13/32	+	289	11.3779	11 3/8	+				
40	1.5748	1 9/16	+	90	3.5433	3 17/32	+	140	5.5118	5 1/2	+	190	7.4803	7 15/32	+	240	9.4488	7 7/16	+	290	11.4173	11 13/32	+				
41	1.6142	1 5/8	−	91	3.5827	3 9/16	−	141	5.5512	5 9/16	−	191	7.5197	7 17/32	−	241	9.4882	9 1/2	−	291	11.4567	11 15/32	−				
42	1.6535	1 21/32	−	92	3.6220	3 5/8	−	142	5.5905	5 19/32	−	192	7.5590	7 9/16	−	242	9.5275	9 17/32	−	292	11.4960	11 1/2	−				
43	1.6929	1 11/16	+	93	3.6614	3 21/32	+	143	5.6299	5 5/8	+	193	7.5984	7 19/32	+	243	9.5669	9 9/16	+	293	11.5354	11 17/32	+				
44	1.7323	1 23/32	+	94	3.7008	3 11/16	+	144	5.6693	5 21/32	+	194	7.6378	7 5/8	+	244	9.6063	9 19/32	+	294	11.5748	11 9/16	+				
45	1.7717	1 25/32	−	95	3.7402	3 3/4	−	145	5.7087	5 23/32	−	195	7.6772	7 11/16	−	245	9.6457	9 21/32	−	295	11.6142	11 5/8	−				
46	1.8110	1 13/16	−	96	3.7795	3 25/32	−	146	5.7480	5 3/4	−	196	7.7165	7 23/32	−	246	9.6850	9 11/16	−	296	11.6535	11 21/32	−				
47	1.8504	1 27/32	+	97	3.8189	3 13/16	+	147	5.7874	5 25/32	+	197	7.7559	7 3/4	+	247	9.7244	9 23/32	+	297	11.6929	11 11/16	+				
48	1.8898	1 7/8	+	98	3.8583	3 27/32	+	148	5.8268	5 13/16	+	198	7.7953	7 25/32	+	248	9.7638	9 3/4	+	298	11.7323	11 23/32	+				
49	1.9291	1 15/16	−	99	3.8976	3 29/32	−	149	5.8661	5 7/8	−	199	7.8346	7 27/32	−	249	9.8031	9 13/16	−	299	11.7716	11 25/32	−				
50	1.9685	1 31/32	−	100	3.9370	3 15/16	−	150	5.9055	5 29/32	−	200	7.8740	7 7/8	−	250	9.8425	9 27/32	−	300	11.8110	11 13/16	−				

NOTE. The + or − sign indicates that the decimal equivalent is larger or smaller than the fractional equivalent.

NOTES

NOTES